ANTIQUES ROADSHOW™

PRIMER

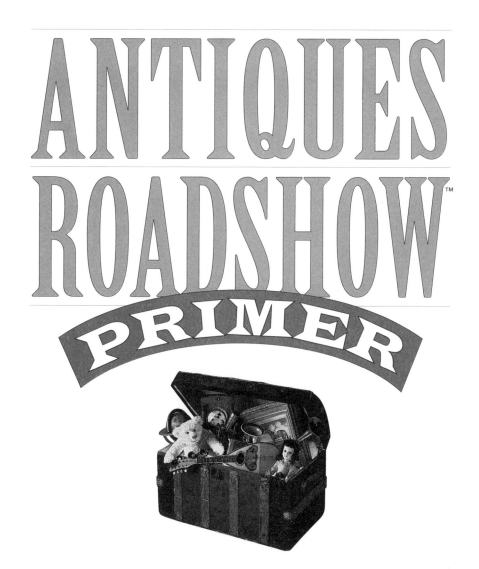

The INTRODUCTORY GUIDE to ANTIQUES and
COLLECTIBLES from the MOST-WATCHED SERIES on PBS®.

by CAROL PRISANT

WORKMAN PUBLISHING, NEW YORK

Foreword © 1999 by Chris Jussel

Antiques Roadshow™ is produced for PBS by WGBH/Boston.
Executive Producer: Aida Moreno
Senior Producer: Peter Cook
Consulting Producer: Dan Farrell
Host: Chris Jussel

Antiques Roadshow™ would like to thank Christie's, William Doyle Galleries, Skinner, Inc., Sotheby's,
our independent dealers and appraisers nationwide, and the staff and crew of the television series.

Special thanks to the Chubb Group of Insurance Companies which generously provide major funding for
Antiques Roadshow™. Additional funding is provided by First Union and by the public television viewers.
Antiques Roadshow Online: http://www.wgbh.org/antiques

Photo credits for front cover, clockwise from top right: Christie's Images; ARS (Antiques Roadshow); ARS;
Winterthur Museum; ARS; Caroline Edelman; Christie's Images, ARS; ARS; ARS.
Photo credits for back cover: *Top right,* ARS; *bottom left,* ARS.
Most ARS photos are by Jeffrey Dunn for WGBH.

Library of Congress Cataloging-in-Publication Data
Prisant, Carol
Antiques roadshow primer: the introductory guide to antiques and collectibles
from the most-watched series on PBS / by Carol Prisant
p.   cm.
Includes biographical references and index.
ISBN 0-7611-1775-X (hc.) — ISBN 0-7611-1624-9 (pbk.)
1. Antiques—United States. 2. Collectibles—United States.
3. Antique roadshow (Television program)   I. Title.
NK1125.P75   1999
745.1—dc21   99-29960
CIP

Workman books are available at special discounts when purchased in bulk for premiums and sales
promotions as well as for fund-raising or educational use. Special editions can also be created to specification.
For details, contact the Special Sales Director at the address below.

Workman Publishing Company, Inc.
708 Broadway
New York, NY 10003-9555
www.workman.com

Printed in the U.S.A.

First printing December 1999
10 9 8 7 6 5 4

To Millard

CONTENTS

Foreword xi

Acknowledgments xv

Introduction xvii

Chapter One

FURNITURE 1

Is It Old? 3

Is It Valuable? 17

American Furniture 25

English and Continental Furniture 31

Seymour card table.

Chapter Two

SILVER 45

Types of Silver 47

Making Silver Objects 50

Understanding Hallmarks 55

American Silver 59

English and Continental Silver 68

Is It Old? 73

Is It Valuable? 75

Georgian silver ewer.

Chapter Three

PORCELAIN, POTTERY, AND GLASS 79

Porcelain 80

Pottery 88

Is It Old? 94

Is It Valuable? 96

Van Briggle vase.

William Aiken Walker painting.

Scottish grandfather clock.

Glass 99
Is It Old? 111
Is It Valuable? 112

Chapter Four

PAINTINGS 115
Is It Legitimate? 125
Connoisseurship 133
Folk Painting 141

Chapter Five

JEWELRY 147
Is It Real? 149
Is It Old? 166

Chapter Six

CLOCKS AND WATCHES 177
Anatomy of a Timepiece 179
Clocks 184
Watches 194

Chapter Seven

METALWORK 201
Bronze 202
Brass 211
Copper 217
Pewter 221
Iron 226
Folk Art 230

Josiah Harrison weather-vane.

Chapter Eight

RUGS, QUILTS, AND SAMPLERS 233
Rugs 235
Quilts 247
Samplers 255

Chapter Nine

TOYS, DOLLS, AND COLLECTIBLES 263
Toys 264
Dolls 274
Teddy Bears 284
Collectibles 288

Chapter Ten

BOOKS AND MANUSCRIPTS 301
Books 303
Manuscripts 315

Glossary 321
Suggested Reading and Resources 325
Finding an Appraiser 327
Auction Houses 328
Appraisal Organizations 328
Antiques Roadshow™ *Appraisers* 329
Photo Credits 337
Index 347

Pennsylvania sampler.

Titanic *luncheon menu.*

Book of botanical illustrations by Redouté.

FOREWORD

Antiques Roadshow™ set out, in early June of 1996, on a journey across the United States "in search of America's hidden treasures." What we discovered astounded us.

That first year was tough going—no one had heard of *Antiques Roadshow™*. We traveled to thirteen different cities in seventeen weeks, arriving in a city on a Tuesday or Wednesday and spending the next few days trying to drum up a crowd for Saturday's event. We often begged the local media for advance coverage. By the time we reached our last event of the season, in Villa Park, Illinois, and more than 1,000 people came through the door during the day, we felt we were making some headway.

It wasn't long after our television debut the following January that we knew we'd have no trouble drumming up crowds the next summer. As of this writing, on the brink of our fourth season, we're the most-watched series on public television, with more than 14 million viewers per week. We accommodate as many as 7,000 people (and their objects) at each location during the summer tapings of the show.

Chris Jussel, the host of the Antiques Roadshow™.

I've always said that everyone has at least one thing that is "old." (I once suggested we call the series *This Old Stuff* but fortunately no one took me seriously.) We were amazed at what America produced—at the kind and quality of antiques that just came through the door at the events. Items from many centuries were represented: beautiful examples of the highest craftsmanship, exquisite folk art, and, of course, even a few fakes and reproductions. There were those times when a hitherto-unrecognized piece of great worth was revealed—these were moments of high excitement for the experts and the *Antiques Roadshow*™ crew.

One thing that continually surprises me in my travels with the show—something remarked on by other *Roadshow*™ experts who are also old hands in the antiques business—is this: Most people are *not* primarily interested in how much their item is worth. They are much more interested in the other questions: Who made it? When was it made? Where was it made? How do I care for it?

Becky MacGuire discusses the history of blue-and-white china with Chris Jussel.

At the show we give people a chance to have their questions answered by professionals—all of them with a great deal of experience in their respective fields—in a forum free of any pressures to either buy or sell the object. And our experts answer those questions in order of their importance: first, what it is; then, who made it and when; and finally, by the way, what it's worth in today's market. Fairly often the object isn't worth much, but the owners are pleased, nevertheless, to have learned more about a cherished possession.

The show has captured a large television audience because these are the faces of America, telling America's stories about their own heirlooms, about objects from their own homes. These are real people on the screen, not actors in a drama or a comedy, but folks just like us.

All of which confirms my feelings about the wonderful world of antiques. I have been in the business since the early 1970s, and my dad had been in the business since the 1920s, so it's "in my blood." I've always said that collecting antiques is for everyone, that it cuts across all social and economic boundaries. The person collecting eighteenth-century hairy-paw-foot Philadelphia Chippendale furniture worth several hundred thousand dollars is no more passionate and knowledgeable about collecting than any of us who collect antiques, whether it's the person who collects penny toys from the 1930s or the woman who collects late-nineteenth-century glass bottles that cost five dollars each, or the youngster collecting 1960s lunch boxes—or the oldster after the very same items.

And there's always room for one more. Anyone starting out as a collector is beginning his or her own journey "in search of hidden treasures." There's plenty to learn, discoveries to make, and it's all fun—and that's what's most important in life.

—CHRIS JUSSEL

ACKNOWLEDGMENTS

MY THANKS TO . . .

Peter Workman, for his confidence in me and his topflight team.

The far from old but enormously valuable Anne Kostick, without whose careful editing, level head, diplomacy, and fine intelligence, this book would be Old News.

The following appraisers from the *Antiques Roadshow*™: Noel Barrett, Frank Boos, Chris Coover, Nick Dawes, Nancy Druckman, Leila Dunbar, Alan Fausel, Rudy Franchi, James Ffrench, Andrea Blunck Frost, Kathleen Guzman, John Hays, Joyce Jonas, Selby Kiffer, Leigh Keno, Leslie Keno, Gloria Lieberman, Louise Luther, Mary Jo Otsea, David Rago, Peter Schaffer, Eric Silver, Larry Sirolli, Jeanne Sloane, Jonathan Snellenburg, Arlie Sulka, Barry Weber, and Richard Wright, who generously volunteered their valuable time and expertise to read the draft manuscript or to be interviewed. It has been a privilege to learn from them all.

Nick Dawes, Leila Dunbar, James Ffrench, Selby Kiffer, and Paul Provost, whose thoughtful suggestions and scholarship contributed so substantially to the book's accuracy and content.

The staff of *Antiques Roadshow*™, including executive producer Aida Moreno, senior producer Peter Cook, and consulting producer Dan Farrell, for their hard work in gathering and disseminating information about the series; David Bernstein, Betsy Groban, Caroline Chauncey, Amy Carzo, Stephanie Coyle, and Lisa Abitbol for being the book's guardian angels within WGBH.

Margaret Caldwell, Don Fennimore, and Jane Shadel Spillman, who offered their erudition and expertise, and made evenhanded, insightful, and constructive comments.

Jeni L. Sandberg, for her perfectly timed assistance, innovative and excellent research, and general cheer.

Katie King, for her meticulous and conscientious work on the text, and for tolerating the process with remarkably little complaint.

Writers/editors Francine Almash and Janet Hulstrand; thorough and painstaking photo researchers Giema Tsakuginow, Joan Meisel, and Anita Dickhuth.

The Design Group, for their admirable minds, the unstinting benefit of their experience, and their occasional shoulders—especially those of Dylan and Bo. Morrison Heckscher, for his timely assistance.

Waldo Hutchins, for his helpful intercession.

Sanford Goldstein, for his unfailing interest and excellent advice.

Vladimir Piskacek, for his friendship and support.

Mother, for her $200.

Barden Prisant (young), for being so utterly bribable in countless antiques-ridden circumstances.

Barden Prisant (grown), for his acumen and logic, his generosity, his counsel, his bottomless database, and his droll sense of humor.

And Millard—the wings beneath my wind—for all the rest.

—C.P.

INTRODUCTION

Like millions of other Americans, you probably wander away from the TV set at the end of the *Antiques Roadshow*™ and roam around your living room, picking things up, turning them over, measuring your chairs and lamps with a newly critical eye, and generally wondering if you really should have given that dreary ancestor portrait to your third cousin, once-removed. You've learned a lot from watching the show every week, but now you want to know more. If that's the case, this primer promises you immediate help. Help in deciphering those cryptic stamps on silver; help in spotting valuable first editions; help in locating maker's marks on dolls; help in recognizing the difference between the imitation sapphire and the genuine sapphire; help in judging the actual age of ostensible "Old Master" paintings. Help, even if you're not remotely mechanical, in determining when to flip that drop-leaf table upside down and take a long look underneath, and when to walk on by.

Victorian Gothic Revival chair

Georgian silver tureen.

This book is a primer. This means, of course, that it will introduce you to the basics of antiques—not presume to make you an instant expert. Acquiring expertise is a lifelong task. The *Antiques Roadshow*™ experts themselves have become the specialists they are just through years of looking, listening, and reading. You can't go to school, after all, to evaluate quilts, distinguish run-of-the-mill pocket watches from rare watches, or determine the age of brass andirons. Nor can you earn a doctorate in recognizing an original finish or dating a cast-iron toy bank. Experience (and that occasional painful mistake) is the definitive bottom line. Consequently, samplings of appraisers' experience have been included here to help you determine for yourself if your Tiffany look-alike or Windsor chair is indeed old; and if it is old, whether it has unexpected value.

Pearl, diamond, and yellow gold bar brooch.

Because there are thousands of decorative objects out there, I've selected categories based on antiques-world staples—silver, glass, pottery and porcelain, books, paintings, jewelry, rugs, clocks, and furniture. Traditional "blue-chip" antiques. And there are newer collectibles as well, such as dolls, toys, advertising and movie memorabilia—though you won't find 1950s Scandinavian chairs, for instance, or 1920s beaded bags, glass insulators, or Barbie dolls. This is not because they are not as valuable or as interesting as other collectibles, but because the field is huge and always in flux, and far beyond the scope of a basic primer. Which means, too, that there are no newly emerging (or expiring) categories in this book, and nothing, therefore, that's likely to be enormously expensive one year and valueless the next. It's a group that's good for the long haul. The front hall, as well.

Pewter teapot by William Will.

Primarily, I've focused on American antiques, because that's what Americans often own and what American collectors usually like to buy. As a result, several European and English areas of collecting are barely touched upon, a deletion allowing me to include two important categories that seldom appear in general books on antiques: paintings and jewelry. Along with new and useful information on how to examine and evaluate both, you'll find practical advice on feeling, sniffing, weighing, and even listening to innumerable other collectibles, from chests to clocks to paperweights. You'll learn, among other things, that the "fancy" object is not necessarily the valuable object and that the well-known and typical work of an artist or craftsman is generally more desirable than the atypical work. And along the way, I hope you'll find yourself less intimidated by the process of detection and the ostensible majesty of age.

Cuckoo clock.

While I've only skimmed the surface of the great European and British works of art, there are several categories of traditional antiques I've utterly excluded. Prints, for instance, which are a field unto themselves. Antiquities. Sculpture. Photographs. Judaica. And all of the superb arts of Asia. These were hard choices to make, but choices I based, to some extent, on the objects appearing most frequently at *Roadshow*™

Cast-iron dentist mechanical toy bank.

appraisers' tables. I've opted to tell you, too, only about things that had appealing histories or were likely to be most valuable. This is not to say that Depression glass, music boxes, Fiesta Ware, model ships, and crocodile luggage aren't appealing and costly. But meat-and-potatoes knowledge about traditional antiques will always stand you in good and discriminating stead.

Two very important subjects don't appear here: prices and any discussion of fakes. Prices go out of date so fast that they're virtually worthless. A five-year-old price guide—even a two-year-old price guide—is useful in only a relative fashion, especially in volatile markets. (If A was more valuable than B two years ago, for instance, it will still be more valuable today.) Then, too, prices differ in various regions of the country. What sells for $300 in Missouri may be worth only $30 in L.A. This book will be useful, wherever you live, for years to come.

Recognizing fakes requires real expertise. Reproductions are fairly easy to spot, but fakes are intended to deceive. And reading about fakes at the same time you're acquiring the basics can be fatally confusing. So I've excluded them. Should you ultimately arrive at the point where you know all the attributes the genuine object ought to have, and the piece you own seems to meet all criteria, consult a specialist—any object worth faking deserves a professional second opinion.

For the reader who plans to spend fortunes on his or her first time out, however, I have one piece of advice. Read plenty of books. No single book can hope to tell you all you'll need to know. Even encyclopedias can only give you a taste of the vast world of beautiful, interesting, curious, and possibly overpriced objects out there. So read widely, choosing, perhaps, from the list of excellent books appended to each chapter or from the carefully selected general list at the back.

Navajo rug

The point of this book, of course, is to help you to detect the old and recognize the valuable for yourself. To send you confidently into antiques shops and shows, flea markets and auctions with solid, usable facts and your eye sharp and sure. You're capable of developing antiques expertise, and you're more than capable of doing some amateur appraising. As we've seen, America's hidden treasures are still out there by the thousands, waiting to be discovered—by you—in your living room, at home.

Chapter One

FURNITURE

I n the last few centuries every household, no matter how spare, had at least a bed, a table, and a chair. These furnishings—unlike cups, plates, and cooking utensils—were just too large to be lost. This, of course, is why we see so much more old furniture today than we do other early decorative objects. Glass and china are fragile, and silver is intrinsically valuable as well as meltable. So glass, china, and silver disappear, while attics full of furniture—battered, nicked, and stained—endure.

Some American furniture, in fact, has endured since 1650, when the first furniture is thought to have been made in the New World by Pilgrim craftsmen who, naturally enough, copied English styles. Their oak chests, cupboards, and Brewster and Carver chairs (named for *Mayflower* passengers) were distinctly Jacobean in style, although the following William and Mary style found the colonists quite ready for lighter, smaller, Dutch-influenced walnut furniture. Colonial cabinetmakers were ready to flex a bit of creative muscle, too, by devising the uniquely American chest of drawers on a drawered stand—colloquially called the highboy. (The stand, by itself, is

An extremely rare Queen Anne stained maple side chair with rush seat.

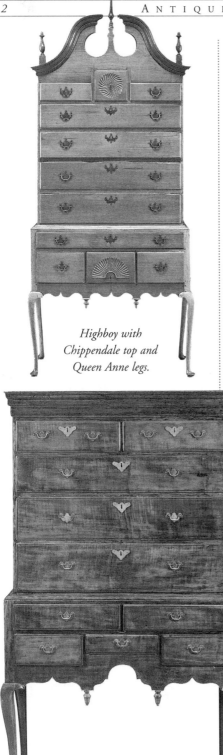

*Highboy with
Chippendale top and
Queen Anne legs.*

*Flat-topped Provincial
Queen Anne highboy.*

a lowboy.) Even smaller and more graceful than its predecessors, Queen Anne furniture (c. 1725) found an increasingly hospitable and prosperous country happy to embrace its wavelike, and expressly British, "line of beauty" in the new wing chairs, mirrors, and curved side and armchairs. But by 1760 American craftsmen were more than ready to turn Thomas Chippendale's very English brilliance into their own, all-American style. Every rich ornament of the fashion—interlaced scrollwork, ball-and-claw feet, fretted chinoiserie—was embraced and translated by sophisticated craftsmen in New York and Philadelphia, but it flowered best in seafaring Newport, where block-front, shell-carved desks, bookcases, and chests of drawers—true mahogany "sculptures"—were superb examples of American muscularity and grace.

In 1776 the War of Independence blocked trade with England, preventing the Adam style from ever gaining a foothold in America. But by 1800 emigrant Scotsman Duncan Phyfe's interpretations of Hepplewhite and Sheraton furniture were welcomed to its parlors. After about 1810 Phyfe, now inspired by French Empire style, Americanized sheaves of wheat and lyres and borrowed French Classicism for sofas, tables, and beds. Simultaneously, the far more stately furniture of the French-born Charles-Honoré Lannuier—pier tables and consoles, particularly—rivaled Parisian originals.

For eighty-five years thereafter, Americans sorted through various revival styles, trying to decide whether they wanted to be scholars in Gothic libraries, Rococo Revival coquettes, Renaissance princes, or all of these and more. By the beginning of the nineteenth century (following a short fling with reactionary Aesthetic and Eastlake styles), the country had learned to mingle the Beaux-Arts, Belle Epoque, Arts and Crafts, Colonial Revival, Louis XV and Louis XVI styles—and to be comfortable with a decorative mix which, in essence, thoroughly represented the melting pot America had become.

IS IT OLD?

But how much of this 300-year accumulation of perhaps old-looking furniture is actually antique? And even if it is antique, is it necessarily valuable?

The United States government legally defines an "antique" as any object 100 years old or older. There are very important distinctions between "period," "antique," and "used" furniture, however, so when you come across a desk or an interesting-looking chest of drawers in your great-aunt's attic, before you haul it down the stairs and spend your valuable time and money cleaning it up or having it repaired, you should ask yourself two key questions. Is it old? If it is old, is it valuable? Sentimental value apart, it may not be worth your effort.

How old *is* old? Is your grandmother's Chippendale coffee table old enough to be an antique? Probably not, sorry to say. "But why not?" you might sensibly ask. "She lived to be 101." Well, perhaps she purchased her table from a neighbor when she was in her fifties. Or moved to an apartment when she was seventy-five and sold her old table, replacing it with this one. She may have been an inveterate redecorator who, at ninety-two, was still buying Chippendale reproductions from the local consignment shop. Yet such complicated speculations are in the end unimportant, because the fact is, even if she purchased her coffee table as a young bride in 1925, the whole idea of a coffee table is a fairly recent invention—far too recent to be legitimately "antique." Antique tables might be made of the same mahogany or be of similar design, but you will *never* find an antique coffee table, because the coffee table was not even in use until about 1920.

Antique furniture is furniture that was made at least 100 years ago, and though it has certainly been "used," it does not fall into the category of **used furniture,** a term that describes secondhand furniture less than 100 years old. Twentieth-century designer furniture from Charles Eames or Heywood Wakefield, for example, may be historically

EIGHTEENTH-CENTURY CHIPPENDALE CHAIR

Appraiser John Hays was "thrilled and dazzled" when he saw this gorgeous Chippendale armchair on the floor. The chair had been in the same family for fifty years, passed on from first son to first son, and had all the classic characteristics of c. 1770 Philadelphia style: the wonderful scallop shell crest, the magnificent scrolled arms, and the molded "banana" supports. What makes this item particularly exciting is the fact that, for every eight to ten side chairs made, there were only two armchairs, so it's rare that one comes to light.

The owners once had this chair appraised for $500. They were stunned when Hays informed them that it was worth not less than $60,000 to $90,000. And that's a markdown, because it doesn't have its original surface!

Furniture Styles and Periods

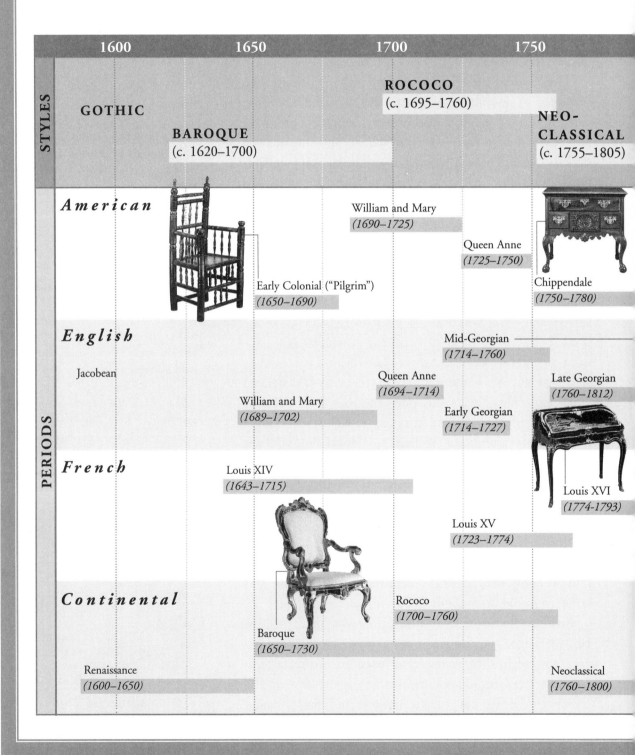

	1600	1650	1700	1750

STYLES

GOTHIC

ROCOCO
(c. 1695–1760)

BAROQUE
(c. 1620–1700)

NEO-CLASSICAL
(c. 1755–1805)

PERIODS

American

William and Mary
(1690–1725)

Queen Anne
(1725–1750)

Early Colonial ("Pilgrim")
(1650–1690)

Chippendale
(1750–1780)

English

Mid-Georgian
(1714–1760)

Jacobean

Queen Anne
(1694–1714)

Late Georgian
(1760–1812)

William and Mary
(1689–1702)

Early Georgian
(1714–1727)

French

Louis XIV
(1643–1715)

Louis XVI
(1774-1793)

Louis XV
(1723–1774)

Continental

Rococo
(1700–1760)

Baroque
(1650–1730)

Renaissance
(1600–1650)

Neoclassical
(1760–1800)

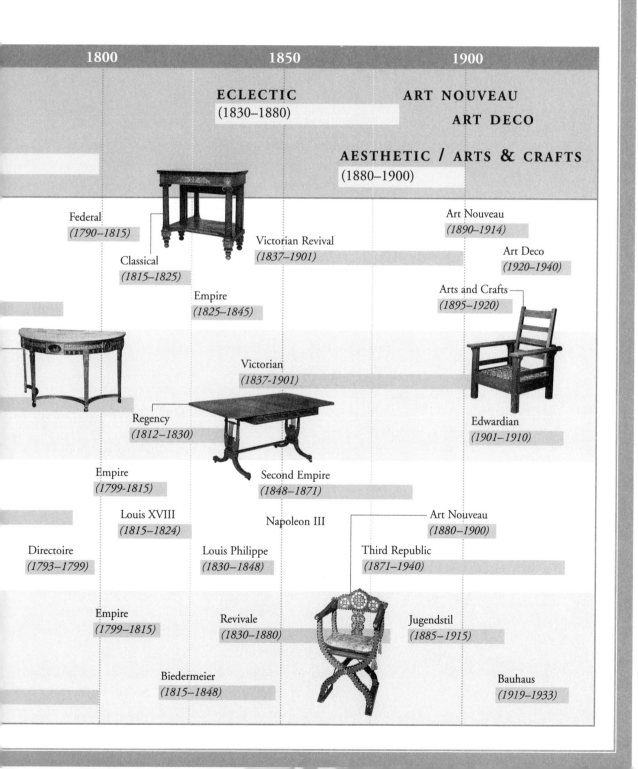

1800	1850	1900

ECLECTIC
(1830–1880)

ART NOUVEAU

ART DECO

AESTHETIC / ARTS & CRAFTS
(1880–1900)

Federal
(1790–1815)

Art Nouveau
(1890–1914)

Art Deco
(1920–1940)

Victorian Revival
(1837–1901)

Classical
(1815–1825)

Arts and Crafts
(1895–1920)

Empire
(1825–1845)

Victorian
(1837-1901)

Regency
(1812–1830)

Edwardian
(1901–1910)

Empire
(1799-1815)

Second Empire
(1848–1871)

Louis XVIII
(1815–1824)

Napoleon III

Art Nouveau
(1880–1900)

Directoire
(1793–1799)

Louis Philippe
(1830–1848)

Third Republic
(1871–1940)

Empire
(1799–1815)

Revivale
(1830–1880)

Jugendstil
(1885–1915)

Biedermeier
(1815–1848)

Bauhaus
(1919–1933)

*BOSTON
HIGHBOY*

This highboy, passed down through nine generations, was traced to the guest's ancestor, Benjamin Gale of Williamstown, Massachusetts. People looked to Boston as the "style center" during Colonial times, and this classic Boston piece dates from 1740. The fan-carved ray on the center drawer represents a sunburst, and the meticulously inlaid drawers are graduated (they increase in depth). The chest has cabriole legs and a nice combination of dark and light woods and original brasses.

Leigh Keno admired the 250-year-old inscription on the back of a drawer, but, unfortunately, noticed in the same drawer a remnant of the original finish. The chest has been cleaned. According to the Kenos, if the old finish had been retained, this chest would be worth $100,000 to $120,000! But its value is now reduced to $50,000.

interesting and valuable, but technically it's still "used," not antique. A piece of furniture can actually *be* antique, however, and still be worth less than its modern counterpart, because there were mediocre craftsmen working a century ago, just as there are today.

A second category of antique that has only moderate value is the antique **reproduction** of a style or design of an even earlier period. A "Baroque" chair made in 1879 is, strictly speaking, antique because of its age, but it is not period. It is an old reproduction.

Period furniture is the plum in the pie, the pinnacle of the antiques pyramid. It is furniture that was made in the period when its design was first popular and new, and it is generally the most valuable of antique furniture. ("Period" is a term commonly used to refer to furniture made before the Industrial Era, or pre-1840.) A Baroque chair of the period ought to have been made around 1600. A Duncan Phyfe chair is period if it was made c. 1801–1825. Period furniture may be of mediocre quality, but it is always a legitimate product of its time.

As an example of the distinction between "period" and "antique" furniture, consider the following: In 1876 there was a great centennial celebration in Philadelphia, and excellent copies of the American furniture that was popular in 1776—elaborate highboys and hand-carved Chippendale-style chairs—were reproduced in quantity, often beautifully. These are termed "Centennial" pieces today, but they may look disconcertingly "period" because, in addition to the accuracy of their imitation, they have acquired 100-plus years of patina. Of course, since they are over 100 years old, they are legally antiques, and they are generally far better crafted and made of finer materials than today's reproduction highboys. But they are not period furniture, and they don't compare to it in value.

Following are some suggestions for distinguishing antique and period furniture from used furniture. Keep in mind that you may be dealing with antique and valuable furniture, and proceed with great caution.

♦ Run your fingers underneath or over the back of the piece: very sharp edges and corners can indicate recent manufacture.

♦ If the muslin dustcover is not original, carefully tear back one of its corners from beneath an upholstered chair, and use your fingers (a flashlight is helpful, too) to feel the blocks of wood glued in the corners and the undersides of the chair rails. Edges and backs should feel hand-finished, slightly irregular and uneven to the touch, rounded and soft, and never razor-sharp.

♦ If the upholstery is not original, lift one edge at the chair rail to check for the innumerable nail holes which, to a trained eye, are the reassuring sign of many reupholsterings over the course of a long life.

♦ Look for the distinctive curved pattern left in sawn wood by the teeth of a circular saw. It is one important sign of manufacture after 1840.

♦ Remove one screw in some inconspicuous spot. An old, handmade screw will have irregular widths between the spirals, running the whole length of the shaft. The slot in the head may be off-center. (New screws have sharp points and regular, evenly spaced threads.)

♦ When scratched lightly with a fingernail, old pine and poplar wood (look for it behind chests of drawers and beneath drawer bottoms) will show a light line on the age-darkened surface. Aged poplar has a greenish tinge.

♦ Wood veneers on antique furniture are of thick and somewhat irregular widths, rather like home-sliced bread. (You can judge this by noting the veneer edges on the backs of chest tops, for instance, or wherever bits of veneer have broken away.) Modern veneers are thin, with every slice exactly the same width.

The underside of an old chest of drawers: hand-hewn, darkened with age, revealing no new elements—just what you hope to see.

Circular saw marks.

A brass rosette conceals the bolt head on this handsomely carved Federal mahogany bedpost, c. 1790–1810.

VICTORIAN REVIVAL

From c. 1840 on, coinciding with advances in furniture manufacturing technology, furniture design became a cavalcade of styles revived from the past. Lacking in originality, such reworking of designs of earlier eras tended to debase the originals they emulated, and all such revivals are lumped, today, under the general heading "Victorian." This retrospective era yielded ultimately to the innovative end-of-century styles of the Aesthetic Movement, Art Nouveau, and Arts and Crafts—all of which looked forward to the modern era.

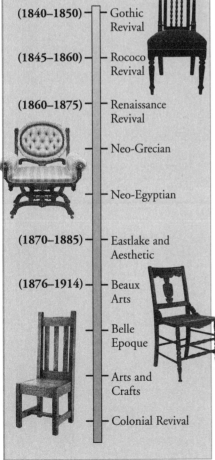

(1840–1850)	Gothic Revival
(1845–1860)	Rococo Revival
(1860–1875)	Renaissance Revival
	Neo-Grecian
	Neo-Egyptian
(1870–1885)	Eastlake and Aesthetic
(1876–1914)	Beaux Arts
	Belle Epoque
	Arts and Crafts
	Colonial Revival

♦ Check for wear on the top rails of chairs (where dust cloths have smoothed away the original edge) and under the runners of drawers, which will be very smooth. Dining table legs may be scuffed and nicked from generations of restless feet. Some wear is good, of course, and worn, though not worn-out, is perfect.

♦ Old tables don't have metal or plastic taps on the bottoms of their feet. (Sometimes these have been recently added to an old piece. Usually, they haven't.)

♦ Turn over a tripod table. Period table pedestals are often reinforced with a hand-hammered metal disk or a tri-part metal strap where the legs join. Twentieth-century tables may be reinforced with large, crimped staples. A one-board top, made from a single piece of wood, is a good indication of age.

♦ See if the piece is branded with the name of a manufacturer. Look for a pencil, chalk, or ink inscription on the underside of a table or drawer. A name of any kind, appearing anywhere on an antique piece, is always interesting and worthy of research. (Stenciled numbers, however, are late-nineteenth- to early-twentieth-century factory inventory numbers.)

♦ Until 1800, all the mirror glass in America was imported. Antique glass is thin (less than ⅛ inch thick), variably wavy, and somewhat gray in color. To determine if a piece of mirror is old, hold the tip of a key to the glass. The closer the tip of the reflected image is to the tip of the actual key, the more likely it is that the glass is old.

Don't be misled by *where* you've found an old piece. Used furniture is as easy to carry up to the attic as antiques are, and gets equally dusty. On the other hand, valuable antique desks have been found in laundry rooms, being used as ironing boards and hidden beneath layers of scorched sheets.

Forms Characteristic of Their Era

SEVENTEENTH CENTURY

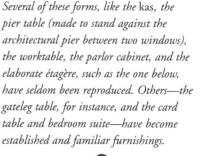

- The gateleg table
- The *kas* (a Dutch wardrobe)

EIGHTEENTH CENTURY

- The high chest (known colloquially as a highboy) and the accompanying dressing table (lowboy)
- Gaming (or card) tables
- Block-front secretary bookcases (third quarter of the eighteenth century)

EARLY NINETEENTH CENTURY

- The Neoclassical *récamier* sofa, an early-nineteenth-century version of an ancient Greek design

- Worktables, swivel-top card tables, pier tables, and center tables (early to mid-nineteenth century)

VICTORIAN (LATE NINETEENTH CENTURY)

- Highly elaborate parlor or side cabinets
- Bedroom suites
- Whatnots or étagères

Several of these forms, like the kas, the pier table (made to stand against the architectural pier between two windows), the worktable, the parlor cabinet, and the elaborate étagère, such as the one below, have seldom been reproduced. Others—the gateleg table, for instance, and the card table and bedroom suite—have become established and familiar furnishings.

PERIOD OR NOT?

In the late nineteenth century, a cabinetmaker named Ernest Hagen, once an employee of the famous craftsman Duncan Phyfe, began to reproduce his deceased employer's output of fifty years before—leg for leg, chair back for chair back. And because, by century's end, Phyfe's genuine furniture was beginning to succumb to age, Hagen also extensively repaired, remade, and reworked the pieces in need of repair that came his way. Today, these copies and restorations are confusing even to experts. By now, they are technically antiques. But they're not period antiques, and no matter how old they become, they never will be, nor will they be as desirable or costly as Phyfe's originals. (Although they'll probably continue to confuse scholars for years.)

A classical carved and inlaid mahogany breakfast table by Duncan Phyfe, 1800–1820.

FORMS

"Form" refers to a type or shape of furniture—a certain style or design of desk or table, for example. Some forms exist more or less unmodified for decades or even centuries; other forms were invented at a particular time and fell out of use, fashion, or favor sometime later. Understanding the history of forms can help you date a piece as well as determine whether the piece is a reproduction or even a fake.

Certain furniture designs and pieces were typical *only* of certain periods, as shown on the previous page.

WOOD

The woods used in furniture can indicate the region of manufacture. Primary woods are used on the exposed, visible portions of a piece. Secondary woods, less hard or attractive, are employed where they won't be seen, as on the backs of chests and the bottoms of drawers. Poplar and pine are secondary woods commonly used on American furniture.

Although some woods are relatively easy to identify, wood recognition is not for the casual attic-browser. The following general descriptions may help somewhat.

Pine, widely used in both America and England as a primary wood for inexpensive furniture and as a secondary wood, is very soft. It dents easily with just the pressure of a fingernail.

Oak, on the other hand, is quite hard and has a distinctive coarse and open grain. It is durable, though hard to carve, and is often used as secondary wood on English, French, and Dutch furniture.

Rosewood (named for its scent when freshly cut), found in India, Brazil, and the West Indies, is a very expensive, fine-grained, faintly oily wood with bold, almost black streaks.

Mahogany, from Africa, the Dominican Republic, Honduras, and other islands, is often stained a reddish

Woods Commonly Used in American Furniture

STYLE	WOODS COMMONLY USED
Seventeenth Century	Pilgrim-style furniture is primarily oak
William and Mary *(1690–1725)*	walnut, maple, cedrella (Spanish cedar)
Queen Anne *(1725–1750)*	walnut, birch, maple, cherry, mahogany
Chippendale *(1750–1780)*	mahogany, birch, cherry, maple, walnut
Federal *(1790–1815)*	mahogany, often with contrasting inlays and veneers and numerous other woods, including satinwood
Classical *(1815–1825)*	mahogany, maple, rosewood
Empire *(1825–1845)*	rosewood, grained maple, mahogany
Victorian Revival *(1840–1880)*	rosewood, mahogany, walnut
Country and Shaker *(1690–1900)*	Pine, maple, birch

Above: Showing Sheraton influence, a Philadelphia carved mahogany arm-chair attributed to Henry Connelly, c. 1800.

Upright and foursquare, Pilgrim-style furniture is easily identified by the multitude of turned spindles.

The shield-shaped back reveals the Hepplewhite influence in this American Federal chair.

brown, but is also seen in its natural golden brown state. It is undoubtedly the most popular furniture wood. Used to make both solid cabinetry and veneers, it can be recognized by markings of fine, short, blackish "hairs." It is often highly figured.

Cherry is commonly used in its solid form rather than as veneer. The color of cherry wood, a rich and warm red-brown, is distinctive.

Walnut was used both for veneers and in solid form in mid-eighteenth-century furniture. Sometimes handsomely figured, walnut takes an exceptional polish.

A Visual Guide to Styles

When our ancestors ordered furniture, they chose every detail, from the wood to the style of carving. There was no one way to create a chair, which is why there are so many different "Chippendale-style" chair backs, not to mention chairs of mixed styles—for instance, Hepplewhite backs married to Queen Anne legs. The chart below shows some examples of the major styles. Learning to recognize the typical part will help you to see the harmonious whole.

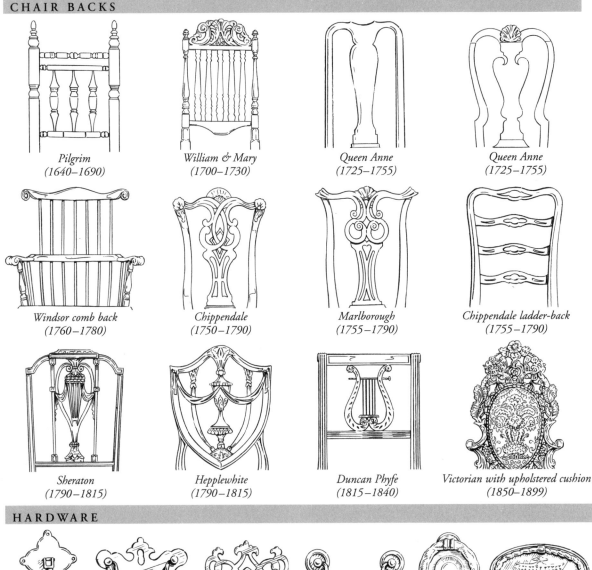

CHAIR BACKS

Pilgrim
(1640–1690)

William & Mary
(1700–1730)

Queen Anne
(1725–1755)

Queen Anne
(1725–1755)

Windsor comb back
(1760–1780)

Chippendale
(1750–1790)

Marlborough
(1755–1790)

Chippendale ladder-back
(1755–1790)

Sheraton
(1790–1815)

Hepplewhite
(1790–1815)

Duncan Phyfe
(1815–1840)

Victorian with upholstered cushion
(1850–1899)

HARDWARE

Diamond with
teardrop pull
(1700–1730)

Solid batwing
(1750–1790)

Pierced backplate
(1750–1790)

Plain curved batwing
(c. 1800)

Brass ring drop
(1800–1820)

Stamped drop
(late eighteenth
century)

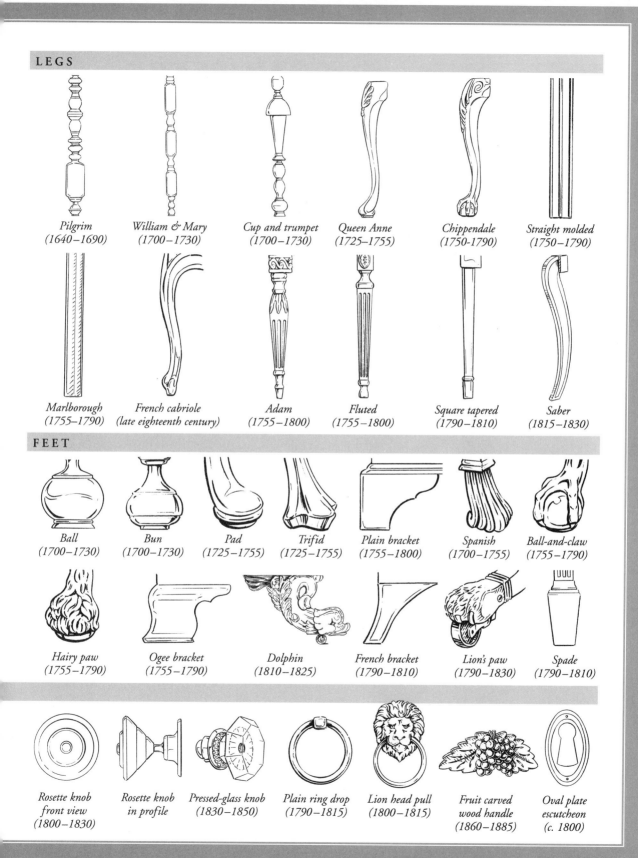

LEGS

Pilgrim
(1640–1690)

William & Mary
(1700–1730)

Cup and trumpet
(1700–1730)

Queen Anne
(1725–1755)

Chippendale
(1750–1790)

Straight molded
(1750–1790)

Marlborough
(1755–1790)

French cabriole
(late eighteenth century)

Adam
(1755–1800)

Fluted
(1755–1800)

Square tapered
(1790–1810)

Saber
(1815–1830)

FEET

Ball
(1700–1730)

Bun
(1700–1730)

Pad
(1725–1755)

Trifid
(1725–1755)

Plain bracket
(1755–1800)

Spanish
(1700–1755)

Ball-and-claw
(1755–1790)

Hairy paw
(1755–1790)

Ogee bracket
(1755–1790)

Dolphin
(1810–1825)

French bracket
(1790–1810)

Lion's paw
(1790–1830)

Spade
(1790–1810)

Rosette knob
front view
(1800–1830)

Rosette knob
in profile

Pressed-glass knob
(1830–1850)

Plain ring drop
(1790–1815)

Lion head pull
(1800–1815)

Fruit carved
wood handle
(1860–1885)

Oval plate
escutcheon
(c. 1800)

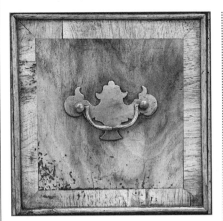

Indications of wear and use surround the hardware on this drawer from an eighteenth-century English dressing table.

Sandwich glass knobs can sometimes be found on mid-nineteenth-century American furniture.

A "through-tenon" seen emerging through the back of a chair.

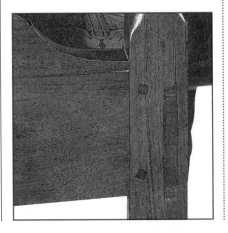

HARDWARE

Most pre-1800 hardware is handmade, hand-forged, and hand-tooled. (Be aware that many antiques have replacement hardware.) Wrought iron was used for hinges and escutcheons (the metal surrounds of keyholes) until about 1690, after which cast brass became the metal of choice for drawer pulls and toe caps. If a drawer pull has not been polished smooth (and if it has, that's a good indication of age), it may still show evidences of the workman's file or hammer.

♦ Screws were invented in the sixteenth century, but until the nineteenth century they were expensive. Screws with perfectly pointed tips and centered slots in the head became more common in the early nineteenth century.

♦ Victorian hardware is frequently embellished with the florid designs typical of the period.

♦ Original nails on antique furniture should be crude, handmade or machine-cut. The steel-wire nail we see today wasn't in use until c. 1880.

♦ Hardware can be original to the period and to the piece, or it can look quite unlike other hardware of that era, which means the original hardware may have been replaced at a later date. Drawer pulls are often replaced, for, as screws become stripped, the original hardware falls off and gets lost. Hardware fashions do change, too, though fairly slowly, and owners like to update their furniture. Look for the "ghosts" of the original hardware beneath newer brass fittings.

♦ If you find an escutcheon that's marked (on the back) or if a drawer has a labeled lock, it can help to identify the age of the piece, although there's much less information on hardware identification than there is on cabinetmakers. Most hardware on antique American furniture was imported from England. (And if the hardware is stamped "Made in England," look no further for clues to its age. The words "made in" for *any* country always indicate a manufacture date later than 1890, when the McKinley Tariff Act required labeling denoting the country of origin.)

Mortise-and-tenon construction.

CONSTRUCTION

Early furniture was constructed by woodworkers known as joiners. These craftsmen "joined" pieces of wood to make the basic furniture forms of the day, using for the most part the mortise-and-tenon method of joining, in which the two pieces of wood to be held together were shaped to lock together. The resulting join was held in place by a wooden peg or a dowel rather than a screw or glue. Dovetailing, a later construction method, was a technique connecting the drawer front to the drawer side, most easily seen on the sides of drawers and still in use today. Glued joints were often used with dovetailed construction as well.

♦ In general, the fineness and evenness of the construction method is some indication of age: early wooden pegs or dowels were irregular; later ones were perfectly symmetrical. Nails and screws also progressed from irregular and uneven to smooth and uniform.

♦ If, when you're examining a piece of supposedly early furniture, you find anything remotely resembling plywood or staples, you can turn off your flashlight. Both are signs of modern construction.

♦ Dovetails, the triangular wood "teeth" that enable the sides of drawers to slot into each other, are an excellent aid to dating. On period furniture, they are handmade, and each tooth can differ slightly from the others. Although, in the Pilgrim era, cabinetry dovetails were quite crude, as techniques and tools improved during the eighteenth century they became increasingly fine. The legs of tripod tables are usually dovetailed into the central pillar, but the dovetails

Dovetail joints.

The inscribed line left by the cabinetmaker is visible along the edge of this drawer with its hand-cut dovetails.

JOHN QUINCY ADAMS CHAIR

Although it is known as a "Senate Chair," this chair was actually issued to John Quincy Adams in the United States House of Representatives. Because it is also the chair he died in, in February 1848, the chair was considered bad luck and relegated to the office of the sergeant-at-arms. It went from there to a private home in upstate New York, was donated to the local chapter of the DAR, and was then bought at auction by the present owner.

Said expert Wendell Garrett, "The chair is a piece of history," for John Quincy Adams was part of a famous American family, the son of a president, a president himself, and the only former president to return to the House as a representative. Garrett put a price tag on this aesthetically undistinguished bit of history of $4,000 to $6,000.

may be concealed beneath a piece of reinforcing metal. Eventually, dovetails were machine-made and thus completely regular in size.

♦ After c. 1850, the back panels of centrally recessed sideboards were usually screwed on rather than tenoned through the back.

♦ Look for dovetails, evidences of hand-planing, hand-made screws and nails.

♦ Philadelphia manufacture is a possibility if the end of the tenon affixing the side rail of a chair to the rear leg shows through on the back of the leg, and if the pegs that "nail" the tenon in place also show.

DECORATIVE DETAILS

INLAY

Inlay is ornament created by insetting variously shaped pieces of wood, ivory, or metal into a recessed surface. Inlays were frequently fashioned by craftsmen who sold them to local cabinetmakers who then incorporated the inlays into their designs. The fashion for inlay comes and goes. Figural inlay—in the form of shells, fans, shields, and, lastly but most desirably, American eagles—is most often found on delicate Hepplewhite furniture. It lost ground to elaborate carving until late in the nineteenth century, and reappeared in the 1870s on Aesthetic-style pieces. It can be found in Oriental, Egyptian, and Classic Greek motifs.

BRONZE APPLIQUÉS

Gilded bronze mounts on American furniture were almost invariably imported from England and France. They first appeared here early in the nineteenth century, depicting Classical figures and other Greek motifs on high-style American Classical furniture. Revived for use on French-style Victorian furniture in the mid- to late nineteenth

century, when designs became elaborate and gilt-ridden once more, they are nevertheless atypical of American furniture, for on the whole Americans prefer their wood unmounted and metallically unadorned.

CARVING

Fine carving is always well executed and usually highly realistic. Repetitive motifs like reeding and gadrooning should show unevenness and variations in width and depth; if such elements are completely regular throughout their length, they are likely to have been machined. There should be a nice buildup of dirt and wax in the recesses. And especially on ostensibly eighteenth-century pieces, the originally sharp edges of the carving should feel smooth—with no sharp edges—on every prominent spot.

IS IT VALUABLE?

Value, in furniture, depends chiefly on four criteria—rarity, provenance, quality, and condition. Of these, only condition and provenance are fairly simple to establish. The other two usually require time, research, and experience—and probably the help of an expert—to apply accurately. Three other elements—patina, finish, and color—are also important in considering furniture's value.

RARITY

The words "rare" and "antique" are somehow linked together in our minds, although an antique piece can be quite rare, in fact, and still be of absolutely no interest to anyone. Take United States Vice President Daniel D. Tompkins' gout stool, for example. One of a kind? Absolutely! But desirable?

Above: An inlaid fan enriches a drawer from a mid-eighteenth-century Boston dressing table.

Examples of reeding (right) and gadrooning (below).

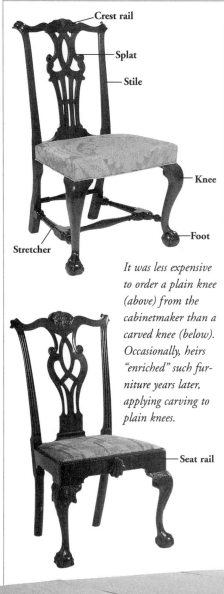

Crest rail

Splat

Stile

Knee

Foot

Stretcher

It was less expensive to order a plain knee (above) from the cabinetmaker than a carved knee (below). Occasionally, heirs "enriched" such furniture years later, applying carving to plain knees.

Seat rail

From J. and J.W. Meeks of New York, c. 1825–1845, an Empire drop-leaf table with somewhat clumsy proportions and undistinguished design.

Consider how the antiques market functions. Dealers and curators want to buy the best and most remarkable pieces. In this case, neither the form of our example—a gout stool—nor its provenance (who was Daniel D. Tompkins, anyway?) would merit inclusion in an important collection. And museum and dealer preferences are closely followed by and highly influential with the public, which hopes to buy for itself, if not identical pieces, then pieces similar to what the trendsetters are buying. All enthusiasts, curators, dealers, and scholars are constantly in search of the rare. But when they all agree that a particular antique, despite its rarity, has nothing aesthetically interesting or significant to say about the era in which it was created—in other words, when it is simply a bit of historical trivia—it might be as one-of-a-kind as a vice president's gout stool, but no one will want to own it.

Another exception is the piece that is genuinely rare, a fine example of its type, in excellent condition, but from a period in which there is not much scholarly interest at the moment (though in the future, of course, there may be). And, sadly, there is also the piece that just isn't as rare as one believes it is. When friends, and the owner of the local antiques shop, agree they have "never seen another one like it," it's easy for the novice to believe that he or she has the only example of a particular type of chair, table, or gout stool in the country. Yet in New York, Chicago, and Los Angeles, there may be hundreds of identical objects going unsold in antiques shops and at auctions.

PROVENANCE

Most people also believe that an important pedigree, or provenance, adds thousands of dollars to the value of an antique. Families hand down stories about "the bed George Washington slept in" or Napoleon's anything at all. Not so long ago, when the antiques world was less rigorous and scholarly than it is today, such "histories" *could* convince the unwary and may have driven up value. Today, however, we require actual proof that Washington laid his head to rest somewhere—something on the order of a notation in a fellow officer's journal that "the General enjoyed Mr. Smith's hospitality overnight, and breakfasted well next morning." Naturally, such documentation is exceedingly hard to come by, but without some proof—a letter, a contemporary reference or, best of all, traceable descent through the Washington family to you—your bed, despite that "G.W." carved into the bedpost, has no useful provenance at all.

QUALITY

In antique furniture, value depends to a large extent on the quality of craftsmanship or construction and the quality of the design. Naturally, these are not always found together in a single piece. But how can you tell a good piece of furniture from a mediocre one (known colloquially as "brown wood")?

First of all, keep in mind that there's quite a lot of bad antique furniture around. "Old" is not necessarily "good." And "old" is not necessarily "valuable," either.

The very best of antique furniture was expensive when it was new and was entirely custom-made. A client could order a table with a plain or carved knee, with hairy-paw or hairless feet, in an expensive, rare wood or a common, affordable one, and each element was individually priced. The best piece, the one that we value today, is always crafted of rare or beautiful woods or cased in beautifully matched veneers. If carving is called for, it is highly sculptural, with every detail crisp. The proportions of the best pieces are always excellent: legs neither too short nor too chunky for the height; backs and arms in perfect balance with leg-length and seat-width. The hardware—if there is hardware—is an adornment integral to the whole design, not stuck on like some shiny afterthought. If it was costly then, it will be valuable now. For "the best" is generally a

Superior carving on the crest rail and back splat of a Philadelphia Chippendale mahogany side chair, 1760–1780.

An example of a carved knee.

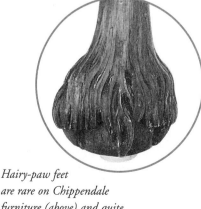

Hairy-paw feet are rare on Chippendale furniture (above) and quite desirable on most types of pre-Victorian era furniture.

WINDSOR CHAIR

Stephen Fletcher was appraising furniture in a summer home in Martha's Vineyard when he happened across a beautiful chair which, according to him, is "a perfect New England example of a Windsor chair" and thus worth ten or twenty times the value of similar chairs in the house. Why? First, it has its original paint. Two to three coats of early paint can be seen underneath the seat of the chair— the newest layer, about 100 years old. Second, although there is evidence of wear, the legs are intact (that is, they have never been cut down). Dating from the last quarter of the eighteenth century, such a chair is worth at least $1,000.

The comb-back Windsor is a characteristically American form.

An example of freehand painting on a slide-lid box.

work of art, and, like any great art, it's expensive and in short supply.

You can learn to judge quality for yourself. Read books on furniture, look at the pictures carefully, make objective comparisons with photos from museum collections, or better yet, see them in person. Cultivate your eye. The mission of museums is to present visitors with examples of the finest artifacts from the past. If you observe the best, you can train your eye to recognize it when you see it. One or two similar details shared by your own piece and a museum piece aren't enough to qualify your piece as a valuable antique, for your piece may have "problems." Perhaps the upper and lower sections of your chest don't really match, making them a marriage—two parts that were not "born" together. An otherwise well-crafted piece may have clumsy-looking inlay, indicating that the inlay was added later. When hardware looks wrong—too big, too small, or just vaguely out of period—it may have been added later or replaced. And when a piece lacks design cohesion, or when a handsome design seems carelessly carved, it may be that the joiner and carver were two individuals, born fifty or even a hundred years apart.

PATINA AND FINISH

The dictionary defines "patina" as "the sheen on a surface caused by long handling." Alternatively, you could say that the accumulation of wax, soil, stains, and oils that human hands have left on the furniture over the course of many years have created a smooth film of—well—dirt.

Museum curators, dealers, and auction house experts are the ones who establish styles in finishes, and their theories about patina seem to change each generation or so. At the moment, it is considered heretical to remove patina or to refinish any antique. The more buildup, the better. Such "original finish" is *de rigueur* today, because that finish reflects the whole history of a piece and cannot be reproduced. (Twenty years ago, however, museum curators were cleaning, polishing, and regilding their furniture collections, so dealers and collectors did the same, and much good furniture—by current standards, at least—was compromised.) Yet America's early manufacturers certainly sent their wares out into the world looking shiny and new—without a smudge of patina on their freshly shellacked tops and drawers. So some antiques experts disagree with today's emphasis on original finish. Expert John Hays observes that, in the evaluation of American furniture, the validity and beauty of the form of the piece are most important: "Original finish should not be allowed to become more important than these qualities, or the tail will be wagging the dog."

COLOR

Old furniture has either acquired a rich, deep color or it has faded. If you want to see what color it was when it left the cabinetmaker's bench, just remove a piece of hardware. (Difference in color can also be a good indication of age.)

Furniture tops and drawer fronts, exposed to sun, are often a different color from hidden areas like backs and drawer bottoms. These reveal a mottled, uneven darkening and might be almost black. (If they seem too uniformly darkened, however, they may have been stained at a later date to hide a replacement or repair.) The outsides of old drawers, where they are exposed to air, will have darkened, but drawer interiors are often close to the original shade of the wood.

A considerable amount of American furniture, from the Pilgrim era to recent times, was painted. Paint is a handy and affordable cloak for covering unlovely wood grain or concealing unmatched wood. "Graining" was one technique by which woods that were more expensive than the customer could afford were imitated, sometimes extremely well, in paint. Paint also made a decent imitation Oriental lacquer (a painstakingly

A stenciled detail on a chair splat. Lower end of splat marked in gold paint "W.P. Eaton," for William Page Eaton of New England, 1830–1850.

Graining, painting, and stenciling on an individualistic American washstand with eagle heads, c. 1830–1845.

S E Y M O U R   C A R D   T A B L E

Thirty years ago, this guest unwittingly bought a fine example of a John Seymour card table for $25 at a garage sale. The Seymour workshop in Boston, owned by a family of well-known British cabinet-makers, crafted this inlaid demilune card table.

Leigh and Leslie Keno admitted that their hearts were pounding when they saw the piece, for it is labeled, still has its nice old color, and is in fine condition. The front is meticulously inlaid with the beautifully tapering bellflowers that also decorate the legs. According to the Kenos, the piece could bring $200,000 or more.

built-up accretion of extremely hard, waterproof varnish). Stenciling and freehand painting were used in the nineteenth century to simulate the costly gilt or bronze ornament decorating European court furniture. But much of this paint today, perhaps because the surfaces weren't well prepared, perhaps because of rough treatment, is flaking or chipping away and lacks the brilliance it had when new. Now, as long as this is original paint, its condition won't enormously affect its value as an antique. What you *don't* want to see is repainted paint—no matter how well done or how like the original it is. That first surface, once gone, is lost forever.

Shellac, a common antique finish, deepens in color with age, turning painted, stenciled, and gilt areas brownish-orange. Any stained or painted area that appears somehow different from the finish on the remainder of a piece may have been repainted, repaired, or altogether replaced. If a finish is fresh and gleaming, suspect either refinishing or a modern reproduction of an antique style.

CONDITION

We seldom find antique furniture in perfect condition. When we do, the furniture may have been of such fine quality to begin with that it was exceptionally well cared for along the way. But even when furniture is not pristine—as is usually the case—the piece that retains the most value is the piece that can be returned to its original state with the least amount of restoration. A replaced arm is a lost arm and represents a significant loss in value. Most families know this and treasure their good furniture. They are justifiably appalled, therefore, when the 200-pound guest crushes the delicate Hepplewhite chair or when the veneer on the locked drawer maddeningly breaks long before the lock comes open.

Still, a certain amount of normal wear and tear *is* allowable on an antique piece of furniture. Wherever the human hand, foot, or bottom has come into constant contact with it, you can expect to see wear. Consequently, when you look at a piece, try to imagine how *you* would use it today. If a chair is actually old, for example, and especially if it is the sort of chair that gets much use, the hand rests should be smooth and the carving slightly worn away. If you were sitting in the chair, would your feet naturally hook in the stretchers? If so, those stretchers should be worn just where your heels would go. If hardware has been polished for years, there should be "halos" around the brass plates where the polish has abraded and bleached the surrounding wood. Tops can be stained, nicked, sun-bleached, and scratched without significantly altering value. It's presumed, too, that original upholstery will have disappeared entirely, to be replaced, frequently, by something inappropriate, like orange flocked velvet. (Still, it's a nice plus when the original upholstery is found, often under layers of the new.)

Legs are expected to be slightly worn down (especially on the rear legs, which are continuously being slid backward) and marked with dings from generations of close encounters with mops and vacuum cleaners. Despite years of abuse, legs should never be cut shorter, and if a leg is broken, yet is still affixed to a piece, that is not desirable, but it's infinitely better than having a piece with a replaced leg—or no leg at all.

Missing parts of any kind—except hardware—seriously diminish the value of antiques. The only exception to the rule is the piece that's one of a kind, which will never be found again. In that case, "as is" simply has to do.

Expect to find shrinkage on furniture over 100 years old. Because wood contracts across the grain, circular tabletops, for instance, become slightly ovate over the years. Secondary woods to which veneer is glued tend to be soft woods that shrink readily, so veneers, especially in America's exceptionally dry heat, will shrink and crack and sometimes fall off altogether. Drawer bottoms shrink away from drawer sides, and in extreme cases even solid wood tops, and most particularly the sides of chests, buckle, warp, and ultimately crack—an unhappy and virtually irreparable form of damage.

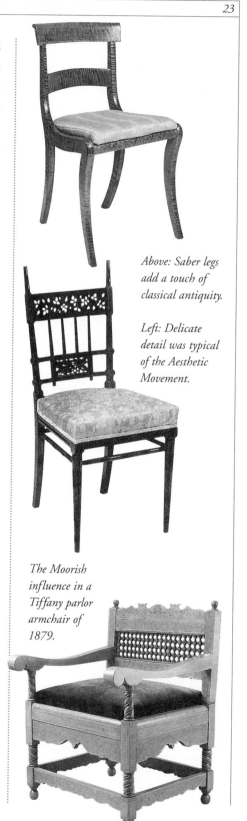

Above: Saber legs add a touch of classical antiquity.

Left: Delicate detail was typical of the Aesthetic Movement.

The Moorish influence in a Tiffany parlor armchair of 1879.

TIPS *from the* *experts*

Leigh Keno, Leslie Keno, and John Hays tell what to look for in furniture.

If, in looking at a piece of American furniture, you think you're seeing all kinds of styles mixed together, the piece is usually Victorian.—J.H.

There can never really be hard-and-fast rules about antique furniture, but here are some generally useful observations:

Replacement of the ends of chair and table legs is a common repair, for fragile leg tips wear down, break off, or rot away. To learn if legs have new ends (if they've been "ended out"), use dental floss to test all horizontal seams. If the floss sinks into the seam, suspect a repair.—Leigh K.

Old paint looks dry, crackled, and softer in color than new paint. —Leigh K.

On painted chairs, a black light can locate areas of new paint, which may be hiding repairs.—Leigh K.

The dovetails on the drawers of the two sections should also be consistent. —Leslie K.

The thickness of the wood, top and bottom, should match, and so should the type of wood. Drawer sides, for instance, shouldn't be pine on the top section and chestnut on the bottom.—Leslie K.

All of the above, incidentally, applies to other types of furniture. Drawers, color, and hardware should all be consistent throughout.—Leslie K.

Any or all of these conditions, however, do indicate genuine age.

In addition, here are a few specific details to watch for when evaluating furniture:

♦ Replaced mirror glass devalues the antique mirror even more than the flaking of its silvered back or (inconspicuous) cracks.

♦ The bonnet-top highboy is usually the most valuable type.

♦ Fine, vigorous carving on a piece of American Chippendale furniture generally increases its value.

♦ The more ornate design requires more handwork. Thus a wing chair with cabriole legs (curved legs ending in an ornamental foot) is more valuable than a block-leg chair, for instance.

♦ Exceptionally large pieces of furniture—pieces that are too big for modern homes and apartments—are always less desirable than smaller, more versatile pieces.

♦ "Fancy chairs"—delicate side and arm chairs decorated with gilt and paint—lose most of their resale value if they have been repainted. (Scratch through in an inconspicuous area to check for layers of paint.)

♦ Original upholstery lends value to seat furniture, especially when it is in good condition.

♦ Saber-leg chairs of the Classical period are more valuable than straight- or turned-leg chairs, particularly if the feet end in carved or brass paws.

If you are still convinced, after this iceberg's tip of cautions, that you own a piece of furniture that is old, is of superior quality, and has the exquisite carving, proportionate embellishments, elegant lines, and graceful curves of a masterpiece, and if it also seems to be the twin of one in the Metropolitan Museum of Art—well, perhaps you actually are the lucky owner of a fine and important antique, a rare museum piece. It happens.

AMERICAN FURNITURE

In America, not surprisingly, we find far more American furniture than we do Louis XVI commodes. Also not surprisingly, antique American furniture has considerably more value in this country than it has anywhere else in the world. (Collectors are chauvinists, worldwide.) That is why you'll want to learn how to distinguish genuine American pieces from confusingly similar-looking European examples. (For more help on this, see pages 32–33.)

In the eighteenth century, New York, Philadelphia, Boston, and Newport each developed its own style of furniture, often using recognizably different construction techniques and types of ornamentation. Every settled area in America had its peculiar regional characteristics of construction, carving, and design, generally based on its own cultural heritage. Boston furniture has a strong English bent; Pennsylvania's aesthetic is German. Regional preferences account for differences in small elements like ball-and-claw feet: Massachusetts, New York, and Pennsylvania examples all differ. Scholars research locations of eighteenth-century output, for the piece that can definitely be attributed to its place of manufacture becomes more valuable. Recent scholarship, for example, has begun to identify several Southern cities of manufacture, with a corresponding rise in value of those pieces that can be firmly attributed to the South.

Rural versions of American furniture have changed surprisingly little over time. The same chair designs have been used for 100 years or more, a fact which makes certain styles, like provincial ladder-back chairs and Windsor chairs, hard to date. After all, the "provinces," places like Vermont and Ohio, were far more provincial in past centuries than they are today. In the Colonial era, there were no magazine illustrations for craftsmen to copy, and the city, with its stylish shops, could be at a distance of many days' ride away. So a cabinetmaker in South Carolina

TIPS (Cont'd.)

About 99.9 percent of Windsor chairs were painted to unify the several woods used in their manufacture. To determine if yours has been repainted, turn the chair over and look under the seat for traces of the old paint (although an old repaint, done within the first several years of the chair's history, is acceptable). Original paint is highly desirable. —Leigh K.

The scalloped edge around the top of an eighteenth-century tilt-top table will never be applied: it will be carved from the piece of wood itself. (An applied edge will reveal telltale seams.)—Leigh K.

There should be anywhere from three to five plugged holes beneath the top of a tilt-top table. These reveal where the wood was held while being turned on a lathe.—Leigh K.

It is crucial to the value of case pieces (highboys and chest-on-chests) that their tops and bottoms belong together. Start by comparing the grain and the color of the wood. Grain should be consistent. Color, however, might vary, simply because a piece may have sat for years in a position that bathed its top, but not its bottom, in bleaching sunlight.—Leslie K.

Also check the "hardware history." Both top and bottom hardware should be made of the same material, be of the same age, and be affixed by the same types of screws. If hardware is removed, it ought to reveal identical "ghosts" on the wood, top and bottom.—Leslie K.

American Furniture Craftsmen

Phyfe

Duncan Phyfe was in fact a Scot. Along with manufacturing delicately reeded and carved mahogany furniture, he was an accomplished salesman of his own well-made and, usually, moderately stylish wares. Phyfe's furniture was so popular that, at one point, his New York shop employed over 100 men.

CHARLES-HONORÉ LANNUIER *(fl. 1790–1819)*

NEW YORK A Frenchman, Lannuier crafted the best high-style Classical furniture in America, employing gilding, figured mahogany, rosewood, bronze mounts, and caryatid and other figural carvings. His work is often stamped.

Lannuier

WILLIAM SAVERY
(1721–1788)

PHILADELPHIA The work of this Quaker craftsman is, in its simplicity, restraint, and dignity, an unusual interpretation of the generally ornamental and rococo Chippendale style. Savery shared Affleck's preference for working from English pattern books.

GODDARD-TOWNSEND SCHOOL *(fl. 1725–1785)*

NEWPORT, RHODE ISLAND A family of superbly talented cabinet-makers and their apprentices, noted for their rhythmically sculptural block-front case furniture embellished with robustly carved shells.

Goddard-Townsend

JOHN COGSWELL
(1738–1818)

BOSTON Cogswell is best known for the case pieces he manufactured, often in *bombé* shapes. Although his Chippendale furniture is unusually elaborate for Boston, Cogswell's Neoclassical output (made in partnership with his son) resembles that of the Seymour firm in its use of tambour doors and painted interiors.

THOMAS AFFLECK
(1740–1795)

PHILADELPHIA One of the premier manufacturers of Philadelphia Chippendale furniture, Affleck masterfully translated that very English style into the American vernacular. His elegant, restrained cabinetry occasionally incorporated elements from Chippendale's "Director" verbatim.

DUNCAN PHYFE
(1768–1854)

NEW YORK The best-known and most influential American proponent of the "Grecian Style" in furniture,

JOHN AND THOMAS SEYMOUR *(fl. 1790–1820)*

BOSTON The Seymour shop was known for sophisticated Federal furniture of elegant proportions. It employed exceptionally fine inlay, contrasting veneers, and a particular shade of robin's-egg blue paint, frequently used for the interior of pigeon-hole desks.

GUSTAVE AND CHRISTIAN HERTER
(1830–1892; 1839–1883)

NEW YORK Herter Brothers worked successfully in many Revival styles. The brilliance of its Aesthetic Movement designs and its Japanese-style furniture in cherrywood and ebony were unsurpassed in the nineteenth century.

JOHN HENRY BELTER
(1833–1867)

NEW YORK Among the best known of America's mid-nineteenth-century cabinetmakers, Belter produced elaborate and highly ornamented Rococo Revival parlor furniture. A patented wood-laminating technique allowed Belter to manufacture elements with unusually deep curves on chairs, tables, and beds, which were also often pierced and lavishly carved with realistic carved flora.

ALEXANDER ROUX
(fl. 1837–1881)

NEW YORK A French immigrant, Roux worked in all the revival styles, successfully manufacturing everything from bronze mounted furniture to faux bamboo in order to meet the eclectic tastes of the times. Roux also imported and retailed furniture made in France by his brother.

Roux

GUSTAV STICKLEY
(1857–1942)

NEW YORK Several members of the Stickley family were engaged in manufacturing furniture, but Gustav's rectilinear Arts and Crafts-style oak wares, with their exposed tenons and strong clean lines, are preferred today. In reaction to the materialism of late-nineteenth-century America, Gustav Stickley called his firm the Craftsman Workshop. In 1916, it was taken over by his brothers and renamed Stickley Mfrg. Co.

Stickley

POTTIER AND STYMUS
(fl. 1859–1880s)

NEW YORK Purveyors of fashionable revival furniture, Auguste Pottier was a cabinetmaker and William Stymus was an upholsterer. Their work often makes use of bronze mounts, inlay, and porcelain plaques.

FRANK LLOYD WRIGHT *(1867–1959)*

CHICAGO An iconoclastic Midwestern architect, Wright believed, along with proponents of the Arts and Crafts movement, that there was a need for high-quality, machine-made furniture— pieces for mass consumption.

Wright

His spare (and often uncomfortable) furniture, usually of dark-stained oak, tends to be highly linear and strongly vertical or horizontal in design.

CHARLES AND HENRY GREENE
(1868–1957; 1870–1954)

PASADENA The Greene brothers, like many architects who designed furniture to complement their clients' houses, launched the California Bungalow style from their Pasadena shop. Greene pieces combined the Arts and Crafts tenets of Wright and Stickley with those of Englishman Charles Eastlake, incorporating various materials such as ebony, silver, and semiprecious stones. Oriental details and ebony pegs are typical of Greene and Greene manufacture.

Roycroft

ROYCROFT
(1895–1938)

NEW YORK Elbert Hubbard, the founder of Roycroft, was highly influenced by British Arts and Crafts design and made Arts and Crafts furniture in East Aurora, New York. Roycroft doors and cupboards have exposed copper hinges. (See "Roycroft Copper," page 218.)

American Windsor chairs, unlike their English counterparts, almost never have a central decorative splat at the back.

This Rococo Revival rosewood chair by Belter is the essence of Victoriana.

might have been asked to make a chair based on the verbal description of a customer who remembered having seen one like it in Boston or Charleston. Or, if he had access to such a scarce and wonderful thing as a pattern book, like those published by the English craftsmen Thomas Chippendale and George Hepplewhite, he might have been able to copy a design—to the best of his perhaps limited ability. By the nineteenth century, the provincial cabinetmaker was able to reproduce contemporary styles by studying a New York furniture manufacturer or importer's brochure. But he still had to rely on local materials and his own, usually unsophisticated eye. For all these reasons, there is an enormous amount of very ordinary antique furniture in existence today. (Which is not to say that good "country" pieces can't be wonderful, or that quality furniture was never manufactured outside the great cities. Or, for that matter, that so-so pieces were never made by urban craftsmen.)

AMERICAN FOLK FURNITURE

While high-style Belter furniture was being made in 1850 in New York, provincial cabinetmakers were content to be fashioning simple pieces in the Federal and Classical styles of forty years before. The designs of folk and country furniture may have lagged behind those of urban wares because the clientele of frontier and country cabinetmakers were conservative or because the craftsmen's pattern books, if any, were probably out of date. Thus, dating country furniture can be difficult.

Such chests (and chairs and tables) were usually crafted of local woods, several kinds in combination, which is why they were often given a concealing coat of paint or hidden beneath a painted faux-wood grain that imitated richer materials like rosewood or mahogany. This painting is unquestionably a form of folk art in itself, as are these sometimes surprisingly elegant and well-executed pieces of furniture. Folk art collectors are particularly enthusiastic about the eccentric and usually idiosyncratic country pieces of the eighteenth and early nineteenth centuries. Yet, while numerous rustic pieces, like Windsor chairs, country cupboards, blanket chests, pie safes, and farm tables, were certainly of excellent quality, it was the Shaker community that produced some of America's finest country furniture.

SHAKER 1790–1900

The Shaker religious sect emigrated from England to America in 1774. The life the Shakers sought was simplicity itself, based on concepts of self-sufficiency and commonly owned property. The Shakers believed that "utility is beauty," and the furniture they designed was exceptionally well constructed and almost effortlessly practical. It was generally made of fruitwood, pine, or naturally seasoned maple. Seat furniture was fashioned of wood and the characteristic woven tape or was made with cane, splint, or wicker. The best and earliest Shaker work was either painted, palely stained, or dark red, and the best period of Shaker furniture manufacture is considered to have been between 1790 and 1840. Much light, strong Shaker furniture was manufactured in the area surrounding New Lebanon, New York, but it was also made in Massachusetts, Maine, Ohio, and Kentucky, and it was sold commercially.

A handsome, practical, typical Shaker rock maple taped side chair.

Shaker red-stained tall chest, New Lebanon, New York, 1820–1840.

IS IT VALUABLE?

Nineteenth-century furniture, once neglected, has become increasingly valuable in the past twenty years and is well worth researching. A few guidelines:

♦ Before 1880, the casters on Shaker beds were set sideways to keep the beds from rolling away from the wall. Shaker beds made after 1880 have casters that swivel.

♦ Around 1900, there was a revival of Jacobean furniture, in which dark-stained, shallowly carved elements on chair backs, for example, were often centered by

English Furniture Designers and Craftsmen

Hepplewhite

(1791–1794). He carried the popular furniture styles of Hepplewhite to new levels of fashion and ornamentation. His design repertoire, replete with delicate husks and swags, inlays and flutings, carved and inlaid ornament, highly figured contrasting woods, and clever "mechanical" furniture, made his work immediately and lastingly fashionable.

CHARLES EASTLAKE *(1836–1906)*

A designer and art critic, Eastlake published the highly influential *Hints on Household Taste* in 1868. Today his name is primarily associated with furniture having medieval Gothic characteristics (often termed Modern Gothic). The pieces are generally of walnut or ebonized wood and highly architectural, with turned, pierced, and inlaid trefoils, quatrefoils, spindles, as well as incised linear decoration, often relieved by gilding.

A watered-down American version of an Eastlake design.

GILLOWS *(1695–c.1885)*

Known for fine-quality, conservative, and stylish furniture, Gillows of Lancaster began to impress its name on its wares after c. 1780. Look on the front edges of drawers and on the backs or seat rails of chairs.

Chippendale

THOMAS CHIPPENDALE *(1718–1779)*

His book of designs (and self-advertisement), *The Gentleman and Cabinet-maker's Director* (1754–1762), gave this brilliant Rococo designer a widespread influence on English, Irish, and American furniture manufacture.

ROBERT ADAM *(1728–1792)*

Adam's restrained and coolly intellectual Classical architecture, delicately embellished with mirrors, gilding, mythological bas-reliefs, and an austere, updated vocabulary of Classical ornament, inspired the fine furnishings he designed in the late eighteenth century for the residences he created.

GEORGE HEPPLEWHITE *(d. 1786)*

His 1788 volume, *The Cabinet-maker's and Upholsterer's Guide,* was published (posthumously) to instant success. Hepplewhite's designs gave curves to Adam's lines and were less costly. His influence is identifiable in shield-back chairs and sideboards with concave corners.

THOMAS SHERATON *(1751–1806)*

Sheraton was a designer and drawing master, and author of *The Cabinet-maker's and Upholsterer's Drawing Book* caned oval panels. These reproductions are never as heavy as the originals.

♦ Massive central pedestals and legs with animal-paw feet on dining room tables date from the mid-nineteenth to the early twentieth century.

♦ The top drawer of late American Empire (1840–1850) chests of drawers usually overhangs the drawers below. Despite elaborate embellishments like gilding, stenciling, or Sandwich glass pulls, the design is ponderous and, for that reason, of relatively little value.

ENGLISH AND CONTINENTAL FURNITURE

Because American furniture was, to the smallest drawer pull, usually based on European and English designs, it is illuminating to examine the prototypes. For centuries, American furnishings of all kinds tended to reproduce those of England (with a Dutch overlay on the earliest pieces), while England itself often elaborated on French designs. By the nineteenth century, the increasingly sophisticated American cabinetmaker followed suit, also imitating French designs, so both can look quite French. Nevertheless, European furniture is usually very different from the American product in line and proportion, although the American eye can have difficulty distinguishing period French or English furniture from each other and from later revivals, especially from reproductions. Even specialists in American furniture are sometimes hardput to discriminate between the eighteenth-century Rococo chair made in Rome and the related chair made in Austria. Both can look a lot like the similar chair made in Germany or Sweden. If, because of provenance or style, you believe the piece you own is probably not American, the following information may help you sift through alternatives.

The sofa table is a form that originated in the Regency period; here, an example with lyre-form supports, from 1802.

The Davenport desk is only (and always) an English form—usually in walnut, as is this 1860 piece.

DISTINGUISHING AMERICAN FROM ENGLISH FURNITURE

GENERAL:

English secondary woods are oak, mahogany, and deal—a soft pine that *Antiques Roadshow* appraiser J. Michael Flanigan differentiates as having more knots than American secondary wood.

The backs and interiors of English furniture, the parts constructed of secondary wood, often have a red wash, meant to retard insect damage.

♦ **Eighteenth century:** Antique American furniture often combines the quite out-of-date with the newly fashionable on a single piece, freely mixing Queen Anne, for example, with Chippendale motifs. (Such pieces are often termed "transitional.")

♦ **Eighteenth–nineteenth centuries:** Certain antique furniture forms tend to be English: the davenport (a small vertically oriented desk with drawers down one side) and the Carlton house desk (a writing table with a semi-circular second tier partially enclosing the writing surface), among others.

This console table is a superb example by Robert Adam.

ENGLISH FURNITURE

A great deal of English furniture turns up in America: first, because the colonists initially imported more goods from England than they manufactured; second, because Americans were (and still are) enamored of English style, which has always mixed swimmingly with American taste. This is not surprising, since American taste, after all, was shaped by English taste in the first place.

English taste, in turn, traditionally hankered after the French. France's style and sophistication were far superior to that of any other country in the world (as the English, despite being France's perennial enemy, would readily acknowledge.) It wasn't until 1754, when Thomas Chippendale, an English cabinetmaker, altered that fact with the publication of *The Gentleman and Cabinet-maker's Director,* that England developed its own Rococo style. The *Director* teemed with engraved illustrations of the highly carved, asymmetric scrollwork, Gothic spires and crockets, and the whimsical chinoiserie ("Chinese Chippendale") characteristic of Chippendale. Its author's version of Rococo style swept England in a welcome ornamental storm.

Just a dozen years later, however, Chippendale sold up his stock, having perhaps seen the writing on architect Robert Adam's cool Neoclassical walls. For Chippendale was suddenly outmoded. Chinoiserie disappeared without a trace, and Gothic returned to its cathedrals, as the elegant and uncompromising ovals and straight lines of Adam's chairs and tables turned English design on its decorous head. (Though Adam's work was not without its detractors. No less a figure than Horace Walpole derided its "gingerbread and snippets of embroidery.") It wasn't long, however, before his critics were appeased, for Adam in his turn was supplanted by George Hepplewhite, who made Adam's ovals into shields, his lines into curves, and his scholarly and austere style palatable to an emerging middle class. Hepplewhite accomplished this only with the 1788 publication of *The*

Cabinet-maker's and Upholsterer's Guide, for to this day no trace of a piece of furniture or even a bill from George Hepplewhite's shop has ever been found.

The fruitful and amazing progress of eighteenth-century English furniture design closed with the work of Thomas Sheraton, whose elaborate, feminine, and highly artistic furniture caused an almost immediate backlash in the form of the seriously masculine and relatively unornamented dark mahogany surfaces of Regency furniture, the English equivalent of French Empire style. Following this, both countries tumbled into the Neo-isms of Victoriana for fifty-odd years.

CONTINENTAL FURNITURE

Many Americans, if asked to imagine a piece of European furniture, might conjure up something curved and grandiose, decked with heavily carved heads of animals—most particularly lions and griffins—or something with sinuously arranged, partially clad bodies. They would not be altogether mistaken in their imaginings, though what they would actually be visualizing is, specifically, the seventeenth-century Baroque style—which was not necessarily asymmetrically carved and florid, but was certainly exuberant and lush. It flourished particularly in Italy, from 1650 to 1730, but also in Germany and Holland, where it could be heavy, symmetrical, and solemn.

The Baroque evolved gradually during the reign of Louis XIV (1643–1715) into the rich, formal, and somewhat lighter furniture of the rococo style (from *rocaille,* a French word for "rock"), possibly inlaid with exotic woods (though still heavily carved) or fashioned—just for the Sun King's court—in fabulous Boulle marquetry of tortoiseshell and brass. Large mirrors and lavish upholstery completed this palatial fashion. And though furniture was manufactured in every country in eighteenth-century Europe, there is little

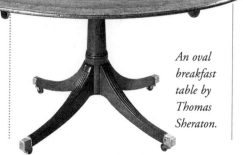

An oval breakfast table by Thomas Sheraton.

An exuberantly Rococo French commode.

*Louis XVI ormolu-mounted small
mahogany secretaire à abattant, c. 1785.*

question that the *crème de la crème* of the era was made in France. (It is worth noting that the sheer amount of seventeenth- and eighteenth-century furniture *attributed* to France and England is far more than it would have been possible for all of their combined craftsmen to make.) Certainly, much of what we customarily attribute to France or England was actually made in Belgium, Portugal, Ireland, or the Scandinavian countries. But it is also true that the most talented craftsmen in the world flocked to Paris, hoping to be admitted into the selective artisans' guilds that were not only producing these royal commissions, but simultaneously inventing furniture forms of an effervescent, feminine delicacy, superbly executed.

Throughout the century to come, furniture that was innovative, beautiful, and useful was consistently produced in France. The French *commode* (French for "handy" or "commodious") typifies the style. A chest of drawers is first and foremost a utilitarian storage piece—a top and drawers standing on four legs. But in the hands of the French cabinetmakers, it became a stylish confection. The fronts of the drawers were given a serpentine curve (a form quite difficult to fabricate and, for obvious reasons, termed *bombé*—French for "bulging"). The little apron that stretches between the two front feet (also curved) was elegantly shaped as well. The top might be a piece of rare and richly patterned marble or a rectangle of elaborately inlaid wood. And the large panels of veneer that sheathed the whole would be glued to the surface in handsome matched patterns, while, in order to disguise the homely function of the piece, its front and sides would be inlaid in patterned exotic woods, bordering the drawers and sides in fantastic intertwining flora. Richly detailed bronze, sculpted into foliate scrolls thickly plated with gold, provided drawer pulls, corner protectors, and toe caps. Such a chest would be a work of art—the collaborative effort of a designer, a cabinetmaker, a metal sculptor, and a gilder. Not a "chest of drawers" anymore. Nothing less than a Commode.

Continental Furniture Craftsmen

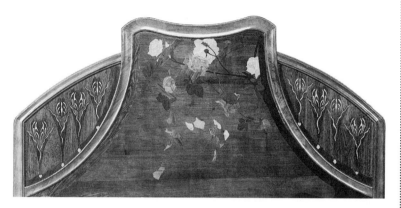

A French headboard with sinuous Art Nouveau marquetry by Louis Majorelle, c. 1899.

A.C. BOULLE *(1642–1732)*

FRANCE A master cabinetmaker of the Baroque era, Boulle perfected a technique for veneering furniture in elaborate patterns of tortoiseshell and brass.

EMILE GALLÉ *(1846–1904)*

FRANCE Perhaps best known for his work in glass, Gallé also produced naturalistic Art Nouveau furniture, sinuously organic and often inlaid with floral marquetry.

CARLO BUGATTI *(1855–1940)*

ITALY Working in the Art Nouveau period, Bugatti produced exotic and fantastic Moorish-influenced furniture, frequently paneled in vellum.

LOUIS MAJORELLE *(1859–1939)*

FRANCE Influenced by Gallé, Majorelle created both carved and inlaid Art Nouveau furniture in mahogany and exotic woods, occasionally mounted in bronze. His workshop was one of the largest at Nancy.

JOSEF HOFFMANN *(1870–1956)*

AUSTRIA Trained as an architect, Hoffmann was a founder of the Wiener Werkstatte. His cubist-influenced designs, often incorporating openwork elements, were geometric and severe.

ÉMILE-JACQUES RUHLMANN *(1879–1933)*

FRANCE Designer of the most elegant and expensive Art Deco furniture in France. Ruhmann's exceptionally well-crafted pieces were, to some extent, an updating of Louis XV forms, although veneered in rare woods like amboyna and ebony and inlaid with ivory. His work is always branded with his name.

GERRIT REITVELD *(1888–1964)*

HOLLAND An architect, Reitveld worked at first in the Arts and Crafts style, but, after World War II, made furniture that was distinctly avant-garde.

JEAN-MICHEL FRANK *(1895–1941)*

FRANCE A decorator working in the Art Deco style of the 1920s and 1930s, Frank designed furniture for his clients' homes. These creations, frequently veneered in sharkskin or vellum, seldom employed either applied or carved ornament.

Josef Hoffmann chair.

BIEDERMEIER: FURNITURE FOR THE BOURGEOISIE

A provincial German and Austrian version of the French Empire style, Biedermeier furniture (named for a fictional middle-class German and known in France as Charles X) was popular in Sweden and Denmark. Designed for the middle-class market in the 1830s, it lacked the refinement of the French original, but the attractive, light-colored figured woods from which it was constructed (ash and maple veneers) belie its rather plain and dignified demeanor. What ornamental detail it did have—columns or restrained inlay—was usually executed in contrasting ebony or ebonized woods.

An unusual, but typically architectonic fruitwood Biedermeier settee (detail) from Vienna, c. 1825.

Ultimately, of course, this fantasy, exuberance, and high-style formality provoked a sober backlash, arriving gradually during the reign of Louis XVI. A return to Classicism—spare, restrained, as severe as the French could get—became the court style. Eventually, the discoveries of the ruins at Pompeii and Herculaneum found their echo in carved, fluted columns and *paterae* (rosettes) on secretaires and chairs, and curving cabriole legs became columnar, while sober woods, especially mahogany, reigned as veneers.

We'll never know how the Louis XVI style might have evolved, for the French Revolution cut it short, so to speak, to be followed by Napoleon's somewhat bellicose Empire style—strict and linear, with sparse ornaments of swans, trophies, and victors' wreaths.

Meanwhile, traces of Parisian modes were making their way to small rural villages, where families often lived in one room and local cabinetmakers copied the lines and the substance, if not the icing, on Marie Antoinette's dainty cakes. Actually, the craftsmen who made this furniture weren't technically "provincial" at all. French village cabinetmakers customarily apprenticed themselves to craftsmen in regions distant from their own homes and then returned to their communities with increased knowledge of their craft and a little serendipitous sophistication about furniture fashion and design. Their work in oak, walnut, and cherry armoires, their commodes and ladder-back, rush-seat chairs might have a rose or two on a crest or a door, or might be only marginally less sophisticated than the furniture seen at court, but their "French Provincial" style had its own lasting charm. It is, to the sophisticated creations at the courts of the French kings, as good American pieces are to the London-designed furniture of Chippendale and Hepplewhite.

So brilliant was the French design of these hundred years that it swept all of Europe before it and has remained hugely influential to this day, for it exemplified a meld of aesthetic and historical moment in a way never seen before or since. The dominance and excellence of this style explain why, especially today, all the European furniture that looks remotely like it is identified as "French." But of course, Italians made chests of drawers for their villas, and Belgians made tables, and Russians made chairs. And many look French, incontestably. But they are not.

For our purposes, it's not so important to know if a piece is French, or German, or Tuscan. It's far more important—because of the hundreds of thousands of "Louis XV" and "Louis XVI" chairs produced since Madame Defarge sat knitting on her very authentic one—to recognize an old one when we see it.

IS IT OLD?

English and Continental furniture is frequently more elaborate than similar American examples, and is often made of fruitwood. Beyond these generalities, there are several other differences:

♦ Woodworm is common on English and Continental furniture, but it is also quite commonly faked. To know if wormholes are authentic, insert the tip of a straight pin into several holes. If the pin goes straight down, the hole is artificial, for worms meander: they never eat in a straight line. They also do not tunnel on the surface of the wood. If you can see a length of worm tunnel sliced in half, that furniture is made from sawn boards of old wood and is not antique.

♦ In eighteenth-century Europe, large bookcases were status symbols and could be quite elaborate. (English examples tended to be more subdued.)

♦ If a desk has brass sockets that once held candle-holders or (worn) pull-out wooden slides on the bottom, it's quite likely to be antique.

♦ If the shelves of bookcases rest either on pegs inserted into holes in the side or on supports of any kind, the piece was made after c. 1820. Before that, shelving slid along grooves.

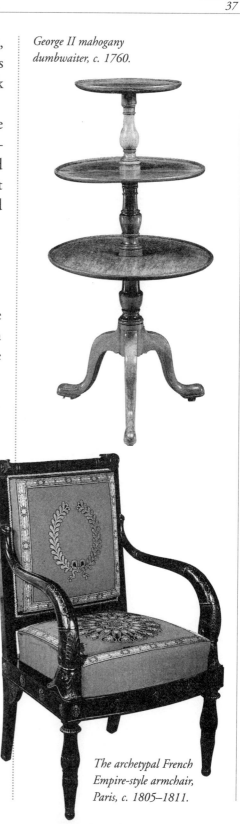

George II mahogany dumbwaiter, c. 1760.

The archetypal French Empire-style armchair, Paris, c. 1805–1811.

TIPS *from the experts*

Antiques Roadshow appraiser Larry Sirolli shares his expertise in identifying and determining the age of English and Continental furniture:

On any antique tilt-top or other type of portable table, expect to see darkened and smudged areas underneath the top edge. This is where fingers gripped as the table was moved. (Such fingerprints will have been polished off the top.)

Chests of drawers, because they were always expensive, were often "refreshed," rather than replaced, when they went out of style. The two areas most often subject to such alteration were a chest's feet and its hardware.

Before 1730, the wood grain of English drawer bottoms runs front to back. After that date, the grain runs side to side.

When you examine furniture with marquetry, run your hands over it. Because woods shrink at different rates, the antique piece will never feel perfectly flat.

English furniture didn't become highly popular in the United States until the 1920s. At that time, innumerable large, ungainly, and unsalable Queen Anne bookcases and cupboards were stripped of their walnut veneers. These were used to make even more numerous little (and therefore salable) "Queen Anne" tables.

♦ Portuguese furniture of the Baroque era often has numerous bulbous, lathe-turned elements.

♦ English cabinetmakers, unlike those in most European countries, made considerable use of mahogany between c. 1740 and 1770.

♦ In the Adam era (c. 1765–1800), satinwood, even more costly than mahogany, became highly popular in England.

♦ In the late eighteenth century, marquetry in the form of figures and Classical mythological subjects was a particular favorite of Italian cabinetmakers.

♦ The French Empire style of the Napoleonic era, ornamented with sphinxes and bees, was copied widely, even in Russia—enemy of France.

♦ After c. 1850, mortise-and-tenon construction was replaced by construction using round dowels. Similarly, hand-cut dovetails became machine-cut.

♦ Most of the Dutch floral marquetry seen in the United States was made during a nineteenth-century revival of this mid-eighteenth-century style.

♦ During the second quarter of the nineteenth century, there was a widespread Gothic Revival. Much highly architectural furniture was ornamented with quatrefoils, arches, and clustered columns, and the best work was done in expensive materials like rosewood.

♦ High-shine, shellac-polished ("French Polish") furniture became popular at the beginning of the Victorian era. Only in the provinces did natural finishes endure.

♦ In the last quarter of the nineteenth century, there was a revival of the fashion for furniture veneered with the tortoiseshell and brass inlay created by Boulle in the seventeenth century. Almost any Boulle furniture found in America today will be of Victorian vintage.

♦ Holland and Scandinavia continued to make rococo *bombé* chests long after France moved on to Neoclassical designs.

IS IT VALUABLE?

Fine French cabinetmakers of the eighteenth century were required by their guilds to stamp their work. Look for such marks on the back of a case piece or under the chair rail. On commodes, you might also look for a maker's name to be stamped on the wood beneath the marble.

♦ French "signatures" can be in ink, impressed into the wood with a stamp, or on a paper label.

♦ Well-done carving on the columns and feet of a chest of drawers, and/or a brushing slide—a narrow pull-out slide just above the drawers, covered with baize and used for brushing clothes upon—add value to a chest.

♦ Gilt wood was fashionable on furniture throughout Europe in the eighteenth century, especially in France.

♦ Period French furniture makes use of rabbets on the lower surfaces of drawer bottoms instead of chamfered edges. The interiors of drawer fronts may also be veneered.

♦ Irish furniture, which is often exceptionally well carved, is commonly mistaken for English furniture. It is collected in its own right, however, and can be quite valuable.

♦ Oak was the secondary wood of choice in France and Holland.

♦ Sets of eight or more chairs are always more valuable than sets of four or six. "Assembled" sets (in which the chairs have been acquired a few at a time), however, are less valuable than sets of chairs made at the same time in the same shop.

A late-seventeenth-century William and Mary chest of drawers with characteristic walnut veneer and marquetry.

The urn-form backs on this pair of unusual, but only moderately successful chairs show the influence of Robert Adam.

Fine Furniture:
Learning by Comparing

There's only one way to learn about antiques, and that's to look, look, and look some more, and at as many examples as possible. The best way to train your eye is to compare, compare, compare. Here are four mini-lessons that do just that.

LABELS, STYLES, AND DUNCAN PHYFE

In the course of a business, successful manufacturers had to adapt their initial styles to changing tastes and make furniture in various fashionable designs. These less typical pieces are sometimes difficult to attribute to a particular workshop, but experts try. The presence of that rarity, a label—especially the label of a highly collectible maker—is a genuine serendipity.

The Duncan Phyfe firm fashioned this labeled, marble-topped work-table in New York, c. 1812, in the popular Federal style. Crafted of figured mahogany, with discreet touches of brass, it has delicate proportions, fine craftsmanship, and that Phyfe label—a combination that makes it precisely the type of piece that collectors of American furniture covet.

On the basis of criteria like details of design and workmanship, original bills of sale, and similarity to other, labeled pieces from the Phyfe workshop, this marble-topped sideboard, made at about the same time as the piece at left, is *attributed* to Duncan Phyfe. It has no label, but even if it did, its heavy and architectonic classical lines would make it less attractive to collectors than the easy-to-like, easy-to-accommodate worktable at left.

THREE HIGHBOYS

The highboy—known in its own time as a chest on frame, or high chest—is a uniquely American furniture form. Balanced on four or more legs, its tall upper section is fitted with a stack of graduated drawers, while its stand has three or more drawers of various sizes. Three versions of the eighteenth-century New England flat-topped high chest are seen here, and one is a cautionary tale.

The earliest example (c. 1710), from the William and Mary era, has six sturdy trumpet-turned legs, with connecting stretchers for added strength. Crafted of oak, it was made near New Haven, Connecticut. With its scalloped skirt, elaborate pendant finial, and handsome hardware, this highboy is unquestionably sophisticated. But curiously, its brass pulls are all attached upside down, indicating that they were removed at least once: perhaps when the piece was painted, c. 1738, by a folk artist or perhaps by an artistic housewife—who inscribed her initials and that date on the inside of the central top drawer. This type of documentation, along with the unusual blending of the formal and naïve, adds interest and dimension to a rare and early piece.

Like the majority of highboys, this Queen Anne example (c. 1720–1740) is unpainted. Its legs are solid walnut and its case is embellished with dramatic matched walnut veneers. Fashioned in Essex County, on the North Shore of Massachusetts, it is taller than its William and Mary era predecessor, but also more elegant—perhaps because its flat top is deeply molded and therefore more architectural; or because a curved apron lends it lift and grace. Certainly the batwing brasses and turned pendant finials (and a secret drawer) augment its high-style air: but the biggest difference between this highboy and the earlier model is the newly invented cabriole leg, a triumph of engineering that can support the entire weight of the cabinetry, without stretchers.

Early in the twentieth century, with American furniture scholarship in its infancy, many handsome pieces were acquired by museums and collectors that later turned out to have "problems." Although it looks as fine as the example to its left, this handsomely proportioned maple highboy has been caught in a scholarly crunch. The museum that owns it once believed it was made in New England between 1750 and 1780, but a recent reexamination revealed drawers that fit badly, brasses that weren't original, and a top that appeared to be unrelated to the bottom, all of which combined to suggest a possible "marriage" of top and bottom, or worse, a piece entirely made from fragments of older chests. In other words, a fake.

BALL-AND-CLAW FEET

The ball-and-claw foot, so prevalent on eighteenth-century Chippendale furniture, may have derived from a Chinese motif depicting a dragon clasping a pearl in its claw. Certain styles of ball-and claw feet exemplify regional differences in furniture manufacture and, in conjunction with other characteristics, allow experts to determine, fairly confidently, where a piece was made.

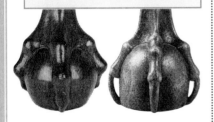

In the two examples above, the foot on the left, from a mahogany card table carved in Boston, nicely suggests an actual talon, but the foot on the right is a tour de force of masterful carving. The ball is clasped by rare and difficult-to-execute "open" talons, and the talons themselves are well-defined, continuing up to a distinct suggestion of a tendoned ankle. The entire foot—almost a sculpture in itself—has a muscularity and strength that one sees only in the finest furniture: in this case, a Goddard-Townsend School high chest from Newport.

SHAKER AND VICTORIAN FURNITURE COMPARED

There are no absolutes of taste. Only the artist's competence in carrying out his design can explain why it is that utterly dissimilar pieces can actually be equally fine.

or dislike both, you can judge an important piece of furniture (and all types of decorative art, in fact) by asking yourself if the piece is an excellent example *of its kind.*

In these examples, a fine example of Shaker furniture—characteristically simple, severe, and utilitarian, is seen beside an equally fine Victorian sideboard—characteristically exuberant, florid, and similarly utilitarian. Both were made around the same time (the second half of the nineteenth century), and both succeed completely in being the best of their kind. While you may prefer one to the other,

FURTHER READING

Andrews, John. *Antique Furniture (Starting to Collect Series)*. Wappingers Falls, NY: Antique Collectors Club, 1996.

Bishop, Robert C. *Guide to American Antique Furniture*. New York: Galahad Books, 1973.

Bishop, Robert, and Coblentz, Patricia. *Furniture 1*. Washington, D.C.: The Smithsonian Institution, 1979.

Butler, Joseph, and Skibinski, Ray. *Field Guide to American Antique Furniture*. New York: Henry Holt, 1987.

Davidson, Richard. *Miller's Antique Checklist Furniture*. New York: Viking Penguin, 1991.

Dubrow, Eileen and Richard. *Styles of American Furniture*. Atglen, PA: Schiffer Publishing, 1997.

FitzGerald, Oscar. *Four Centuries of American Furniture*. Radnor, Pennsylvania: Wallace-Homestead Book Co., 1995.

Forrest, Tim. *The Bulfinch Anatomy of Antique Furniture*. Boston: Little, Brown, 1996.

Hinckley, F. Lewis. *The Directory of Antique Furniture*. New York: Bonanza Books, 1950.

Kaye, Myrna. *Fake, Fraud, or Genuine*. Boston: Bulfinch Press, 1991.

Ketchum, William C. *Furniture 1*. New York: Alfred A. Knopf, 1982.

Learoyd, Stan. *The Guide to English Antique Furniture: Construction and Decoration, 1500–1910*. New York: Van Nostrand Reinhold, 1981.

Lipman, Jean, and Winchester, Alice. *The Flowering of American Folk Art*. New York: Viking, 1974.

Naeve, Milo. *Identifying American Furniture*. New York: W.W. Norton, 1989.

Petraglia, Patricia P. *Sotheby's Guide to American Furniture*. New York: Fireside, 1995.

A typical Victorian Renaissance Revival chair.

The tilt-top variation in a tripod table is found on Chippendale and later round tables.

Types of frequently seen furniture which, 95 percent of the time, are not valuable:

♦ Boston rockers

♦ Savonarola chairs

♦ Pine six-board blanket chests without interesting detail, like original paint

♦ Windsor-style kitchen chairs

♦ Chairs with an impressed (rather than hand-carved) design of scrolls or flora on the crest rail

Egyptian Revival reflected Victorian interest in the ancient world and the Middle East.

Philip, Peter, and Walkling, Gillian. *Field Guide to Antique Furniture.* Boston: Houghton Mifflin, 1992.

Schwartz, Marvin. *Furniture 2.* New York: Alfred A. Knopf, 1982.

Shea, John G. *Antique Country Furniture of North America and Details of Its Construction.* New York: Van Nostrand Reinhold, 1975.

Weinhagen, Robert F., Jr. *Assume Nothing.* New Albany, IN: Highland Publishing House, 1993.

Chapter Two

SILVER

Pick up a silver spoon, tray, or creamer and turn it over. Is the back or bottom impressed with the name of the maker, odd-looking symbols, or the word "sterling"? If not—if it's stamped, instead, EPNS—you know two important things about it. It isn't very old. And it isn't silver.

It may look like silver, polish like silver, even have a firm place in your family's history as being silver—but it's unquestionably **E**lectro-**P**lated-**N**ickel-**S**ilver. Base metal, unfortunately, beneath a silvery skin.

This is one of the most useful bits of information the novice can have about silver.

Before plated silver was invented in the eighteenth century, an object that appeared to be silver generally *was* silver, with a small amount of copper added to harden it. (Pure silver is simply too soft to be of practical use.) Silver was the most valuable material commonly used for the decorative arts, second only to gold. And, like gold, silver was meltable—which is why so much of what was made in silver has been lost forever. Kings and conquering armies melted down enormous quantities of splendid silver wares, minting coinage, buying swords, and wreaking their customary havoc. Art depicting church interiors and grand banquets tells us just how much was lost. Even

The once-crisp edges on this American cream pitcher, made by Myer Myers in the eighteenth century, are worn from years of polishing.

SILVER SPOON

John Culme quizzed the owner on her knowledge of this beautiful silver spoon. It belongs to her mother, it turned out, and neither one of them could remember where she bought it or anything about its history. When she said they suspected it was from the late 1800s Culme couldn't contain his smile. It turned out that this rare diamond-point spoon was over 600 years old, having been made in England around 1380 when Richard II was on the throne.

Although the spoon had quite a bit of restoration—the bowl was cracked on both sides, and the diamond point would have originally been gilded—Culme still valued it at $10,000 to $20,000. Upon hearing this, the owner laughed, stating that she would not tell her mother just yet. She would tell her to watch the show first.

as recently as the 1980s, the manipulation of the American silver market brought tons of suddenly high-priced metal—much of it reasonably antique—to the smelter.

Luckily, a good deal of wonderfully worked silver has survived, thanks to the fact that so many fine objects were fabricated after the seventeenth century, when demand rose and workshops flourished, and it was simply impossible to demolish it *all*. Interestingly, in the American colonies a kind of reverse process took place in which great quantities of silver objects were created out of bushels of foreign coins, melted down to provide us with tea trays and Revere bowls.

Silver was traditionally worked with a hammer, but also with engraving tools, punches, casting molds, and dies. It could be enameled and jeweled, and fashioned into baby rattles, cups, and gravy boats, and grandmother's pride and joy—that prominently displayed silver tea service.

There are styles in silver, as in all furnishings, and while less is decidedly more in most cases, silver often seems to have been designed on the assumption that any piece that is sufficiently ornate will look inordinately valuable. This is because silver has always reflected the status of its owner, and—before beauty, before usefulness, before antiquity—the possession of great quantities of silver has historically been a symbol of substantial wealth. Only gold, over the centuries, has surpassed silver's cachet, but gold could not be kept on constant display. One never had to put one's silver away in a jewelry box. In fact, the more it was used, the smoother and more lustrous it became. Today, sadly, while most people still appreciate old silver, they don't like the upkeep. "All that polishing," they complain. "Who has the time anymore?" Which may explain why such quantities of silver come up for sale.

Yet, as it loses popularity and travels to the auction block or into attic trunks, we will find ourselves with less and less fine sterling to enjoy. And, eventually, the stainless, aluminum, and silverplate utensils that are taking its place will have our dining rooms all to themselves. Except that dining rooms are rarely built anymore.

TYPES OF SILVER

I n the hierarchy of metals, silver is less valuable than platinum and gold, and more valuable than bronze, brass, copper, pewter, and iron (in that order). Unlike gold, silver doesn't occur in a natural state; it must be extracted from ores such as argentite or galena. Yet, like gold, silver is a precious metal and has enjoyed this status since antiquity. Although little Greek and Roman silver remains, writers of the Classical era referred to silver frequently, and most often (amusingly) to silver drinking cups and wine vessels, for its earliest use seems to have been reserved for objects relating to the consumption of alcohol. This might also explain its continued popularity throughout the Middle Ages, when men of wealth commissioned and amassed elaborate wine jugs and goblets as well as serving pieces for lavish banquets, then stored these gleaming hoards of silver table objects in their treasuries—often using them as payment for debts.

Beautiful, attention-getting, utilitarian, and luxurious, silver was also infinitely recyclable. One's worn or outmoded silver objects could be melted down and fashioned anew. Unfortunately, this attribute also made it easy for unscrupulous craftsmen to adulterate the metal and defraud the purchaser. So standards of metal purity had to be devised. In England in the fourteenth century, a legal silver standard was established, requiring 925 parts of silver in 1,000 parts of the metal, with a symbol to be punched into each piece attesting to its silver content. (See "Understanding Hallmarks," page 55.) The same proportion of silver to alloying metal, 925/1,000, became the standard for coins as well and conveniently

Ornate Russian silver spoons, early seventeenth century.

Rare two-handled silver cup made by Richard Conyers, Boston, c. 1696–1708.

Art glass and silver paired in a 1910 Silver Gallé cameo compote with an unusual squash blossom motif.

allowed Great Britain, in uncertain economic times, to convert candlesticks into shillings.

FLATWARE

The term "flatware" is used to describe cutlery: eating utensils and serving knives, forks, ladles, and spoons of all types. Matching services of flatware are a rather recent development in the history of civilized dining. Although the Romans were familiar with spoons, the fork was invented in Italy only in the seventeenth century, when one critic deemed it "coarse and ungraceful to throw food into the mouth as you would toss hay into a barn with a pitchfork."

On the whole, however, the fork was surely an improvement over eating one's meal from the blade of a knife, especially since early knives didn't hold up well. Their steel blades were attached by a long rod to hollow silver handles filled with a core of pitch (tar residue), and heat, cold, and even water could easily break the seal and render a table knife useless. For this reason, early sets of flatware are often found without any knives at all.

HOLLOWARE

Holloware, as opposed to flatware, comprises silver vessels and serving wares, like bowls, vases, tea services, trays, and baskets, chiefly—but not always—designed to be used at the dining table. Silver lighting devices, such as candlesticks, candelabra, and even the occasional lamp, come under that classification as well.

Made in Colonial Boston, c. 1732–1735, this oval tobacco box was a gift from his pupils to a teacher named Rogers, whose coat of arms is engraved on the top.

PRESENTATION SILVER

Presentation silver is commemorative silver. Most of us have seen it—usually in glass cases—but few of us own it. The Super Bowl trophy is presentation silver, as is the America's Cup, for silver has always been the medium of choice for commemorating important events. But important "custom-made" trophies, rewards, and tokens of appreciation are expensive, so they are usually commissioned by groups or organizations rather than by individuals. Such items might range from silver-topped walking sticks and swords with silver hilts to magnificent dinner services like those with which the British and Americans marked naval victories and official retirements. Invariably, presentation pieces are as lavishly designed and decorated as the client's pocketbook will allow, and for these tours de force the silversmith gives his all.

Consequently, despite the very specific nature of presentation silver (which is often decorated with racehorses, marine life, or images of the archetypal Native American) and the fact that it is always inscribed (and therefore ill-suited for casual display in the average home), the best of such silver is highly valued by collectors for its often superb artistic merit. Ordinary modern sterling trophies, prosaic vases, or silver trays engraved by the local jeweler, however, are worth no more than the scrap value of the metal they're made of. Most silver collectors aren't interested in displaying other people's awards.

A presentation piece: maidens, waves, and flora—all the elements of Art Nouveau on a 1916 Gorham silver punch bowl.

SILVER TROPHY

While Jeanne Sloane examined a silver trophy at the Seattle *Roadshow,* the owner explained that his grandfather had won it at Madison Square Garden in 1892 for his hackney stallion (carriage horse). Inscribed on "The First American Championship Cup" are the names of the grandfather and his horse Bonfire.

"A very impressive punch bowl," Sloane remarked. She said the manufacturer was Whiting and Company, as fine a silvermaker in the 1890s as Tiffany. The sculpted carriage wheels and etched horse would make it the ultimate symbol of the gilded age in America. In today's market, the specially commissioned trophy might be worth $10,000 to $15,000 to a collector of presentation silver.

Art Nouveau pen tray of copper with applied silver.

Small silver box by Kalo, c. 1910, sized for pills or stamps.

Complicated or highly detailed elements, such as the leg shown on this sauce boat by Nathaniel Richardson, Philadelphia (c. 1785), were molded separately and then attached to the body.

SMALL SILVER COLLECTIBLES

Anything that can be made in gold can also be made in silver. And because silver is so much less expensive, there is much more of it. From thimbles to elaborate match safes (match holders), from letter openers to toilet sets and vinaigrettes (tiny containers containing a vinegar-soaked sponge, used in the malodorous eighteenth century for disguising odors), from snuffboxes to card, cigarette, and needle cases, artistically wrought silver makes any perfectly common object grander and more beautiful than it would be if made of a lesser metal. Small decorative pieces, in silver as well as gold, are sometimes called *objets de vertu* ("excellent objects").

MAKING SILVER OBJECTS

Silver is a highly forgiving metal. It is malleable (it can be hammered into a thin sheet) and ductile (it can be drawn into fine wire). It has the highest electric and thermal conductivity of any metal. It takes well to being chiseled, raised, or cast. And, unlike gold, it has always been inexpensive enough to be practical for massive forms, such as wine cisterns and heavy trays, while remaining strong enough and fine enough to be fashioned into graceful flatware and luxurious trinkets.

MANUFACTURING TECHNIQUES

Over the centuries, various techniques have been used to shape and decorate silver.

Hammering Beating a sheet of metal with a hammer, thereby forming it into a desired shape, is the most primitive method of working silver. Hammering makes the metal brittle, so the silver object must be repeatedly annealed (or heated and then slowly cooled) to soften it before further hammering. In the nineteenth century, the traditional method of hand-hammering silver was supplanted by pressing disks of the raw metal against a lathe-spun form, then finishing it by hand.

Casting Small but important parts like feet, spouts, finials, and handles, plus bits of decorative ornament, are made by pouring molten metal into a mold. When cool, these additions are attached to the body of the object by heating the facing surfaces or by soldering them together.

Spinning Modern holloware is frequently spun into shape. A flat disk of silver is formed over a mold to the desired shape, and both are spun together while a shaping tool is pressed against the silver disk.

Aesthetic Movement mixed-metal wares, like these hand-hammered Tiffany bowls, often combined silver with copper, brass, silver, gold, and steel.

DESIGN TECHNIQUES

Once the silver object has been created, the exterior of the silver can be treated in one (or in combinations) of the following ways.

Embossing In use from the earliest times, embossing is a method of tooling the metalwork to ornament it, or to refine the detail. Raised designs in the forms of leaves, flowers, figures, and animals can be fashioned from smooth silver by placing the sheet metal on a bed of soft wood or wax and using punches and a hammer to shape it from the back. This technique is also called *repoussé,* meaning "pushed out." Another variant of the same technique involves hammering out domed patterns in relief, called "bosses." The patterns are raised above the surface of the object and can be seen or felt in reverse on the interior or underside.

Floral repoussé *and an unusual handle with a goat-head finial highlight this American coffeepot by A.F. Warner.*

The piercing technique is beautifully exemplified in this pair of German reticulated compotes with glass liners, late nineteenth century.

Bright-cut decoration enlivens the handles of Paul Revere tablespoons.

Chasing This technique adds detail to *repoussé* work and to flat surfaces. A series of small punches are used to give texture or create lines that can resemble engraving.

Piercing Practiced since the eighteenth century, piercing is a method of making delicate openwork holes or patterns by using a fret saw, a tool that creates precise, parallel cuts. Practiced since the eighteenth century, piercing is a time-consuming and therefore expensive process, superseded late in the 1700s by the invention of the flypunch.

Engraving Unlike chasing, engraving requires cutting away metal with a pointed tool to create designs on the surface. Engraving on early American silver is somewhat rare, although Colonial craftsmen like Nathaniel Hurd and Joseph Leddel made good use of the technique.

Bright-cutting This design technique also cuts away metal. Bright-cut patterns are created with a steel tool that polishes as it chisels small light-reflecting facets into the silver surface. This ornamental technique was developed by silversmiths in the late eighteenth century in response to the rising popularity of silver plate, which imitated silver by fusing a thin layer of silver to a copper base but which could not be engraved, since the copper showed through. Bright-cut decoration sought to capitalize on this distinction.

Gilding In this technique, all or part of a finished piece of silver is coated with gold. Gold-plated silver is also called *vermeil*—French for silver-gilt. Besides slowing the tarnishing process (for goldplate tarnishes much more slowly than silver), gilding glamorizes (or vulgarizes, depending on one's school of thought) silver.

Enameling A method of coating all or part of a silver object with brightly hued molten glass, enameling goes in and out of fashion. Medieval silver was frequently enameled, as was Russian silver, but in the intervening centuries before the resurgence of Western European interest in the process during the Arts and Crafts and Art Nouveau eras, large silver pieces were seldom enameled. Niello, a type of black stain, is common to Russian silver as well.

Silver can also be ornamented with delicate filigree wirework as well as semiprecious and precious stones.

SILVER PLATING TECHNIQUES

Solid silver is, of course, more valuable than plated base metal. Consequently, the difference between silver and silver plate is usually one of intrinsic value, rather than eloquence or even inventiveness of design. In fact, without looking for distinguishing hallmarks, it is often impossible to tell the two apart. But the quality of old plated silver (known as Sheffield plate) is far superior to that of modern electroplated wares.

ANTIQUE (SHEFFIELD PLATE)

As long ago as the ninth century, craftsmen tried to imitate silver by coating copper, brass, and iron articles with thin layers of the metal. It wasn't until 1742, however, that an Englishman, Thomas Boulsover of Sheffield, discovered how to fuse silver to copper. Eventually, Boulsover devised a way to make a "sandwich" of silver-copper-silver, providing durable and handsome silver plate that could, at long last, perfectly replicate silver. Of course, when the sandwich was viewed from the side—on the edges of trays, for instance—the copper edges would be exposed and thus had to be hidden by a U-shaped section of silver wire. Naturally, too, plated wares could not be engraved (the underlying copper would show through) but a rectangle or oval of solid silver could be inlaid into the piece, usually in the center, and safely monogrammed there. The invention of Sheffield plate, as it came to be called, enabled the middle class to own highly convincing "silver" tablewares and

Russian enameled spoon dating from the late nineteenth century. The paneled stem is picked out with enameled stringing.

Four pieces from an American silver flatware service by International in the Wedgwood pattern.

decorative objects that were similar to silver in *almost* every way. Only years of polishing would eventually reveal the telltale copper beneath the silver skin.

Much early Sheffield plate is unmarked, although some marks from the last quarter of the eighteenth century—those of such noted manufacturers as Matthew Boulton and Dixon and Company—are well known. Crossed keys, bells, bows and arrows, and an open hand are also marks that are frequently encountered.

MODERN (ELECTROPLATE)

Though highly successful, fused plating was an expensive process and required considerable manpower. In the 1840s, however, a method for successfully electroplating base metals with silver was discovered, and the old Sheffield technique was replaced by this newer, faster, and less costly process.

In electroplating, objects to be plated are immersed in an electrolytic tank that contains a pure silver ingot. A current of electricity is passed through the tank, and a thin coat of silver is transferred from the ingot and deposited onto the metal objects.

Several types of metal could be plated in this fashion: brass, copper, a tin alloy called Britannia metal (similar to pewter), and German silver—the term for an alloy of copper, nickel, and zinc. The latter two are gray-white in color, and when used beneath silver, the electroplated object seems to be silver even when its real silver coating has been polished or worn away. For that reason, no doubt, all electroplating was eventually executed over nickel-based alloys, and such wares were stamped EPNS—electroplated nickel silver. The Elkington Company, in Birmingham, England, which was the first firm to employ the plating technique extensively for commercial applications, manufactured exceptionally fine original-design objects in electroplate along with well-done replicas of antique silver.

This fine and very early Sheffield plate coffeepot (c. 1760) looks—as it was intended to—much like genuine silver. It was made from single-sided plate.

Some American firms, among them Tiffany and Gorham, made electroplated wares—even flatware—as well as sterling silver. Occasionally, these firms produced the same pattern in both versions. Numerous flatware patterns were made in electroplate. In addition to being marked EPNS, sets of plated flatware may also be marked A1, to indicate that there were two ounces of silver deposited on a gross of teaspoons, for instance, or XX to indicate that four ounces of silver had been deposited on every gross of teaspoons.

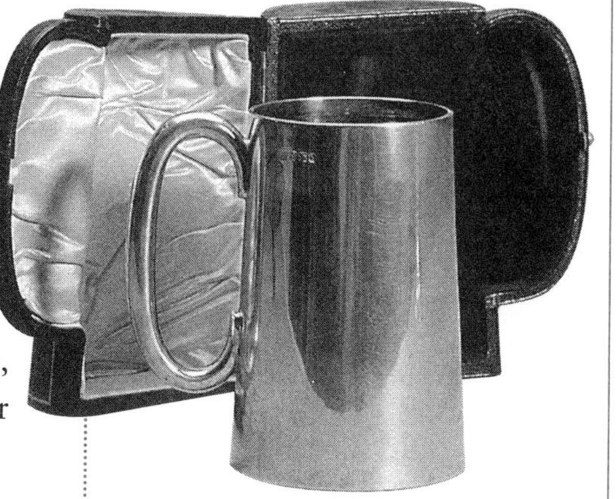

Made in Sheffield: a sterling silver tankard in its own fitted leather case.

UNDERSTANDING HALLMARKS

Because of its intrinsic value, silver has always been subject to fairly rigorous regulatory controls—elaborate but easily deciphered systems of punches, or stamps, known as "hallmarks." Hallmarks may be the arcana of silver, but they are also one of its pleasures. Few mysteries in the field of antiques succumb so readily to the amateur sleuth as does silver, for, armed with a silver hallmark book, one can often track the "footprints" left behind by centuries of talented silversmiths.

It's actually not difficult to distinguish the genuine silver object from the plated one, for authentic silver comes to you impressed with useful information.

A typical early-nineteenth-century shape, the boat-form on a pedestal foot, is seen here in an English sugar basket. The hallmarks are visible on the foot rim.

ENGLISH HALLMARKS

The British hallmarking system, the world's most stringent, was established in the fourteenth century. Due to rampant fraud, all English goldsmiths (as crafters of both silver and gold were called) had to take their wares into Goldsmiths' Hall to be assayed (analyzed for their silver content). Hence, our term "hallmark." The system requires

DUTY·DODGERS

Sometimes a silversmith lived too far from his local assay office to find it convenient to haul his products there (although probably more often a resentful craftsman simply didn't care to pay the duty). In either case, he would strike (or impress) his work with his own initials four or five times in an effort to imitate the required hallmarks.

Scrolled and pierced English Victorian wine coasters engraved with a heraldic crest. Hallmarks are visible on the foot rings. London, 1846.

that small stamps be impressed on objects of any consequence. These stamps, struck into the metal with dies, indicate the year a piece was made, the standard of the silver used (i.e., the proportion of actual silver to base metal), and where it was made (London, Sheffield, Birmingham, etc.). Hallmarks, literally, are those required by the Hall. Thus, the maker's mark is not, strictly speaking, a hallmark. English silver has a minimum of three hallmarks (plus the maker's mark), as shown on the facing page.

THE STERLING STANDARD MARK

Originally, a shaped punch, its outline altering over the years, depicted at its center a crowned or uncrowned leopard's head. In 1544, this was replaced by the most famous British hallmark—the lion passant (a walking lion). The mark indicates that a piece is indeed "sterling," or 925/1,000, and that the metal meets British legal requirements. (For the brief period from 1697 to 1720, 950 silver became obligatory and during that time was stamped with the figure of Britannia.)

THE MARK DENOTING THE MAKER'S NAME

Unscrupulous goldsmiths eventually created the need for another hallmark, one identifying the maker of a piece by name. Each artisan became obliged to register his name with Goldsmiths' Hall and to stamp his creations with his own mark: usually, his first and last initials.

THE MARK OF THE YEAR OF MANUFACTURE

Signified by a single letter of the alphabet—in Gothic, Roman, or script typeface, among others—the date stamp is enclosed in variously shaped punches and throughout Great Britain is used in twenty- to thirty-year cycles. It denotes the year, from 1478 until today, when the piece of silver was made.

THE MARK DESIGNATING THE ASSAY OFFICE

Initially, the lion passant was the hallmark of the London assay office, but it ultimately became the famous British "sterling" mark and London's mark became the leopard's head crowned. The town of Birmingham's mark was an anchor. Edinburgh's was a thistle. Newcastle's town mark was three castles. Dublin's hallmark, fittingly, was the lyre.

British hallmarks, despite their apparent clarity, can sometimes be knotty to decode. All too often, one or more were badly struck (the die made a weak, overlapping, or partial impression on the metal) and can be frustratingly difficult to read. Moreover, a hallmark on the shoulder of a piece of silver, or in any location where it has been subject to regular polishing, can be partially or even completely worn away.

In 1784, a duty was levied on silver to pay for the American War of Independence. The hallmark indicating that the duty had been paid was the head of the ruling monarch, who at that time was George III. The duty was finally discontinued in 1890. Thus, from 1784 to 1890, there were four hallmarks (plus the maker's mark) on each piece of English silver.

EUROPEAN HALLMARKS

European silver (which can be either better-than-sterling quality or more highly alloyed, i.e., 950 or 800) was assayed and marked as well, although each country, confusingly, devised its own marking requirements. Both English and Continental hallmarks are struck on the bottoms of vessels, the edges of foot rings, or the bodies of mugs; in addition, European marks, unlike those on British silver, often hide among the scrollery or foliage of the design and can even be buried in the bottom of candle sockets. It's often a challenge just to *find* the marks on Continental silver.

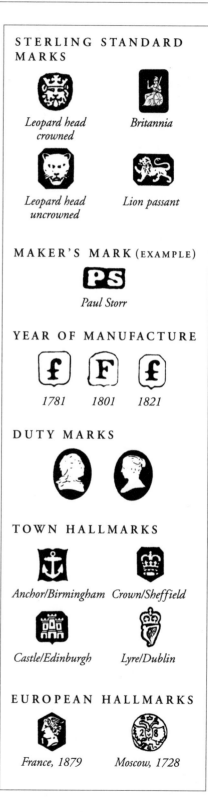

STERLING STANDARD MARKS

Leopard head crowned

Britannia

Leopard head uncrowned

Lion passant

MAKER'S MARK (EXAMPLE)

PS

Paul Storr

YEAR OF MANUFACTURE

1781   *1801*   *1821*

DUTY MARKS

TOWN HALLMARKS

Anchor/Birmingham   *Crown/Sheffield*

Castle/Edinburgh   *Lyre/Dublin*

EUROPEAN HALLMARKS

France, 1879   *Moscow, 1728*

SMOKE-UP

Appraiser Jeanne Sloane has passed along this tip—better than a rubbing, even better than a photograph—for deciphering hallmarks.

Hold the hallmarked area of your piece of silver over a burning candle, just close enough to allow the soot from the flame to blacken the immediate area of the marks. Then, take a piece of Scotch tape and press the sticky side against the row of blackened marks. Remove it carefully, and press the tape against a sheet of white paper. You will have a perfect, beautifully clear reproduction of the hallmarks.

A Philadelphia salt cellar, c. 1820, by Thomas West (who also made clocks and watches).

A pair of coin silver serving spoons, Jacob Hurd, Boston, 1702–1758.

European silver is hallmarked with nothing like the satisfying dependability of English hallmarks. Germany and France were fairly rigorous in marking their wares, and France, in fact, in 1272, was the first country ever to require silver marks at all. Russia, from about 1700, was also punctilious in maintaining silver standards. Not until the nineteenth century did the Netherlands and Italy adopt the French marking system, while the Scandinavian countries based their hallmarks on the German model. Throughout the Continent, it was common to use heraldic town marks on silver, and there are hundreds, if not thousands, of these, many forever undecipherable.

AMERICAN HALLMARKS

In America, there was no standardized format for marks. Although American silver has always been sterling (925 parts of pure silver in 1,000, or a little less, called coin), the country's oldest wares—porringers and jugs—are marked simply with the maker's name or initials.

Therefore, American silver has never been subject to the scrutiny of any assay office, although, from 1814 to 1830 in Baltimore, an ultimately unpopular attempt was briefly made. In the absence of any regulating body, early American silversmiths marked their wares with their individual guarantees of quality, such as their names or initials, or symbols like an eagle's head or, capitalizing on the impressive reputation of English silver, variations on the trustworthy British lion.

By the middle of the nineteenth century, however, American makers had been stamping their first initial and full last name on silver wares for some time, as well as employing a second punch to indicate the silver standard. "Coin" (or "C"), "Dollar" (or "D"), and "standard" were typical American hallmarks. Occasionally, American silversmiths marked their wares with the word "sterling," and though their metal was indeed of that purity, it wasn't until after the Civil War that the use of the word became common. Only in 1907 did America legally require "sterling" to be stamped on its wares. (America and Ireland, in fact, are the only countries in the world to use the word "sterling" on their silver.) This is why, on a fairly modern piece marked Gorham or Tiffany or Reed and Barton (despite the occasional convincing-looking hallmark), if the word "sterling" does not appear, you can be very certain it's not silver.

AMERICAN SILVER

A silver tankard by the versatile Paul Revere, Jr., Boston, 1772.

E arly American silver is relatively rare, and spare in design, while post–Civil War silver is readily available and distinctly luxurious. Between these two eras, the Industrial Revolution, patriotism, and wealth combined to consolidate both America's confidence and its style in the decorative arts.

SEVENTEENTH- AND EIGHTEENTH- CENTURY SILVER

T he average Colonial dinner table was unlikely to be set with silver, for most early Americans were simply not wealthy enough to be able to afford that luxury. Those few who were would often purchase their "plate" (silver) in London, and what silver *was* fashioned in this country was largely ecclesiastical.

Nonetheless, as early as 1650, flourishing urban centers like Philadelphia and Boston were able to support a few silversmiths, although the majority had been trained in England and their

A fine silver punch bowl with the maker's mark of Myer Myers.

COLONIAL SILVER CANN

The Colonial silver piece below was inherited from the guest's mother-in-law, who lived in the Boston area. This makes sense, according to Christopher Hartop, for some of the nicest silver was made in Boston in the eighteenth century. Crafted by well-known silversmith Jacob Hurd, the piece dates from c. 1740 to 1750 and is a typical Boston "cann," or mug.

The cann has a clear maker's mark (usually found at the left side of the handle) as well as the family's initials. According to Hartop, collectors will pay a premium for early pieces with family provenance. In fact, such pieces are worth more than those that have changed hands several times. This, and its good condition, make the mug worth $15,000.

wares reflected their origins. New York also had its share of immigrant craftsmen, but its silver strongly reflected the predominant Dutch background of its residents. Because American silversmiths had to compete with sophisticated foreign imports, most early colonial silver was particularly elegant, although it was also relatively plain. Wealthy Southern colonists continued to prefer English silver, and silver created in the South, especially in Charleston, was designed to look as much like the British prototype as possible.

Most American Colonial silver was solid, heavy, and unadorned. Where a British piece might be engraved with an impressive coat-of-arms, its American counterpart, if it had any decoration at all, was likely to display its owner's initials, simply engraved. Also, fashions arrived late in the colonies and remained in style long after they had fallen into disuse abroad. As a result, there could be several years' time lag between the emergence of a style in England and its subsequent appearance in America.

TANKARDS

When they did own silver, what kinds of silver objects did Americans own? Mostly, pieces that displayed, served, or contained food. Like the ancient Romans, Americans preferred their alcohol in silver cups, though instead of the Roman and medieval goblets, they imbibed from tankards—tall, cylindrical, covered mugs. Of the eighteenth-century American silver still in existence, in fact, much is in the form of tankards. Boston tankard designs were quite plain, reflecting plain New England taste, but tankard handles in New York and Philadelphia were often ornamental with bases embellished by foliate bands. Tankards were primarily used for ale and were heavy when full. Yet several have women's names engraved on them, which tells us that women could hoist them. These unique drinking vessels only disappeared from the American table around the Federal period (1789–c. 1820), when wine and liquor replaced ale as the popular drinks.

CANNS

The "cann," known in England as a mug, was also used for cold beverages. Paul Revere is known to have made canns, as well as tankards. In general, American canns can be distinguished from the British variety by a slight belly in their cylindrical shape.

TEA ACCESSORIES

Because tea was initially a fashionable, luxury beverage, all its appurtenances were, appropriately, crafted in silver, beginning with the teapot itself. And because tea was so expensive, early teapots were quite small, and American examples are exceptionally rare. The New York teapot, not surprisingly, was frequently pear-shaped in imitation of its Dutch antecedents, while Boston and Philadelphia pots displayed the globular shape of their English prototypes. Many early teapots also had wooden handles to save the hand from being burned.

That odd bowl, usually around six inches in diameter, that accompanies many late eighteenth- to nineteenth-century tea services (though much more frequently found orphaned and alone) is a waste or slop bowl: a receptacle meant to hold used tea leaves and exhausted lemons. Early American tea caddies, almost never seen today, were rectangular flask-like containers with small round covers for storing tea leaves, and were not part of the tea service but separate, ornamental objects. Hot-water urns, large and fashionable spigoted containers for water, (kept piping hot by the heated iron rod inside) were popular from about 1800 and might or might not match the tea set.

And should you be in doubt as to whether your family tea service is English or American, look for a waste bowl. American services have them.

An elegant American cann with a particularly ornamental handle.

Early tea accessories: a sugar nips (above), and a tea strainer (below).

PORRINGERS

A humble object (and, except for spoons, the most common type of early American silver), the porringer was a

Early American Silversmiths

MYER MYERS
(1723–1802)

A New York silversmith and president of the New York Silversmith's Society, in business from c. 1753 until 1802, Myers held part interest in a Connecticut silver mine. His best work was done in the rococo style.

JEREMIAH DUMMER *(1645–1718)*

The first American-born silver-smith, Dummer apprenticed in Boston; he engraved the plates for the first paper money made in Connecticut.

American sauceboat by Nathaniel and Joseph Richardson, c. 1785.

JOHN CONEY *(1655–1722)*

Coney was a Boston silversmith whose work was often plain and substantial, but who could also create high-style, highly Anglicized luxury wares.

PHILLIP SYNG, JR.
(1703–1789)

The son of a silversmith, Syng was a versatile Philadelphia craftsman, assisting Benjamin Franklin with his electrical inventions, becoming a trustee of the academy that eventually became the University of Pennsylvania, and, most memorably, fashioning the inkstand used at the signing of the Declaration of Independence.

JOSEPH RICHARDSON
(1711–1784)

The son of a silversmith and a prolific Philadelphia craftsman, Richardson created presentation silver to be given to Native Americans.

PAUL REVERE
(1735–1818)

Though best remembered for the famous midnight ride, Revere, the son of a Huguenot silversmith, was not only a patriot but a well-known silver-smith in his day. He was the creator of the "Sons of Liberty Bowl" and the maker of much plain, English-influenced domestic silver.

Salver by Myer Myers, 1745–1776.

small, shallow bowl with a slightly domed bottom and, often, a pierced tab handle. Perfect for soups, puddings, and, of course, porridge, it remained popular in America well into the nineteenth century—long after it had gone out of favor in England.

SAUCEBOATS AND TUREENS

Prosperous households set their tables with impressive silver tableware such as sauceboats and soup tureens. Sauceboats were usually made in pairs, while tureens (usually oval in America) were among the most important and expensive silver items one could own. The earliest examples rested on four small feet and often had a matching stand—an oblong tray—beneath it. After 1780 or so, silversmiths set their tureens on pedestal bases.

CRUET SETS AND CASTERS

Cruet sets as well as casters, which contained the sugar, dry mustard, and pepper to "cast" over the food, were important to the eighteenth-century table since food was often far from fresh and off-tastes needed to be disguised. Casters commonly came in sets of three and were often held in silver cruet frames along with oil and vinegar bottles.

SALT CELLARS

Salt, sprinkled either with the fingers or a small spoon, was served in tiny footed silver bowls called salt cellars. Cellars were either lined with glass or gilded to protect the metal from the corrosive effects of the salt. It wasn't until the nineteenth century that salt shakers replaced them on the table.

LIGHTING

The matter of lighting was of great importance in the days before electricity, when evening entertaining necessitated scores of candles. With brass and pewter so readily available, silver candlesticks were a great luxury to be indulged

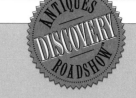

SILVER TANKARD

Appraiser Frank Boos was interested when he saw this silver tankard come out of the bag, and was anxious to hear more about it. The owner said it had been given to his father years earlier and he knew nothing more than that, although the owner of a retail store had offered to buy it for $300. A look at the markings explains why the owner was right not to take the man up on his offer.

Luckily, the English hallmarking system was very precise, and from a few simple marks on its lid and side Boos was able to identify the vessel as having been made in London in 1731, during the reign of King George II, by silversmith Robert Brown. Crafted of solid silver, with a beautiful scrolled handle, the tankard is worth $4,000 to $6,000.

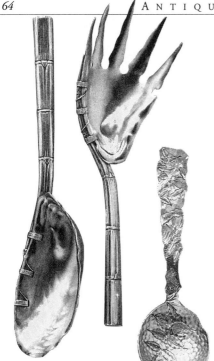

The Victorians (and their heirs) had the right silver flatware for every conceivable food, from berry spoons to ice-cream and bonbon spoons and dessert knives.

in by only the wealthiest of early Americans (who nonetheless, for status and nostalgia's sake, still set their tables with silver candelabra long after the advent of electric light).

Many silver candlesticks and candelabra were weighted at the bottom with pitch or plaster of paris covered by a felt pad, because they were generally top-heavy and prone to tipping over. (This filling also prevented thin, lightweight silver from being too easily dented.) Chambersticks, made low and portable to light the way to bed, were made in pairs and individually. Although early American silversmiths are known to have made candlesticks, few examples have been found.

NINETEENTH-CENTURY SILVER

With the turn of the nineteenth century, a newly sophisticated populace began to want not just silver but *heavy* silver. Substantial weight became (and remains today) synonymous with quality. And although factory production of silver began at this time, it wasn't until the discovery of America's great silver mines in Nevada in the 1850s that a mighty surge of technical innovation led to a distinctive, uniquely American silver style: strong, vigorous, and sometimes florid, to be sure, yet a style that could not be confused with English, Dutch, or any other silver wares.

Naturalistic motifs, grapevines especially, decorated every type of object, and self-confident tablewares shimmered with *repoussé* fruits, leaves, and chock-full horns of American plenty. By century's end, sober forms like the tea service had grown larger and more elaborate, and often included a matching and usually heavy tray that might be three feet wide. The making of serving pieces and other flatware grew exponentially, with special utensils for serving berries, jam, asparagus, and cold meats, and even— for cake and ice cream—the fabled runcible spoon.

Sterling silver objects were available, at last, for everyone. And almost everything that *could* be made of silver, was: hairbrushes, pin-holders, buttons, and card cases.

Nineteenth- and Twentieth-Century American Silver Makers

FLETCHER & GARDINER (1810–1827)

Thomas Fletcher and Sydney Gardiner of Philadelphia manufactured elegant and monumental presentation silver. The firm was commissioned to commemorate the naval victories of the War of 1812, for example, but it also sold its handsome domestic wares to stylish homes from Louisiana to New Hampshire.

SAMUEL KIRK & SON (1815–1979)

Best known for its highly elaborate *repoussé* work, this Baltimore firm produced tea sets, flatware, and serving pieces that were virtually blanketed in high-relief flowers and leaves.

GORHAM & COMPANY (from 1831)

Founded in Providence, Gorham was the nineteenth century's largest producer of silver. Although it competed with Tiffany in standard domestic wares, the firm also created its own special line of "Martelé" silver between 1897 and 1920. This innovative ware (which after 1900 was made of 950 parts of silver in 1,000 and thus was of higher silver content than other American silver) was embellished with naturalistic Art Nouveau motifs. Gorham made only 5,000 or so pieces of Martelé, generally recognizable by its characteristically sinuous form and the clearly visible imprints of hand-hammering.

TIFFANY & CO. (from 1834)

The wit and invention of Tiffany silver made this firm, founded by Charles Louis Tiffany (father of Louis Comfort Tiffany, creator of Tiffany glass), the preeminent American silversmith of the nineteenth century. Its New York designers created the finest work yet seen in Renaissance Revival, Neo-Egyptian, Moorish, Art Nouveau, even Native American styles. Tiffany's best nineteenth-century work was in the "Japonesque" style.

KARL WEBER (1889–1963)

Weber's clean and functional designs are austere, with very discreet ornamentation at the base or on the cover. In plated silver as well as sterling, his best work was done after 1927.

THE INTERNATIONAL SILVER COMPANY (from 1898)

The International Silver Company of Connecticut was formed as a consortium of small silver manufacturers. During the 1920s and 1930s, the firm also employed outside designers, among them, artists Karl Weber, Donald Deskey, and Gilbert Rohde. In addition to the company mark, their work bears the mark of the designer.

KALO (1900–1970)

Founded in Chicago by Clara Wells, Kalo is among the oldest and most important firms producing handcrafted silver.

PETER MÜLLER-MUNK (1904–1967)

The creations of this archetypal New York designer, fabricator of fine Art Deco silver in the 1920s and 1930s, are sophisticated and, also, rare.

Silver fruit stand with gilt details, Gorham, Providence, Rhode Island, 1872.

Example of mixed metals: a Tiffany pitcher.

AESTHETIC MOVEMENT SILVER

In the late nineteenth century, an edict of the Japanese government banned samurai swordsmen from wearing their swords and turned the talents of the emperor's armorers to domestic metal objects. Consequently, at the Philadelphia Centennial Exposition of 1876, Americans suddenly became aware of, and enthralled by, the highly sophisticated mixed-metal objects on view in the Japanese display. Tiffany, and to a lesser extent Gorham, quickly capitalized on this fad for Japanese objects by manufacturing their own mixed-metal items for the domestic market—restrained combinations of copper, brass, bronze, gold, and silver on all types of decorative wares. Such "Japonesque" pieces were sparingly studded with insect and floral motifs in the new Japanese-influenced Aesthetic taste (advocated by Oscar Wilde in England, among others) and were marked "sterling silver and other metals."

An elaborate late-nineteenth-century coffee service by Unger Brothers.

ARTS AND CRAFTS SILVER

Toward the end of the nineteenth century, the proliferation of what were now perceived to be banal, machine-made objects ultimately caused a reaction among small groups of influential artists, who decreed a return to simpler, handcrafted wares: objects with visible soul. Thus, after years of manufacturers' trying to hide all evidences of handwork, it suddenly became fashionable to call attention to the work process, with its more than occasional—and human—imperfections. Handmade pieces and hand-hammered silver became synonymous with genuine artistic merit. In fact, even machine-made articles were occasionally hammered to give them the desirable "human touch."

SILVER-MOUNTED GLASS

At the end of the nineteenth century and the beginning of the twentieth, glass overlaid with silver was a minor fashion. There were two types of silver-mounted glass. The better examples—vases, bowls, and perfume bottles sinuously mantled in actual ribbons of curving silver—were often engraved and hallmarked in some inconspicuous spot. The less expensive type had chemical or electrolytic silver designs bonded right to the surface. The designs were thin, virtually on the same plane as the glass itself and not a separate piece of silver, and pieces look more valuable than they actually are.

TWENTIETH-CENTURY SILVER

In the years following World War I, the sleek Art Deco style, first viewed by Americans at the Exposition Internationale des Arts Décoratifs et Industriels Modernes in Paris in 1925, rocked the design world. Influenced by Cubism and "moderne" geometrical motifs, its clean, unembellished surfaces spoke to a hopeful generation. That same year, Gorham hired Erik Magnussen, a well-known Danish designer, to create designs in the new style, and American silversmiths also began to experiment with strong angles and lines.

Modernist silver, less stylishly ornamented than Art Deco silver, perhaps, but still

Silver-overlaid perfume sphere of teal green glass.

Art Deco three-piece demitasse set: coffeepot (with green Bakelite handle) and open sugar bowl and creamer, Durgin/Gorham, 1929.

GEORGE III SILVER EWER

Belonging to this guest's great-(six greats!) grandmother, an eighteenth-century mono-grammed ewer has great sentimental value; the owner even has an old family photo showing it. Jeanne Sloane noted that it's important to look at the hallmarks on a piece of silver first. The marks here, including the maker's mark, CW, indicate that the pitcher was made in 1771 by Charles Wright, a well-known London silversmith.

Most intriguing is the unusual shape of the piece. Highly decorative, it probably would have been displayed on a sideboard near a basin. The lion's mask beneath the spout is a nice detail that adds to its quality. It is valued at about $10,000.

spare and inevitably reminiscent of the New York skyline, was created by several Bauhaus designers who had fled to America from Europe.

ENGLISH AND CONTINENTAL SILVER

English and Continental silver has a more illustrious history and a far greater sophistication than silver made in America. In fact, American silver can seem somewhat provincial by comparison. Between the fifteenth century and the nineteenth (some would say twentieth) century, generations of European silversmiths created innovations in both technique and form in the craft—the art—of silver.

ENGLISH SILVER

Because England has always had a fairly stable government (compared with the governments of France and Italy, for instance), and because English silver has been reliably hallmarked (see "English Hallmarks," page 55) for four hundred years, English wares have long been the silver of choice, not only in America but throughout the world. Yet English silver was desirable not just for the quality, luster, and probity of the basic metal, but also for the genius of its silversmiths.

Although England produced fine silver in the late seventeenth century and crafted its share of highly superior rococo scrollwork throughout the early eighteenth century, English silver truly came into its own in the latter half of the eighteenth and beginning of the nineteenth centuries, when British artisans broke away from the French aesthetic at last and developed a uniquely English silver style. It began with craftsmen translating the Neoclassical filigree

English Silversmiths

Silver tea caddy, Hester Bateman, c. 1790.

century until the middle of the nineteenth century. Bateman pieces are usually Neoclassical in style and frequently decorated with bright-cut patterning. They are widely collected.

PAUL STORR *(1771–1844)*

During the Regency period, Storr manufactured—first for other firms and, eventually, for his own—bold and elegant heavy-gauge silver soup tureens, service plates, and entree dishes, among other items. Storr's eminence was such that the British Admiralty commissioned him to create "The Battle of the Nile Cup," England's gift to its great naval hero Lord Nelson.

RUNDELL, BRIDGE & RUNDELL *(1788–1842)*

One of London's most successful makers, Rundell, Bridge & Rundell was patronized by the royal family and had warrants from the both the Prince of Wales and Duke of York. They commissioned silversmiths Paul Storr and Benjamin Smith for their more important wares and were known for good-quality but less elaborate pieces as well.

PAUL DE LAMERIE *(1688–1751)*

A French Huguenot who emigrated to London in the first decade of the eighteenth century, this celebrated English artisan crafted spectacular objects for George II and the English aristocracy along with relatively modest domestic wares. De Lamerie's reputation is based on exquisitely fashioned wares incorporating the fanciful, naturalistic motifs, elaborate scrollwork, and asymmetry characteristic of the rococo style.

THE BATEMAN FAMILY *(1761–1840)*

The work of this family is most notable because its owner was a woman—Hester Bateman. With her sons, Peter and John, and her grandson, William, Bateman manufactured pleasant (though, some think, relatively undistinguished) table silver for the English middle classes from the mid-eighteenth

Pair of English George III covered sauce tureens, London, 1804.

George IV covered presentation soup tureen, London, 1821.

English muffineer (small sugar caster), Britannia standard marks, London, 1899.

of English architect Robert Adam into elegant, impeccably made silver wares of dazzling utility—tea urns, table centerpieces, banks of airy candelabras—and influencing silversmiths in Scandinavia, Russia, and America. It blossomed with British silversmiths reinterpreting the work of Thomas Hope and other remarkable English architects ofthe Regency era (named for the regency of George IV, 1811–1820) and fashioning handsome wine cisterns, sets of entree dishes, and massive, elaborate urns in heavy silver. These bold and sturdy wares, of distinctly noble bearing, were as wholly British—and proud to be—as the victorious heroes at Waterloo.

CONTINENTAL SILVER

On the whole, it is safe to say that most Continental silver is more elaborate in design and decoration than either English or American silver. But there is much less of it, because the waves of political turmoil that have periodically shaken Europe have frequently resulted in the loss of tons of its finest decorative and utilitarian silver. A suite of solid-silver French furniture, for instance, was melted down in 1689 to add to the war chest of King Louis XIV, and the losses of silver during the great upheaval of the French Revolution can only be imagined.

Continental silver can be 800 to 950 parts silver in 1,000. Containing somewhat more copper than English or American silver, it is slightly stronger, yet often thinner, lighter, and grayer in appearance. On occasion it may not look or feel at all like silver and can even be mistaken for tin, but the workmanship is often superb. This is especially true of sixteenth- and seventeeth-century examples, most of which, unfortunately, are seldom seen in America except in museums. Americans are far more likely to find eighteenth-century English silver than great sixteenth-century Augsburg wares or works by French or Italian silversmiths. Early German silver does occasionally turn up, and when it

European Silversmiths

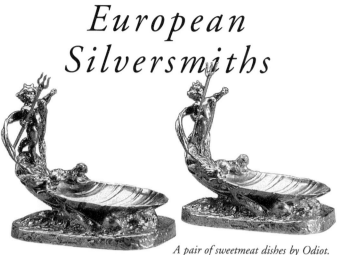

A pair of sweetmeat dishes by Odiot.

WENZEL JAMNITZER

(1508–1585)

In sixteenth-century Nuremberg, Jamnitzer created marvels of silver, fantastically shaped or elaborately encrusted with insects, shells, and reptiles.

NICOLAS DELAUNAY

(1655–1727)

The most important French silversmith of his era, Delaunay fashioned highly ornamented Baroque wares for the court of Louis XIV at Versailles.

JOHANN MELCHIOR DINGLINGER *(1664–1731)*

The best work of this famous silversmith of the German Baroque was created at the behest of Augustus the Strong.

JUSTE-AURÈLE MEISSONNIER *(1693–1750)*

Only a single snuffbox is known to have been struck with Meissonnier's hallmark, but his influence on French Rococo silver design is immense. He was jeweler to King Louis XV, as well as an architect, medallist, and designer; an interpreter of the Rococo at its most florid.

ROBERT-JOSEPH AND HENRY AUGUSTE

(1723–1816)

Working in Paris in the Rococo and Neoclassical styles, this father and son were commissioned to make silver for Madame de Pompadour and Catherine the Great and for the coronation of Napoleon I.

JEAN-BAPTISTE-CLAUDE ODIOT

(1763–1850)

A Parisian silversmith whose architectural and elegant wares, ornamented in the fashionable Empire taste with swan, dolphin, and ram's-head motifs, brought him numerous imperial commissions.

FRANÇOIS FROMENT-MEURICE *(1802–1855)*

Proponent and leading craftsman of all popular and eclectic mid-nineteenth-century styles—Gothic Revival, Renaissance Revival, and Rococo Revival—Froment-Meurice was the most fashionable French silversmith of his day.

JEAN PUIFORCAT

(1897–1945)

The sleek designs of French silversmith Puiforcat, created in the first decades of the twentieth century, launched the Modernist movement in silver.

WIENER WERKSTATTE

(1903–1932)

Dagobert Peche and Josef Hoffmann were silver designers and artistic directors of the Wiener Werkstatte, an Austrian group workshop noted for its simple, functional, and occasionally fantastic Art Deco creations. All Wiener Werkstatte pieces were handmade, and most were individually commissioned.

GEORG JENSEN *(from 1904)*

This Danish firm is noted for clean-lined silver, discreetly embellished by naturalistic Art Nouveau foliage, vine-like tendrils, and pod-like finials and feet. Jensen specializes in tablewares.

Sterling centerpiece bowl by Georg Jensen.

A silver kovsch made by Ovchinnokov, c. 1896

Silver-gilt lobed cup and cover by Melchior Bayer, Augsburg, c. 1600.

does, it can be recognized by the rather deep, zigzag assay scrape in some inconspicuous spot. This characteristic, and the fact that the hallmarks may be very hard to find (they should be there, however), can help you to distinguish German and Scandinavian/Baltic silver from English and American wares.

FRENCH SILVER

The vaunted genius of French design is revealed in its silver: most particularly, in the wares of the seventeenth and eighteenth centuries, when the style, invention, and superb craftsmanship of the sophisticated Parisian silversmiths (there were 500 before the Revolution) influenced silver designers throughout Europe—not only in their own time, but for centuries to come. Because eighteenth-century French silver was hallmarked *before* it was finished, rather than afterward (as in England), French hallmarks are often stretched out of shape.

RUSSIAN SILVER

The Russian court was ever in thrall to Western and, especially, French design. Its aristocracy, therefore, ordered great silver services from Western silversmiths. Much of Russia's native silver, however, has a folk-like, distinctively Slavic character. Even the forms are Russian. The *kovsh,* an elliptical bowl with a long handle, resembles a long-necked bird; it is a typical Russian form and, like the porringer in America, the article most frequently encountered. *Kovshi,* and Russian silver of the nineteenth century in general, are often overlaid with cloisonné enamels in primary colors. Pastel shades are favorites of collectors, although they are less common. Russian wares, which are 825 parts silver in 1,000, have been reliably marked since the eighteenth century.

GERMAN SILVER

German silversmithing reached its zenith in the sixteenth and early seventeenth centuries, with Nuremberg and Augsburg the centers of the craft.

Drinking vessels of all kinds are a German specialty, for sixteenth-century doctors prescribed that medications be drunk from vessels of precious metals. These were turned into masterpieces of lavish design; coconut cups, for instance, and nautilus shells were set on fantastic silver stems. The *nef*, a typically German wrought-silver galleon, and "wager" cups in the form of windmills or a woman holding a swinging cup aloft, were produced prolifically in Germany from the late fifteenth century until 1900. (Don't confuse the imitation of silver known as "German silver" with the solid silver wares of German manufacture.)

IS IT OLD?

You can determine the age of silver as follows: First, consider the shape of the piece. Then, examine the metal's patina, heft its weight, compare its style of decoration to a style chart, and check its condition. Next, look for any inscriptions that may be engraved on it. *Finally*, look at its hallmarks. It has been suggested by some that the smell of silver is quite distinctive and can be used to distinguish silver objects from pewter, for example. (However, one *Antiques Roadshow* appraiser believes that if you've reached the point where you need to smell the silver, things have become desperate!)

♦ Preindustrial silver shows evidences of being hand-hammered, particularly beneath the foot or on the inside. (On some Arts and Crafts and twentieth-century silver, hammer-marks were treated as a decorative device and consequently will be highly visible on the exterior.) On the antique handmade object, such marks were not intended to show and therefore are more discreet, but there.

♦ Until 1770, most forks were made with three prongs. Thereafter, four prongs became the norm.

♦ Teapot handles of the Georgian period (1714–c. 1830) were usually made of wood. Teapots of the

EXETER SILVER SPOON

The owner had taken a chance at a country auction and bought a locked box for $65. This silver spoon was inside the box.

"It's probably the oldest piece of silver ever seen on the show," said expert Christopher Hartop. Made at the end of the sixteenth century, the spoon might have been a family's only piece of silver and a precious possession.

Silver marks on the piece show that it was made not in London or another well-known silversmithing city in Elizabethan England, but in Exeter, in those days an important trade center. The bowl is worn from centuries of use, but otherwise the piece is in quite good condition.

Because it was made in Exeter rather than London, Hartop estimated that this rare spoon would command three or four times the price of a contemporary London spoon—about $2,000 to $2,500.

TIPS *from the experts*

Andrea Blunck Frost, Jeanne Sloane, and Frank Boos offer some rules of thumb for silver:

Breathing lightly on a questionable spot can reveal a repair site. The repair will show up as a pale and frosted area. Soldering, the usual form of repair around the joins and hinges, leaves a brown stain.—F.B.

A largish dimple in the silver's surface often indicates where engraving might once have been, as does a shiny but smeared look on the surface.—F.B.

If a piece appears to be handmade and has at least two hallmarks, it may be Continental.—A.B.F.

Mixed-metal wares weren't valued in Grandmother's day, but they certainly are now.—F.B.

A heraldic-looking mark will be the town mark.—A.B.F.

American marks must be *exactly* like those in the books of hallmarks if an accurate attribution is to be made. —A.B.F.

Never wrap your flatware with rubber bands or *any* silver in cling wrap. Both leave impossible-to-remove stains.—J.S.

If a piece has just a maker's mark, don't assume it's American. It is more likely to be the mark of a Scottish maker or an Englishman who lived a long way from the assay office.—J.S.

Age, in silver, isn't enough. A good piece should also be representative of its period.—J.S.

nineteenth century were fitted with silver handles interrupted by small ivory ferrules to provide insulation from the heat of the liquid in the pot.

♦ Shafts of eighteenth-century candlesticks were cast in two pieces and soldered together, then soldered to a cast base. Antique candlesticks, therefore, should show vertical seams along the sides of the shaft.

♦ An engraved date on silver should not be mistaken for the date of manufacture. Very often it commemorates an event that took place many years earlier. For example, parents might be given a piece of old silver to commemorate an important anniversary, with the date of the celebration engraved on it.

♦ On old silver, the owner's initials can help in determining the date and origin of a piece. Sometimes the lettering itself—punched in with little dots (sixteenth and seventeenth centuries) or in florid or Gothic (Victorian)— can be helpful.

♦ On eighteenth-century American cups, pitchers, and tankards, the hallmarks will be found to the left of the handle, while English pieces of the same era are usually marked to the right.

♦ A tankard's thumb-rest (the tab depressed by the thumb to raise and lower the lid) may have left a dent in the top of the handle. This type of damage is considered a desirable indication of age.

IS IT STERLING OR SILVER PLATE?

Check the high spots (raised parts of the design) for evidence of the base metal showing through beneath the silver skin.

♦ In the nineteenth century, it was uncommon to mark plated wares. Occasionally, however, a disk bearing the manufacturer's name was applied in some inconspicuous place.

♦ Plated trays are usually heavier than silver trays.

♦ To see the rectangle of genuine silver that was often let into the center of a Sheffield plate object for monogramming, breathe on the suspect area. The rectangular outline will be revealed. Sometimes the let-in plate was never engraved at all.

♦ Silverplated wares tend to tarnish to a deep, gun-metal black shade, often having a certain iridescence. Sterling usually tarnishes to brown or gray.

♦ A piece stamped "Sheffield plate" was made in Sheffield in the nineteenth century. It is *not* genuine old Sheffield plate.

♦ In England, it is illegal to sell articles as genuine Sheffield plate unless they were made by the correct Sheffield process within the period when Sheffield was manufacturing fused-plate objects.

Two-handled silver centerpiece with the maker's mark of Tiffany & Co., c. 1881–1887.

Silver candlesticks by Nathaniel Morse, c. 1730.

IS IT VALUABLE?

Silver is usually weighed by the pennyweight (24 grains equals one pennyweight, 20 pennyweights equals one troy ounce, and 14 troy ounces equals one pound). It can be weighed accurately only on a special silver scale (not on a bathroom scale). Most of us assume, quite correctly, that the weightier the piece of silver, the more valuable it will be, and there are several excellent reasons that this should be so. Heavy silver withstands polishing better, it is less susceptible to dings from falls, and it feels gratifyingly substantial in the user's hand.

POLISHING SILVER

Museum conservators currently recommend lacquering heirloom sterling that is not in daily use, since overenthusiastic elbow grease can damage the silver surface. Early lacquers were brittle and may have chipped away, and the silver can be badly tarnished where it is exposed to air. Modern lacquers, presumably more elastic, are reversible as well, but *all* lacquers somewhat alter the patina and finish of antique silver.

A late nineteenth-century silver samovar, Orest Kurlikov, Moscow.

Many silver items, especially candlesticks and vases, have hollow bases filled with plaster or resin. Such wares have been "weighted" with this filler material and are therefore unweighable for actual silver content. (Knives always have base-metal blades, as silver is too soft to cut with. In consequence, they are also unweighable.) As one specialist succinctly described some modern silver, "It seems almost to be made of tinfoil." Most of this lightweight or unexceptional silver is of banal design and valued only for its "scrap" weight—that is, the weight of the silver itself, melted down.

The condition of silver is important but, as with all antiques, if an example is particularly uncommon and it would be rare to find that particular piece in perfect condition, imperfections will be overlooked. In addition, consider these details.

♦ High spots and projections on silver pieces (such as the raised areas on *repoussé* design) should be examined for wear and holes caused by decades of polishing.

♦ The quality of a piece of silver has nothing at all to do with its scrap or melting price. Beautiful silver and prosaic silver can weigh exactly the same.

♦ Any kind of repair or alteration—removing the engraving, engraving a piece that was once plain, making a pitcher out of a mug, adding decoration or removing it—devalues a piece of silver.

♦ Because there will always be a market for large, expensive pieces of silver by well-known makers, these will inevitably be high-priced. Small pieces, however, tend to be priced according to their utility as well as their beauty.

♦ Until the mid-nineteenth century, an "I" or an "i" denoted the initial "J." Thus the mark IC could as easily designate one of early America's best-known silversmiths, John Coney, as it could the far-from-famous I. Clark or even a previously unrecorded maker.

♦ Specialized forms of antique silver, such as tea caddy spoons, vinaigrettes, and marrow scoops (long-handled utensils for reaming marrow from beef bones), tend to be more valuable than more common wares like teaspoons and tablespoons.

♦ Southern silver—from Charleston or Virginia, for instance—is rare and thus highly desirable.

♦ Western silver—that of San Francisco, for example—is valuable because it's rarely seen. But its value will be greater in the West, perhaps, than in other regions.

♦ Old Sheffield plate is always less valuable than sterling, but it cannot be considered inexpensive, especially if it's in excellent, unworn condition.

♦ Pieces with unusual designs—those that incorporate the human figure, animal heads, or mythological ornament—often are more valuable than pieces with more commonly seen leaf, flower, and fruit motifs.

♦ Tea and coffee services, which can include as many as twenty pieces, are worth considerably more if all the pieces remain together.

♦ Among sets of flatware, the most valuable are those called "straight sets"—sets made by a single manufacturer in the same year.

♦ In general, oblong tureens are not as valuable as tureens of round or oval form.

♦ The typical work of any silversmith is always more highly valued than his atypical work.

♦ Many silver objects from the late nineteenth century exhibit intentionally discolored or unusually textured surfaces. *Never* try to polish or repair these seeming "flaws." The object's value (which often far outweighs its size) will be destroyed.

♦ Original inscriptions or the names of well-known people on silver add to value. Religious inscriptions

Seven-light silver candlebra with maker's mark of Tiffany & Co., 1902–1907.

Silver and colored stone chalice by Archibald Knox for Liberty & Co., 1903.

O·L·D N·E·W·S

There are a few kinds of silver items that experts see all too often at the *Roadshow*. The fact that these items are common usually indicates that their value cannot be very high:

♦ Modern silver plate

♦ Coin silver spoons

♦ Plated Renaissance Revival compotes supported by human figures

(and most silver made for religious purposes) are, conversely, seldom desirable.

♦ Early American silver, particularly porringer handles, is occasionally engraved with three initials in a triangle. The upper letter indicates the surname and the lower two the first names of the husband and wife who owned the piece.

FURTHER READING

Drury, Elizabeth. *Antiques, Traditional Techniques, etc.* New York: Doubleday, 1986.

Ensko, Stephen G. *American Silversmiths and Their Marks.* Mineola, NY: Dover Publications, 1983.

Fennimore, Donald L. *Silver and Pewter.* New York: Alfred A. Knopf, 1984.

McClinton, Katherine. *Collecting American 19th-Century Silver.* New York: Charles Scribner and Sons, 1968.

Okie, Howard. *Old Silver and Old Sheffield Plate.* New York: Doubleday, 1928.

Truman, Charles. S*otheby's Concise Encyclopedia of Silver.* London: Conran Octopus Limited, 1996.

Wilson, John. *Miller's Silver and Plate Antiques Checklist.* London: Reed Consumer Books, 1994.

Wyler, Seymour. *The Book of Old Silver.* New York: Crown Publishers, 1979.

Art nouveau-style yachting trophy, possibly by Gorham, c. 1916.

AMERICAN FURNITURE

In the hierarchy of the decorative arts, fine furniture is unquestionably king. At its best, as in the pieces seen below, it exhibits nobility and dignity, a distinctly sculptural presence, and—with royalty's usual good manners—a common touch, obligingly conforming both to our anatomy and workaday use.

Above: Chest of drawers of carved and painted wood, Thomas Dennis, c. 1678.

Left: Mahogany Chippendale scroll-top block-and-shell-carved chest-on-chest, Rhode Island, c. 1760–1785.

Below: A sprightly apron and exceptional carving on an ideally proportioned Chippendale dressing table, or lowboy.

A classical chair from Baltimore, 1815–1820; possibly by John and Hugh Finlay.

Left: An eighteenth-century high chest of drawers exemplifies the art of lacquering.

Right: The fine and delicate craftsmanship of this tambour-door desk is typical of the Seymour workshop.

Left: A chest with bracket feet, c. 1800, decorated with vivid and imaginative freehand painting.

American (Cont'd.)

An effective pairing: a small chestnut table (tabouret) by Gustav Stickley, inset with a Grueby faience tile, c. 1901.

An undulant and vigorous Chippendale card table from Newport's Goddard-Townsend workshop, c. 1760–1780.

Gilded bronze mounts, cut brass panels, and rosewood graining make this a highly sophisticated Grecian couch; Boston, c. 1820–1830.

Below: A stenciled, grained, and marbleized game table. The folding top rotates, and game pieces are stored in the well; Baltimore, c. 1820–1825.

Herter Brothers, purveyors to the wealthiest Americans, worked initially in Renaissance Revival and Neo-Grecian styles, as seen in this ladies' desk. Herter's later, Aesthetic-style work was more innovative.

ENGLISH

The center table, like this English Regency example of costly rosewood with brass mounts (c. 1820), was a fixture of nineteenth-century parlors.

An English version of an Empire bed.

Below: This walnut arm-chair, 1740–1780, blends elements of Queen Anne and Chippendale styles.

The prototype of the Edwardian piece: a period-painted satinwood secretaire cabinet, c. 1800.

Edwardian satinwood dressing table, painted with figural scenes and floral sprays.

George III painted arm-chair, c. 1768; attributed to Thomas Chippendale.

CONTINENTAL

Louis XIV silvered and parcel-gilt lit de repos, *late seventeenth century.*

A French cabinet, painted, mounted with gilt-bronze, and inset with rare, pink-ground Sèvres porcelain plaques, 1824–1826.

A rococo commode with Boulle marquetry encrusted with bronze mounts.

A Louis XV ormolu-mounted Japanese lacquer bureau, c. 1750–1755.

An amusing Continental Empire daybed on realistic gilt-bronze feet.

Right: A painted and gilded canapé with tapestry upholstery, from the last quarter of the eighteenth century; stamped "Jacobi."

SILVER

Silver is the only precious metal to be used for household objects. Consequently, antique ceramics, brass, glass, and pewter are often imitative of expensive silver teapots, tureens, and tankards, and most other silver forms. But no other material comes close to simulating the quality of genuine silver: its warmth and luminosity; its rich effect; or the satisfying crispness with which it can be engraved, embossed, and ornamented.

The Belle Epoque style: a richly embellished punch bowl by Tiffany & Co.

Allover embossing has always been a specialty of the Kirk firm in Baltimore. This teapot, an early example, dates from 1828.

AMERICAN

Right: Vermeil and applied decoration combine in an unusual covered punch bowl by Whiting, c. 1875.

A tureen with an eagle finial is a superb example of American presentation silver.

The Dutch influence: a pear-shaped teapot from New York, c. 1740.

Below: A graceful pair of Myer Myers sauceboats, made in New York between 1745 and 1776.

A rare and sophisticated Philadelphia cruet stand with its original condiment bottles intact.

A Boston Colonial era porringer with monogrammed pierced-scrollwork handle.

Left: Chased with swags, bows, and Greek key borders, this elaborate Philadelphia hot-water urn, c. 1825, looks distinctly English.

The waste bowl from a c. 1820 American tea service.

Art Moderne at its best in a silver and Bakelite cocktail set by Magnussen for Gorham.

Above: An Art Nouveau vase with enameled chrysanthemums, made by Tiffany & Co. for the Columbian Exposition of 1893.

A rare enameled silver box, set with turquoise and opals, by Louis Comfort Tiffany, c. 1910.

Flatware by International Silver.

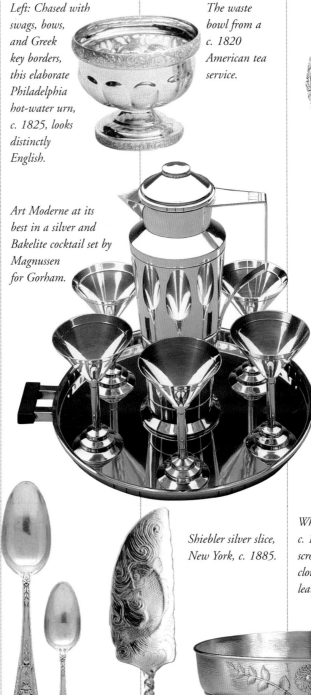

Shiebler silver slice, New York, c. 1885.

Whiting centerpiece bowl, c. 1885. Japonesque, on four scroll feet, with stylized clouds; chrysanthemums and leaves rising from each foot.

ENGLISH

CONTINENTAL

An aquatic theme in a nineteenth-century French centerpiece by Froment-Meurice.

Paul Storr, the foremost English silversmith of the Regency period, fashioned this exceptionally well-detailed figural candelabra in 1815.

Above: Not to be confused with Sheffield plate, this solid silver chamber stick was made in Sheffield, c. 1820.

Below: The essence of Art Deco: a luxurious and sleek silver-and-jade bowl by Puiforcat.

Below: Pieces of Elizabethan silver, like these London beakers, are seldom seen.

Below: The anthemion borders and animal-form spouts of a French tea service by Odiot are characteristic of Neoclassical design.

PORCELAIN

Below: A circular covered dish and plates from a much larger Minton and Boyle ironstone service, c. 1840.

An early blue-and-white Royal Worcester mug attempts to replicate Chinese porcelain.

PORCELAIN, POTTERY, AND GLASS

We particularly treasure our ceramics and glass for having escaped the slippery fingers and cruel knocks of time. Like butterflies, they're admired not just for their diversity of hue, shapeliness, and variety, but also for their inherent fragility.

Left: A covered vase, part of an eighteenth-century Royal Worcester mantel garniture, actually looks Chinese.

Everyday china: Canton and Nanking wares in characteristic blue-and-white patterns were so inexpensive they were used as ships' ballast.

Left: Competing with English and European imitators, much Chinese porcelain was made specifically for export, like this famille rose tureen from the eighteenth or early nineteenth century.

Copies of Sèvres porcelains—and there are thousands —never compare with the genuine thing, like this potpourri vase with gilt bronze mounts attributed to Thomire, c. 1785.

Superbly modeled and painted Meissen figures: fish, fruit, and milk vendors.

Paris porcelain: a two-handled ornithological ice pail, cover and liner, c. 1820.

POTTERY

Nineteenth-century blue-and-white Staffordshire pictorial plates, transfer-printed like decals.

A triumph of English soft-paste: the figure of a Thames waterman painted in vivid enamels, c. 1753–1755.

Minton pâte-sur-pâte decoration on a "pilgrim flask" vase by M.L. Solon, c. 1875.

A remarkable early-nine-teenth-century Sèvres breakfast service, decorated with finely painted reserves of birds, butterflies, and shells, c. 1813.

Below: An example of the type of Rockingham glaze book-form flask made by the Bennington factories.

Above: Like many others, this Staffordshire pot-tery figure from the latter half of the nineteenth century depicts a famous personage; here, Edward, Prince of Wales.

An American majolica shell-and-seaweed pitcher, Griffen, Smith and Hill, late nineteenth century.

Classical blue-and-white Wedgwood pattern.

Classical figures were the favorite subjects of Parian wares, which were intended to simulate marble.

Perhaps made for America's Centennial, a late Chinese export plate depicts the signers of the Declaration of Independence.

A rare Wedgwood Queen's Ware "Frog Service" dessert plate, manufactured in 1774 for Catherine the Great of Russia.

A fine Sèvres cabinet plate, made early in the nineteenth century, in a style much imitated in the early twentieth century.

A mid-eighteenth-century version of the Chinese famille verte palette by Worcester.

A nineteenth-century stoneware butter churn with sprightly cobalt decoration, made in Albany, New York.

Many English porcelain painters are known. George Complin painted this Derby plate in 1790.

A view of England's Apsley House centers this early-nineteenth-century Berlin porcelain cabinet plate.

Above: A slip-decorated glazed redware two-handled jar, attributed to John Bell, Waynesboro, Pennsylvania, nineteenth century.

Left: A sturdy and business-like spongeware pitcher.

Topographical subjects are desirable, like this view of Cheltenham on a flower-encrusted Chamberlain's Worcester plate, c. 1820.

Emerging from the body of an Artus Van Briggle vase, a low-relief blossom, c. 1929.

Right: Refined workmanship, subtlety of color, and graceful lines characterize the work of Adelaide Alsop Robineau, c. 1910.

GLASS

The color gradations of a summer sunset on this New England peachblow vase are produced by combining gold and uranium oxide with sodium nitrate.

Below: The familiar Sandwich Glass dolphin candlestick, molded between 1840 and 1860.

This handsomely faceted English or Irish Waterford glass dish, c. 1785–1810, is the essence of British glassmaking.

Seventeenth-century glassblowing masterpiece: a whimsical Venetian glass goblet wrapped in glass flowers.

Double-overlaid and etched glass form the base and shade on a Gallé lamp fitted with silver mounts, c. 1890.

Right: The celebrated "Bristol Blue" glass, of a royal blue color that results when cobalt dioxide is added to clear molten glass. The glass was actually made throughout Europe, and not at Bristol at all. It entered England through the port of Bristol, which accounts for the name.

In an Art Nouveau vase, a dramatic swirl of Tiffany favrile glass seems still molten.

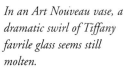

René Lalique Bouchon Fleurs de Pommier perfume flacon.

Blown-glass single-flower vase, Daum-Nancy, France, 1902.

Hovering over a clump of lily pads and a stand of bulrushes, Tiffany's brilliant dragonflies in glass and lead, 1900–1910.

PAINTINGS

Seen singly, the majority of works by most listed artists seem attractive and competent. But pleasant colors, scenes, and subjects can cloud our judgment as to quality. By comparing an artist's paintings with those of his or her contemporaries, or with those of other painters attempting similar subjects, we can better distinguish the "choice" from the second-choice.

The single iris in the painting Fleur de lys *by American Frank Vincent Dumond (above) is competently and accurately rendered, "pretty," and altogether lacking in the sort of fresh, exciting, and idiosyncratic vision that coalesce to make the* Irises *by Vincent van Gogh (right) "Great."*

The restoration of Marriage at Cana *by Paolo Veronese removed centuries' worth of smoke and grime (detail, far left) to reveal remarkable detail and the artist's original, brilliant palette (near left). Viewers can become so comfortable with brown and aged varnish, however, that such cleanings provide a shock.*

A comparison of techniques can be of some help in dating art. In Still Life with Flowers and Fruit *(below, left)*, by seventeenth-century Dutch artist Jan Davidsz de Heem, the flowers are painted with jewel-like precision. Compare the impressionistic brushwork of the 1864 still life by Claude Monet *(right)*, Spring Flowers *(below, right)*, and the theorem (Still Life, *right*, attributed to Elizabeth W. Capron), not painted at all, but composed with stencils by a mid-nineteenth-century American amateur. Each technique is characteristic of its era.

Deprived of Europe's great and ancient architecture, a natural spectacle like Niagara Falls was irresistible to American nineteenth-century artists. Frederick Edwin Church's Niagara *(right)*, Louis Rémy Mignot's Niagara *(above)*, and Alvan Fisher's The Great Horseshoe Falls *(above, right)* render the falls in styles that range from able to dazzling. Which captures their grandeur most effectively?

AMERICAN ARTISTS

From the Revolutionary War to the close of the nineteenth century, American art—its subject, America—grew resolutely, if in fits and starts, toward a wholly indigenous style.

The splendor of the American landscape was a prime subject for nine-teenth-century artists. In Creek Near Gloucester, Massachusetts *(above),* Fitz Hugh Lane *freezes one light-struck moment,*

augmenting it with his own dreamy vision. By comparison, Mount Tom on the Connecticut River *by Edmund C. Coates (left) seems unimaginative and lack-luster.*

The gentle composition and effortless flow of Mary Cassatt's warm pastel, Mère et enfant *(left), far out-shine a conventional and badly composed portrait,* Lady in White, *by her contemporary, Wilson Lockwood (below).*

Western subjects, blending nostalgia and grandeur, have always been popular with Americans. The Native Americans pictured by Oscar Edmund Berninghaus in Pueblo Indians on Their Reservation *(right) are neither posed nor stereotypic and were actually painted outdoors. A similar but stilted work by Victor Casenelli,* Landscape with Indians *(above), lacks its interest and immediacy.*

Matthew Pratt was a student of Charles Willson Peale in London. Yet Peale's 1788 Mrs. Richard Gittings (far left) displays a distinctly American independence, compared with the formal, well-observed, but stiff rendering of Pratt's Portrait of Abigail Willing (near left).

Marine paintings, with their highly accurate detail, may be useful documents for marine historians, but they sometimes lack spon-

taneity. Antonio Jacobsen was enormously prolific and rendered highly precise paintings of ships, as seen in The East African in Full Sail (above).

John Henry Mohrmann's Kilmeny, viewed from the same angle and enjoying the same weather, is almost a twin.

The successful academic still life should depict its subject realistically. In two renderings of a favorite mid-nineteenth-century

subject—huge, bountiful tiers of fruit—only Severin Roesen (above) truly succeeds. A similar work by Charles Baum (top) lacks three-dimensionality and "juice."

STONES AND ORGANIC MATERIALS

Diamond

Zircon

Ruby

Citrine

Sapphire

Star sapphire

Emerald

Aquamarine

Topaz

Pearl

Almandine garnet (pyrope)

Demantoid garnet

Jadeite

Turquoise

Nephrite

Opal

Amber

JEWELRY

Size, color, and stone quality are crucial to the valuation of jewelry, but design (and particularly design that can be attributed to a famous craftsman or firm) is important to collectors as well. The exceptionally fine pieces illustrated here either exemplify the work of the best artists and goldsmiths of the mid-nineteenth to mid-twentieth century or epitomize the best of popular jewelry design.

STYLES

VICTORIAN

Diamonds delineate a ring shape favored in the late nineteenth century.

Amethysts were popular choices for Victorian jewelry.

Gold, seed pearl, and carnelian bracelet by master jeweler Castellani, c. 1860–1865.

Ring set with rose-cut diamonds.

Rose- and table-cut diamond ring.

Jewelry motifs reflect the furnishings of the period, as seen in this gem, enamel, and gold bangle bracelet, c. 1880.

Demi-parure of Victorian amethyst and gold.

Aquamarine, garnet, turquoise, and pearl brooch, set against a background of "bloomed" gold.

Stone cameo with finely carved bust in an "Etruscan" gold frame.

ART NOUVEAU

A jeweled landscape in plique-à-jour with enamel, pearls, and diamonds by René Lalique.

A typical Art Nouveau combination: opals, diamonds, cultured pearls, and enamel in a necklace.

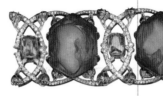

Dragonfly designs, as in this aquamarine, pearl, diamond, and plique-à-jour enamel necklace, were Art Nouveau favorites.

Enamel and unusual materials like citrine and ever-glass are used in a Lalique bracelet.

BELLE EPOQUE

A diamond necklace, c. 1910.

Filaments of platinum spin a diamond-set floral pendant, c. 1905.

The French influence: a pin of fire opal and diamonds with bows and garlands, c. 1905–1910.

ART DECO

Hard-edged and modern: an Art Deco diamond brooch signed by Cartier, c. 1920.

Exotic Asian motifs, as seen in this carved jade pendant, typify the era.

"Fruit salad" necklace of carved rubies, cabochon emeralds, diamonds, and yellow gold.

Ruby and diamond "skyscraper" clips.

Jabot pin with a diamond-mounted Buddha: a typical Art Deco form.

Below: Repetitive pattern in an Art Deco diamond bracelet.

The sautoir was high-fashion in 1925. This one was created from natural pearls, ruby beads, and diamonds.

Art Deco diamond and emerald bracelet, c. 1925.

Right: A ruby, sapphire, emerald, and diamond Egyptian Revival bracelet by Lacloche, Paris, c. 1925, combines the finest in period design with a famous label.

DESIGNERS

Guilloche enamel two-color gold picture frame, characteristic of the work of Carl Fabergé, 1896–1903.

RETRO

Bold, "industrial strength": a diamond "rouleau" bracelet, c. 1938.

Diamond, cabochon ruby, enamel, and gold berry bracelet by Tiffany & Co, with matching earrings.

Retro citrine, diamond, and gold necklace.

Citrine ruby and diamond cocktail ring. Asymmetric scrolls and semi-precious stones typify Retro style.

A set chock-full of cabochon rubies, emeralds, sapphires, and diamonds; bracelet signed by Van Cleef & Arpels.

Glass beads are clasped by thorn-like prongs in a Lalique necklace, c. 1908.

Retro ruby and diamond brooch.

CLOCKS AND WATCHES

O n the wall or stairs, on the wrist or in the pocket, centuries' worth of clocks and watches, in materials as varied as bronze, wood, and gold, share a face and hands as familiar to us as our own, and bear orderly witness to our hours and days.

The elephant and howdah on this bronze mantel clock illustrate the eighteenth-century French preference for exotic subjects.

TALL CLOCKS

Far left: A mid-eighteenth-century Dutch spectacular in marquetry, gilt-bronze and brass with moon phases on the dial.

Left: A George III chinoiserie lacquer longcase clock with alarm.

Right: A Massachusetts carved and inlaid mahogany tallcase clock, c. 1796. The movement is by Caleb Wheaton; the labeled case is by Ichabod Stanford, who worked in the cabinetmaking shop of one Luther Metcalf.

Wrought-iron mantel clock in the distinctive Art Deco style, its case designed by Edgar Brant.

Below: A very rare example of a clock by Louis Comfort Tiffany, incorporating alabaster and mosaic glass.

Empire Revival black marble and gilt: bronze mounted mantel clock.

Just another pretty face: a typical and common Royal Bonn-style mantel clock made in Germany, c. 1900.

Right: English clockmakers were particularly noted for their fine bracket clocks. This George III clock with its three-train movement and ebonized case is an excellent example.

Below right: A highly decorative green lacquer chinoiserie case makes this eighteenth-century clock rare.

Right: In a display of technical virtuosity, a George III bracket clock chimes the hour and quarter-hour, amazes with automata, and entertains with music as well.

Antoine-André Raviro bronze French Empire mantel clock.

POCKET WATCHES

Set with half-pearls, an enameled hunter-cased watch with push-down stem repeater.

Gold quarter-repeating skeletonized jacquemart watch. The arms of the figures move and strike the bells.

A view of the movement of an unusual gold hunter-cased pocket chronometer with chain.

BRONZE

Tiffany bronze and favrile glass wall sconces.

Probably an English example, but common in early America: a bronze-and-iron kettle, dated 1708.

METALWORK

From the simplest cooking pot to the stateliest candelabra, several varieties of metals contribute their strength, weight, and beauty to an amazing miscellany of decorative objects. Humble or grandiose, they often outlast the ages, growing lustrous with the passing years.

BRASS

A famous bronze by Frederic Remington: Coming Through the Rye, *cast in 1907.*

Pair of brass candlesticks, stamped "Joseph Wood," 1730–1740.

A rare signed and dated eighteenth-century American brass sundial.

American andirons, fashioned with characteristic Chippendale flame finials and ball-and-claw feet.

Pierced fretwork and American eagles decorate a fine serpentine fireplace fender, c. 1800.

Brass (Cont'd.)

Small andirons,
c. 1791–1821, their
plinths decorated with
Adamesque urns.

COPPER

Copper-and-zinc grey-
hound: an uncommon
subject for a weathervane.

Brass precision: nineteenth-
century compass, clinometer,
and telescope.

Doubly functional: this
Scandinavian tobacco box,
dated 1787, has been
engraved with a perpetual
calendar.

A stately, lobed goblet
with ribbon-like
handles, fashioned
by Josef Hoffmann,
c. 1925–1931.

Below: A mid-nineteenth-
century Boston brass-
and-glass argand
lamp, fitted for the
display of a small
bouquet.

An
"American
Beauty" floor
vase, made by
Victor Toothaker
for Roycroft,
c. 1912.

Eighteenth-century
Philadelphia kettle
of copper, brass, and
tin in unusually fine
condition.

Left: This curiously
shaped pot was termed
a "saucepan" in
Colonial America.

PEWTER

A rare and important pewter flagon, Johann Christophe Heyne, Lancaster, Pennsylvania, 1752–1781.

Close-up of marks on the bottom of the pewter flagon above.

Enamel-decorated Art Nouveau desk accessories from London's Liberty & Company.

Below: A collection of eighteenth- and nineteenth-century American lighting devices and tablewares.

IRON

On a trade sign, wrought-iron spectacles frame eyes painted on tin.

A splendid molded-copper weathervane with a horse-drawn pumper and fireman showing a fine turquoise patina.

The champion trotter Black Hawk: one of the most popular nineteenth-century weathervane subjects.

RUGS

A neatly designed bag face by nomadic Yomud weavers.

RUGS, QUILTS, AND SAMPLERS

With astonishing grace and deftness, the human hand paints colorful patterns with textiles, creating brilliant squares and rectangles of warmth: quilts to cover beds; rugs to cover cold floors; samplers to warm fond parental hearts.

Typically vivid: a geometric Kazakh rug from the Caucasus.

Ladik prayer rug with mihrab *(niche).*

A playful pattern on an American hooked rug.

A sophisticated Persian Tabriz shows a marked abrash, *or change in wool.*

Fiery against a dark background, boldly drawn freehand leaves and flowers on a hooked rug.

Right: A droll and highly detailed Navajo pictorial rug depicting the drive-in audience for a tribal ceremony.

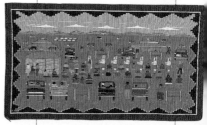

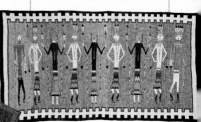

A Navajo rug with images of yei, *the holy people commonly depicted in sandpaintings.*

QUILTS

Resonant and bold: a pieced Amish bar quilt, 1880–1910.

A virtuosic display of needlework on a trapunto and appliqué presentation quilt, 1861.

Bits of expensive chintz are adornment for a pieced appliqué quilted coverlet, c. 1830.

A pieced Sunburst quilt, 1840–1860, radiates outward in carefully arranged gradations of color.

Four wedges of calico "flying geese" and a meticulous feather-quilted border embellish an old quilt.

A medley of brilliant starbursts on a Mennonite pieced appliqué quilted coverlet, late nineteenth-century.

Derr Family pieced cotton quilted coverlet, Berks County, Pennsylvania, 1820–1850.

A conventional blue-and-white jacquard coverlet has a whimsically "architectural" border.

Pieced appliqué quilted coverlet, Lancaster County, Pennsylvania, 1820–1850.

Right: A rare and fine American sampler entitled "Washington City" dates from the Federal era.

SAMPLERS

Farm animals, dogs, swans, and stylized flora on an embroidered appliqué quilt, c. 1825–1845.

Left: An imaginative eighteenth-century American alphabet sampler by eleven-year-old Elizabeth Crowninshield.

A well-wrought and thoughtfully composed mourning sampler.

TOYS, DOLLS, AND COLLECTIBLES

Because playthings and collectibles—especially dolls, teddy bears, and rock memorabilia—have usually been subjected to more than their share of affectionate use, those that come down to us in pristine condition are considered the most desirable.

Made in France: a Citroën fire truck (center), key-wind ladder truck (left), and Pinard ladder truck (right).

Graceful and elegant: a Lutz tinplate oversize phaeton.

Rare tinplate Märklin Ferris wheel, c. 1890s.

The last word in firefighting: a Märklin horse-drawn live-steam fire pumper.

A very rare prewar Bentalls van.

A prewar double-decker bus with painted passengers.

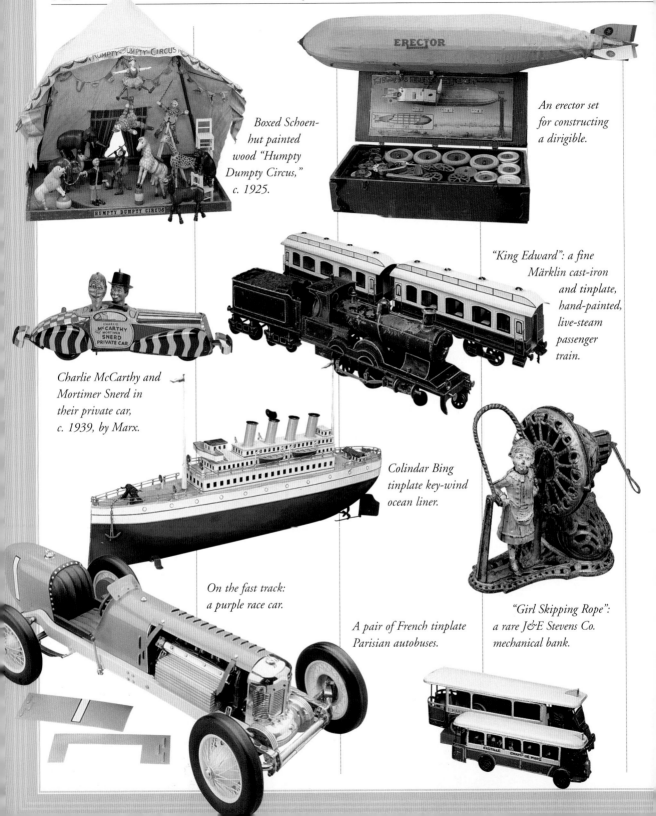

Boxed Schoen-hut painted wood "Humpty Dumpty Circus," c. 1925.

An erector set for constructing a dirigible.

"King Edward": a fine Märklin cast-iron and tinplate, hand-painted, live-steam passenger train.

Charlie McCarthy and Mortimer Snerd in their private car, c. 1939, by Marx.

Colindar Bing tinplate key-wind ocean liner.

On the fast track: a purple race car.

A pair of French tinplate Parisian autobuses.

"Girl Skipping Rope": a rare J&E Stevens Co. mechanical bank.

Called a "Queen Anne" doll, this English example postdates that period; it was made c. 1750–1770.

Greiner doll, c. 1858.

English poured wax doll by Pierotti, c. 1890.

An endearing Kewpie doll with bisque head and glass eyes; made between 1910 and 1920.

Left: A Kestner doll, c. 1905–1910.

Left: Armand Marseille's most successful doll, made c. 1899–1920.

Left: A lovable little rag doll.

Right: A china head with molded, center-part hair suggests a c. 1840 date for this German doll.

Right: Despite the fragility of wax, this wax-over-composition German doll by Dizessel, c. 1885, is in excellent condition.

Babe Ruth's signature, right on the sweet spot—where it ought to be.

Their sleeves rolled up, Ulysses S. Grant and Henry Wilson symbolized the workingman's friends on their 1872 campaign poster.

A film collector's prize: the souvenir program from Welles' masterpiece, Citizen Kane.

Baseball was popular even before the Civil War, and depictions of the game were subject for song-sheet covers.

A clever but ultimately ineffective campaign button from 1944.

Teddy Roosevelt 1904 campaign button.

Republican campaign button from the 1936 presidential election.

The epitome of speed: a stylized Mobil Oil porcelain Pegasus from the 1930s has a rare, embossed body.

Ten pounds of peanuts were doled out from a "store tin" that retains its cover, scoop, and glassine bags.

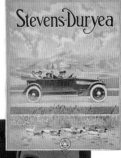

A reminder of the 1955 "subway series": the Dodgers/Yankees program.

A vintage automobile ad from the golden era of motoring.

Democratic party banner, celebrating the repeal of Prohibition.

Though both the coffee and the company are long gone, this collectible tin remains.

All they need is love and the box they came in: a set of Beatles nodder dolls.

The famous Red Goose on a painted wood sign.

Animation cel of Mickey Mouse in The Prince and the Pauper.

BOOKS AND MANUSCRIPTS

Every aspect of the written word, from calligraphy to autograph to inscription, attracts enthusiasts. We can't tell (the importance of) a book by its cover, its age, or its paper, however, though penmanship on manuscripts is beautiful by itself and illustrations invariably enrich simple prose.

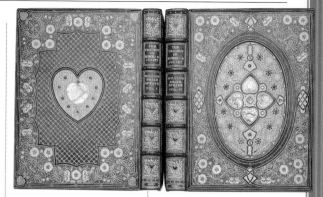

A truly splendid jeweled binding (with 24 jewels), of Romeo and Juliet *by Sangorski & Sutcliffe, binders and calligraphers; illuminated manuscript, c. 1920.*

Some Poems by John Keats, bound by Sangorski & Sutcliffe in a jeweled binding (with 1,027 jewels); illuminated manuscript, c. 1912–1914.

Illustration by Arthur Rackham for Hans Christian Andersen's "The Emperor's New Clothes."

An Arthur Rackham illustration captioned "She was Sitting Under the Christmas Tree," painted in 1932 for Hans Christian Andersen's "The Little Match Girl."

Ptolemaic atlas.

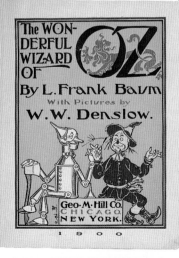

Title page, L. Frank Baum's The Wonderful Wizard of Oz, *illustrated by W.W. Denslow; first edition, 1900.*

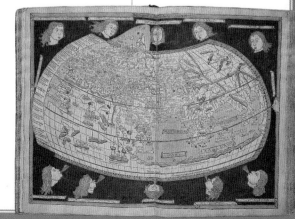

On the
Origin of
Species by
Means of
Natural
Selection
*by Charles Darwin;
first edition, 1859.*

*Lincoln's Gettysburg
speech and second
inaugural address
(1865), bound in a
Union blue Levant
morocco cover by
Riviere & Sons.*

Mark Twain's Tom Sawyer; *first English edition (which preceded the American first by six months), London, 1876.*

Louisa May Alcott's Little Women *and* Little Men; *first editions, 1868–1871.*

"Ode to a
Nightingale" by
John Keats, page 1,
verso, 1819.

*Right: Letter
from Thomas
Edison to Isaac
Norris, dated
January 22,
1880.*

Bank check in the amount of $250, signed by George Washington and dated October 22, 1798.

Autographed manuscript excerpt of Wolfgang Amadeus Mozart's unfinished Requiem, *with the chorus "Requiem, aeternam dona eis, Domine" (Give them eternal peace, oh Lord), 1791.*

Left: First page of the Nicolay copy (known as the "First Draft") of the Gettysburg Address, written in Washington, D.C., shortly before November 9, 1863. This is the earliest extant version in Abraham Lincoln's handwriting.

"The Rite of Spring," original score, written in 1913 by Igor Stravinsky.

Second and final page of the Nicolay copy of the Gettysburg Address.

Inscription and opening page of "A Visit from St. Nicholas," written by Clement Clarke Moore for his children, Christmas Eve, 1822.

Chapter Three

PORCELAIN, POTTERY, AND GLASS

The most devastating development in the long history of ceramics and glass was the discovery of electricity and the use of electric lighting in the home. It led, unfortunately, to a new type of furnishing—the table lamp, that highly wired despoiler of Ming vases, dainty Meissen milkmaids, Staffordshire dogs, and glittering Waterford urns.

In the early part of the twentieth century, if an object was moderately attractive and stood still for too long, decorators bought it, drilled it, and made it into a lamp. Thus arose the antiques dealers' favorite axiom: if a thing *can* be drilled (or planted), it *will* be.

We're grateful, however, for the still vast numbers of ceramics and glass that the drillers missed, modest or magnificent. The manufacturers who produced them were justifiably proud of their wares, which is why, when you turn over a plate or a glass, you will often find marks—the factory name, a pattern name, a country of origin, or some

A graceful American wine glass, blown, cut, and engraved by the New England Glass Co.

The arrival in Europe of pieces like this seventeenth-century Chinese brush pot launched a race to learn the secrets of porcelain manufacture.

Extremely fragile but intact, a unique American Belleek mirror frame, wholly encrusted with realistically modeled white blossoms.

not-too-cryptic symbol. To puzzle fans, the marks are fun, for reference books list thousands of marks that, properly deciphered, tell how old a piece is, where it was made, and whether or not it's rare. Famous names dot those pages—Royal Crown Derby, Worcester, Sèvres, Tiffany, Lalique—names of wares that families hand down for generations. But there are mystery marks as well: Japanese? Chinese? Eighteenth-century Viennese?

We are leaving them mysterious, for the moment, and confining this chapter to the kinds of porcelain, pottery, and glass Americans are most likely to find: European and American nineteenth- and twentieth-century ornamental wares. Chinese pieces are notoriously difficult to identify in any case—first, because their marks differ so from those on Western wares, and then, because even when they've been interpreted, they can't be trusted. Throughout China, the copying of fine early ceramics is considered an homage to the originals, and since porcelain has been made in China since the tenth century, a great deal of such "homage" exists.

In America, there is an enormous variety of eighteenth-century European, Asian, and domestic ceramics and glass. The European output alone comprises a large and rarefied field—a field encompassing all the stars, from Capodimonte to Chelsea, Delft, Wedgwood, Baccarat, Royal Crown Derby, and Royal Copenhagen. Though spoiled for choice, we will try in this chapter to touch on some of the lamp escapees you might someday find.

PORCELAIN

Our English term "china" for porcelaneous objects derives, as you might expect, from the country in which this ceramic material originated. Chinese potters were creating exquisite ceramics of porcelain over a thousand years ago, yet the formula for porcelain remained their secret for centuries, and seventeenth-century Europeans, trading with China, were desperate to learn it.

Would-be porcelain makers experimented with a variety of materials and eventually created a mixture of clays and glass that produced, not true porcelain, but a rather soft, moderately translucent porcelaneous material called soft-paste. Once the Meissen factory near Dresden in Saxony unlocked the secret of true (or hard-paste) porcelain in 1708, this artificial porcelain was abandoned, although it continued to be made in England. Eventually, the magic formula of hard-paste porcelain—kaolin mixed with petuntse (feldspar), two forms of decomposed granite that fuse together in the kiln—spread gradually throughout the Continent and to England, and porcelain began to be produced in the West in earnest.

AMERICAN PORCELAIN

There *is* early American porcelain, but it is so rare that it is seldom seen. In the Colonial period, most of the better tablewares were imported from Britain and China, for elaborate dinner services could be commissioned with monograms or commemorative motifs and, after the Revolution, with highly popular patriotic emblems—eagles in particular. A short-lived Philadelphia firm, Bonnin and Morris (in business only from 1770 to 1772), produced such a minuscule amount of porcelain that the few pieces that occasionally turn up today are enormously valuable. The Tucker firm, also of Philadelphia, is best known for the stolid white and gilt pitchers it produced from 1825 to 1838. But American porcelain certainly never offered any serious competition to the European product. Throughout the nineteenth and well into the twentieth centuries, well-to-do Americans continued to prefer French,

A great American rarity: a soft-paste porcelain basket made by Bonnin and Morris.

More common are examples of Belleek, like this small, lobed teapot by Ott and Brewer.

The stocky shape of Tucker pitchers (above), c. 1830, is easily recognizable. Tucker wares are not quite as elegant as they are scarce.

The substantial wares of the Union Porcelain Works sometimes incorporate "monkey" handles like this one or, in patriotic mode, bison heads.

English, German, and Chinese porcelains for their increasingly grand table settings.

Toward the middle of the nineteenth century, however, sparked by waves of immigration, America began to establish its own ceramic tradition. In Greenpoint, Brooklyn, for instance, an immigrant Englishman named Charles Cartlidge established a factory and was soon joined there by the Union Porcelain Works. Cartlidge porcelains looked very much like their English forebears, but tended to be heavily gilded and of hefty design and "potting" (the fabrication of porcelain or earthenware). All-white bisque-like wares (Parian), along with quantities of porcelain and pottery, were also manufactured in the area around Trenton, New Jersey. So many ceramics were made there, in fact, by the late nineteenth century it came to be known as the "Staffordshire of America," a reference to England's great center of ceramic manufacture.

In the third quarter of the nineteenth century, an American interpretation of Irish Belleek china—crisp, thin, and white beneath an iridescent glaze—was also made in Trenton by the Lenox factory and was an immediate success. Ott and Brewer, another Trenton firm, manufactured Parian ware on the English model, along with highly sophisticated figures and decorative objects, although they, too, produced the eggshell-thin, Belleek-type wares that came to be known as American Belleek.

As the century and industrialization progressed apace, porcelain moved steadily from a degree of creativity and genuine artistic merit to a sheer, mechanistic virtuosity, and ceramics in general became slicker, more elaborate, and altogether lacking in any evidence of having been fashioned by the human hand. Many late-nineteenth-century ceramics were so perfectly wrought and decorated, in fact, that they seemed almost to have been made by machine (a feature that characterizes most twentieth-century porcelain). Large European bisque figures in elaborate costume with naturalistic flesh were typical of the period and were commercially successful throughout America. Millions of these inexpensive, flashy figures were produced in France and particularly in Germany, and exported to America, as were the "cabinet pieces" made solely for display. American and Japanese firms manufactured these wares, copying well-known European factories in Berlin and Vienna. Often heavily gilded plates were decorated with gilt-bordered portraits of European royalty or tediously competent copies of Old Master paintings, all edged in borders of rich claret or royal blue.

EXPORT PORCELAIN

Quantities of mass-produced porcelains, decorated with conventional patterns, were made for export to the United States and England from Canton and Nanking, China. Armorial patterns (which could be ordered decorated with one's own heraldic device), Fitzhugh patterns in green, orange, brown, and blue (with borders composed of honeycombs, circles, and butterflies), and rose medallion patterns (in which four or more panels of birds, butterflies, and flowers abut a central medallion of related design) were the usual contents of the two hundred or so boxes of china in the hold of every ship returning from the Orient. Although Chinese wares first arrived here in the late eighteenth century, much of what has survived today is from the nineteenth century. During that era, popular styles were in *famille rose* (rose-pink family) shades which, along with *famille verte* (predominantly green) porcelains, were often purchased in large services. Export wares frequently have small scenes of figures interspersed with flowers. Both *famille rose* and *famille verte* Chinese porcelains are still made today, but the earlier wares, ordinary as they were at the time, are far superior to these too brilliantly colored and carelessly painted later pieces.

A Canton mug and covered vegetable dish, nineteenth century.

Nineteenth-century Chinese platters reveal the prototype of "Blue Willow" patterns— a pagoda, a bridge, and a willow.

Manufactured for export to European and American markets, blue-and-white Canton wares were Western in shape with perfunctorily painted Chinese designs.

Early-nineteenth-century blue-and-white English transfer ware is still reminiscent of Chinese prototypes.

BLUE-AND-WHITE

Blue is by far the most common single color used on white ceramics, because it is attractive, of course, but also because its cobalt pigment (which is gunmetal gray when first applied) is the most reliable pigment in the heat of the kiln and therefore easiest (and cheapest) to produce.

Blue decoration on a white ground—popularly called blue-and-white—can be printed or painted. Meissen's blue onion pattern has been popular for more than two hundred years and has been endlessly reproduced. The Royal Copenhagen factory in Denmark still successfully manufactures its two-hundred-year-old Blue Fluted Lace pattern. The Blue Willow pattern, also originating from the late eighteenth century, usually depicts an arrangement of willows, bridges, figures, and pagodas, a Westernized pastiche of Chinese motifs. Most often, Blue Willow is found printed, not painted, on earthenware.

Blue-and-white Canton ware, made in China in the eighteenth and nineteenth centuries and shipped from the port of Canton, is a perennially popular type of export porcelain. Frequently it is crudely potted, and its decoration (painted by an assembly line of artists) tends to be slapdash. But Canton was affordable—so inexpensive, in fact, that the merchant ships carrying it from

Ceramic Makers and Marks

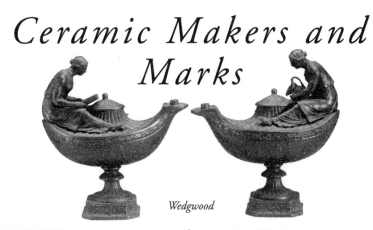

Wedgwood

MEISSEN *(from 1708)*

GERMANY The first European factory to make hard-paste porcelain, and ceaselessly imitated, Meissen is famous primarily for superb eighteenth-century wares with floral designs and chinoiserie decoration and is valued especially for its brilliantly colored porcelain groups and figures, all seeming to have a lifelike sense of movement. In the nineteenth century, the company revived its early styles, among them flower-covered "Snowball" wares.

BERLIN *(1761–c. 1860)*

GERMANY The Royal Factory was one of several to make hard-paste porcelains in Berlin in the eighteenth century. During the nineteenth century, it was perhaps best known for its production of realistically painted porcelain plaques.

WORCESTER *(from 1751)*

ENGLAND Worcester porcelain incorporated soapstone, a substance that allowed it to hold boiling water with-out cracking. This functional aspect, along with beautiful underglaze-blue wares, polychrome enamel chinoiseries, flower sprays, and European figural decorations, made the firm highly successful. During the Victorian era, Worcester produced elaborately pierced cabinet wares.

ROYAL CROWN DERBY *(from 1750)*

ENGLAND Known in the mid-eighteenth century for high-quality soft-paste wares, especially figures, after 1770 the works of the factory were valued particularly for their pure white porcelain body and brilliant glaze. Nineteenth-century Derby wares often have gilt-work in relief and enamel beading. Japanese Imari patterns have always been popular as well.

MINTON *(from 1796)*

ENGLAND Although the factory made much blue-printed pottery in the eighteenth century, in the Victorian era it created one of the most interesting of modern ceramic innovations: *pâte sur pâte*—a built-up "paint" of clay and water that could be used to create finely shaded, cameo-like decorations on porcelain. Minton is also known for its often elaborate and richly enameled majolica.

SÈVRES *(1756–1851)*

FRANCE In eighteenth-century France, Sèvres, the national porcelain factory, created international styles in ceramic design. When the Meissen factory foundered during the Seven Years' War, Sèvres became the dominant manufacturer of porcelain in Europe. Known particularly for its brilliantly colored enamel grounds, its use of lavish (and often tooled) gilding, and "jeweled" decoration, Sèvres wares were imitated by competitors in England and throughout the Continent.

SPODE *(from c. 1770)*

ENGLAND Josiah Spode was the inventor of the hard, white, translucent porcelain, made with calcined bone ash, known as bone china. In the nineteenth century, the Spode factory also produced earthenware, creamware, and copper luster wares.

WEDGWOOD *(from 1754)*

ENGLAND The Wedgwood factory was founded by Josiah Wedgwood, who perfected creamware (called Queen's ware), pearlware, black basalt, jasper, and the blue-and-white stoneware for which the firm has been famous for centuries. In the nineteenth century, Wedgwood also manufactured luster-wares, most notably Fairyland luster.

PARIS PORCELAIN *(c. 1780–1840)*

FRANCE Several factories made porcelains in Paris early in the nineteenth century, and together their wares, often imitative of Sèvres design, are known as Paris porcelain. The best of the Paris porcelain output were objects made in the Neoclassical style.

TIPS
from the **experts**

Nick Dawes outlines the types of imported ceramics likely to be found in this country in various periods:

(1750–1800)
— Chinese export porcelain
English soft-paste porcelain
Meissen
English creamware
Delftware
Nanking ware

(1800–1850)
— English pearlware
English porcelain
Chinese export: Canton ware *(mostly blue-and-white)*

(1850–1900)
— Canton ware
Staffordshire *(ironware, White Granite Ware)*
Ornamental Dresden porcelain
Limoges porcelain
Continental porcelain *(especially from Bavaria, Austria, and Central Europe)*

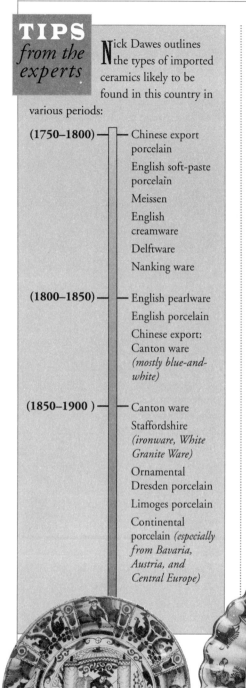

the Orient to America and England used it as ballast. It is a favorite in the United States because it is so appropriate with eighteenth- and nineteenth-century American furniture.

THE EUROPEANS: A QUICK REFERENCE

Porcelain is one of the triumphs of European decorative arts. Hard-paste porcelain was produced at Meissen in 1710; within fifty years, it was being manufactured in Italy, Germany, France, and England, its secret traveling with Meissen's deserting employees. Yet the early porcelain of Meissen, painted with chinoiserie (pseudo-Chinese) landscapes or formed into exquisitely sculpted and realistically colored human, animal, and bird figural groups, was constantly imitated then and even today. In France, however, the hard-paste porcelain factory at Sèvres eventually outshone even Meissen with elaborate, inventive, and brilliantly hued enamel grounds (the basic applied color of the porcelain object) in turquoise, rose pink, and royal blue, among other colors. The best Sèvres porcelains had painted white reserves (scenes within a frame) depicting figures, flowers, and landscapes, the whole embellished in rich gold relief (surface projection).

Eighteenth- and early-nineteenth-century Sèvres wares were largely reserved for French consumption, but as relations improved between France and its former enemy, England, the Sèvres factory began to export to both England and the United States. Throughout the rest of the century, Sèvres continued to make the highly formal porcelains for which it had become renowned, although, by the end of the era, Limoges, a city in south-central

Examples of early German and Swedish blue-and-white-faience.

France, had superseded Sèvres as the most important center of French porcelain manufacture. Many factories in Limoges, while continuing to produce wares in the style of the eighteenth century, also worked in the more flamboyant Victorian style. (Several of these nonchalantly imitated the famous crossed-L mark of Sèvres as well.)

In Germany, during this period, the Meissen factory near Dresden retained its traditional importance, continuing to manufacture its own most popular wares. But these were also widely reproduced by other German firms, one of which copied them so successfully, even counterfeiting Meissen's mark, that Meissen legally forced it to use, instead, a crown above the word "Dresden." The factories of Berlin, Nymphenburg, and Vienna also worked in styles of the preceding century. Berlin, however, became particularly successful with figural and portrait porcelain plaques in the 1880s, while in Austria the Vienna factories continued to manufacture handsome and showy vases and plates in the Sèvres style, embellished with courtly scenes in the manner of French artists Fragonard and Boucher or like those of Angelica Kaufmann, a Swiss painter known for Neoclassical figural subjects. Throughout the nineteenth century, all of these

Pearlware is pottery, less expensive than porcelain and thus particularly suitable for children's tableware.

A mid-nineteenth-century Spode partial dessert service, comprising sauceboats, a fruit bowl, and cake and dessert plates, is indicative of the extensive services that the Victorian household required.

HOW TO TELL PORCELAIN FROM POTTERY

Pick up a cup, pitcher, or vase, and the first thing you'll need to know, before you can determine if the piece is old or has value, is whether its "body"—the combination of clays and minerals that make it a ceramic—is porcelain or pottery.

Pottery is:

♦ Usually thicker than porcelain

♦ Made in a variety of colors; may be multicolored

♦ Often utilitarian and frequently found as kitchen and table wares

♦ Nonresonant (lacking a "ring")

♦ Porous, requiring a glaze or impervious coating if intended to hold liquid

Porcelain is:

♦ Hard and glassy (especially if it's hard-paste porcelain)

♦ Not porous

♦ White in color

♦ Generally translucent

♦ Resonant, especially in bowl form

Twentieth-century American redware jar, sgraffito-decorated with a large and confident eagle.

elaborate commercial porcelains (and others like them from Bavaria and Central Europe) occupied prominent spots in American parlors. And even today, their names—Dresden and Limoges, especially—retain a touch of magic.

Josiah Spode, an English manufacturer, introduced bone china c. 1800. Bone china contained bone ash, making it harder and more "creamy" than Continental porcelains. Throughout the nineteenth and twentieth centuries, bone china, produced by firms like Minton, Worcester, Coalport, and Royal Crown Derby, became England's most successful commercial porcelain.

POTTERY

Pottery (earthenware), like porcelain, is made from clay baked in a kiln. It's the metal or mineral content, particularly the amount of iron in the clay, that creates its basic color. A high iron-oxide content, for instance, makes clay red, but clay can also be yellow, white, brown, or gray. Pottery is most frequently used for less expensive, utilitarian wares.

In England, long before Josiah Wedgwood introduced his tough, inexpensive, elegant creamware (cream-colored earthenware with a cream-colored or clear glaze) c. 1760, other potteries were making creamware, although it was coarse and yellow. Wedgwood's earthenware was as thin and delicate as porcelain, lead-glazed in translucent shades, and could be molded into objects as varied as caster sets, ewers, coffeepots, and egg separators. When Queen Charlotte, wife of George III, ordered nine hundred pieces for the palace, the justifiably proud manufacturer renamed it Queen's ware.

Pearlware, another Wedgwood specialty, is a bluish white version of creamware, often decorated in blue glazes and chinoiserie designs. Pearlware figures and tablewares, by Wedgwood and other English factories, are common in the United States today.

The six most frequently seen varieties of nineteenth-century American pottery are redware, yellowware, stoneware, spatterware, spongeware, and majolica. The first three are body composition types; the last three, decorative techniques.

Redware, not surprisingly, is the name for objects made of red clay. Redware is the crudest of pottery and has been made for millennia. It can be "thrown" on a potter's wheel or simply molded by hand. Often brittle and easily damaged, it is always coated with glaze (often of a green color) because it is porous and would otherwise absorb liquids.

Yellowware is an English or American earthenware commonly used for kitchen items like mixing bowls. It is seldom marked.

Stonewares are refined earthenwares comprising a combination of clays and vitreous (glassy) ingredients. After firing in a kiln, stoneware may become impervious to liquid, which is why it can be left unglazed, although most often it is decoratively glazed. Most stonewares range in color from light gray to brown and are durable, dense, and relatively lightweight when thinly potted. If common rock salt is thrown into the kiln with stoneware, it acquires the characteristic brownish, orange-peel surface of "salt-glazed" stoneware. In the late eighteenth century, the Wedgwood factory made highly refined colored stonewares simulating natural stone, among them, jasper ware and black basalt. These are still being made.

Spatterware and **spongeware,** both produced in the nineteenth century, are types of decoration. Spatterware is earthenware that has been daubed (spattered) with colored slip (liquefied clay), usually cornflower blue or red. It was produced earlier than spongeware and was often made in England and then imported to the United States. Though English, these wares are today as collectible as the American versions.

Spongeware is earthenware made for everyday use. More heavily potted and more primitive than spatterware, it is crudely decorated with dabs of color applied with a sponge.

American majolica is a mid- to late-nineteenth-century product, a colorfully glazed Victorian invention and was a

Nineteenth-century salt-glazed flowerpot with a tree in cobalt blue.

A sgraffito fantasy flower decorates an American pottery pie-plate; signed and dated by the artist in 1783.

"Demon drink" is drolly exemplified in folk-art devil jugs like this 1930s version from North Carolina.

TIN·GLAZED WARES

All the following are terms for a common type of earthenware with a coating of glaze, made white by the addition of tin.

Majolica, made in Italy and England (but maiolica—don't confuse the two—is early Italian or Spanish tin-glazed earthenware)

Faience, made in France, Germany, or Portugal

Delftware, made in Holland and England

A 1510 maiolica plate depicting a painter at work.

Salt-glazed and cobalt-decorated stoneware vases typify the style of Henry Remmey II and his son, Henry Remmey III, who worked in the Baltimore and Philadelphia area between 1818 and 1835.

specialty of the firm of Griffen, Smith, and Hill, of Phoenixville, Pennsylvania. American majolica tends to be less detailed and more heavily potted than comparable English majolica, which was made most successfully by Minton, George Jones, and Wedgwood.

Another variety of pottery is ironstone, an early-nine-teenth-century type of white earthenware that is sometimes called Stone China, or in America, White Granite Ware. Tough and thick, plain or transfer-printed, it was frequently used for large dinner services or as commercial tableware.

Most American and European Arts and Crafts potters of the late nineteenth century worked in pottery rather than porcelain. True to the tenets of the style, their wares were naturalistic and "organic" in color and shape, and typically were handmade.

BENNINGTON POTTERY

Bennington, Vermont, was a major center of ceramic production in the nineteenth century. Several factories manufacturing Parian porcelain and Rockingham and salt-glazed stonewares flourished in the town. The largest and most successful of these was the United States Pottery Company, known for its "Rockingham" glaze (a glossy, mottled brown glaze named for an English prototype). The typical Bennington example, however, had a thickly potted yellow body and was usually somewhat cruder and larger than related English pottery.

Many figures of lions, deer, cows, spaniels, and poodles were made in America in this distinctive glaze, and most are attributed today to the United States

American Art Potters and Marks

Grueby

CHARLES VOLKMAR
Corona, New York

Volkmar's early pottery, often decorated with landscapes and animals, reflects his training as a painter. Volkmar is known for underglaze blue-and-white pieces and matte-finish art pottery, occasionally lined in a vivid color.

CHELSEA KERAMIC
Chelsea, Massachusetts

After 1895, Chelsea became the Dedham Pottery and made blue-and-white tablewares.

ROOKWOOD *Cincinnati, Ohio*

Many of the best art potters trained initially at Rookwood, which was founded by Maria Longworth Nichols. This extremely influential factory developed numerous innovative techniques, among them, the Tiger Eye glaze, silver-overlay ware, and an ethereal vellum glaze. The firm also made lamps, mantels, and wall plaques, among other unusual items, and its imaginative wares were imitated throughout the country. Rookwood is always well marked, and numerous Rookwood decorators' marks are known.

LONHUDA *Zanesville, Ohio*

Best known for a high-gloss brown glaze on a yellow body (resembling Rookwood), Lonhuda imitated Native American pottery shapes and some-times incorporated images of Native Americans themselves into designs employing a yellow, red, and gray palette. Several Lonhuda artists are known. Their signatures can be found on the factory's vases and bowls.

WELLER *Zanesville, Ohio*

In the first decade of the twentieth century, Weller was one of the largest pottery works in the world, manufacturing everything from standard matte-green art pottery to the sinuously iridescent, oil-slick glazes of Jacques Sicard to Dickens Ware, depicting characters from the popular English novels. In the 1920s, the factory produced much commercial relief-work that resembled carved wood.

GEORGE OHR
Biloxi, Mississippi

A self-proclaimed eccentric and genius, Ohr made thousands of pieces of pottery—no two alike—that incorporated a variety of techniques, often reflected in his signature folded, crimped, and ruffled style. Some of Ohr's most singular wares were made of paper-thin clays, twisted or pleated into unusually shaped vases and bowls and decorated with earth-colored mottled and bubbled glazes.

NEWCOMB COLLEGE
New Orleans, Louisiana

Every piece of Newcomb pottery is marked with the initials of the college (which trained women potters), its designer, and its potter. These often inventive and highly artistic wares, frequently glazed in a characteristic blue-green shade, were each one-of-a-kind.

GRUEBY FAIENCE
Boston, Massachusetts

Made primarily by hand, Grueby pottery compared favorably with those of Rookwood. The factory was known both for its art pottery and its architectural tiles, although the matte-glaze vases and bowls, particularly those with carved and molded naturalistic decoration, are favored by collectors.

ADELAIDE ALSOP ROBINEAU
Syracuse, New York, and St. Louis, Missouri

America's finest woman potter, Robineau most often worked in porcelain, and her creations are idiosyncratic and extremely rare.

ARTUS VAN BRIGGLE
Colorado Springs, Colorado

Early Van Briggle pottery, with its gentle matte glazes and subtle reliefs suggesting natural forms, seems quintessentially Art Nouveau, especially the factory's most successful designs: those that incorpate the female form, the famous "Despondency" among them.

American Arts and Crafts pottery of all types has become increasingly popular. It is one of a few ceramic styles in which Americans excelled. David Rago shares his expertise.

The great years for Art Pottery were short—from 1900 to 1915.

Art Pottery collectors prefer vases to almost any other form.

Hand-decorated holloware is likely to be more valuable than flatware (plates, etc.).

A "dream team" of Art Pottery artisans worked at the University City Porcelain Works in University City, Missouri, between 1909 and 1910. They were Mabel G. Lewis, Adelaide Alsop Robineau, and Taxile Doat.

Ninety-five percent of Grueby pottery is green. The other 5 percent is multi-colored and the most valuable sort. The Grueby Pottery company also made bases for Tiffany's leaded shades.

Roseville pottery reached its peak in 1906, manufacturing wares with fruit and flower patterns in relief. After World War I, pieces were cast in molds and not made by hand. If you look within these postwar pieces, they will show the inverse of the relief pattern on the surface.

A good piece of art pottery will have an even foot ring, a straightforward shape, and a die-stamped or incised mark.

Blue and green matte glazes, entire plants (rather than individual plant elements), and trees draped with Spanish moss were popular subjects for Newcomb College pottery. This piece dates from 1912.

Pottery Company at Bennington. Yet other, smaller factories also made these wares. Few Bennington pieces are marked, and reproductions are common.

The Rockingham glaze is found on American pie plates, bowls, mugs, jugs, flasks, and, less commonly, figures and even desk sets. As with the animal figures, not all such wares were made at Bennington. (Flasks attributed to Bennington always have a circle of beaded dots around the spout.)

Crocks are salt-glazed stoneware storage vessels made throughout the East Coast for commercial patrons in the eighteenth and nineteenth centuries. Those made at the Bennington factories in Vermont are salt-glazed stoneware and usually decorated in underglaze blue.

Stamped marks of crock makers will often appear on the shoulder, and marked wares of early manufacture, especially those of unusual shape or decoration, are particularly valuable.

AMERICAN ART POTTERY

An enormous interest in ceramics developed in America in the 1860s and 1870s. Influenced by well-attended international exhibitions and by a growing wave of interest in Japanese ceramics, some painters and sculptors turned to making pottery. This new direction was part of an international reaction to a perceived loss of humanism in the arts.

American art pottery, then, was Art Nouveau or Arts and Crafts in style, but it was invariably artist-made and decorated. The fashion for art pottery lasted just a short while—from the 1870s until just after World War I—but it became so popular that it was manufactured by scores of factories in the United States. Several serious and innovative potteries were founded in that period, the largest and most famous of which was the Rookwood Pottery of Cincinnati.

Art pottery is often decorated in earthen shades like browns and greens, and has a carefully applied glaze, glossy or matte. Although most American art pottery is clearly marked, the marks are not always easy to decipher.

FOLK CERAMICS

Vernacular earthenwares and stonewares were fashioned by provincial potters for their own or local use. Regional American ceramics, like those of the West Virginia potteries, Moravian potteries, and Pennsylvania redwares, are representative of the work of these talented craftsmen, who lent their own often whimsical and individualistic styles to purely utilitarian crocks, pots, plates, jugs, and bowls.

Redwares are frequently decorated with yellow slip. Redware plates, bowls, or pans, unmarked and ornamented with decorative and somewhat elaborate floral design, may be Moravian pottery, produced in North Carolina between 1770 and 1860.

Many kinds of utilitarian jugs and crocks, most notably gray-bodied stonewares decorated in blue, were made throughout the eighteenth and nineteenth centuries. These come in three basic shapes: ovoid; chunky and ball-shape; and straight-sided with a sloping shoulder. Some experts equate these shapes with dates of manufacture.

Shape is not the only determinant, however. Decoration is often a useful key to place of manufacture. For example, sgraffito decoration (a technique in which the watered-down opaque clay or slip decoration coating the piece is scratched through in designs that expose the red body beneath) may indicate Pennsylvania, New Jersey, or North Carolina origins.

On stoneware crocks and jugs, the most common motifs (and often the least desirable) are flowers. Landscapes, birds, and commemorative images are the designs most highly sought after.

This slip-decorated salt-glazed stoneware inkwell, c. 1790–1810, is a rare form in American pottery. Decorated with birds, it was also initialed by its unknown artist.

Glazed Moravian sugar jug, North Carolina, 1802–1810.

STAFFORDSHIRE FIGURES

Many nineteenth-century (and even twentieth-century) American homes decorated their mantels with Staffordshire figures, those naïve and endearing earthenware dogs, shepherds, images of the famous, and cottages that were so popular in England for decades. Staffordshire figures first appeared in the mid-nineteenth century, and it's worth knowing how antique examples differ from their modern counterparts.

Mid-nineteenth-century Staffordshire figures do not have a uniform network of cracks (crazing) in the glaze that covers the surface, and figures tend to be well-worn at the extremities. If colored, colors are rich and appear to be sloppily applied. There is some loss of crispness of detail in twentieth-century versions, which may also be crazed and more matte on the surface. Vibrant color and gilding, as well as printed marks, are signs of twentieth-century origin.

Perhaps made in Bennington, Vermont, a nineteenth century pottery figural flask, mantled in his own cloak and a mottled brown Rockingham glaze.

IS IT OLD?

One of the pleasures of ceramics is that, because they are often marked, there are (almost) hard-and-fast rules. Below are a few guidelines for distinguishing what factory made a piece, when it was made, and how you can distinguish the old from the new.

MARKS

Miraculously, a single mark on a ceramic can reveal the country and, often, the factory it was manufactured in as well as the year the pattern or shape was registered for production. In the case of English registration marks, the mark can denote the very month.

Despite our frequent and accurate warnings that ceramics marks are not to be trusted (on pre-nineteenth-century English, Continental, and Chinese ware especially), it is equally true that the marks on most nineteenth-century pottery and porcelain—particularly those of American origin—ought to be believed. The fact is, until rather recently, no one was interested enough in this field to make forgery monetarily worthwhile.

Marks are most commonly printed under the glaze, using a stamp or transfer technique, and appear on the bottom or back of an object. Sometimes they are painted over or under the glaze. Incised marks are scratched into the foot or back of the body before the piece is fired at all, and impressed marks are stamped before firing. Sometimes the painter of a portrait plate (see above) will sign his or her work on the front, within the painting. More rarely, a factory artist will inscribe or sign the back.

Interestingly, if a piece has *no* mark, it may predate the use of marks and thus be worth researching. (On the other hand, thousands of late-nineteenth- and twentieth-century wares are *un*marked, so you have to determine general age by shape, design, and body—which you ought to do in any case before you check for marks.)

A pattern number alone on the back of tableware indicates that the piece is probably English and likely to have been made in the early nineteenth century.

Marks that include "Made in [x]," "Bone China," "English Bone China," or (as with every vintage object) the country of origin indicate twentieth-century manufacture.

For English ceramics, marks that use the words "Limited" or "Ltd.," or the word "Trademark," indicate a date of manufacture after 1861–62.

Sometimes, along with the factory mark, an inscription will have been painted on the back or bottom of an especially finely painted piece of porcelain. Very often, this identifies the subject of the scene or landscape on the front; almost invariably, it also indicates a particularly high-quality piece. (Inexpensive imitations have *printed* inscriptions and decoration.)

Numbers on the reverse of identifiably marked ceramics often refer to patterns. If a company's records are accessible, these can help you to date your own ceramics. For the same reason, actual pattern names can be somewhat helpful in dating.

DESIGN AND DECORATION

Initially, in order to compete with Asian markets, eighteenth-century Continental porcelain was designed to reproduce the shapes, types of decoration, and colors of Chinese porcelains. Even the marks were often a European-flavored interpretation of Chinese calligraphy. (Still fashionable today, Chinese wares are being reproduced by factories here and in Asia.) Ultimately, however, some porcelain design began to imitate the valuable silver of its own era. Any general book on silver can help you recognize

NEWCOMB COLLEGE VASE

David Rago shows us that an art object is always more interesting when we know something about the social and historical issues involved in its production. This Newcomb vase, made by a woman,

embodies his point. With so many men lost in the Civil War, women became part of the workforce. At Newcomb College, the New Orleans-based pottery company (1900–1940), women often decorated and "carved" the firm's vases, incorporating flowers indigenous to the area.

This vase has a bayou scene of Spanish moss and live oak trees—evocative of the Old South. Made about 1913 to 1915, it is marked CN on the bottom. It has a deeply mottled surface and employs the blue palette typical of Newcomb pottery. According to the guest, the vase survived a Los Angeles earthquake. Rago estimates its worth at $2,500 to $3,500.

CERAMIC DAMAGE DETECTION

In Richmond, expert David Lackey demonstrated how to go about inspecting porcelain for damage—the sort that isn't immediately evident:

1) **T O U C H** : Run your hands and fingers all over every surface of the piece. You may discover differences in texture, indicating a crack or a repair. Your fingers will hunt down tiny chips too small to be seen.

2) **L I S T E N** : Balance a cup or plate on its foot and gently "ping" it with your fingernail. If it rings, that's good; if it thunks, that's bad—it means there's a crack in the body, which you will probably discover by sight or feel.

3) **L O O K** : Aside from cracks, chips, and visible evidence of repairs look for inconsistencies in glaze (is the piece mostly shiny with a small matte area?) and color (are the handles a lighter shade of green than the foot?). Both indicate a less-than-perfect repair. White and gold colors are especially hard to match in repairs.

4) **A S K** : Finally, ask the representing dealer, expert, or auction house to tell you what they know about any damage or past repairs.

These Japanese characters mean "Made in Japan." Though frequently thought to indicate age or fine quality on Asian ceramics, they are of no more importance, in fact, than "Made in USA."

the shapes common to each design period and enable you to readily date these ceramics.

♦ Transfer printing was not common on American pottery until the 1840s. After 1880, combinations of print and hand-painting sometimes appear.

♦ Decorations of calla lilies or sunflowers, favorites of the English and American Aesthetic movements, often indicate a late-nineteenth-century date of manufacture.

IS IT VALUABLE?

More than that of many other decorative objects, the value of ceramics is dependent on condition. A cracked vase or bowl is useful only as a "cabinet piece," for it can't be handled, used, or displayed in the round—rather a drawback. And it is important to know that while pieces from the eighteenth century may be old, they are not always valuable. The following guidelines should enable you to better evaluate your own pottery and porcelain.

Ornamental objects—those made for decorative rather than practical purposes, like vases and figures—are usually more valuable than utilitarian pieces like cups and saucers, the most common (and least sought after) of ceramic wares. Large or complicated forms, like tureens and groupings of several figures, were hard to fire in the kiln. As a result, these elaborate objects were costly when new and are correspondingly valuable today. In general, decorative ceramics and luxury items of limited use, such as large vases, table centerpieces, and candelabra, will be more valuable than utilitarian wares.

Although all ceramics are inherently fragile, collectors will only accept very *rare* pieces with damages. On run-of-the-mill objects, chips, cracks, and replaced parts destroy value. However, firecracks (cracks that appeared in ceramics at the time the piece was fired, rather than by misadventure) are acceptable to most buyers, especially in pieces that are rare. You can recognize a firecrack by its random shape—it never proceeds in a straight line.

Should a piece of porcelain have a well-known or rare mark, like that of Sèvres, the quality of the potting and decoration should absolutely meet the standards for which that factory was famous. Lifeless painting, careless workmanship, or crudely applied gilding would never have been sold by Sèvres, or by any factory with a reputation to maintain. Consequently, poor technique is always a telltale sign of a later reproduction or forgery.

Because of their documentary value, any signatures or monograms (both are different from factory marks) tend to increase the value of the object; naturally, the original signatures of well-known ceramic artists—and there are many—make a piece that much more valuable.

Although numerous American luxury tableware firms imported European porcelain in the last quarter of the nineteenth century and imprinted their own names on these wares (in addition to the manufacturer's mark), only porcelain sold by Tiffany and Co. enjoys increased value from the association. Unmarked ceramics can occasionally be definitely attributed to particular factories, but marked pieces will generally have more value.

Many of the European factories peaked in creativity and design during the eighteenth century. But even nineteenth- and early twentieth-century reproductions of their own early styles can be so far superior to those made more recently that they bring substantial prices.

Hand-painted designs—borders, flowers, figures, and landscapes—are executed with fine brushes. Such brush strokes are frequently visible. Hand-painted wares also exhibit the slight mistakes and irregularities that usually exist in work created by the human hand.

Eagles and patriotic emblems on Chinese export porcelain increase value, as do ships flying American flags and other recognizably American motifs.

Printed designs on porcelain and pottery are usually less valuable than hand-painted designs.

VAN BRIGGLE VASE

The marks on the bottom of this very large vase tell the story: the name (Van Briggle) and date (1906), as expert David Rago explained, mean that the piece was made at the famous Colorado pottery after the master's death in 1904, but while his wife was still running the business.

Its form is very rare—the largest dated piece Rago had ever seen. The color is a "really nasty green"—so ugly that the owner's wife hid it in a corner as an umbrella stand. But Rago had a surprise for the owner. Pulling out a knife, he scraped off the green to reveal the original shade beneath the paint: the robin's-egg blue that Van Briggle was known for.

Although there's a lot of Van Briggle pottery around, the rarity of this form and its extra-large size led Rago to appraise it at $10,000— only one in 5,000 pieces is so valuable. A bath of acetone would remove the rest of the green and clean up this

"dirty puppy," advised Rago. "And keep the umbrellas out of it." The owner said he certainly would from now on.

NATIVE AMERICAN POTTERY

An Acoma polychrome water jar, with traditional decorations of geometric patterns and black bars.

A Laguna Pueblo jar from the late nineteenth century with characteristic foliate and geometric motifs rendered in reddish and dark browns on a cream-color slip.

Maria Martinez' subtly dramatic black-on-black pots.

Native American pottery, often thousands of years old, turns up in archaeological digs in the Southwest, but the wares we currently find are far more likely to be nineteenth-century descendants of these early pots.

Bowls, water jars, storage jars, and dippers fashioned of decoratively painted earthenware are typical of today's highly collectible Southwest pottery. Such wares, naturally, are utilitarian, yet they are dual-purpose, too—useful for barter, for burial with the dead, and (the most elaborate pieces) for ceremonial occasions.

The traditional technique for making and decorating Native American pottery was handed down like a treasured recipe from mother to daughter. A girl was taught how to grind the paste for the pots, what mix of ingredients would make her pots more durable or take the highest burnish, and how to knead the resulting amalgam to a workable consistency. The technique used for "baking" pots was critical, since Pueblo pots were never fired in kilns, but rather, in carefully controlled outdoor fires. Most engagingly, girls were encouraged to hunt for distinctive designs in the content of their dreams—in other words, to complete the recipe analogy, to season their creations "to taste."

Stimulated by the advent of tourism in the 1880s, the pottery of the Southwest—Pueblo pottery—became not only more commercial, but also more inspired. The husband-and-wife team of Julian and Maria Martinez created such innovative wares (she made the vessels, he decorated them) that Pueblo pottery began to attract an international following. The most sought-after of the Martinez ceramics were the "black-on-black" wares, with their contrast of matte black backgrounds and subtly glimmering, polished black designs. In the 1920s, Maria Martinez began to sign her pots. Also influenced by the tourist trade at the turn of the century were Cochiti potters, who crafted ceramic human figures in contemporary dress.

Nineteenth-century Zuni wares are often decorated with graduated bands of geometric design symbolizing stacked thunderhead clouds, a formation certainly crucial to the arid locale. Zuni jars are also painted with stylized barnyard fowl and flowers, designs that may reflect their artists' increasing familiarity with Eastern folk art designs.

Acoma and Laguna potters worked in a thousand-year-old tradition. Although their pots appear to be top-heavy, with round shoulders dropping to the typical conical base, they also display bold and handsome polychrome decoration; this is especially true after 1860, when geometric patterns blanket each vessel in undulant design from top to bottom.

Nampeyo, a Hopi artist, found fame in reinterpreting the tribal designs she found on ancient shards. Her success in producing and marketing large, painted vessels brought an invitation to appear at the 1910 Chicago Land and Irrigation Exposition, where she demonstrated her craft and was touted as "the greatest maker of Indian pottery alive."

GLASS

Why bother to define glass? It's been around since the Bronze Age and we all know it well. Here, however, is a remarkable eighteenth-century definition:

It is an artificial concrete of salt and sand or stones. It is fusible by strong fire. It is flexible and elastic. It is capable of being cut only with diamond or emery. It is diaphanous, whether hot or cold. When it is red hot, it is ductile, and it may be fashioned into any form. It will receive any color or dye, both externally or internally. Neither acid juice, nor any other

Blown by a Roman glassblower in the second century B.C., a long-buried jug is encrusted with the opalescent patina that Louis C. Tiffany, among others, attempted to emulate.

A simple glass jug, made in New Jersey between 1830 and 1850, looks much like certain catalog wares offered today.

This tumbler, made in Sandwich, Massachusetts, between 1825 and 1850, represents, perhaps, our idea of "glass."

A brilliant allover cut rose bowl might best exemplify the term "crystal."

matter, extracts either color, taste, or any other quality from it. It will lose neither of weight or substance, by the longest and most frequent use. Neither wine, beer, or any other liquor will either make it musty, or change its color or rust it. A drinking glass filled with water and rubbed on the brim with a wet finger will yield beautiful notes.

And even lacking that last whimsical quality, glass would certainly seem to be among the most amazing of man-made materials, especially taking into account—as this old definition seems not to have done—that it can also be astonishingly beautiful.

Composed simply of silica (sand, flint, or quartz) that is heated with an alkaline flux, such as soda (used for the bubble-like glass of the Venetians) or potash (for thicker German wares), glass is infinitely capable of being tinted, painted, engraved, inlaid, even—and not least of all—rolled flat for windows.

"GLASS" VS. "CRYSTAL"

In America, there has always seemed to be some semantic distinction between "glass" and "crystal." "Glass" is what we drink Coke from, while the crystal tiptoes from its cupboard only for guests.

The early glassmakers, in fact, hotly pursued a reliable glass formula that would make their metal (as glass is termed) less airy, bubbly, and fragile than it was and altogether more like natural rock crystal: strong, thick-walled, cuttable, and white in color (unrefined glass had a greenish tinge). When, at the end of the seventeenth century, Englishman George Ravenscroft finally discovered that substituting oxide of lead for soda would produce a lustrous, heavy metal of diamond-like brilliance, he invented both "flint glass" and a British glass industry. Ravenscroft's discovery means that there is indeed an actual compositional difference between our water glass today and our champagne flute, for the best of the latter contains lead. The term "crystal" remains a tribute to his success.

In the centuries following this breakthrough, the outstanding quality and variety of the glassware manufactured in Great Britain, America, and Europe created such an enormous field for collectors that, currently, glass is outranked in popularity only by stamps and coins.

MANUFACTURING TECHNIQUES

Fundamentally, there are only three ways to make glass: free-blow the liqueous material, mold it, or press it.

Free-blown glass is made by picking up a glob of the molten metal on one end of a long pipe, blowing and working it into a basic shape, then transferring it, while still soft, onto a "pontil rod" for further crafting—swirling, perhaps, or pincering-in a spout, or applying a handle. When a glass vessel is complete, it is broken off the rod and left with an irregular, often rough scar, called a pontil mark, on its bottom. (In the late nineteenth century, free-blown glass could be held in a snap-case, however, which left no mark at all.) Despite myth, a pontil mark is not necessarily an indication of age, for free-blown glass is often made in precisely the same way today that it has always been. (What a pontil mark does indicate, however, is that the piece was blown.)

Blown-molded glass results from placing the hot glob of glass within a patterned mold and blowing into it until the molten glass fills the walls of the mold. When the glass has cooled, the mold is opened, and the imprint of the pattern—a sunburst, a waffled motif, or a vertical rib—remains on the outer surface of the piece, while its interior reproduces the pattern's concavity. The adoption of this ancient, neat, efficient, and relatively inexpensive technique provided early Americans with an affordable imitation of expensive, Anglo-Irish cut glass and also heralded the beginnings of a distinctly American style of clear glass.

Its simplicity and elemental shape make it almost possible to envision the glassblowing process employed to create a c. 1750 dark green New Jersey wine bottle.

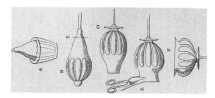

"Molded Roman Pillars," from Pellatt, Apsley, Curiosities of Glass Making *(London: David Bogue, 1849).*

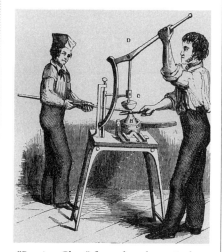

"Pressing Glass," from the volume cited above.

PEACHBLOW

Relatively rare and expensive today, peachblow, a type of free-blown glass that gradually shaded from white or yellow to pink, was manufactured by at least three American companies.

The New England Glassworks in Cambridge, Massachusetts, patented its "Wild Rose" color in 1886, and pieces sometimes retain their paper labels marked "Wild Rose/N.E.G.W."

Peachblow was also made by Hobbs, Brockunier & Co. of Wheeling, West Virginia. This has a white glass lining and is cased in a shaded but transparent peachblow layer.

The rarest of the type, Mount Washington peachblow, is purple-pink, shading to gray-white, and may have a raspberry-like dollop of glass over the pontil mark.

The gradations of color on a Mount Washington peachblow vase manage to outweigh its stubby contours.

Glassmaking techniques are demonstrated in this 1849 view of the furnaces in an English glasshouse.

Pressed glass: In the 1940s, collecting pressed glass cup plates was a fad. What is a cup plate? A round and dainty, busily patterned bit of glass, about 3 inches in diameter, crucial to the fashionable and ladylike early-nineteenth-century ritual of tea. Because early teacups had no handles (in imitation of Chinese teacups), hot tea was poured into the saucer to cool while the cup was placed on a cup plate. A mechanical press for making these glassy confections (and thousands of bowls, plates, and compotes as well) was invented in the United States in the 1820s, when a technology allowing a dollop of glass to be pressed with a plunger into a metal mold and formed immediately into a shaped and decorated object, created a cheaper, speedier substitute for hand-worked wares. But when the technique was new, the shock of the cold metal mold on the molten glass caused it to wrinkle, so glass manufacturers found a clever solution: camouflage the flaws with decoratively stippled or beaded backgrounds. Coincidentally, this created "lacy glass," long considered to be the finest type of American glass. (In the

1840s, when glassmakers learned to keep the molds hot, such "lacework" was no longer necessary.)

Pressed glass can be distinguished from blown-molded glass by its perfectly smooth inner surface, its somewhat thicker walls, and the mold lines on its outer surfaces, which may be seen or felt. The edges of pressed glass decoration, in comparison with *cut* glass, feel rough, not sharp.

ORNAMENTATION

Glass designers seem never to have resisted the temptation to gild or otherwise embellish their work. Glass has been universally subjected to techniques like "hot" decoration, where spirals, beads, and molten bits of glass are applied before the object cools; to being painted, when cool, with realistic or stylized designs with colored glass powders bound with oils in a flux (enameling); to being encrusted with thick or thin applications of gold leaf, which lend glass (should it need any) extra flash; to being frosted over its entire surface, for an iced and wintry effect. And one technique, first used in ancient Rome and not rediscovered until the mid-nineteenth century, places layers of different hues of glass one on top of another (cased or overlay glass), then carves a design through the layers. This process, a particularly difficult one, creates cameo glass. A less costly way to achieve a somewhat similar result is to coat the glass with molten colored glass and cut through the transparent surface to the clear metal beneath. (The Bohemians did this splendidly.) Cheaper still was "flashing" the surface with a thin coat of colored stain or paint and scratching the design through. (Inexpensive flashed copies, principally of twentieth-century origin, are often scratched elsewhere as well.)

COLORED GLASS

Impure glass is green or grayish. Refined glass is colorless. Such "white" glass, however, can easily be tinted or quite deeply colored ruby, cobalt, or amber, for instance, with metallic oxides in powder form. Before the 1860s, bottles were colored (it was cheaper), as were tablewares of every type. American pressed glass can be found in amethyst, green, blue, turquoise, and yellow. After the 1870s, colored glass came to be used extensively for the decorative wares known as "Art Glass."

A liquor flask impressed with a portrait by Stebbins & Stebbins, a Connecticut firm, meets up once more with the brass mold into which it was blown.

In the nineteenth century, incoming presidential families customarily sold the household furnishings of the previous administration when they took up residence in the White House, an odd practice that has allowed presidential glassware to come on the market from time to time.

In addition to traditional "frosted" engraving, glass can also be decorated with stipple engraving; Above, a virtuosic 1974 example by Englishman Laurence Whistler.

Engraving can be polished as well, as seen in the lavish decoration on the body and stopper of this decanter, c. 1905.

A 1913 vase exemplifies the art of acid etching, another technique used for surface ornament on glass.

Three common types of ornamentation actually involve cutting the glass.

CUT GLASS

Cut glass is made by carving a free-blown or mold-blown shape into geometric patterns with variously sized, power-driven sandstone or limestone wheels and grinding with a mixture of water and sand. The pontil mark, if there is one, is either polished out or hidden by a cut sunburst or hob-star beneath the foot. In this fashion eighteenth-century British glass—thick-walled, weighty, and highly light-reflective—became a first cousin to the natural crystal it was intended to imitate, for its metal lent itself particularly well to being cut. English and Irish glass of that era was, in fact, more elaborate than American efforts, although from 1810 until around 1850, a great deal of American cut glass was produced, especially in the strawberry diamond pat-tern. However, the finest moment for American cut glass lay ahead, in the period from 1880 to 1915, when large, elaborate, and brilliantly sparkling punch bowl sets, odd-shaped relish trays, mustard jars, bowls, lamps, and even novelties like baseball bats were manufactured for a newly wealthy and innocently ostentatious middle class. How better to reflect those nouveau riches, after all, than to spread one's tabletop with glassy diamonds?

Identification: In distinguishing cut glass from pressed glass, run your fingertips along the edges to be sure they're very sharp. Look for mold marks, too, which are typical of pressed wares. The best-quality cut glass is always quite carefully cut, and miters meet neatly. Check to see, too, that the pattern doesn't stop awkwardly at the rim; this signals a repair and significant loss of value.

Old American cut glass (made in the first half of the nineteenth century) tends to be decorated with simple designs that use only a few motifs in repeating patterns. In contrast are the brilliant-cut patterns from later periods, which can completely obscure the object's surface with explosions of pinwheels, hobstars, and diamonds.

Cut glass, like all antiques, becomes more valuable when the factory that produced it can be identified. After 1900, it was often trademarked with an acid stamp, visible under a strong light.

ENGRAVED GLASS

Engraving cuts or carves the glass surface (usually free-blown) with stone or copper wheels. These wheels, of various sizes, are lubricated by a continuous stream of oil and sand while being turned by a foot treadle—something like an old dentist's drill. Engraved designs can be left matte, giving them a frosted appearance, or they can be polished and clear. Fine, high-quality engraving can also be achieved with diamond points, creating stipple engraving with its realistic subtleties of shading. Because the engraving process is more superficial than the cutting process, thin-walled pieces like wineglasses are especially suitable for such work, although engraving can be done on all thicknesses of glass. In the nineteenth century, Bohemia specialized in elaborate engraving, and by mid-century engraving was internationally fashionable.

Under a magnifying glass, engraved glass is identifiable by the curved edges on the cuts that form the design. Acid-etched glass is often confused with engraved glass, but remember that the engraved edge is always deep and sharp. Engraved glass is valued according to the intricacy of its craftsmanship and the beauty and originality of its design.

ACID-ETCHED GLASS

Initially introduced as an inexpensive alternative to wheel-engraving, acid-etching is a technique in which the entire piece of glass is coated in wax or resin and the design is scratched through the coating with a sharp tool. After the piece is exposed to the fumes of hydrofluoric acid, or dipped into it, the acid eats away the exposed portion, and as the coating is removed, the design is revealed.

TIFFANY FLORIFORM VASE

About fifty years ago, this guest received her vase as a wedding present from a judge and his wife, who was a collector.

According to appraiser Barbara Deisroth, the vase was made around the turn of the century by Louis Comfort Tiffany. A rather early piece, it is formed as a tulip and its colors, among them lime green and salmon pink, are quite lovely. The number on the bottom, preceded by an X, indicates that the vase was an experimental piece and, as such, is worth $20,000 to $30,000 today.

A stoppered decanter is a typical example of "cut-to-clear": nineteenth-century glass, cut back through the cranberry-colored layer to expose the clear glass beneath.

The finial and handles of this sophisticated covered cup, blown in South Jersey at the Wistarburg Glassworks sometime between 1739 and 1737, were pincered into shape.

A charmingly provincial Stiegel glass flask.

The wares of John Amelung are far grander than those of Stiegel, as seen in this extensively engraved glass-covered tumbler made in Frederick, Maryland, in 1791.

The gray matte finish of acid-etched glass can easily be mistaken for engraving, but fortunately it can be distinguished by examination under a magnifying glass (see page 105) and by the feel of its edges, which are cut vertically into the glass (rather than curvilinearly, as with engraving). A great deal of inexpensive etched glass was made during the 1920s and 1930s.

AMERICAN GLASS

Although it has long been known that German and Polish glassblowers worked briefly at Jamestown, Virginia, in 1607, America's early colonists seem to have imported most of their glass from Europe and didn't attempt it again themselves until, in the early eighteenth century, Caspar Wistar made window glass and bottles in New Jersey.

Two types of eighteenth-century American glass, the products of the glasshouses of German immigrants Henry William Stiegel and John Frederick Amelung, are notable and rare. Stiegel owned three Pennsylvania glasshouses, where he manufactured the greenish glass bottles and tableware that, with their stylized flowers and hearts, perfectly reflected the English and German roots of his glassblowers. Many ostensible "Stiegel" wares, with their "Pennsylvania Dutch" (German, in fact) designs were actually imported, and perhaps 90 percent were imported in the 1920s, when the ware first became fashionable among American collectors.

Amelung's more sophisticated goblets and tumblers, however, were favored even in the eighteenth century by luminaries like the governor of Pennsylvania. Amelung produced blown-molded glass whose distinctive and Germanic engraving of scrolls with monograms, of inscriptions within a floral wreath, or of a crown above a garland makes it easily recognizable today (along with the lucky fact that about half of Amelung's presentation pieces are signed). If there are any to be found, that is: Amelung glass is hen's-tooth rare and exceptionally valuable.

In the nineteenth century, the itinerant American glassworker migrated west in pursuit of the supplies of coal and water he needed for glass manufacture and transportation. Consequently, great glasshouses were founded in coalmining areas like Pittsburgh, Pennsylvania, and in West Virginia and Ohio. Fortunately for the growth of America's glass industry, these native blown-mold wares were an agreeable substitute for costly European cut glass. In Brooklyn and New England, far from Bohemia's woods and fields, immigrant glassworkers also produced affordable versions of Middle European red-cased and engraved glassware and countless types of everyday glass. By century's end, there were over a hundred known glass factories active in the United States, plus numbers of anonymous shops that only engraved or enameled that output.

Keeping pace with America's burgeoning industrial growth, glass became a particularly prominent industry in the nineteenth century. The Boston and Sandwich Glass Company, founded in 1825 and in business until 1888, attained international renown for its affordable pressed glass objects, its furniture knobs, dolphin candlesticks, and the glittery, lacy glass (see above) manufactured between 1825 and 1850. The company's products, along with those of other American manufacturers, were shipped throughout the United States and even exported to South America and the West Indies. They became so popular, ultimately, that by the 1920s *all* pressed glass had come to be known as "Sandwich."

In 1903, the Steuben Glass Works was established in Corning, New York, by Englishman Frederick Carder and Irishman Thomas Hawkes. Steuben initially produced several types of colored glass and even outsold rival Tiffany with its own gold-and-blue iridescent glass called Aurene (from the chemical symbol for gold, Au). After 1935, however, the factory turned to making the clear, shapely wares, frequently engraved, for which it is known today. Since 1933, *all* Steuben wares have been marked, generally beneath the foot, as have numerous other American wares, Libbey and Sinclair among them.

A "cire perdue" sculpture by Frederick Carder: a group of three translucent colorless glass dolphins leaping from ocean waves.

A lacy glass compote, molded at Sandwich c. 1830–1845, replicates the form of Regency silver tablewares, while the decoration on the bowl adds a touch of American "lace."

ANTIQUES
DISCOVERY
ROADSHOW

TIFFANY LAMP

There are actually thousands of Tiffany lamps in existence, especially those with designs of flowers or fruit. But the Tiffany lamp with a history, in excellent condition, and sporting a fish motif is a rarity.

This is what expert Louise Luther encountered when she examined a lamp that had belonged to the guest's great-great-aunt, formerly a private secretary to J.C. Penney in New York City. The fish on this shade, made of iridescent glass, appear to be swimming in a sea of rippled, striated, confetti-like glass. "Bubbles" at the top of the shade complete the watery illusion.

Although a quick check of the bronze base revealed a "Tiffany Studios" mark, Louise Luther observed that "in Tiffany lamps the value is in the shade, not the base."

The owners had a recent appraisal "in the high 20s," but Luther was ready to surprise them: because of the rarity of the design and its unusual form, she appraised their lamp at $100,000. "It's a beauty," she said.

ART GLASS

Art glass, to many enthusiasts, represents a peak moment in the history of glass: a product of the 1870s, when the Aesthetic Movement turned away from factory-made objects and encouraged hand-crafts from the artist's studio. For thirty or so years, until the end of the century, naturalistic objects in porcelain, pottery, and glass, were fashioned, as they had historically been, by hand.

TIFFANY GLASS

Born in 1848, Louis Comfort Tiffany, the son of the founder of the well-known jewelry store, is undoubtedly the best-known of American art glass manufacturers and, possibly, the most famous and versatile talent in the history of American decorative arts. After a privileged youth spent traveling in North Africa and Europe, the unconventional and inventive Tiffany returned to New York in 1879 to found a decorating firm, Associated Artists, with three other advocates of innovative design. Eventually, however, he broke away to create his own company, producing leaded glass windows, art glass, metalwork, and, primarily, the inspired lamps for which he is renowned.

Tiffany's hugely popular, iridescent "Favrile" (a variation on the Old English for "handmade") glass, first created in 1892 or 1893, was actually inspired by archaeological Roman and Islamic glass. This material, buried for centuries, had acquired an oily, opalescent crust that Tiffany yearned to reproduce. When he ultimately discovered that he could mimic those ancient relics by exposing glass treated with metallic oxides to acid fumes, he incorporated his invention—favrile glass—into ravishingly beautiful blown glass and leaded glass lampshades, scarab jewelry, small and large-scale glass vessels, bronze wares, and mosaic tiles. (One contemporary critic nonetheless carped that his sinuous vegetable, plant, and floral-form vases, were highly impractical—"hardly ever suited to holding flowers.")

Tiffany table and floor lamps (made as early as the 1890s) reached the height of their popularity between

1899 and 1916. The lamps, and imitations of them (see page 108) were so ubiquitous during that era that it's almost impossible today to imagine any turn-of-the-century interior without its jewel-like lamp—more useful for ambiance, unfortunately, than for reading by.

Genuine Tiffany bronze or gilt-bronze lamp bases were vinelike and naturalistic, often simulating tree trunks or stylized plant motifs. Their shades, however, are their glory, with rich, glowing arrangements of daffodils, trailing wisterias, lacy dragonflies, and a wide variety of growing things all composed of carefully selected pieces of colored, often iridescent glass leaded together, like church windows. Thousands of Tiffany lamps were made, and all are far more valuable today than when they were new. Their value is judged by their patterns, color, execution of design, rarity, and condition.

Many lampshades were labeled. One of the more common labels is found on the inside bottom edge: a copper tab, usually marked TIFFANY STUDIOS, New York, and sometimes bearing a style number. The bases are usually impressed with the firm's mark and often a style number as well.

OTHER ARTS AND CRAFTS LAMPS

Tiffany's great success invited innumerable, inexpensive, and generally less talented competitors. The best and most collectible of these are lamps made by Handel & Co. and by Pairpoint.

Handel lamps, marked with the company's name (with or without a design number), can be leaded, like Tiffany lamps, or painted on the interior of their all-glass shades to display colorful scenes when lit.

One variety of Pairpoint all-glass lampshade is known today as a "puffy" because shades of this type were mold-blown in relief into plump floral forms before their interiors were painted. Some Pairpoint shades are stamped THE PAIRPOINT CORP and are occasionally marked with a patent date. Pairpoint bases made of metal and wood are usually labeled, but the all-glass bases don't have permanent marks.

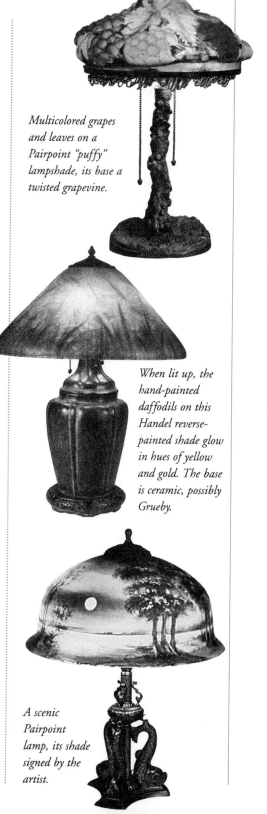

Multicolored grapes and leaves on a Pairpoint "puffy" lampshade, its base a twisted grapevine.

When lit up, the hand-painted daffodils on this Handel reverse-painted shade glow in hues of yellow and gold. The base is ceramic, possibly Grueby.

A scenic Pairpoint lamp, its shade signed by the artist.

EUROPEAN MANUFACTURERS

Although Germany and Bohemia were the heart and soul of Continental glassmaking, the best-known European manufacturers in America are Waterford, Baccarat, and Lalique.

Waterford glass, first produced near Waterford, Ireland, in the eighteenth century, brought the English flint-glass formula (glass made with flints rather than sand and having a high lead content) to dazzling heights. Certainly, the latent fire in this metal lent itself particularly well to the gorgeously cut and faceted candelabra and chandeliers that made the Waterford product famous. Carved into severely geometrical patterns or "steps," Waterford was so plain, classic, and monumental that today its name is synonymous with all Georgian-style cut glass (though, in fact, very little old glass can be firmly attributed to this Irish glasshouse). The cutting on old "Waterford" has quite sharp edges, while the factory's current product feels as soft and round as new pressed glass.

Baccarat was a noted manufacturer of pressed glass throughout the nineteenth century, much as it is today, and provided quantities of ceremonial tableware and lighting for the returning French aristocracy. This famous glasshouse also produced splendidly complex paperweights, and in mid-century it made as much cut glass as pressed glass.

The workmanship of the factory's antique glass was superb. Except for mold-lines, sometimes visible on the base, the product closely resembled blown cut glass. The Baccarat name, sometimes molded in low relief, can often be found on the base. Paper labels appear on wares c. 1900, and if the Baccarat name is acid-etched, the piece dates from the twentieth century.

René Lalique (1860–1945) was a brilliant designer who created, in the course of a very long life, everything from breathtaking naturalistic jewelry, Art Nouveau and Art Deco vases, and perfume bottles to fountains and radiator caps.

Antique mille-fiori paper-weights by Baccarat. Paperweights, especially antique French ones, can be quite valuable. The best French weights were those made by Baccarat and St. Louis, while the rarest weights incorporate glass reptiles and butterflies. Although the finest paperweights were made in France, many were also made in America. If the surface of a paperweight seems not quite round, it may have been ground down to repair a damage.

A fragile, trumpet-shaped Venetian glass, made with soda at Murano, c. 1670.

From 1910 until 1945 he made unusually stylized and, typically, frosted objects in blown-mold and pressed glass.

The mark R. LALIQUE FRANCE dates from before 1945 (occasionally, without the "France"). Pieces marked Lalique France date from 1945 or after.

Maurice Marinot (1828–1960). A French glassmaker of the Art Deco era, Marinot was primarily interested in the glass itself, not its decoration. To this end, he manipulated the material to feature trapped air bubbles and streaks of internal crackle or metals, and created thick-walled, monumental (though small) wares, each of which he made by hand.

Emile Gallé (1846–1904). The premier French glassmaker of the Art Nouveau era, Gallé worked in Nancy in Lorraine, where he was the nucleus of a center of creativity in several of the decorative arts—glass and furniture among them. Large factories produced the glass he designed, which incorporated organic and naturalistic influences into vases, sculptures, and glass lamps.

Daum (August, 1853–1909, and Antonin, 1864–1930). Part of l'Ecole de Nancy, the Daum brothers worked in the aesthetic of Gallé, though usually less inventively. Their factory produced naturalistic wares in the typical dragonfly and lily pond motifs of the period, and, with Louis Majorelle (a furniture and metal artist), manufactured decorative lamps.

IS IT OLD?

Glass doesn't reveal its age. It can be five thousand years old and still look a hundred years old, or it can be new and, with a slightly sanded bottom, masquerade as old.

Bubbles in glass don't necessarily indicate age, either. Sometimes they simply mean that the glass has been carelessly manufactured. Consequently, you should always consider the form of a piece (is it a modern form or an old one?), its provenance (if it has one), and evidences of wear.

TIFFANY CYPRIOTE VASE

In the 1950s, this guest shopped at the famous Lillian Nassau store on New York City's Madison Avenue. Torn between a Tiffany wisteria lamp and this Tiffany vase, she finally opted for the signed vase. According to appraiser Louise Luther, it's worth less than the lamp today, but the guest still made an excellent decision, for it is in uncompromised and beautiful condition.

Tiffany strove to design a type of glass that would *look* as ancient as if it had been buried in the ground, and he called his innovation a Cypriote. This example displays Tiffany's "button pontil," a characteristic of his early 1890s work. (Lillian Nassau threw in an extra vase as well; though damaged, it is still nicely designed with a pond lily decoration.)

Bought by this careful shopper for $600, the Cypriote vase is worth $20,000 today.

Louise Luther and Nick Dawes comment on evaluating art glass and glass in general:

Lalique from the early nineteenth and early twentieth centuries is marked on the bottom with the molded word "Lalique." Modern Lalique marks are etched on the bottom.—L.L.

The signature on Gallé glass is acid-etched, usually on the side.—L.L.

The Tiffany signature is scratched into the glass.—L.L.

Don't scrub or polish the base of leaded glass lamps.—L.L.

On Tiffany lamps, you should always find the Tiffany label both on the inside of the shade rim and on the bottom of the base.—L.L.

If you tap lightly on the rim of a shade with the palm of your hand, a genuine Tiffany shade will reward you with the "Tiffany Whisper" created by the slight loosening, caused by age, of the leaded glass components.—L.L.

Before 1935, Steuben manufactured colored glass.—L.L.

The object should always authenticate the signature, not the other way around, and confirm the maker's reputation in every respect.—N.D.

Any damage to glass removes almost all its value.—N.D.

Here are some guidelines:

♦ English glass of the late nineteenth century is often impressed with the same sorts of lozenge-shaped registration marks seen on English porcelain and pottery (called, in England, "kite" marks).

♦ On enameled glass, quite brilliant colors tend to indicate nineteenth-century work.

♦ The elaborate and technically virtuosic designs of Baccarat paperweights can include glass rods centered by the letter "B" and, often, a date. Always examine paperweights under a magnifying glass.

♦ One hallmark of gilded glass of French manufacture is a black outline surrounding flat, thin gilding. This type of gilding is often found bordering the edges of vases and plates.

♦ Twentieth-century cut glass is polished in an acid bath (rather than by hand). Consequently, it never feels as sharp as genuine antique glass and, naturally, no longer reveals the marks left by the cutting wheel.

IS IT VALUABLE?

Value in glass has much to do with supply and demand, and is not necessarily related to age. Glass collectors—more than other collectors, perhaps—seem to prefer those pieces that can be easily identified. Rare and unusual art glass can bring the highest prices, while the most expensive pieces of glass are often those that are one of a kind.

♦ Nineteenth-century French glass can frequently be identified by its gilt metal mounts.

♦ Sometimes the unusual piece, the one that doesn't look expensive, *is*. For example, a quite rare Lalique perfume bottle that sold not too long ago for $60,000 cost less than $10 new. (Remember, however, that the Lalique factory has produced over 10 million glass objects, most of which—while still collectible—are not nearly that valuable.)

♦ The only types of glass that collectors will accept in less than perfect condition are important ancient glass and Venetian glass. The latter, being soda glass, is very fragile.

♦ Surprisingly, much ancient Roman glass is not all that rare and, despite its great age, is not especially valuable.

♦ Layered glass, on the whole, is more valuable than opaque or semitranslucent single-color ware.

♦ On pieces in which the applied design is more important to the beauty of the object than its color, shape, or historical importance, the value will be diminished if gilt is rubbed away or the enameling lost.

♦ Rare examples of American mold-blown glass exist in blue or purple.

♦ Antique glass enameled or painted with *unusual* birds, animals, or flowers is more valuable than glass with conventional decoration.

♦ Mass-produced glass is only valuable to the degree that it is difficult to manufacture—like certain types of cameo glass.

♦ Overlay glass was made principally in Bohemia. The red examples are more sought-after than the blue or amber types; however, by far the most desirable of cased glass items is English cameo glass, especially that made by Thomas Webb & Sons, much of which is signed.

Scenic pitchers in cranberry cut-to-clear were made at American firms by Bohemian craftsmen.

Tricolor cameo glass, like this example by the firm of Thomas Webb and Sons, is the most desirable type.

A glass pitcher, c. 1830, with lily-pad decoration on the body and threading encircling the neck.

FURTHER READING

Battie, David, and Cottle, Simon. *Sotheby's Concise Encyclopedia of Glass.* Boston: Little, Brown, 1991.

Drury, Elizabeth. *Antiques, Traditional Techniques, etc.* New York: Doubleday, 1986.

Forrest, Tim. *The Bulfinch Anatomy of Antique China and Silver.* Boston: Little, Brown, 1998.

Frelinghuysen, Alice Cooney. *American Porcelain.* New York: Metropolitan Museum of Art/Harry N. Abrams, 1989.

Hayes, Allan, and Blom, John. *Southwestern Pottery.* Flagstaff, AZ: Northland Publishing, 1996.

Ketchum, William C., Jr. *Pottery and Porcelain.* New York: Alfred A. Knopf, 1983.

Kovel, Ralph and Terry. *Kovels' American Art Pottery.* New York: Crown Publishers, 1993.

Lang, Gordon. *Miller's Antiques Checklist: Pottery.* London: Reed Consumer Books, 1995.

Miller's Antique Checklist Porcelain. New York: Viking Penguin, 1992.

Penney, David, and Longfish, George. *Native American Art.* Southport, CT: Hugh Lauter Levin Associates, 1994.

Spillman, Jane Shadel. *Glass Tableware, Bowls & Vases* New York: Alfred A. Knopf, 1982.

———. *Glass Bottles, Lamps, and Other Objects* New York: Alfred A. Knopf, 1983.

Tait, Hugh. *Five Thousand Years of Glass.* London: British Museum Press, 1991.

West, Mark. *Miller's Antique Checklist: Glass.* London: Reed Consumer Books, 1994.

Chapter Four

PAINTINGS

T his chapter is not about famous artists, schools of painting, or the long and gorgeous history of art. Instead, it offers some useful rules of thumb to help you evaluate the paintings you own, plus tips for recognizing legitimate paintings (as opposed to prints of paintings and oil-on-canvas copies of originals in museums) and for determining whether or not they're as old as they appear to be.

The hard part will be learning that you probably don't own a painting by some undiscovered genius, because there are almost no undiscovered geniuses left. All the "diamonds" have been ferreted out, even the roughest ones, because most of the artists who were occasionally undervalued twenty years ago are overvalued today. No matter how seemingly obscure or forgotten, every deceased artist whose work has appeared in a significant auction gallery in the United States or abroad, and any living artist whose work has appeared in an important gallery, has been assessed by the artistic community and given his or her place in the artistic pantheon.

The good news is that the work of any one of those 150,000 artists could be on your wall or in your basement or attic right now, and worth a good deal more than you

Cherokee Roses in a Glass,
Martin Johnson Heade (1819–1904).

An Albert Bierstadt oil (above), a Winslow Homer watercolor, and a Mary Cassatt pastel. Contrary to the usual hierarchy of media value, all three works by American artists are considered to be among the best of their kind.

imagine. It may even be art with capital "A." So it's crucial to learn if your painting is really a painting or just a photograph, print, chromolithograph, brush-stroke reproduction, or some other unlovely facsimile of a painting. You'll also want to find out what makes a collectible painting collectible, and what distinguishes a mediocre painting by a well-known artist from a pretty good painting by a mediocre artist. Such discrimination has absolutely nothing to do with whether "the eyes follow you around the room" or whether the hands are well-painted. On the contrary, a painting's value is determined primarily by the opinion of the artist's contemporaries and that of later generations—ours in particular.

In art, as in so many fields, there is a hierarchy of value. And painting is the accepted pinnacle of all artistic endeavor. This means that disproportionate sums will be readily paid for oil paint on canvas, a material that, unlike jewelry or silver, has absolutely no intrinsic value. Paintings and drawings, in fact, are considered "Fine" Art, while everything else—porcelain, silver, glass, furniture—is herded into the "Decorative" Art category. (Sculpture is the exception.) Of all the arts, only painting offers the possibility of emotional profundity and thus—unlike the Decorative Arts—fetches shockingly high auction prices. Only paint is glorified by critics and the media, luring wealthy tyros into believing they can "invest" in art. And it is paint, chiefly, that packs museums worldwide.

Michelangelo and other Renaissance artists ground native plants, insects, and semiprecious stones and mixed them with oil to make their medium: oil paint. Artists of all periods, in fact, worked with the technology at hand (enabling today's experts to accurately date and attribute paintings by determining the composition of paints

Common Media in Order of Market Value

If an important artist works in only one medium, or
does his best work in one medium, that will supersede the usual order of value.

TYPE	USUAL SUPPORTS	CHARACTERISTICS
Oil paint	Canvas, wood panel, board (The flexibility of oil allows works to be painted on portable supports, like canvas, which can be rolled.)	Pigment mixed with vegetable oils (linseed, poppy, walnut). Oil is flexible and long-lasting, and adds sheen to pigment. It takes years to dry fully and must be varnished.
Tempera	Wood panel, board	Pigment mixed traditionally with egg yolk. Fast-drying. Especially associated with fourteenth-and fifteenth-century Italian artists, but sometimes used by twentieth-century American artists.
Pastel	Textured paper	Powdered pigment mixed with resin or gum, employed in stick form. Fragile and easily dislodged from the paper. Always framed under glass. Seen frequently in the work of eighteenth-century portraitists, and revived in the late nineteenth century by Degas, Mary Cassatt, and William Merritt Chase.
Watercolor	Textured paper	Pigment mixed with water-soluble gum. Fast-drying and transparent. No white is used, as the white of the paper creates highlights. Employed most notably in Britain in the eighteenth and nineteenth centuries. Always framed under glass.
Gouache	Textured paper	Pigment with an opaque white filler mixed with water-soluble gum; not transparent and not as luminous as watercolor; has a chalky appearance. "Body color" is a synonym.
Charcoal; colored chalk	Paper	*Charcoal:* charred twigs, used predominantly for preliminary sketching. *Chalk:* comes in red, black, and white, and is not manufactured, as are pastels, but cut from soft stones and colored earths. Both are used for drawing. Chalks are fragile and usually framed under glass.
Pen and ink; pencil	Paper	*Ink:* colored fluid or paste, usually employed in drawings. *Pencil:* a rod of graphite encased in wood, most often used in preliminary sketchwork.

Fine works by Canaletto (above) and Boucher (below) are both extensively copied "Old Masters." Works of such quality would always require the careful examination of one or more experts.

through microscopic examination). Oil paint, however, is one type of medium—the material or combination of materials that the artist uses to create his or her work. Pencil, crayon, even chicken wire and broken plates—all, when used with artistic intent, are media. And there is a monetary hierarchy of media.

Surprisingly, perhaps, this chapter doesn't deal with authenticity. There are numerous experts for that, and it is definitely not something one can learn in a book. The legitimate art most of us do own—or stumble across at tag sales or buy in small antiques shops—doesn't really require authentication in any case. It is probably genuine, because the majority of artists never sold for enough money to have been worth copying—either in their lifetimes or today. Art Is Long, as the saying goes, and life is short. But eating well on Art has always been hard, which is why most apparently real, legibly signed works are usually just what they seem to be—pleasant wall decorations by moderately talented artists. So, if you have a landscape signed, for example, Gaugengigl (see opposite)—a nineteenth-century American artist, by the way—that's *exactly* what it is.

IS IT OLD?

Our initial concept of what constitutes good art is often based on the works displayed in local museums. And as museums tend to have works by safe, established artists, many of us grow up believing that valuable pictures must be dark, religious or mythological works by Old Masters, rife with beseeching eyes and tangles of fleshy limbs. But the paintings we'll find stacked in the shadowy corners of attics are far more likely to be stiff and unattractive portraits or assorted somber landscapes of indeterminate age in which herds of cows or sheep mooch endlessly around picturesque streams, for in the days before photography, portraiture was the artist's bread and butter while landscape painting was the amateur's Sunday afternoon pastime. Many of the paintings we find, buy, or inherit look "old." But are they? And how old? Ten years? One hundred years? And are they genuine (though not necessarily valuable) Old Masters? You can begin to determine a painting's age by examining the following features.

CANVAS AND OTHER SUPPORTS

The support is the flat surface that holds the paint. The most basic and familiar support is canvas, usually a piece of linen primed with a coat of gesso (a mixture of gypsum and size) to keep it from absorbing the paint. The linen is pulled tight over the edges of a wooden frame—the stretcher—and nailed to the back. In preindustrial times, linen was hand-woven. Consequently, when we examine the back of an early work on canvas, we should expect to see rough, uneven weaving and the somewhat lumpy raised threads that indicate handwork. Old linen canvas also darkens with age, as it has often hung for decades in rooms lit by wood fires, candles, and gas. Naturally, these accretions of smoke will have darkened not only the varnish on the picture's surface, but the back of the canvas as well. If that back isn't nicely aged, if it's too clean, too white—and especially if it's flawless and machine-woven—the canvas (and the painting on it) are likely to be new.

RELINING

Sometimes the back of a canvas will look newer than the painting does, for quite legitimate reasons. When paintings have been damaged or when the paint has begun to

VAN DER WEYDEN & GAUGENGIGL

Gaugengigl

These two paintings from Boston had been in the family for years—probably a hundred years, judging from what Colleene Fesko told the owner about the painters.

The paintings represent "the golden age of Boston high style" in the late nineteenth century, according to Fesko. One is by Cornelius Van der Weyden, an oil on canvas estimated to be worth $3,000 to $5,000 (left). The other (above) is by Ignaz M. Gaugengigl, originally from Bavaria, who entitled this work *Schmertz Vergessen*. Gaugengigl's genre painting on wood was appraised at $5,000 to $7,000. Each painting, according to Fesko, is "a classic example of what Boston was collecting at that time."

Van der Weyden

Alan Fausel, Nancy Druckman, and Nan Chisholm on examining pictures:

D O N ' T examine a picture without a magnifying glass.—A.F.

R U N your fingers lightly all over the painting's surface to feel for three-dimensionality. Watercolor paper has tactile structure. Counterfeit watercolors and even drawings seem flat and seamless.—A.F.

L O O K for handmade nails in the stretcher. These indicate age.—A.F.

Paper tape on a painting's edges generally means that the painting has been relined—an indication that it has at least *some* age.—A.F.

"Paintings" under glass are prints 90 percent of the time.—A.F.

A rectangular impression in the paper surrounding a work on paper indicates that it is a print. That impression is the plate-mark of a printing plate. —A.F.

The legitimacy of watercolor can sometimes be identified by the size of the paper it's painted on: standard paper sizes are 30" x 22", 15" x 22", and 11" x 15".—A.F.

Any painting on a mahogany panel was done after 1820, and consequently cannot be an Old Master.—A.F.

Typically, American folk artist Erastus Salisbury Field painted cloudy backgrounds and "Mr. Spock" ears. —N.D.

chip or flake off, careful owners take them to restorers to be relined. Relining provides the old support with a new, backup layer of canvas "glued" (commonly, with a resin-wax mixture) to the reverse of the original to double its strength. (That backing, coincidentally, also hides—and, unhappily, obliterates forever—any and all helpful inscriptions.) With the passage of time, even the relining itself acquires age and darkens.

In order to tell if a picture has been relined, you will have to very carefully remove the picture from the frame and examine its edges. There, if relining has been done, you can often clearly see two layers of linen, one on top of the other, where the margins of the original canvas have been trimmed so that they no longer roll over the sides of the stretcher. On occasion, however, that original canvas was not cut, and you can easily observe the double layer wrapping around the sides and the back of the stretcher, although, frequently, paper tape can hide the evidence.

Expert relining doesn't affect a picture's value, although a poorly done job certainly does. Still, it's an acceptable and often necessary conservation technique.

LAYING DOWN

A procedure that *does* affect value is "laying down," a relining technique that was popular early in the twentieth century but is frowned upon today. Laying down a picture means gluing the painted canvas to masonite (or "board," as it's commonly called). The back of the painting then looks like masonite, and the casual viewer might assume, just from looking at the back, that it was actually executed on board. But a close examination of the edges at the sides of the laid-down picture reveals the woven, fabric edge of the trimmed, original canvas.

Market value is significantly damaged by a painting's being laid down, although the process *is* reversible. It is very expensive damage to undo, however, and not the sort of expense one undertakes for unimportant works.

MARKS ON THE CANVAS

Sometimes, the back of a canvas will have retained the original stamp of a purveyor of artist's supplies. Such stamps—most often seen on nineteenth-century pictures—can be helpful in determining the painting's (or at least the canvas') country of origin. Even if a portion has been obliterated, the remainder may still contain a word in a foreign language or a significant address. (A stamp reading So-and-So et Fils, for instance, might indicate the canvas is French.) Keep in mind, however, that numbers of American expatriates bought canvas and painted in Europe, so such stamps are not infallible indicators of an artist's nationality.

PANEL AND PAPER

In addition to canvas, there are several legitimate types of hard supports (masonite among them). Wood panel had the advantage of being widely available and somewhat portable (in small sizes, of course), but it was also subject to worms and warping. Early panel can be distinguished by the rough tool marks of hand-planing on the reverse and, occasionally, by wormholes. (Fakes, by the way, show the "half-tunnels" of worm activity, rather than just the pinholes of entry.) *Very* rarely, panels are branded with the initial of the joiner who crafted them. Modern wood panels are often thin, exhibiting little or no evidence of hand fashioning.

Old panel frequently splits and is repaired by an elaborate lattice of wood strips, or "cradle," applied to the back. Cradling is a technique that stabilizes the movement of wood and keeps it from warping and cracking further. The expense of cradling a painting is usually justified only for valuable works of art. If you find a painting on a cradled panel, therefore, further detective work is worthwhile.

Watercolors and pastels are typically on paper: a fragile support in far too many ways, but also the most successful ground for these delicate media. Usually protected under glass, works on paper, if they are handled at all (not to be recommended), are handled *very* carefully, for they can be incredibly brittle, falling to crumbling, worthless dust in

W I L L I A M   A I K E N
W A L K E R
P A I N T I N G

Before examining this painting, believed to be by William Aiken Walker, Nicholas Maclean explained why it is sometimes tricky to identify the work of this particular artist. Walker, one of the only artists specializing in rural scenes from the Deep South around the turn of the century, had a somewhat crude technique. Because he's easy to copy, there are many reproductions of his work. This painting, however, had all the signs of an original—right down to the inscription on the back listing its price when it was new: eight dollars!

The current owner, a collector of African-American memorabilia, was reluctant to say what she'd paid for the painting, but was clearly elated to hear Maclean's estimate of $20,000 to $30,000.

your hands. Use a magnifying glass to determine if a work under glass is on paper. Old paper, for instance, may have developed brown spots, or "foxing." Photos of paintings printed on paper are often mistaken for watercolors or even oil paintings. If, under a magnifier, you see the comic-book-like dots of a photo process on a work signed "Winslow Homer," the "watercolor" is a worthless reproduction.

STRETCHERS

The wooden stretcher to which the canvas has been nailed both supports it and establishes the painting's size. Before the eighteenth century, artists usually constructed their own stretchers, nailing together four pieces of inexpensive wood (usually pine) in the widths and lengths required. Since then, however, commercially made stretchers have made homemade stretchers obsolete. Commercial stretchers come in several sizes. (American standard sizes, incidentally, differ from European standard sizes.) Usually, stretchers are formed as squares and rectangles, put together with mortise-and-tenon joints. After assembly, most nineteenth- and twentieth-century stretchers had "keys" inserted into each of the four right angles. Keys are pairs of triangular wood tabs inserted into the corners, where they can be tapped down (usually by a restorer) to tighten the canvas ever so slightly as years of humidity and heat combine to buckle and loosen its fit on the stretcher. Some keys, over the years, may have fallen out of their slots.

In addition, look for these details:

♦ Old stretchers, like old furniture, should *look* old, and their wood should be age-darkened, not stained a dark brown. Edges should feel soft.

♦ Old stretchers may show evidence of having been hand-hewn and coarsely made. On paintings presumably created before 1840, they should not show the curved kerf marks typical of a circular saw.

♦ Old American stretchers are usually of soft pine. You can lightly scratch an old pine stretcher with your fingernail and reveal lighter wood beneath.

♦ Old stretchers sometimes have more than one set of nail holes in them, an indication that either they've been reused or the painting has been taken off the stretcher at least once, to be relined, and then renailed. (Though it might also mean that a frugal artist reused an old stretcher.)

♦ Old stretchers often have writing on them: cryptic letters or numbers, the title or location of the painting, the name of a previous owner, a date, or, occasionally and most gratifyingly, the name of the artist. Such information was often written on the soft pine in pencil, and it may be necessary to tip the back of the painting to the light to read the impression a pencil has made in the wood.

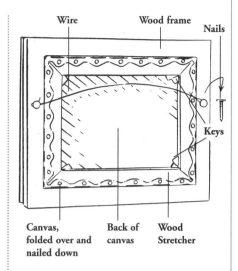

Above, a rear view of a framed oil painting on canvas, with the commonly seen protective piece of brown paper removed.

FRAMES

What can the frame tell you about the age of the painting it surrounds? There are many styles of frame, after all. There are elaborately Rococo gilt frames, Western frames bristling with carved weaponry, unadorned ebonized frames, sleek Art Deco frames, ad infinitum. Although frames can be changed with the decor, occasionally one actually finds the proper-style frame on a contemporaneous picture—an eighteenth-century frame on an eighteenth-century picture, for instance.

The earliest paintings had no frames. They were painted right on walls or on large wood panels, which made the works immovable. By the sixteenth century, however, the frame was a well-established form of protection for the painting as well as an attractive piece of furniture.

A gilt wood rococo frame surrounds François Boucher's painting of 1755. It is a perfect example: a period picture enclosed by period frame bearing an accurate plaque.

Antique frames are very fragile. Because wood shrinks, mitered corners may no longer meet; because the bottom edge, in particular, has been constantly dusted, the red or yellow undercoating (bole) may show through the worn gold leaf. Bits of carving or entire chunks of gesso may have broken off and gilding may have flaked entirely away.

Though rarely seen, tabernacle frames, like this sixteenth-century Italian example, were intended to hold devotional pictures. They were often hung high on the wall and lit by candles from below.

The frame, in fact, was as much a piece of furniture as a table and, like a table, was usually the work of a cabinet-maker or joiner, seldom the work of the artist himself.

Keep your eyes open for these signs of age:

♦ If a frame was made in the same time period as an old painting, i.e., if it was contemporary to the painting, it should show its age on the reverse, where the bare wood is exposed, and at the back and corners, where the construction techniques will be like those on antique furniture.

♦ Naturally, a seventeenth-century landscape would not have been framed in chromed metal strips.

♦ And if your handsome gilt wood frame is held together at the corners with big crimped staples, the frame is new.

♦ It's new, too, if the wood on the reverse is pale, or rough and splintery to the touch. Old wood should be brown and smooth.

♦ Sometimes the colored undercoating of the gilding can be seen on the back of the frame as a mustard or terra-cotta wash. Such washes conceal new wood well.

♦ If a new frame surrounds a seemingly antique painting, then either the old painting has been recently reframed or, despite an old-looking picture, both frame and painting are modern.

Frames can be gilded, painted, or ebonized, and now and then they are designed by the artist himself. The work of the finest framemakers, either artists or craftsmen, has recently become a pricey subspecialty of art collecting, for enthusiasts are newly aware of the aesthetic advantages of setting a fine painting in its proper period frame. (A Victorian still life, for instance, will look its ornate best in an elaborate gilt Victorian frame.) While it's preferable that the painting and frame be born together or at least be of conforming styles, the value of a fine painting will certainly *not* be affected by a poor frame. (Conversely, even an incredible frame will never increase the value of a pedestrian painting.)

Frames have long had a function other than the protection and enhancement of paintings. They're also, frequently, a kind of billboard. The center of the bottommost rail of a gold-leafed frame has always seemed the ideal spot for listing the "credits" of a painting: its title, its creator, his or her birth and death dates. More often than you might suppose, these credits are wrong. Many (if not most) paintings were purchased from the artist with no frame at all, and when they were framed later, these plaques were added. Sometimes, then, a title might be invented for the picture by the buyer and/or the framemaker, who all too often also misspelled the artist's name, mistook the dates, or misread the signature.

Because paintings so frequently have their frames changed to suit fashions in decoration, never rely on the plaques. More than likely, they were placed on the frame centuries after the fact by a modern dealer or by a restorer hired to clean and reframe the painting. (If your painting and frame seem to have aged simultaneously, there is hope.)

Sometimes misidentification is even intentional. The I-wish-I-were Canaletto with a little creative engraving on that brass plaque somehow *becomes* Canaletto when passed down to unsuspecting heirs. Then the family "Canaletto," with its incorrect (though flattering and valuable) attribution, becomes firmly fixed in the minds and the often all-too-empty pocketbooks of descendants.

IS IT LEGITIMATE?

Legitimacy is even more important than the construction details that indicate a painting's age, because even if we've established age, we can't establish a painting's legitimacy unless certain details on the

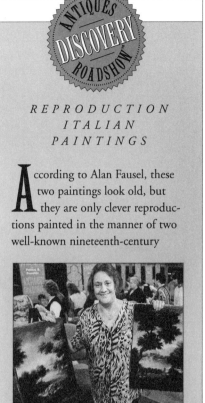

REPRODUCTION ITALIAN PAINTINGS

According to Alan Fausel, these two paintings look old, but they are only clever reproductions painted in the manner of two well-known nineteenth-century Italian artists, Zuccarelli and Ricci. They have been made to look much older than they actually are. A dirty varnish has been added, and they have been baked in the oven to give them an aged *craquelure* (or crackle) effect. But the rough canvas is not that old; the stretchers are machine-sawn and appear to be new. Most tellingly, because the mark on the back reads "made in Italy," the paintings cannot be any earlier than the 1890s. Their worth: $500 to $700.

Especially with the works of important artists like Edgar Degas, there are thousands and thousands of reproductions in circulation.

Female portraiture is among the most common subjects. Here, a portrait by young Rembrandt, c. 1633.

front of the canvas—on the actual painting itself—agree and are *consistent* with that age.

Don't confuse legitimacy with authenticity, however. The procedure for determining authenticity (is it really Degas? a genuine Fitz Hugh Lane? a Rembrandt?) is straightforward, but not always easy, especially with famous names. Authenticating art is always the realm of the expert, definitely not within the scope of a primer. Be assured, however, that somewhere in the art world there is an expert who has studied every aspect of the work of every artist of note (possibly your artist), and often a catalog of all his known works—when they were painted, who owned them last, and where they are today. This catalog (known as a *catalogue raisonné*) might list a painting of the description and date of yours and establish its authenticity—if your painting first passes the following tests.

THE SUBJECT

Many subjects are so universal that they predate history. Cave dwellers, for instance, enlivened their dank homes with charcoal images of cows. Thus bovine and similar timeless subjects, like landscapes, won't tell you much about a picture's age. Yet many subjects definitely do bespeak their times. Religious scenes, for instance, were the only form of pictorial art until the Renaissance era.

Of course, there are religious works from later eras, but as the Church became less influential, artists rendered biblical subjects less often. Ultimately, they acquired wealthy patrons for increasingly acceptable secular subjects—masterful portraits in Italy, magically lit interiors in Holland, and lighthearted scenes of courtship in France. America, of course, came late to the field. Most of America's eighteenth-century artistic output consisted of portraits, although in the nineteenth century American artists turned to the country's remarkable native topography—brilliant autumn woods, waterfalls, rugged canyons, soaring peaks. These typically dramatic natural subjects enable us to recognize their work as American today, but often with an enthusiasm resulting in misidentification. Every other picture of a river, it seems, has become "Hudson River School."

A subject should be contemporary with its own time, and when it is, dating, for instance, becomes remarkably easy. On the simplest level, pictures of locomotives must be nineteenth- or twentieth-century. You should never find an eighteenth-century painting of a steamboat, either, because steamboats weren't in use until the nineteenth century.

A New England landscape: view near Pittsfield, Massachusetts, by Thomas Cole.

Yet there are landmark subjects in the history of art: the Dutch interior, the Madonna and Child enthroned, the French Impressionist landscape. And all such seminal combinations of subject with style—created by visionaries and pioneers—are henceforth unrecapturable. Meaning that everyone after Turner who has chosen to paint the atmospheric light effects of storms, shipwrecks, and fires follows in his brilliant wake. Everyone who produces two-dimensional blocks of primary colors connected by black lines stands on the squared shoulders of Piet Mondrian. Originality is unique. And the art world and market values originality.

A typical religious subject: Madonna and Child with the Infant Baptist, *ascribed to Pontormo.*

A study in pointillism by its chief practitioner, Georges Seurat.

Virgin and Saints *by David*
(detail of an open book).

TECHNIQUE

Most of us can recognize the techniques of Impressionism: a water lily or a bridge, rather than being presented realistically, is rendered as a flurry of brush strokes and bright colors laid side by side, blurring into an "impression" of its subject. Monet, Impressionism's grand master, portrayed wisteria vines in a colorful shorthand of wisteria—the embodiment of a May moment. His works don't replicate nature at all, nor do they wish to be replicas.

Pointillism is also a technique—one in which thousands of minuscule paint dots imperceptibly form themselves into a tree, a woman, a dog.

Both techniques were developed around 1880, but they are quite different. If you own a painting that's a rich, formal, botanically accurate still life of massed tulips, peonies, grapes, and insects, all aglow against a dark background, but it's painted in the free, loose brush strokes that the Impressionists employed (or in tiny, pointillist dots), you can be quite certain that while the *subject* may be seventeenth-century Dutch, the painting itself must have been done since Impressionism was conceived. This means it can't be seventeenth-century Dutch or even an 1830 copy of seventeenth-century Dutch. You won't find an eighteenth-century collage, either, or a silkscreen, for instance, because both are modern techniques. Basically, if a work's technique seems too free, too relaxed, too informal for a very traditional subject, look again and look hard.

The signature and inscription in the background of Albrecht Dürer's self-portrait.

SIGNATURES AND INSCRIPTIONS

Signatures are what legitimacy is all about. The signed painting has every chance of having value, while the unsigned painting is a struggle to attribute, to date, and, finally, to sell. There's no doubt that collectors like their paintings to be signed. After all, when one is spending thousands for art, that signature seems to be a "written guarantee" of authenticity. Nonetheless, what appears to be the most straightforward piece of information on a picture can actually be the least dependable, for signatures are often deceptive.

It wasn't until the seventeenth century that signatures became commonplace, though even then they were often obscure. In Holland, for example, artists hid their signatures or devices (monograms or cryptic emblems) in the shadowy backgrounds of their works. Other artists "signed" with symbols: in the nineteenth century American James Whistler (of "Whistler's Mother" fame) signed with a small butterfly. Complete and legible signatures are sometimes hard to come by, for even when the artist's name is there, it isn't always conveniently placed in a lower corner (where it shouldn't be big and red—often a clue to hack work). You might have to search among tree roots or on the bases of marble columns for that signature (where it might be faux-chiseled in). Or look among the painted papers on painted desks and in newsprint, on rocks, or, always, of course, on the reverse of the canvas.

Frequently, the signature *is* actually in one of the corners, but either because the liner (the narrow wood band closest to the picture) is hiding it or because the painting sits so loosely in its frame, it has dropped below the frame's lower edge. If, after checking the reverse of the painting, you think this might be the case, you can remove the canvas or board from its frame and have a look, but you should have great confidence in your own dexterity before attempting this.

Even after finally locating an elusive autograph, sometimes you can discern only a few letters clearly or a single syllable of the last name (first names, followed by indecipherable surnames, are not especially useful). There are computer programs, some accessible by telephone, that can decipher entire illegible signatures

YOU CAN LOOK IT UP

Once you've determined your artist's name, if you'd like to find his or her birth and death dates and biography, it's an easy matter to look up the artist, especially if the artist is European, in the most extensive work on artists of *all* nationalities: the French *Dictionnaire des Peintres, Sculpteurs, Dessinateurs, et Graveurs* (known as *Benezit*). If you think your artist may be American, there is Mantle Fielding's *Dictionary of American Painters, Sculptors & Engravers,* which has American entries that *Benezit* doesn't include. Both reference works can be found in large libraries, university libraries, and museum libraries. Similar specialty publications list the works of marine artists, sporting artists, and artists of individual countries. The artists found in such compendia are colloquially termed "listed."

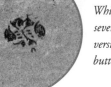

Whistler used several different versions of his butterfly signature.

*WILLIAM SHAYER
PAINTING*

To her husband's dismay, the guest bought this painting simply because she liked it. He did not. Polly Sartori pointed out that she must have good taste because it's actually a work by William Shayer, a nineteenth-century British artist who painted farmyard scenes and scenes of everyday life, a subject termed *genre*. His signature, which is very hard to spot because it's so tiny, is often found on rocks, driftwood, or even on pebbles in the painting. On the back of this picture there are nice old frame labels. Purchased for $125, it's worth about $4,000 to $6,000. Good thing her husband didn't talk her into returning it!

from only a few letters. And you needn't despair if you find no signature at all, for, if your painting meets all the criteria listed here, there are museum experts and scholars who can identify some artists without it. Many works—Old Masters, for example—are enormously valuable despite not being signed.

In addition, consider the following:

♦ It's always reassuring if the signature was incised into the oil paint when the painting was first executed, for then you can be certain it's original to the picture.

♦ Don't be misled by a "floating signature," one that has been added (forged) at a later date. Most counterfeit signatures have been applied on top of the painting's varnish, and by holding the picture at an angle to the light, you can often determine whether the signature's paint has a different finish (is shinier or more matte) than the paint on the rest of the surface; if it's "floating," that is, on the varnish. In the late nineteenth century, amateur and semiprofessional women artists painted many works. To make their work more salable, they frequently signed with a first initial and their surname, or only with initials.

♦ The lettering of the signature should be as old as the rest of the painting. A florid script or the use of the old-fashioned "S" that resembles a script "f" is comfortingly antique.

♦ The antique term "Fecit" (sometimes written "F.," "Fe.," "Ft," or "Fec") is found on paintings until the nineteenth century. "Fecit" means "made by" in Latin. Should your painting be signed "Andrea Mantegna Fecit," it was "made by" (painted by) Andrea Mantegna.

♦ Frequently confusing is the inscription involving the Italian word da, meaning "after." A hypothetical painting signed, for example, "S. Artist da Rubens" is telling us quite clearly that a painter named S. (for starving) Artist painted this picture in imitation of—

or "after"—an existing painting by Rubens. It was quite common, in centuries past and even today, for students to bring their paints to a museum, sit before an Old Master picture, and make an exact copy. This is how they learned technique. Many such paintings (and some are remarkably well done) are signed with the student's name, followed by "da Veronese" or "da Raphael." These are not fakes. They are honest, respectful reproductions, though they are not by Veronese or Raphael. Thousands of such pictures went home with European and American tourists in the nineteenth century.

◆ Another potentially puzzling inscription is "anno," Latin for "in the year of," usually followed by a date. A painting signed "S. Artist, anno 1757" was painted in 1757.

◆ "Pinxit" ("P.," "Pinx.") or "Pictor" is another bit of Latin, meaning "painted by" or "painter."

Any genuine inscription on a painting is interesting to scholars and helpful in documenting origin. Even auction or art gallery labels are useful. Large auction houses, like Christie's and Sotheby's, that maintain sales records for years and years, can occasionally identify property that has sold in their salerooms.

Perhaps the only truly useless written symbols on paintings are those ubiquitous strings of numbers on the reverse of the canvas. Such marks, which are the canvas-maker's inventory or storage notations, are meaningless to us today. Unless they can be matched with the occasional artist's record of his or her own work, they seldom, if ever, pertain to the artist or his art.

DATES

Dates on paintings are a bonus. Not only can they be an aid to identifying an artist if the signature is only partially decipherable, but they can also help to establish a painting's locale. If a painting is dated 1803, for instance,

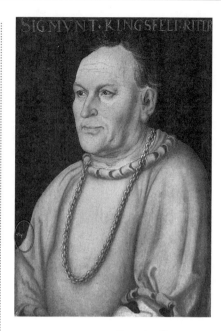

Portrait of Sigmunt Kingsfelt, *Lucas Cranach I (1472–1553)*.

Detail of the above portrait, showing the artist's use of a dragon as a device.

Although the clothing in Edward Lamson Henry's Leaving Home, *is c. 1805, the painting dates from 1889. Its sentimentality and even the postures of the assembled company mark it as Victorian.*

Master's Hat, *by Arthur Wardle, is sweet, likable, and accessible, but is it Art?*

and the artist's biography tells you that he was in Italy in 1803, you can assume your painting was painted there. Yet only when that date seems to concur with all other evidence of a painting's age—the frame, the canvas, the technique, the subject's clothing—should it be considered significant.

♦ Clothing is a giveaway. If your painting of a gentleman in a French musketeer's uniform is dated 1865, it cannot have been painted in the period of the sitter's costume (the seventeenth century) and is unlikely to have significant value.

♦ Even dates painted right on the surface by the artist, as opposed to the often questionable dates engraved on those prominently placed brass plaques (see page 125), are not dependable. Handwriting can be indistinct or frustratingly illegible, making dates easy to misread.

♦ The date ought to be written in the same hand and style as the signature. But even a clearly written date that follows nicely after the artist's signature may have been added later, by the artist or by another hand—perhaps an heir or executor or an overly helpful restorer. It may thus be the actual date of the painting or a somewhat educated guess.

♦ Often the date on a portrait is accompanied by the letters "aet" or the word "Aetatis" (Latin for "at the age of") usually followed by a number. "Aetatis" refers to the age of the sitter. For example, if an inscription on a portrait of a young man reads "William Blackchurch, aet. 16 1784," that means William Blackchurch was sixteen years old in 1784 when this portrait was painted (although it might also be a likeness of him at the age of sixteen, painted years later from memory or from a portrait miniature).

♦ Worth noting is the curious fact that the use of only two numbers to indicate a date—'04 or '95, for example—is very much a phenomenon of the late nineteenth and twentieth centuries.

CONNOISSEURSHIP

"I don't know much about art," goes the cliché, "but I know what I like." In fact, most of us, especially if we don't know what we like, don't really feel capable of judging quality in paintings. We may have taken Art History 101, but it probably didn't teach us much about art criticism. Consequently, we're in plenty of good company when we find ourselves drawn to pretty pictures of flowers, puppies, happy couples dancing, thatched cottages, bubbling brooks, and square-riggers on the high seas rather than to huge black squares centered by one red dot. A recent book, basing its conclusions on a questionnaire about the art the average American would like to own, created a composite painting on a computer—an imaginary "perfect picture." It turned out to be a landscape about the size of a dishwasher, depicting a disproportionate quantity of very blue sky and water (it seems Americans love both the color blue and Nature), portraying several people, including the figure of George Washington, and animals (Americans also like paintings of fellow humans and animals). This composite tells us quite clearly that if most of us were to collect art in a big way, we would never give houseroom to a late Picasso or even the smallest Jackson Pollock.

Art is judged, however, by standards other than the median taste of the times. For while size, color, and subject often make "pretty" art expensive (many more people want

BENTON ROLL-IN

This guest's father and the American artist Thomas Hart Benton once hunted and fished together, and in many ways this painting of the Grand Teton Mountains in Wyoming reflects the artist's love of the outdoors. Nan Chisolm explains that the guest's picture was executed in egg tempera paints and "en grisaille"—in shades of gray. Because the painting is in excellent condition, and because it bears a correct, clear signature, Chisolm estimates its worth at $10,000 to $20,000.

Tondal's Vision, a difficult subject by a brilliant artist, Hieronymus Bosch.

to own it), art critics and scholars tucked away in universities and museums use far more stringent criteria to determine what, exactly, makes art "fine." Creativity and innovation are integral to the formula, but the artist's handling of color, command of technique, and his or her painting's emotional impact on the viewer are equally important. When critics and scholars find an artist who combines all these elements successfully, they term that artist "great" and his or her works "masterpieces."

And, much of the time, the public agrees, standing in long, respectful lines to view Van Gogh and Degas, Ingres and Vermeer. It seems that standards of connoisseurship actually overlap agreeably often with popular taste.

If your painting *is* old and legitimate, therefore, how good an example of its kind is it? While you might not consider yourself a connoisseur, you can still learn to judge intelligently the works you already own and thus buy discerningly in the future.

SUBJECT

First, don't dismiss a work just because you hate its subject. Goya painted executions, Bosch depicted the torments of the damned, and both are decidedly geniuses. Admittedly, certain subjects are simply not desirable and not readily marketable: paintings of dogs attacking stags, for instance, or still lifes incorporating dead game. Most Americans don't care to look at pictures of savage hunting scenes, so even competent seventeenth-century paintings of such subjects—except those by well-established artists famed for just those subjects—are simply not as valuable in America as cheery depictions of dogs, foxhunts, horse races,

Portrait of an 83-Year-Old Woman, *Rembrandt, 1634.*

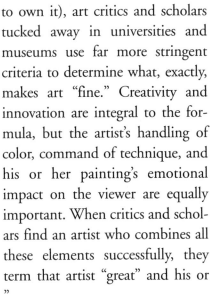

or geese on the wing, all of which attract similarly sporty collectors. Run-of-the-mill portraits won't be desirable, either, especially those of aged sitters, unless they're beloved grandparents or Rembrandt's noble oldsters. Plain husbands and wives captured past their prime by far-too-honest painters lack the required charisma. Still, even "bad" subjects, if painted by important artists, will ultimately find homes—though for far less money than the same artist's attractive subjects. Even grand and beautifully painted religious pictures, so desirable in more pious times, are far from universally marketable today.

There's a market for "name" as well, regardless of subject. Works by celebrity painters, like Winston Churchill and Anthony Quinn (but not Lionel Barrymore), bring prices unexplained by talent or the lack of it.

On the other hand, numerous "good" subjects, sometimes with no signature at all, sell as well: for instance, the aforementioned historically significant subjects—Washington Crossing the Delaware, Nelson Expiring at Trafalgar, Covered Wagons Heading West. Battle scenes are popular, even when unsigned or painted by an unlisted artist, and there's always an empty wall for a spectacularly smoky marine engagement, as well as even naïvely rendered Little Big Horns, or anything at all to do with America's Civil War. We want to view such subjects at a clinical distance, of course. Should a painting depict too much in the way of devastation or gore, it won't find wall space.

Paintings of children—even badly done portraits (especially folk portraits)—and renderings of flowers are also marketable. And paintings of pretty women are traditionally among the most popular of all subjects. If the women are pretty *and* smiling, that's even better (though brooding types have their admirers). And should you happen to have a well-done painting by an important artist of a pretty girl playing with children in a summer garden, well, that's a grand slam.

Riviera Scene *and other works by Winston Churchill have a market despite their lack of significant artistic merit.*

This seventeenth-century hunting scene by Frans Snyders is the sort of subject buyers find objectionable.

Giorgione's superb realistic technique in rendering armor dazzles the viewer of this sixteenth-century Warrior and His Equerry.

While the hands of Solari's fifteenth-century Man with a Pink *are convincingly painted, it is the face of the sitter that grips the imagination.*

COLOR

Color is easy. Today the world loves light bright hues. Somber Old Master subjects, mythological and religious, may have been instructive once and may suit the walls of the cultural striver today—but they're dreary, dark, hard to live with, and much too doleful for homes lit by skylights and hundred-watt bulbs. Modern tastes prefer shimmering waterscapes, pinkly purple sunsets, dappled woodlands, and anything, really, that's not predominantly brown and black. This explains why Impressionists such as Monet, Renoir, and company are internationally beloved (and why much Barbizon art has fallen out of favor). The Impressionists not only paint lovely subjects—gardens, dancers, lush young women—but they paint them in gorgeous colors. And color isn't "intellectual." One needs no training to appreciate color. It's not remotely didactic, and it requires no thought. Consequently, attractive colors make works of art accessible to every viewer, and the more people who admire an artist's palette, the more will compete for that artist's work.

TECHNIQUE

Some artists are born with technique; some have to be taught. Most of us, even if we can't draw the proverbial straight line, can recognize perspective when it's "off"— when a house isn't square to the landscape, or when the waves on a painted ocean haven't a hope of looking like water. We can tell if a drawing of a horse isn't a good representation of a horse, or if the clothes on a human figure barely hint at the body beneath. When we make such observations, we are judging the artist's technique. Conveniently, we ourselves don't have to be able to draw a straight line to know if an artist is doing it well. Technique, or lack of it, shows in the hands, for instance. The old rule of thumb was that an artist could be judged by his rendering of the subject's hands, and a good artist painted real-looking hands. In a way, this is true. Until the mid-nineteenth century, artists tried to be as realistic as possible in their work because, before the advent of photography, their paintings were the only way for most people to own a likeness of their loved ones or view the Rocky Mountains. So, the more accurately they were rendered, the more talented the artist was thought to be. Moreover, the public loved to be amazed by "touchable" velvets and gleaming, perfectly realized brass chandeliers. Such tours de force are not to be despised, for those eyes that seemed to follow you around the room required skill—a facile skill, perhaps, and one not much in demand among critics today, but one that is *still* a useful key to judging how technically able an artist was. (Add intelligence, creativity, and emotional resonance to eyes that seem quite real, by the way, and that's a work of art.) So, if the materials seem old and the perspective and reality quotient seem competent or better, you don't have to know right away if the painting is a work of genius. You can see that it's capably done and merits some research.

In the nineteenth century, Americans were first introduced to their topography via paintings like this example by Albert Bierstadt.

GOOD YEARS, BAD YEARS

Once you've established that a painting is old, made out the signature, discovered at the library that your artist is indeed listed, and made some preliminary judgments about its color, subject, and technique, there is still one more step. Artists have good years and bad years, just like wines, and you'll need to learn about yours.

Some artists, like Salvador Dali, shine early on, then do no more than repeat their early works thereafter. While Dali lived until 1989, most critics agree that he was an early burnout, producing little of consequence after the 1930s. His paintings from the 1930s, therefore, sell for considerably more than his later works. (His prints are another problem altogether.)

Persistence of Memory, *an archetypal surrealist work by Salvador Dali, was painted in 1931—for Dali, a vintage year.*

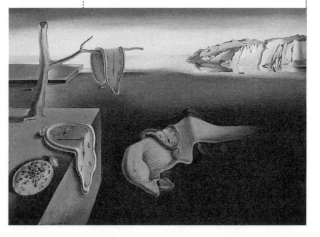

Entitled Woman (Blue Eyes), *this painting by Willem de Kooning was done in 1953 and is a prime example of his work.*

The late work of Willem de Kooning, the twentieth-century American master of Abstract Expressionism who developed Alzheimer's disease at the end of his career, is not as collectible or as valuable as his 1950s output.

Sometimes an artist paints prosaically and academically as a student. Mondrian, for example, painted competent landscapes early on, but became renowned for later break-throughs—like Cubism. Later Mondrians are worth considerably more than the landscapes.

It's the consensus of curators, scholars, and dealers that determines which periods are most important in an artist's development and thus most valuable on the market. Unfortunately, this is not information that the average picture owner, contemplating a late-period S. Artist hanging over the sofa, has immediate access to, for lengthy listings in biographical dictionaries don't really translate into numbers. And, even more confusingly, an owner who has seen a work with his artist's signature in a book or museum may assume that his painting is of museum caliber because it has a similar subject and seems to be old; in fact, he may really own a genuine painting by the same artist, with the right signature, but a work from the wrong period. So the only way to learn the art world's opinion of your painting is to become a self-taught student of the artist's work. Search the Internet, write to museum experts in the city of your artist's birth, contact the author of your artist's *catalogue raisonné* or his or her biographer directly, and do the homework. You are capable of determining for yourself the value of what you own. We all hope we own a Turner, of course. But a Gainsborough's fine, too.

Painted when Piet Mondrian was twenty years old, The Old Church *is authentic but not in his preferred later style.*

CONDITION

We know that a painting is composed of two main elements: its support—canvas, panel, paper, masonite, or even copper—and its medium—pastel, oil paint, watercolors, acrylics, or any number of substances, even shoe polish, wood ash, or string. We also know that oil paints take years to fully dry and must be protected by a coat of varnish against accidental smearing or pockmarking by airborne grime. But canvas and paint are fragile and easily damaged. Over a painting's lifetime, the *least* harm its surface will sustain is from natural aging: the darkening or discoloration of its overcoat of varnish, which turns blue skies green and foliage murky brown. The minute cracking of the paint itself, the result of the infinitesimal movement of the drying paint, is also normal. Allover crazing—*craquelure,* in French—is caused by years of alternating humidity and dryness in the air, and is a good indicator, by the way, of authenticity.

The *worst* damage a painting can sustain is the loss of large sections of canvas or paint. And between these two extremes are all the ordinary dings, wrinkles, gouges, punctures, tears, and bucklings that canvas and paint are heir to. The crucial question to ask about any injured painting, then, is this: How much of the original work remains?

The artist's creation is what we want to save—his lines, his brush strokes, his original paint. Simple cleaning, therefore, seemingly the most innocuous type of restoration, can cause irreversible damage and affect value enormously. Pictures can be overcleaned, changing subtleties of color by removing the artist's glazes—the transparent layers of dilute paint used to create shadow and modeling. Careless cleaning can also alter the relationship of one color to another, so that the picture no longer retains the balance the artist had in mind. Even worse, too zealous a cleaning can actually remove paint (called "skinning"), forcing the inept "restorer" to try to repaint what has been removed.

Although restorers are largely more scrupulous today than they used to be, here is how excessive overpainting

THOMAS HART BENTON PAINTING

Artist Thomas Hart Benton used to hunt and fish with this guest's father long ago. In many ways, the painting of the Grand Tetons in Wyoming reflects the artist's love of the outdoors. Benton used egg tempera paint and worked in what Nan Chisholm refers to as "en grisaille," meaning that the work was done in black, white, and gray. The painting is in excellent condition and has a nice clear signature. Chisholm estimated its worth at $10,000 to $20,000.

Even if it were torn right down the middle, this 1895 oil on canvas by Frederic Remington would still have value.

Unsightly crazing on the face of his muse can be clearly seen in this portrait of composer Luigi Cherubini by Ingres.

occurs. Two fingers of the sitter's hand lie on a newly repaired tear in the canvas. In repainting the faint repair line running across the fingers, the restorer finds that the flesh colors he's mixed don't quite match the remainder of the hand—so he repaints the hand. The hand suddenly looks unrelated to the arm attached to it, so he repaints the arm—and so on. This example may seem excessive, but it does happen. In this way, what began as a minor repair turns into an elaborate and almost always unnecessary and unsuccessful overpaint. Depending on the size and subject of the picture, such manhandling leaves us less and less of the artist's original work for coming generations to enjoy, and while the owner may be left with a brighter, more vivid picture, it's a picture that's light-years from the image that left the artist's easel. Certainly it's not his original work nor his intent. Consequently, though your portrait may unquestionably be by Gilbert Stuart, descended in your family with its original bill of sale (the most impeccable documentation, by the way), if most of Stuart's own work is now lost beneath some anonymous restorer's hubristic hand, that portrait will be considerably less valuable than any unretouched Gilbert Stuart—even one that's dirty or torn.

Over the centuries, to complicate matters, theories about what is an acceptable amount of restoration come and go. Today, for example, the protocol is for conservators to do as little overpainting as they possibly can and even to allow what they have done to show. The theory is that there will be no confusion in years to come as to what is original to the painting and what is not.

The amount and type of restoration done to a picture are generally not something the average owner can judge easily. The owner can certainly see the big and little holes, the flaking paint, the undulating canvas, the repair so amateurish that the mismatched paint colors (or the

Band-Aids patching the holes on the back) are hard to miss. But when dealing with well-done old repairs on potentially valuable paintings, expert X-ray ultraviolet light and microscopic examination are the only ways to determine the extent of the repair. Most damages—old, new, and previous poor repairs—can be readily and often inexpensively remedied, no matter how terrible they seem. Just be sure to find a reputable restorer (contact your local museum), and never throw anything out because it's in poor condition. When you're tempted to chuck some mildewed portrait in your basement or feed a winter fire with some "hopelessly" torn canvas, remember the dealer who toured the smallest antiques shops, asking to buy damaged paintings of Western subjects, "especially anything by Frederic Remington." They bring fortunes, of course, *even* repaired. Hold on to yours.

FOLK PAINTING

We've discussed "academic" art—art by the great and not-so-great artists who had some training, not in the numerous European art academies that became prevalent after the Renaissance, perhaps, but more commonly in the studios of successful, established artists. Such mentors and teachers passed down their techniques and materials to the younger painters who sought them out, who crossed oceans or continents—many of them—to apprentice themselves and learn. But enrolling in an academy of art or finding oneself a teacher a continent away presupposes sophistication and money for travel. And out in the innumerable small towns of young America—in rural Maine or deep in the Pennsylvania farmland—people with the desire to paint might never learn of the existence of such schools, much less the names of artists with whom they might study. Left to their own devices, then, budding painters taught themselves to paint in an unself-conscious, idiosyncratic, and usually inept fashion.

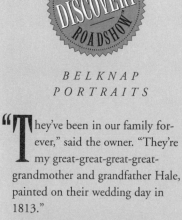

BELKNAP PORTRAITS

"They've been in our family forever," said the owner. "They're my great-great-great-great-grandmother and grandfather Hale, painted on their wedding day in 1813."

Expert (and New Hampshire native) Ron Bourgeault recognized the painted portraits immediately: they are clearly the work of Zedekiah Belknap of New Hampshire, and exhibit his characteristic use of gray paint on the back of the poplar boards. What is especially attractive and unusual, Ron pointed out, is that these portraits were done when the couple were young, happy, and hopeful. In addition, the portraits are in very good condition. Ron appraised them at $8,000 to $12,000 for the pair.

He advised the owner to keep them just as they'd been for almost 200 years: "Don't frame them; don't clean them."

WILLIAM MATTHEW PRIOR PAINTING

According to Colleene Fesko, nineteenth-century American portraiture has a hierarchy of subject matter, and this portrait of a young boy is close to the top. Not only are children preferred as subjects, but this child is particularly appealing in his outfit, holding his horn. In addition, the chair he's sitting in adds dimension, color, and interest. Fesko attributes this painting to William Matthew Prior (1806–1870), a New England painter.

The downside is that this painting no longer has its original frame, and it would be worth more if it had not been restored. Nevertheless, it is still worth $15,000 to $20,000.

Of course, Americans have a long history of self-sufficiency. The sheer distance between our urban centers made men like Jonathan Fisher, a minister in Blue Hill, Maine, who wrote books, worked his farm, studied history and mathematics, devised his own shorthand, built his house and furniture, and not incidentally, painted rather well, more the rule than the exception. Such "provincial" artists had little access to prevailing styles or trends in art, however. What paintings enlivened the walls of their homes were those they created themselves. And the occasionally awkward, but always fresh and naïve efforts of such men (and women as well)—distanced as they were from the currents of European art—constitutes "folk" art, the best of which flourished in the nineteenth century.

There is occasional confusion as to who were folk artists and who were not. Artists who were paid for their work were, technically, professional. But if they were unschooled professionals, they can be considered folk artists. Grandma Moses is a folk artist, for example. But contemporary artists such as Howard Finster and Bill Traylor are Outsiders—the current term used to describe self-taught and naïve late-twentieth-century artists. The distinction between folk artist and outsider artist is mainly chronological.

In their search for examples, early self-taught artists often copied the scenes in English mezzotints or, later in the nineteenth century, lithographs. They tried to reproduce these precisely, but subtle shading and perspective were not their strong points. (Neither, for the most part, were hands and ears.) They countered their failings with lively design and a vivid palette, and if they rendered classic architecture imperfectly, they were often breathtakingly accomplished in their lace collars or carpet patterns. This vivacity and vigor is what attracts us today—along with a glimpse of their simpler, sturdier world. For the folk artist's favorite subjects were his family, his house, his farm and village, the bowl of fruit on the table, the flowers in a vase. His biblical and historical subjects, even the numerous mourning pictures, are ubiquitous and unintentionally droll, with a sense of composition that was often dynamic and inventive. Their sentiments were direct and free, especially in their most familiar works—portraits.

PORTRAITS

In the eighteenth and nineteenth centuries, portraits were painted by limners (a term possibly derived from "illuminers"—painters of medieval manuscripts). Limners were paid for their work, while most folk artists were amateurs. Limning was a highly respectable profession. A notice placed in the *Boston News-Letter* in 1790 read as follows:

> *George Mason, Limner, begs leave to inform the*
> *Public That (with a view to more constant Employ)*
> *he now draws Faces in Crayons for Two Guineas each,*
> *Glass and Frame included; as the above-mentioned*
> *Terms are extremely moderate, he flatters himself with*
> *meeting some Encouragement.*

An artist who found himself without "encouragement" could usually fall back on painting coaches, tavern signs, and even houses, in order to eat. Many limners spent their winters in cities like New York or Boston, but with the spring, they packed their oils and brushes, and set off into the countryside, looking for work. Such itinerant painters occasionally exchanged portraits for room and board.

There is a myth that limners spent the winter months painting all-purpose bodies to which they attached their sitters' heads. This amusing image, so attractive to admirers of assembly-line technology, has been largely disproved. Instead, limners painted (all at one time) sitters facing the viewer fully or slightly turned, often accompanied by tools of their trade: for men, a ship, a sword, a sheaf of papers; for women, books, fans, or needlework. Children

Children are the frequent subject of folk artists, as in this Girl with Flowers, *c. 1840.*

Landscapes, clumsily but charmingly rendered, were often paintings of the artist's own farm or village. Todt Hill, Staten Island, New York, *c. 1850. Artist unknown.*

The Peaceable Kingdom (detail),
Edward Hicks, oil on canvas, 1849.

Twenty-three years separate the version of
The Peaceable Kingdom *above from*
The Peaceable Kingdom *below (1826).*
Numerous versions of exactly the same
scene were painted by Edward Hicks.

were stiffly portrayed with pets or favorite toys, for the limners were heavily influenced by eighteenth-century English portraits, adopting the conventions of British portraiture and occasionally incorporating into their all-American tableaux a building or motif they had seen in a Continental engraving, like Windsor Castle or a Roman ruin. (In most pictures, however, the sitter or family group sits beside a panel of red drapery.) When his work was finished, the limner moved on, leaving the owners with instructions for varnishing their paintings after the oils had dried.

If some of their portraiture seems modern or almost abstract to us today, it often marvelously captured the sitters' essence. "They lacked the ability to describe," wrote folk collector Maxim Karolik of these early artists, "but it certainly did not hinder their ability to express."

SUBJECTS

Folk-art landscape and marine pictures were more often the work of amateur artists than professionals. With few exceptions, they are anonymous today. Because these painters hadn't the skills to capture shadow, the reality of waves, or the perspective of their barns, they compensated with elaborate design or crowded composition. Although the roads in folk landscapes don't necessarily recede into the distance, but remain the same size from the front of the picture to the back, the trees and leaves frequently exhibit a stylized beauty and the fields may be full of botanically accurate flowers. Such carefully observed detail is the delight of folk-art collectors.

Mourning pictures were especially popular in New England in the nineteenth century, an era in which families often lost loved ones too young. Usually painted by the young ladies of a family—trained in the decorous arts of watercolor, drawing, and needlework at ladies' seminaries—mourning pictures were made as gifts for the bereaved or to commemorate a personal loss. Ladies amused themselves also with watercolor scenes of household life or carefully composed still lifes. Those who weren't "artistic" enough made theorems—creations of stenciled fruit or flowers on paper or velvet. Much of the folk art we prize today was simply their hobby or amusement, facilitated by the invention, early in the century, of small cakes of watercolor—an improvement over the old hand-ground pigments. Watercolor painting was an inexpensive, portable, and ladylike pastime, and its popularity explains, to some extent, why so many of these American folk paintings were executed by women, who—in the fine and decorative arts—are generally invisible talents.

Historical scenes were beloved by folk artists, but patriotic subjects like George Washington and the heroes of the Revolution were particular favorites, for veterans of the War of Independence were still alive at the time of the Civil War and the Revolution was fresh in the national memory. Folk art also illustrated great events in paint—floods, fires, rescues, and ship sinkings. Equally worthy of paint and canvas were legends of the Bible, often rendered with all participants in modern dress. Some painters exercised lifelong spiritual missions through their art. The Quaker preacher Edward Hicks painted his naïvely transcendent *Peaceable Kingdom* countless times; in each of these incarnations, the lion lies down with the lamb, while in the background an incongruous and oblivious William Penn signs his treaty with the Indians. Reality wasn't necessarily the issue for many folk artists: events could be juxtaposed on canvas that were impossible in life. Even seemingly realistic landscapes could actually be imaginary composites of several years and seasons in one spot.

Penmanship, in which early Americans were so well trained, led some talented draftsmen to create elaborate exercises in calligraphy—tendriled and sinuous horses and ferocious lions, all drawn in unending and scrolling lines of pen and ink. Among the German settlers of Pennsylvania,

An example of nineteenth-century academic art by American artist J.G. Brown.

An example of a Fraktur: birth and baptismal certificate of Guwenne Catherina Lebo, incorporating hearts, flowers, and the American eagle.

commemorative certificates of baptism, marriage, and death, called frakturs, were vehicles for the elegant calligraphy and stylized, brilliantly colored hearts, flowers, and foliage of talented local artists, who "illuminated" these utilitarian documents.

The invention of photography in the 1840s eventually affected the limners' trade. Why pay an artist for a portrait (always imperfect) when a camera could capture one precisely, realistically, and inexpensively? Ultimately, the brilliance of early-nineteenth-century American folk art dimmed and disappeared. It had never been "good enough," after all: it was only an untutored, countrified imitation of what the trained city artist did better—a do-it-yourself school of painting. But as the tradition of ultra-reality in art began to evolve into "modern" art, traditional, perfectly executed, and banal academic painting came to seem lifeless and stiff. In the light of modernism, American folk art was rediscovered in the 1920s and began to be exhibited as Art. Once despised and neglected, "folk" acquired a sophisticated, enthusiastic audience.

FURTHER READING

Benezit, E. *Dictionnaire des Peintres, Sculpteurs, Dessinateurs, et Graveurs.* Land O'Lakes, FL: Dealer's Choice Books, 1976.

Fielding, Mantle. *Dictionary of American Painters, Sculptors & Engravers.* Temecula, CA: Reprint Service Corporation, 1993.

Gombrich, E.H. *The Story of Art.* London: Phaidon Press, Inc., 1995.

Gardner, Helen. *Gardner's Art Through the Ages.* New York: Harcourt Brace, 1991.

Mendelowitz, Daniel. *A History of American Art.* New York: Holt Rinehart, 1973.

Chapter Five

JEWELRY

matron was having her portrait painted. "Would you paint me wearing a big diamond necklace?" she asked the artist. "Of course," the portraitist said. "But why? You're wearing only a gold wedding band." "Because," said the matron conspiratorially, "if I should die before my husband does, I want his second wife to go berserk trying to find it."

That second wife will search for the jewelry because, as everyone knows, Jewels Have Value. And she'll ignore the Queen Anne chairs, the fishing rods, the mechanical banks, to hunt down the jewelry box—although there's not much chance it holds a significant jewel.

Most of our grandmothers didn't own "important" jewels. (And if they did, they stored them in a vault.) Grandma was far more likely to have owned modest jewelry—a locket, perhaps, or an enameled bracelet, maybe a string of pearls with a ruby clasp. But is her locket gold—or brass? Is the ruby real—or fake? And how are platinum, silver, and antique gold marked? (If, in fact, they are.) Can the untrained amateur, without expensive gem-testing equipment, correctly identify opals, garnets, rose-cut diamonds, lapis, jet, and ruby doublets? Or plique-à-jour?

Absolutely. A quick lesson in stones and design is all it takes, and of the two subjects, the easier is design. Precious

Diamond brooch of round and pavé-set diamonds, openwork foliate design, with diamond collets; mounted in platinum.

Victorian stone cameo of carved carnelian with a bead and wirework frame of yellow gold.

Antique diamond brooch, designed as three old mine-cut diamond flowers mounted "en tremblant" on a mine-cut diamond cascading branch; setting of silver-topped yellow gold.

European-cut diamond ring, mounted in platinum, c. 1930.

stones—diamonds, rubies, sapphires, and emeralds—are not, in any case, difficult to analyze, and many fake stones are quite clearly fake. Once you've established that your ruby is real, all that's left to discover is whether it's a *fine* ruby. For there are inferior rubies, just as there are yellowish diamonds, cloudy emeralds, and watery blue sapphires. Examine them in daylight and see for yourself.

Of course, the process is not always perfectly straightforward. There are suspiciously flawless emeralds and irradiated diamonds that are bright blue-white. Even the experts aren't always able to judge the quality and authenticity of precious stones solely by eye. Judging rubies, like judging Rembrandts, sometimes requires technology, for there are far too many ways to simulate valuable stones, including the old process of heat-treating them and the new one of injecting them with resins—and synthetics are improving all the time. The trained gemologist examines stones for color, clarity, and hardness—and one should always consult a gemologist for analyzing stones of appreciable size. The average jewelry box, however, holds little in the way of significant stones because the average woman couldn't afford them. Historically, precious stones were the prerogative of the rich.

The stones you're likely to find in a vintage or antique piece reflect the fashion trends of that period and help you to date your jewelry. Garnets are inevitably Victorian, for example; most diamond and semiprecious mixes are Art Deco; stone cameos with classic profiles are either genuine classical Roman antiquities or Victorian look-alikes; and snub-nosed profiles on cameos are *always* twentieth-century. You can often tell the age of a piece, in fact, simply by the cut, or faceting, of its stones. Today, rectangular-cut stones are "out" and cushion shapes are "in." The cabochon cut is trendy, and so are pinkish pearls, but yellowish pearls are anathema.

Jewelry design is what turns geology into art. Once you set a stone, in fact, you mix craft—the working of precious metals—with art. Thus jewelry design reflects the aesthetics of the day and, of course, styles in clothing. For example, Edwardian pearl "dog collars"—luxurious necklaces made for formal wear—mimicked their owners' high-necked, daytime shirtwaists; free-swinging ropes of beads epitomized the flappers who wore them; and, in the 1930s, pairs of businesslike clips accented austere, squared-off necklines. As styles spread, they were copied and watered down, so that most of the old jewelry we find today is, sadly, mediocre—and plentiful. This is why great design and workmanship are rare and sought after, and why the work of brilliant jewelers such as Fabergé, Cartier, and Lalique is seen most often in museums.

If you own what you believe to be "designer" antique jewelry (or even unmarked but pleasingly designed old jewelry), be cautious about where you take it to be appraised. Jewelers accustomed to dealing in modern pieces may not recognize, appreciate, or appropriately evaluate jewels of vintage design. Your nineteenth-century Castellani pendant might seem negligible to them, but it certainly isn't. It's art, as a matter of fact. And unlike cash or stocks, it is an "investment" you can wear. It looks nice in portraits, too.

IS IT REAL?

The Romans adorned themselves in real (i.e., valuable) jewelry, just as we do today. Real jewelry is made of intrinsically valuable metal—platinum, gold, or silver—and may be set with genuine stones—precious or semiprecious. "Gold-filled" metal or rolled gold, and paste, synthetic, or reconstructed stones are all types of imitation jewelry. Of course, not everyone can afford real jewelry, so there are innumerable imitations out there, some of which, over the years, have been crafted well enough—with convincing imitation stones, gilt metal, and finely chased mountings—to be mistaken for real. Also, some pieces are *partly* real, with glass stones set in genuine gold, for instance, or real stones in animal-horn mountings.

CONDITION CRITICAL

Appraiser Joyce Jonas repeated an old saying among antiques appraisers. When it comes to value, three things matter: condition, condition, condition. Nowhere is this more evident than in antique jewelry. The first piece Jonas used to demonstrate this lesson was a nineteenth-century brooch which, when turned over, revealed signs of solder and the different-color metals used for repair, making this beautiful pin uninteresting to collectors.

Next was a brooch that began its life as part of a larger piece—one that had become unfashionable. Even though there is a brooch fastener on the back, it is clear that this is a redesign, and that diminishes its value.

The final example was a nineteenth-century cameo brooch. Thanks to the fact that everything on the back was original—the clasp, the gold, the shape—Jonas could date the piece c. 1890 and value it at $600 to $700. The next time an interesting antique brooch catches your eye, remember her advice: the back of the piece tells the story.

A variety of cuts and shapes in a cluster of unmounted gemstones.

Pearls are among the oldest organic materials used in jewelry, although this necklace of pearls, diamonds, and yellow gold dates only from the nineteenth century.

A good-size diamond is wittily displayed in a diamond and demantoid garnet

Consequently, a brief introduction to the indisputably real is important if you hope to tell the diamonds from the rhinestones.

PRECIOUS STONES (GEMSTONES)

Although both design and maker are important, it is stones that catch the eye in a necklace or ring—and indeed are meant to do so. Many jewelers and jewelry collectors, in fact, consider the setting simply a necessary adjunct to the display of stones, for, in identical necklaces, the piece set with stones will be more valuable (and usually more formal) than the one without. It's important, then, to know which stones are most highly valued and which stones look far too convincingly like the real thing.

Three categories of materials are mounted as jewelry:

1. **Crystalline materials** (diamonds and colored stones);

2. **Organic substances** (pearls, amber, ivory, coral, jet, tortoiseshell); and

3. **Simulants** (imitations and synthetics—both intended to deceive).

DIAMONDS

Of the four precious stones—diamonds, rubies, sapphires, and emeralds—diamonds are the hardest, most versatile, and, despite being sold in a carefully controlled market, by far the most common. Diamonds are also considered by most people (engaged couples, particularly) to be the most beautiful of the precious stones. For all these reasons, diamonds, whether white, pink, or canary, are usually the most valuable of the four.

Before the twentieth century, colored

stones were preferred. Diamonds only began to be appreciated when the discovery of South African deposits c. 1870 made them affordable and when the invention of modern cutting techniques ultimately revealed their brilliance. Today, fully 80 percent of the money spent on gemstones is spent on diamonds.

The best diamonds are lively, white, and flawless, as judged on the basis of "the Four C's"—color, clarity, carat, and cut—a foursome well worth committing to memory, as not only diamonds, but most other precious stones are evaluated by these same criteria.

Color: Unlike other stones, diamonds have their own internationally accepted color grading system, ranging from D-color (pure white) to Z-color, quite yellow. Curiously, color H is very good quality—a color most people would be pleased to own, while color I, with the faintest tinge of yellow and a step away, is considered "commercial white." The difference between them would be barely perceptible to the untrained eye, although significant off-colors can easily be seen by the naked eye, especially when set next to whiter examples. (In 1999, a method was developed for making poor-quality, brownish diamonds into E-color stones indistinguishable from genuine diamonds. They are labeled but labels can be ground off.)

Clarity: This term refers to the way a diamond reflects light. Because diamonds are actually crystallized carbon (coal), dark specks of black carbon, plus frosty, smudgy areas and whitish cracks, called *inclusions,* occur within them and affect their clarity. If the rays of light entering the stone meet these inclusions, the light is deflected or broken up, and the stone's "fire" is lessened. The diamond industry has defined six gradations between a flawless stone, one with no inclusions, and a stone with flaws clearly visible to the naked eye. Only the rare, perfectly clear diamond will have no flaws, or be "loupe-clean," which means that, seen under a 10 x 10 power of magnification lens, no flaw would be bigger than a pinpoint. (You can buy a 10x loupe at a jewelry or camera store.) The majority of stones, of

SYNTHETIC STONES

Synthetic stones of all kinds have been made since the beginning of the twentieth century. Synthetics are artificial, man-made stones with the identical chemical composition of the stones they replicate. Thus synthetic stones are hard to recognize, for they're usually internally flawless and the perfect and most desirable hue of the stone they counterfeit. But under a loupe, fortunately, their inclusions inevitably reveal the characteristic record-like grooves that betray their test-tube origins. In synthetic sapphires, for example, color zoning is less obvious than it is in the genuine gem. And interestingly, while sapphire and other precious gem synthetics have been in the trade for only a relatively short while, they have often been used as replacements for missing stones in antique jewelry, and they've also been found in 14-carat gold mountings, flanked by genuine diamonds. (Many of the small colored stones in Art Deco jewelry, however, were always synthetic—which doesn't diminish the value of the piece in which they're found.)

The easily visible small table on these c. 1910 diamond rings makes them less valuable than brilliant-cut stones. (Only larger fine stones are worth recutting.)

GEMSTONE CUTS

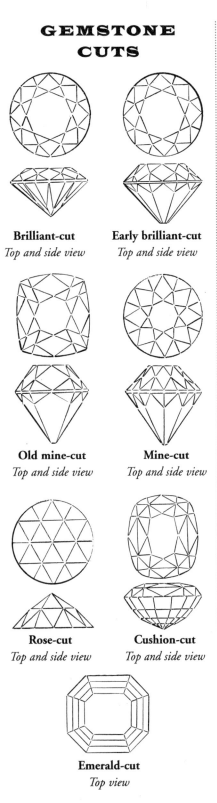

Brilliant-cut
Top and side view

Early brilliant-cut
Top and side view

Old mine-cut
Top and side view

Mine-cut
Top and side view

Rose-cut
Top and side view

Cushion-cut
Top and side view

Emerald-cut
Top view

course, combine various flaws with varying degrees of yellowness. Consequently, when shaping a potentially valuable stone, diamond cutters are carefully treading the fine line between excising its worst blemishes and retaining the clearest, largest gem possible.

Carat: In diamonds, the carat is the *weight* of the stone. (Not to be confused with the use of this term in connection with gold, where a carat is a measure of the purity of the metal.) A one-carat diamond weighs one-fifth of a gram. Stones weighing even slightly over one carat—even 1.1 carat—are worth considerably more than stones that weigh less.

Cut: The cut refers to the faceting of the stone—not its overall shape. A round stone, for example, might be either brilliant-cut or mine-cut. The positioning of flaws within a stone generally dictates its cut. A large, white, uncut diamond, for example, could be transformed into a barely flawed round shape, but, cut into a pear shape, it would reveal all-too-visible flaws. Cut, however, is generally less important than clarity or weight.

Table-cut diamonds feature a large top surface with small (if any) facets around the edges and a flat bottom. They are the earliest cut.

Rose-cut diamonds, despite their name, look nothing like roses and are not remotely pink or red. Rather, they are a simple and old diamond cut, flat on the bottom, with very few facets on top. First developed in Holland in 1640, rose-cut stones, relatively inexpensive as diamonds go, are generally round or oval in shape, have 24 to 36 facets (often less), and are quite common in antique jewels. They look to us like silvery pieces of glass or like marcasites (faceted iron pyrites).

Mine-cut diamonds (also known as European cut) are recognizable by their relatively small table (the flat, unfaceted top of the stone). They are usually round and pointed beneath, with a culet, or flattening of the point. But mine-cut stones lack the fully realized fire of the brilliant-cut we use today. Common in the nineteenth century, mine-cut stones are worth 25 percent less than good brilliants of the same size and quality. Their cushioned, bulky shape reflects light considerably less well.

The *brilliant-cut* diamond has many more facets (fifty-eight, in fact) than either rose- or mine-cut stones. The brilliant cut allows light to bounce off the back of the interior facets, which act as mirrors, increasing the stone's "fire." When diamonds were rare, before the discovery of the great deposits of the South African diamond mines, gem-cutters tried to retain as much of the stone as possible. Today, economy is a consideration for large stones only, and the cutting of brilliants commonly wastes up to 50 percent of the stone.

Simulants: There are several kinds of imitation diamonds, and these are often set in closed settings so that the backs of the stones aren't visible. (Closed settings for genuine diamonds are seldom found after 1800.) The oldest and easiest imitation to recognize is glass, which, when placed against your upper lip, will not feel cold at all. (Diamonds do.) Glass also chips and scratches easily, and exhibits minimal sparkle compared with the real thing. The faceted edges of genuine diamonds are sharp, while glass edges seem rounded and soft to the hand and eye.

Common and not particularly valuable workhorse stones, white zircons, which have a certain amount of brilliance, were frequently used in the nineteenth and twentieth centuries to imitate diamonds—despite the fact that they chip easily and are quite brittle. (Since zircons come in several colors besides white, they were also useful for imitating aquamarines.) The value of zircon is extremely low. Spinel, a semiprecious stone, is another stone that can be confused with diamonds, although spinel and zircon have been replaced as diamond substitutes today by cubic zirconia (CZ), a very convincing twentieth-century synthetic

A combination of rose-cut and old mine-cut stones was used for this platinum Belle Epoque necklace of garland and swag design.

Above: Flower brooch with rose-cut diamond pistil and petals, red and white enamel leaves, and yellow-gold mount.

Right: Brilliant-cut diamonds are employed to great effect in an Art Deco platinum and diamond necklace, c. 1930.

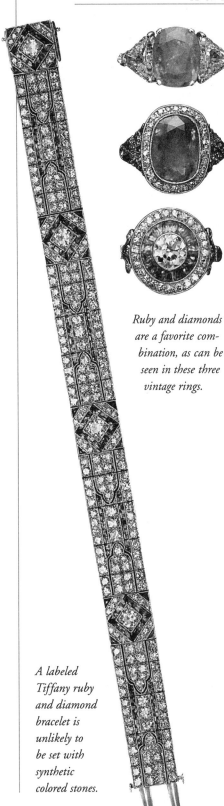

Ruby and diamonds are a favorite combination, as can be seen in these three vintage rings.

A labeled Tiffany ruby and diamond bracelet is unlikely to be set with synthetic colored stones.

that refracts light almost as well as a diamond. Cubic zirconia is hard, too (though not *as* hard) and under magnification is utterly flawless, which is actually its downfall, since every natural stone has imperfections.

RUBIES

Rubies, like sapphires, are the mineral corundum. For centuries, rubies have blazed from maharajahs' turbans and symbolized, in the coronation rings of British monarchs, the sunrise of the Empire. Burma is the traditonal source of the finest rubies, many of which, incidentally, can be more valuable than any run-of-the-mine diamond. Like diamonds, rubies are judged by their color, clarity, carat-weight, and cut. The amount of chromium in the stone determines the hue. Rubies that are too brown, too gray, too pale, or too purple are undesirable. The legendary "pigeon's blood" rubies, which are a brilliant blood-red, are considered the perfect shade—but these are extremely rare.

The color of a ruby should always be determined in daylight, for in artificial light rubies appear to be far more brilliant than they actually are. Viewed in daylight, a "deep red" ruby can become a pallid pink—though conveniently, such variability is also one indication of genuineness. To improve their color, particularly to correct undesirable brown tones, rubies have for centuries been heat-treated. (Heat-treating is a technique in which stones are "baked" at very high temperatures to burn away internal flaws, intensifying both brilliance and hue.) Some respected jewelers, like Tiffany & Co., consider heat-treating rubies and sapphires to be acceptable. But don't try this technique at home. Your own stones will certainly explode in the oven and/or lose all of their color. Of course, natural, unenhanced stones command premium prices, and the fewer their flaws, the higher their prices.

When rubies have so many blemishes that they cannot be salvaged either by careful cutting or by heat-treating, they are sometimes made into beads. They may also be cut into simple cabochon shapes—pillow-like, unfaceted half-domes.

Genuine rubies show very particular kinds of inclusions, like small internal cracks called "feathers," hollow areas within the stone, or intersecting rows of fibers called "silk," detectable under magnification. The presence of silk, in fact, is another proof of genuineness. And it is also the gathering of silk that creates a "star." Rubies are somewhat softer than diamonds and may exhibit surface scratches or abrasions (which can be polished out).

Simulants: There are many imitations of rubies, of which the synthetics are most effective. Synthetics are usually bright red, with internal lines or grooves—like those on old LP records—or with bubbles within the stone. Garnets, though sometimes mistaken for rubies, are usually much darker, purplish-red stones with a distinctly black cast. Red tourmalines are usually too pink to be mistaken for rubies and have telling white inclusions as well. Red glass, full of bubbles, not cold to the touch, and with giveaway rounded facet edges, is even less convincing. Far more problematical, however, are the "rubies" produced in the Orient in the last quarter of the twentieth century, in which a natural corundum top is glued to a synthetic ruby base. This "doublet" provides a stone with all the inclusions we expect to see, plus the exact color of the genuine gem.

SAPPHIRES

Sapphires, like rubies, are the mineral corundum. For most of us, "sapphire" is synonymous with the color blue, but there are also richly colored and extraordinarily valuable "fancy" pink, yellow, and green sapphires, plus a rare pink-orange variety. The highest-quality blue sapphires, those described by the Gemological Institute of America as "medium dark, vivid blue," were discovered in Kashmir at the beginning of the 1880s, and Kashmiri sapphires, from mines that are thought to be no longer producing, are still the most valuable type. Although most sapphires lose some of their color in artificial light, Kashmiri stones do not. (*Very* dark blue sapphires, incidentally, are not desirable.)

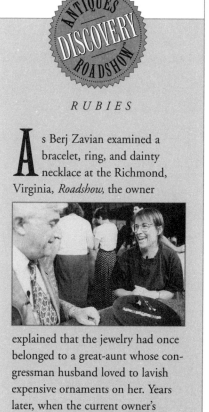

ANTIQUES DISCOVERY ROADSHOW

RUBIES

As Berj Zavian examined a bracelet, ring, and dainty necklace at the Richmond, Virginia, *Roadshow*, the owner explained that the jewelry had once belonged to a great-aunt whose congressman husband loved to lavish expensive ornaments on her. Years later, when the current owner's mother would wear the ring and bracelet, everyone disparaged the "tacky" stuff.

Zavian began by informing the owner that the diamond necklace, though genuine, wasn't worth more than $12,000 (the stones were off-color). The ring, a combination of 3-carat diamonds and a large Burmese ruby, might bring $80,000. But the bracelet, Zavian declared, with its central 3.5-carat Burmese ruby, diamond baguettes, round diamonds, and thirty-one beautifully matched rubies, was the *pièce de résistance*, worth $165,000. Tacky, indeed!

A Belle Epoque star sapphire and diamond pendant, garlanded in a mine-cut diamond frame and mounted in platinum and yellow gold.

Diamonds set in cloudlike floral forms typify Art Deco style in this emerald, diamond, and enamel bracelet.

"Fruit salad": an Art Deco bracelet incorporates both carved rubies and emeralds, c. 1927.

Genuine sapphires share, with rubies, "silky" inclusions—intersecting needle-like crystals, particularly visible under reflected light. Sapphires occasionally contain actual liquid-filled bubbles, like those in spirit levels. Sapphires are also "zoned"—that is, their color is arranged in subtle bands within the stone. And, like rubies, sapphires have traditionally been heat-treated to lighten or darken their color or to improve their clarity by burning away obvious flaws.

Sapphires also appear in starred cabochon shapes, in colors ranging from pale grays to deep blues. The mid-range blues with the clearest six-pointed stars are the most desirable types.

Simulants: Because they are the most popular colored stones, sapphires are very often simulated. Spinel comes in several shades of blue and makes a convincing substitute, though it is more brilliant and has greater clarity than the real thing. Colored glass is also a frequent impostor, especially in antique jewelry, and can be recognized by the criteria used for rubies and diamonds, as detailed above.

EMERALDS

Emeralds are a variety of the mineral beryl. Unlike sapphires and diamonds, they come in one mythical color—green. The finest gems are Colombian, carried to India initially by Spanish traders, centuries ago. (Because emeralds were favorites of Indian princes, they were once thought to be of Indian origin.)

Unlike other colored precious stones, *all* emeralds are flawed. (Emerald inclusions are termed "gardens" in the trade.) They are also much softer than the other precious stones, which is why they can be beautifully carved and engraved, but also why they are frequently found chipped and scratched. In fact, the familiar "emerald cut," a rectangular, stepped cut with clipped corners, was created to protect the emerald from just such damage. For the same reason, emeralds are frequently set in gold rather than platinum since platinum prongs, which are harder than gold, can easily scratch their vulnerable surfaces.

Simulants: The Romans imitated emeralds with green glass, but emerald color has been simulated in the centuries since by several kinds of semiprecious stones: green tourmaline and demantoid garnet, for instance. Synthetic emeralds, however, are especially problematical for the amateur. Early versions, made in the 1930s, were fairly easy to detect, as their "gardens" were obvious, unconvincing white swirls within the stone. Chatham emeralds, modern, man-made synthetics introduced in the mid-1930s, are distinguishable from genuine emeralds by the presence of gas bubbles and veil-like inclusions. But Soude emeralds, stone "sandwiches" of two slices of weakly colored emeralds cemented together with a resinous green-dyed "glue," are far more convincing, as are emeralds enhanced by polymers. Only gem-testing labs can spot resins and polymers.

SEMIPRECIOUS STONES

Although there are scores of semiprecious stones, some of truly rare or wonderful hue, the stones discussed below are the ones you are most likely to find in old jewelry. As with precious stones, color, clarity, and size are of chief importance. The cut of the colored stone is of negligible consideration.

AMETHYST

Amethyst is usually purple quartz crystal, and its color is its most important attribute. Collectors covet the richest, deepest purple shades. They also look for stones with a minimum of color zoning, one of amethyst's characteristics. Until the end of the nineteenth century, when large deposits of amethysts were discovered in Brazil, the stone was both rarer and more popular than it is today and thus it appears frequently in antique jewelry.

ART DECO COCKTAIL BRACELET

John Weschler was intrigued by the brilliance of the diamonds in a beautiful cocktail bracelet. Made of platinum in the geometric style typical of the Art Deco period, the piece contained synthetic sapphires and was unsigned. Yet Weschsler pointed out that neither fact detracted from its overall value. This lies in the 11 carats of clear, European-cut diamonds.

The owner, who inherited the bracelet from her half-sister, had the piece appraised for estate tax purposes in 1984, at which time it was conservatively valued at $2,000. Based on that, the owner could hardly contain herself when Weschler estimated its real value to be $15,000 to $18,000.

A pair of Iberian amethyst and diamond girandole ear pendants. The clustered teardrop shape for earrings has been fashionable since the seventeenth century.

Advice on how to cast a knowledge-able eye on your own jewelry, from appraisers Barry Weber, Joyce Jonas, and Gloria Lieberman.

S O R T your jewelry: spill it out on a soft surface and separate the Recognizably Genuine from the Definite Junk. Have a third category for Possibles.—B.W.

S T E P away from it, forget it's yours, and then use all your senses.—J.J.

S M E L L it: silver, for instance, has a distinctive acrid smell.—J.J.

R U N your fingers over it: jewelry is highly tactile. If a piece has been damaged or repaired, you can feel it. Genuine antique pieces should always look and feel slightly worn.—J.J.

L O O K very closely at the back of the piece. On fine jewelry, the back is as well made as the front. If it's been repaired or assembled from old parts, gold colors may differ.—G.L.

D O U B T the validity of family histories unless you have documented proofs. Be equally dubious about attributing jewelry to the labeled box it comes in: a handsome box can too easily cause the "Tiffany by association" syndrome.—B.W.

H E F T it: good jewelry feels some-what heavy.—G.L.

P I T Y badly repaired jewelry or jewelry that's been converted to some other use (there was a fad in the 1950s, for instance, for making antique watch-chain slides into bracelets); its value is greatly diminished.—G.L.

TOPAZ

The best topazes are the color of fine old brandy. Genuine examples are somewhat rare and can easily be confused with citrine (see page 159), a form of yellow quartz and a much less valuable stone. Heat treatment, which turns the stone pink or blue, has been used on topazes for 200 years. (Blue topazes are often mistaken for aquamarine, which they resemble.) Topaz is very hard and takes wear well, but it is also brittle. Knocked inadvertently against a hard sur-face, it readily cracks.

GARNET

One might confuse garnets with rubies, though garnets are soft and more scratchable. And while the common wine-red dark garnet is universally familiar, garnets come in a great variety of colors—several shades of red as well as a rare, surprising green. There are three types of garnet:

Pyrope: The deep red, faceted stone most often seen in densely set, inexpensive nineteenth-century Bohemian jew-elry. Usually mounted in very low-carat gold or base metal, these pieces cost little when new and are correspondingly low in value today.

Almandine: Formerly called carbuncles, almandine garnets are common in mid-nineteenth-century jewelry, especially in cabochon form. Their deep cranberry-red nat-ural color was often enlivened by a foil backing.

Demantoid: The rarest and most valuable of garnets, demantoid garnets are a bright, grassy green, more yellowish than emeralds. They can be identified by the curved fibers of their "horsetail" asbestos inclusions. Green garnets were frequently used in jewelry made between 1895 and 1914.

TURQUOISE

Affordable and ever popular (the ancient Egyptians simu-lated turquoise), the finest turquoise is a strong sky-blue. Good stones should be free of dark markings, although blemishes, derived from the matrix (parent) stone, are attractive to some collectors. The porousness of turquoise makes it extremely susceptible to staining from the acids and oils on fingers, which is why old turquoise jewelry sometimes turns an unattractive green.

Simulants: There are several types of "composition" and glass turquoise, and genuine turquoise is often impregnated with colored wax to disguise flaws. Currently, simulations are more common in turquoise jewelry than are genuine stones.

OPAL

Exceptionally fragile and iridescent, opals may contain as much as 20 percent water. White opals are light-colored, frequently quite milky, and less valuable than black opals, which are mined only in Australia. The chief characteristic of both types is their attractive "fire"—a sparkling interplay of green, blue, and orange-red silicates. The finest opals show evenly spaced patches of pronounced fire, especially the highly prized reddish-gold fire. So-called fire opals (the choicest come from Mexico) are translucent—a brilliant tangerine-red—and have *no* silicate flash.

Simulants: A deceptive imitation is a thin white opal skin glued to a black stone, which creates a fake "opal" that appears to be the costly black type. Recently developed synthetic opals have a lizard-like skin, visible under magnification. (An effective plastic "opal" has a low melting point.)

CITRINE

Citrine is an abundant form of yellow/brown quartz, also known, understandably, as "false topaz." Being quartz, however, it is softer than topaz and cannot be highly polished. Nor does citrine have the depth of color or subtlety of the stone it resembles. Nonetheless, it has a long history of being sold to unwary buyers as the far more valuable topaz, and though at one time it had modest popularity in multicolor jewelry, citrines have decreased in value over the years. Heat-treated smoky-quartz citrine makes excellent imitation topaz, but it is often set in telltale low-carat mountings.

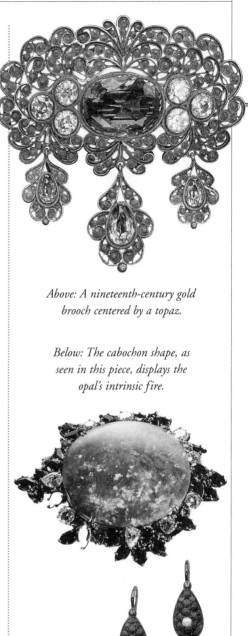

Above: A nineteenth-century gold brooch centered by a topaz.

Below: The cabochon shape, as seen in this piece, displays the opal's intrinsic fire.

Jewelry paved with stones, called "pavé," was fashionable c. 1845, the date of these turquoise and pearl ear pendants.

Above: A demi-parure of Victorian amethyst and gold.

Earrings and brooch of Victorian aquamarine and gold.

AQUAMARINE

Like emeralds, aquamarines are beryl, making the two stones "cousins," like rubies and sapphires. But unlike emeralds, aquamarines can be almost flawless and still be relatively inexpensive, although very large aquamarines are among the most valuable of semiprecious stones. A good deep color—ideally, a Caribbean-sea blue—is particularly desirable. Genuine stones should be quite clear. What inclusions there are should have the appearance of needle-like rain.

LAPIS LAZULI

A complex silicate, usually of a rich azure blue, lapis lazuli was used by the ancient Egyptians for seals and jewelry, while medieval and Persian artists ground lapis to make expensive ultramarine paint. Deep royal blue in color and opaque, top-quality lapis contains flashes of "gold" (actually iron pyrites). A stone's value is substantially decreased by patches of white marbling.

Beware of glass "lapis" and reconstituted lapis, a dark blue, violet-tinged synthetic, sometimes dotted with far too evenly spaced pyrites.

JADE

Jade is so hard and so difficult to carve that the tip of your key or knife won't scratch it. (In case it's not real jade, but just a pretty fake, try this only in some hidden spot.) Genuine jade is one of two distinct minerals: jadeite or nephrite, and jadeite is by far the more valuable of the two. Sometimes it is confused with emerald, for, in its rarest and most valuable form, jadeite is the rich emerald green color known as "Imperial jade." But jadeite is found more commonly in other hues: a radiant white (also quite valuable), lavender, mottled greens, and mutton-fat, which looks very much as its name suggests. The less white marbling jadeite contains, the more translucent it will be, and the more valuable the stone. Jadeite can be distinguished from the less desirable nephrite by its characteristic "orange peel" polish—visible on finished pieces as tiny pits where the allover polish didn't "take." Nephrite, on the other hand, is generally of a deep green English-ivy hue and has an oily, smooth, and relatively unpitted surface.

ORGANIC MATERIALS

Not stones, but outgrowths or derivatives of animals and plants were probably man's first jewels. Organic materials are all adventitious: they are "jewels" that can be found, that don't need to be mined or cut. Pearls, of course, grow in oysters, and tortoiseshell and ivory are animal by-products (protected today), while amber, jet, and coral might be chanced upon in the woods or on a beach. For centuries, all have been incorporated into jewelry.

PEARLS

Until the 1920s, all genuine pearl jewelry was set only with *natural* pearls. These were found in oysters that had built up within themselves successive deposits of calcium carbonate, termed "nacre," around an accidental irritant such as a grain of sand. The lustrous white nacre is the substance that makes pearls luminous and subtly iridescent. And the thickness of the nacre determines the depth and richness of a pearl's luster.

Pearls come in several colors, and color preferences are a matter of fashion. In some countries, yellow or gray-toned pearls are highly valued; in America, pinks and whites are favored. The most expensive pearls are black and pink, not white. Natural pearls are rare today: Most pearls are "cultured," or farmed, in acres of watery beds,

Antique pearl, diamond, and yellow gold bar brooch set with graduated pearls, rose- and old mine-cut diamonds, with openwork yellow gold foliate mount.

THE BURN TEST

How can you tell whether it's real or fake? According to Frank Boos and David McCarron, a simple burn test does the trick.

To distinguish ivory from simulated ivory, simply heat a pin until it's red-hot and place it an area where it won't go into the object. Ivory will smell like burning hair if it's the real thing. Real tortoiseshell will smell like burning hair as well while a plastic reproduction of tortoiseshell will smell strongly of plastic.

When comparing Oriental or European lacquer to plastic, the pin should go in and the lacquer should smell like a tree. If plastic, the pin would also go in but have a plastic smell.

In testing real silk as opposed to fake silk (or "mercerized cotton"), silk will smell like burning hair while fake silk will smell like a vegetable.

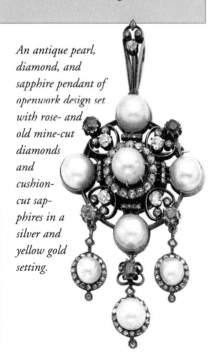

An antique pearl, diamond, and sapphire pendant of openwork design set with rose- and old mine-cut diamonds and cushion-cut sapphires in a silver and yellow gold setting.

from manually inserted, mother-of-pearl bead irritants. Only X rays can distinguish between the two.

All pearls are graded according to the thickness of their nacre, their surface perfection, and their shape, color, and size—in that order of importance. A fine pearl necklace will have virtually spherical pearls and as few blemishes—bumps, surface specks, and discolorations—as possible. The genuine pearl necklace will have a knot between each bead (to keep the fragile pearls from scratching each other) and, often, a precious gold or platinum clasp set with diamonds or other genuine precious stones.

Baroque pearls are misshapen pearls. In the early Renaissance and today as well, they were frequently used to fashion interesting and unusual figural pins, although they can also be drilled for necklaces. Baroque pearl necklaces can be valuable—but seldom as valuable as comparably sized strands of spherical pearls.

"Baby" pearls, called seed pearls, were extremely popular in the Victorian era, as were split (or half) pearls.

TORTOISESHELL AND IVORY

Some materials used in the past are seldom or never used today: tortoiseshell and ivory, for instance, both of which come from animals that are now firmly on the endangered list. (Both were once so popular for jewelry that they were even worth imitating.) Genuine tortoiseshell bracelets, earrings, and pins, inlaid with gold wire and dots in formal patterns called piqué, were categorized as costume jewelry in the Victorian era, as were ivory adornments. Ivory was most often carved into roses, dainty hands clasping bouquets, and similarly feminine motifs. Both piqué and ivory jewelry are of modest value.

CORAL, AMBER, AND JET

Each of these natural, organic materials enjoyed a fashionable moment during the Victorian era. They have in common a general affordability and the likelihood of being found as beads or in brooches.

Jet is a type of fossilized driftwood. Genuine jet is very black and shiny and was primarily worn as mourning jewelry, a fashion created by the perpetually bereft Queen Victoria. Jet jewelry is frequently decorated with ivy, crosses, and floral motifs.

Coral can be found in branch-form pins, bracelets, and necklaces, or as beads. Pale pink "angel skin" and white coral were fashionable tourist souvenirs in nineteenth-century Italy.

Amber, a resinous tree sap, was made primarily into beads and bracelets. Genuine amber, when rubbed on wool, will accrue enough static electricity to lift a piece of paper.

All of these materials are of modest value, even when mounted in gold.

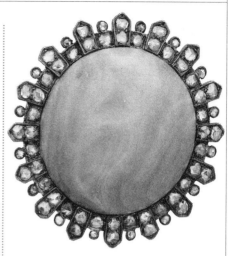

A large cabochon coral is surrounded by a sunburst of rose-cut diamonds in a nineteenth-century brooch.

METALS

Just as paintings do, gems require frames to be displayed to their best advantage. If a gem is rare or large, and especially if it's precious, it deserves to have an equally rare and precious—and correspondingly large, durable, and beautiful—frame. The rarest and most precious of metals, platinum, gold, and silver, have traditionally framed jewels best, though the display of jewels is not always the point, as precious metals have also traditionally been used for their own, unquestionably attractive qualities.

Modern jewelers, as well as Victorians, often carved coral, as in this fantasy brooch, c. 1950, set with diamonds and pearls.

PLATINUM

Platinum, today the most valuable of precious metals, was initially employed in the nineteenth century for such homely items as lightbulb filaments and cooking pots. It wasn't until the twentieth century that the invention of the oxyacetylene torch and a new melting process made it a practical material for making jewelry. In fact, jewelers weren't able to convince the public to accept platinum as a precious metal until they backed it with gold.

Nonetheless, platinum is harder and stronger than either silver or gold. Its silvery-white surface never needs to be polished, although, because it is slightly dull, it is often

This gold Continental sautoir (a very long necklace terminating in a pair of pendants or tassels) is an example of a style only fashionable between 1910 and 1930.

Stamped gold scrollwork makes an elaborate setting for aquamarines in a Victorian bracelet.

coated with a shiny rhodium finish. Millegrain, the minute decorative beading that typically edges stones set in platinum mounts, enlivens that shine.

Marks: French platinum is marked with a dog's head for the domestic market and a left-facing girl's head for export. American pieces might be stamped 10% Irid. (for iridium), Plat., or, most recently, Platinum, Pt950, or Pt. 900. The British import platinum mark is 950 between the two arms of a balance scale within a lozenge-shaped frame. As of 1975, the British mark is an orb surmounted by a cross within a pentagon.

The metal may be combined with white gold and marked "plat. and gold." Look for these stamped marks on the tongues of the clasps on bracelets and necklaces, inside the bands of rings, and on the clasps of pins.

GOLD

Gold has had a long, fabulous, and thoroughly bloody history. These days, it is the queen of the precious metals and the metal of choice for jewelry. Its warm yellow hue enhances every design and kind of stone. (Though yellow gold is the most familiar type, gold can also be tinted to turn it equally attractive shades of green, pink, and white.) And unlike silver, high-carat gold never tarnishes.

A carat, when referring to gold, is the unit of measure for describing the *purity* of the metal—the proportion of gold to an alloying metal (usually copper or silver) that has been added to make the pure (24-carat) gold harder and more serviceable. (Pure gold is far too soft to use in jewelry.) To withstand regular daily wear, jewelry should be no more than 18-carat gold, the usual Continental standard. The British and American standard today is 14-carat (14K) gold.

In the nineteenth century, the invention of very lightweight stamped gold—almost like a heavy aluminum foil—made genuine gold jewelry affordable to all. The hollow gold bracelets and earrings that could be made of this stamped metal were also far less costly than solid gold jewelry.

Marks: 15-carat and 12-carat gold were once common in England, but were discontinued in 1932. Less expensive 9-carat gold is often found in settings of semiprecious or unimportant stones and for chains, where strength is important. Since 1975, 22-carat English gold, used on jewelry from Hong Kong, has been stamped with a crown and the number 916 (meaning there are 916.6 parts of gold per 1,000). Similarly, 18-carat English gold is stamped 750, 14-carat 585, and 9-carat 375. American gold is made in 10-, 14-, and 18-carat standards, while France and Italy export 18-carat jewelry.

SILVER

In the past, silver was used not just for coins and tablewares, but also for royal jewelry. In the eighteenth and early nineteenth centuries, jewelers thought silver the most practical mounting for precious stones—especially diamonds—because its white hue seemed to complement their fire. Silver is seldom used for important jewelry anymore, because the quantity of the metal required to safely hold large stones sacrifices the delicacy of the jewel. Also, silver's unfortunate tendency to tarnish detracts from the stones it surrounds.

Because it is so soft, silver does have the major advantage of being easily formed into fluid shapes. This quality made it a popular choice for jewelers in the Art Nouveau and Arts and Crafts periods, when artists were first creating "modern" jewelry design. And because silver has always been the least costly of the precious metals, craftsmen could afford to experiment with it.

Silver is readily available throughout the world, far more so than gold, and is the metal usually used in Mexican work and for Native American jewelry.

Marks: Modern American and Mexican jewelry is marked "sterling," and twentieth-century Continental silver wares are marked 800 (for 800 parts of silver in 1,000). Modern silver jewelry is always marked. Some large older pieces may also be marked, but small pins, earrings, and silver rings may have no mark at all and need to be tested.

GOLD KANGAROO BRACELET

Australia, once a penal colony, became a desirable destination when people realized its natural resources, such as mines for opals and other minerals, namely gold. A guest's kangaroo bracelet had been in the family for many years, but she was unsure of its history. According to Barry Weber, her bracelet was made up of a series of real gold nuggets; each side segment was raw Australian gold, probably panned in the mid-nineteenth century. Weber claimed that this was only the second piece he had ever seen in his career. Its rarity makes it worth $12,000 to $15,000.

Gold is just as effective when not framing stones, as seen in this wide pierced and chased ring.

EARLY VICTORIAN JEWELRY

The owner's great-great-grandmother received this early Victorian jewelry set as a Christmas present when she was eight years old, around 1830. Ever since, it's resided in its original presentation box, where John Weschler saw it and described its period components.

The set consists of a necklace and earrings of 14-carat gold, handmade filigree work. The style and mode of manufacture identify it as American-made, from upstate New York. The stones are all pink topaz, backed with foil in closed settings to enhance their color (a common practice of the time). The set was appraised by Weschler at $1,200 to $1,500.

IMITATIONS

There are several imitations of gold, most of them fairly effective. Pinchbeck, for instance, an eighteenth-century combination of copper and zinc that looked very much like gold, was named for its English inventor, Christopher Pinchbeck. It was quite successful, both aesthetically and commercially, and has even become something of a collectible itself. But pinchbeck was made obsolete in the mid-nineteenth century by rolled gold, an even less expensive substitute composed of a thin layer of genuine gold adhering to a base metal sheet, rolled to the thinness desired.

Eventually, of course, rolled gold itself was supplanted by the cheap, easy, electroplated "gold" jewelry we know today—confusingly, perhaps even diabolically, called "gold-filled." Such pieces are certainly not gold-filled; they are simply base metal, plated with a thin coat of gold. Twentieth-century pieces of this kind are marked 14K G.F. (for gold-filled) or 1/20K G.F. In the United States, 9K pieces can be marked GF.

Unfortunately, the gold content of gold jewelry from before c. 1900 is unmarked, often causing the uninitiated to assume it isn't real at all. This is why, to determine if an old piece is gold, it must be tested—either with a touchstone and acid or with an electronic gold-tester, available for less than $100 (and far less dangerous than the old-fashioned mixture of hydrochloric and nitric acids). Choose pieces to test that are bright, as gold doesn't tarnish. For pieces that do test gold, the very lack of marks is proof of age.

IS IT OLD?

The great majority of the pieces that Americans discover in their jewelry and safe-deposit boxes comes from the nineteenth and twentieth centuries, although a brooch or ring from eighteenth-century Europe turns up now and then. Even more rarely, a piece of genuine eighteenth-century American jewelry surfaces, for we Americans were far too busy establishing a country to indulge in such frivolous pursuits as manufacturing gold jewelry.

You can easily determine the age of your jewelry by evaluating three key elements: 1) the materials that have been used in its manufacture (the combinations of metals, stones, and other substances), 2) the techniques used to make the piece, and 3) the style of the piece.

An imitation amethyst (paste) and gilt-metal Victorian bracelet.

MATERIALS

METALS

Silver was used in much nineteenth-century jewelry because it was malleable, plentiful, and inexpensive. Many eighteenth- and nineteenth-century diamond-set pieces combine a silver surface with a solid gold back, the silver color setting off the stones handsomely and the gold backing lending added strength. Toward the end of the Victorian era, silver was used not only for thousands of machine-made, mass-produced pins and earrings, but for "art" jewelry as well.

Every era, however, used gold. Gold is hard. Gold is strong. Gold's honeyed warmth complements skin, hair, and, particularly, stones. As the nineteenth century progressed and a newly wealthy middle class found itself with disposable income, more and more jewelry was worn—particularly in England, where good Victorian jewelry was always made of gold. At the end of that century platinum gold was introduced, and soon delicate French-influenced platinum jewelry replaced gold. Platinum's superior strength allowed it to be saw-cut into the lacy designs beloved of the period—spiderweb-thin platinum strands supporting dewdrops of stones, while its gray-white color surpassed silver as the perfect foil for brilliant-cut diamonds. But the platinum craze ran the usual fashionable course, and, eventually, in the mid-1930s gold returned to vogue. Only in the last decade of the twentieth century was there a revival of interest in platinum.

Silver-mounted and gold-backed butterflies and snakes, with pavéd diamonds (as above) or rubies and diamonds (below), were typical late-nineteenth-century motifs.

In the nineteenth century, cameos were among the most popular of "everyday" brooches and were made in a variety of materials. Above: a carnelian cameo with openwork yellow gold frame. Right: a green onyx cameo with rose, yellow gold, and silver wire-work frame. Below: an eighteenth-century Wedgwood and Bentley blue-and-white cameo.

STONES AND ORGANIC MATERIALS

Until the nineteenth century, most stones in jewels were cushion-cut—squarish, with rounded edges. They were moderately well faceted, had gently rounded tops, and came in round and ovate shapes. In the past, colored stones, especially topazes and amethysts, were given the kinds of elaborate presentations used for precious stones today, while the diamonds seen in jewels of the eighteenth century and earlier have relatively few facets: jewelers, limited by their tools, were unable to cut more. Many old colored stones are scratched, of course, although diamonds, thanks to their hardness, have scratched far less. (They *do* scratch, however, despite hearsay.) Such abrasions can easily be ground out, and, if not much stone is lost, a gem will retain its value. (The commonplace that real diamonds will scratch glass is useless as a means of identifying a diamond, for most of the stones currently used to imitate diamonds are also harder than glass and will do the same thing.)

It's interesting to note that old-fashioned rose-cut diamonds were employed well into the twentieth century, mainly when tiny stones, too small to be cut into brilliants, were required. As diamond-cutting techniques improved, diamonds became increasingly more dazzling and, consequently, more popular. Mine-cut diamonds, with their skimpy "tables" but additional facets, were simply steps along the way to the brilliants we're accustomed to.

CAMEOS

Cameos, popular since antiquity, were a particular nineteenth-century passion. With the discovery of Pompeii in the preceding century, Classicism captured the popular imagination, and the collecting of ancient cameos depicting gods, heroes, and noble Italianate profiles became fashionable. During the Georgian period (1712–1820), travelers to Italy and Greece brought home thousands of cameos—both classical antiques and fakes. (Aging fakes was an enterprising rural industry. Italian and Greek peasants stuffed new cameos down the gullets of barnyard geese to create more or less instantaneous antiquity.) Although the trend faltered for a few decades, it flared up in the mid-nineteenth century when hundreds of Sicilian carvers satisfied the demand of thousands of Grand Tourists for inexpensive (sea) shell cameos and the even less expensive lava carvings (of actual lava, usually in shades of brown). In addition to classical subjects, these new and often well-carved renditions depicted Victorianized goddesses, well-known personalities of the day, gamboling cupids, or even the cameo buyer himself. Cameos were often bought unmounted and set by the returning traveler in gold or gold-filled mounts.

Genuine antique examples were always made of stone, usually agate or onyx, while Victorian versions were available in either stone or shell. In each case, the light-colored upper layer was cut back to the darker layer beneath, throwing the subject into bold relief. Stone cameos, the most valuable type, are heavy, almost glassy-looking, and carefully carved—tool marks show.

Check to see if your cameo has been made by gluing a pale stone or white glass top onto a darker base. Genuine cameos, naturally, are all of one piece.

TECHNIQUES

Jewelry craftsmanship reflects the constant interplay between the dictates of fashion and evolving technologies. Sometimes, when a craftsman acquired the tools with which to do some previously impossible thing, the mingling of his imagination and the new technique created a major new style. When Victorian jewelers learned the secret of giving gold a frosted finish, for instance, they touched off a trend for "bloomed" jewelry. When the Castellani firm, in the mid-nineteenth century, discovered a way to imitate the fine gold beadwork of ancient Etruscan jewels, a craze for Etruscan-work began. Even deficiencies have inspired creative and attractive innovations. For example, in the years before

UNCOMMON CAMEOS

Jewelry appraiser Barry Weber gave viewers an important lesson in cameos. "Cameo-carved" refers to any design raised above the surface, and this art form has existed for thousands of years. Most common are shell cameos, carved from Mediterranean conch shells, their value depending on the quality of the carving and the elaborateness of the frame. As an example, Weber displayed some shell cameos brought in that day. The first, a mediocre carving in a plain 10-carat frame, was worth only $100, while the more ornate carvings and settings rose in value to the hundreds. The last, a beautiful, signed piece, quickly jumped to the low thousands.

To illustrate the best work in this medium, Weber brought in a fine cameo featuring an extraordinary carving of Prince Albert, signed by Queen Victoria's personal cameo carver and set in a gold frame signed by the royal jeweler to the court of England. A piece of this rarity, he told viewers, could easily fetch $10,000.

Unmounted Victorian lava cameos.

*Unmounted oval shell cameo
with classical theme.*

*French
brooch of
bloomed
gold, pearls,
and enamel.*

*Late-eighteenth-century diamond pendant,
front and back. The
closed-back silver set-
ting is shown at the
right.*

gem-cutters were able to capture the full fire or color of precious stones, gem-setters often mounted gems in closed-
back settings, with a bit of colored foil cupped within the
metal to enhance the color of the stone. In this fashion, the
color of pale pink topazes or garnets could be enriched, and
genuine stones could be imitated with glass (termed "paste").

Closed-back settings are the earliest settings for stones:
Renaissance, sixteenth- and seventeenth-century jewels are
set in closed backs. Foil-backed stones in closed settings are
usually eighteenth- to mid-nineteenth-century. Frosted
gold is third-quarter nineteenth-century. Etruscan-work
on jewels is always post-1860—unless, of course, it is genuinely ancient Etruscan. Any stone mounted in a closed-
back setting—without exception—should be looked at
twice, especially if there seems to be evidence of discoloration, for foils tarnish and deteriorate with age.

ENAMELS

Enamel jewelry has been made since medieval times, but
the technique reached a creative peak in the nineteenth
century. Enamel is actually pulverized glass suspended in a
medium, and champlevé is an ancient enameling technique in which the medium is poured into the hollowed-
out bed of a heavy gold setting—heavy in order to tolerate
the tremendous heat in which enamels are fired. Cloisonné
enamels are designed with wire "cloisons" (partitions), and
the colors are laid within the frames.

Guilloche enamels are those in which a metal surface is
machine-engraved with concentric or regularly repeated
patterns and then coated with a translucent enamel that
allows the pattern beneath to show through. Guilloche
was a specialty of the Russian firm Fabergé, whose clientele were European aristocracy and whose French-influenced guilloche, cloisonné, and gem-set jewelry had its
fine but fragile moment (as did its patrons) just
before World War I.

Plique-à-jour enamel, a difficult technique in
which transparent, unbacked colored enamel is

suspended like stained glass within metal frames, is particularly hard to find, as little was manufactured and, naturally, much broke; consequently it's rare. But the fluidity of plique-à-jour was the ideal technique for the Art Nouveau designs in which it is usually seen.

STYLES

P robably the easiest way to date jewelry is by style and/or subject. In the sixteenth century, the newly emergent bourgeois matron began to patronize the newly independent "jeweler," who until then had been classed among the goldsmiths. (Interestingly, Renaissance painters like Dürer, Verrocchio, and Holbein were either sons of goldsmiths or their pupils.) Finger rings and pendants were favorites of the era, either encrusted with seed pearls and foil-backed cabochon jewels, or painted with enamel grotesques and arabesques—as were portrait miniatures on vellum. Jewels of the Renaissance were highly pictorial, in fact, until the invention of the rose-cut diamond in 1640, when jewelry was converted from a pictorial to a gem-set art, one in which value became almost wholly dependent, as it remains today, on the size and quality of its diamonds and precious stones. The brooch, the characteristic jewel of the late seventeenth and early eighteenth centuries, glittered with cut gems, particularly in the form of diamond-set bows in unobtrusive silver mounts. At this time, gold was reserved for colored stones such as emeralds.

When the brilliant-cut was devised for diamonds early in the eighteenth century, it found instant popularity, particularly when fashioned into stylish flower sprays, the stones clustered together and the metal practically invisible. Floral-design earrings, brooches, and necklaces were popular throughout the eighteenth and into the nineteenth century, which was when stones first began to be set in prongs, rather than in closed-back metal boxes. This major innovation in stone-setting

NINETEENTH-CENTURY VICTORIAN SNAKE BRACELET

A ccording to appraiser Dianne Lewis, the snake motif in Victorian jewelry flourished throughout Europe after Prince Albert gave Queen Victoria a snake engagement ring in 1839. One example of Victorian snake jewelry brought to the *Roadshow* was made of flexible gold, the top of the head set with diamonds and each eye with a ruby.

The owner suspected that his great-grandmother's snake bracelet was French, and according to the *Poinçons d'Or* (a French book of international jewelry marks) the mark of two heads on the tail indicates that it was indeed exported from France. Lewis dated it from the 1860s and valued it at $3,000.

This French bracelet combines the best of Victorian elements—cameos, frosted gold, filigree, and classical embellishment.

By the fabled Fabergé, a guilloche enamel varicolored gold and silver mounted table clock, c. 1890.

The pieces of glass in this Victorian micromosaic yellow metal pendant and stickpin are coarse and clumsily inlaid. Fine micromosaic is fashioned in colored stone.

meant that it was no longer possible to enhance the color of a poor stone with foil, and accordingly the quality of cut stones improved. Strengthened by a thin layer of gold on the back, silver "open settings" are a fairly good indicator of nineteenth-century origin.

Cameos were also an eighteenth-century fashion, especially after the discovery of Pompeii. Even Wedgwood plaques and cut steel became fashionable and relatively inexpensive substitutes for stones in brooches and rings. Mourning jewelry of painted ivory mounted in delicate ovals foreshadowed the jet and hair jewelry of the Victorian era to come.

VICTORIAN STYLES

Because so much fine jewelry was destroyed during the French Revolution, most of what remains is Victorian. Queen Victoria ruled England from 1837 to 1901, a time of growing prosperity and technological advancement, when, for the first time, the middle class could afford to own fine jewelry. The queen was young when she came to the throne, and everything she did and wore became fashionable. When she married in white, young women chose white for their wedding gowns ever after. When her consort presented her with a snake-form ring, thousands of snake rings turned up to tempt all Europe.

Like Victorian furniture, Victorian jewelry is more than a touch ornate. Certainly, its excesses of bouquets, cupids, insects, scrollwork, engraving, and gem-set hearts seem over the top to modern sensibilities. Yet it has always been popular because—an occasional tendency to ponderousness aside—Victorian jewels are beautifully crafted and essentially feminine.

Every type of jewel was popular during this eclectic period: lockets with glazed compartments for hair, colorful reproductions of Renaissance jewels, realistic floral designs, parures (matching sets comprising variants on one necklace, two bracelets, one brooch, and a pair of earrings), blackamoor jewelry, Scottish pebble jewelry, crescent and

Selected Makers and Marks

CASTELLANI
(1830–1900)

ITALY Rediscovered and popularized, in the mid-nineteenth century, the ancient Etruscan technique for granulated gold jewelry. Castellani wares are almost invariably marked.

TIFFANY & CO. *(from 1837)*

UNITED STATES
Imported jewelry from Europe until 1848, when the firm began to create its own Paris-inspired pieces. Louis Comfort Tiffany, son of the founder and designer of lamps and a small amount of unusual jewelry, took over the firm in 1902.

FABERGÉ
(1842–1920?) **ФАБЕРЖЕ**

RUSSIA Celebrated for its Louis XVI-style enameled and bejeweled clocks, umbrella handles, large and small Easter eggs, and other, often fabulous objects and bibelots. Fabergé did not neglect the Slavic style, making typically Russian, colorful cloisonné enamel pieces. The firm's jewelry often incorporates precisely set sapphires or amethysts, rubies, diamonds, or garnets and ranges from minuscule egg charms to animal and peasant figures carved of semiprecious stones. The name of the firm is most often—not always—written in Cyrillic letters.

CARTIER *(from 1847)*

FRANCE Produced diamond-set jewelry in the *Cartier* elegant, eighteenth-century "garland style" before World War I, but reached its peak in the 1920s, creating quintessential Art Deco bijoux—frosted rock crystal and carved gemstones set in colorful combinations with diamonds, and, especially, fine guilloche enamel and precious stone *objets de vertu.*

BOUCHERON *(from 1858)*

FRANCE Created large scrolled or oval pins, inlaid in geometric and/or stylized shell patterns with coral, lapis, and carved jade. Also produced fashionable zigzag, geometric, and floral jewels, often outlining bouquets in black enamel and diamonds.

GIULIANO
(c. 1860–1914)

**CG
C.&A.G.**

ENGLAND Produced exceptionally finely crafted enameled and jeweled pieces in Gothic and Renaissance styles. The founder's sons continued the firm into the twentieth century, creating jewelry that was more naturalistic and delicate than their father's.

RENÉ LALIQUE *(1860–1945)*

FRANCE Created imaginative Art **R LALIQUE** Nouveau jewels, often in combinations of materials like horn, enamel, and diamonds. In 1914, Lalique stopped making jewelry and turned to glass. Lalique jewelry is quite rare.

UNGER BROTHERS
(1878–1914)

UNITED STATES In contrast to the extensive tablewares manufactured by other American firms, specialized in French-influenced silver jewelry and small household articles. Founded in Newark, New Jersey, the firm was particularly successful with designs in the Art Nouveau style of trailing vines, dragonflies, swirls, and streams. Its line of Art Nouveau jewelry is particularly sought after by collectors.

GEORG JENSEN *(from 1904)*

DENMARK Although Jensen jewelry, with its stylized floral motifs, is always crafted of silver, it is highly collectible today.

VAN CLEEF AND ARPELS
(from 1906)

FRANCE In the mid-1930s, produced the "Ludo Hexagone" bracelet, a wide, flexible bracelet formed of small honeycomb plaques of gold, frequently set with tiny rubies or diamonds. The style was copied, with and without elaborate jeweled clasps, throughout the following decade.

GEORGES FOUQUET

FRANCE Along with **Raymond Templier, Gerard Sandoz,** and **Jean Despres,** joined the Union des Artistes Modernes in 1929. Artists and jewelers, this group designed and crafted its own geometric, Cubist, linear, and altogether novel jewels.

1 9 4 0 S
B R A C E L E T

Appraiser Joyce Jonas was completely enamored of a gold bracelet purchased by its owner at an estate sale. Jonas described the bracelet as a wonderful example of what 1940s jewelry was all about. All the elements of that time were perfectly reflected in its design, for not only is the linked pyramid design meant to mimic tank tracks, but the various shades of gold (yellow and green), and the small rubies and diamonds coupled with large semiprecious stones from South America, typified an era hampered by the tremendous shortage of materials during World War II.

The real value of the bracelet, however, was in the fact that it is just as wearable today as when it was made. Its timeless quality is the reason that this piece, purchased for $1,500, is valued at $6,000.

Machinery translates into a massive diamond bracelet, c. 1940, the essence of Retro style.

star shapes, and micromosaic jewelry. The Victorians favored turquoises, amethysts, dark blue or green enamels, half-pearls, carbuncles (almandine garnets), and agates. Examples of Victorian jewelry are readily available today and are a collectors' treasure-trove.

T W E N T I E T H - C E N T U R Y   S T Y L E S

Art Nouveau jewelry, a brief style of 1895 to 1910, was sinuous, flowing, and vaguely surreal with naturalistic overtones. For the first time, the entire female figure appeared in jewelry, often depicted amid scrolls of hair, water, peacock feathers, foliage—or all of the above. Pastel enamel work, in both cloisonné and plique-à-jour, was characteristic of the period.

More jewelry was purchased in England between the years 1900 and 1920 than ever before in history. During the Edwardian period, called "the Belle Epoque" in America, brilliant white diamonds caught in webs of platinum were inspired by the feminine aesthetic of eighteenth-century France. Edwardian jewels were delicate in appearance, with fine-spun platinum detail and every possible edge mille-grained. Flowers, leaves, hearts and pairs of hearts, tassels, bowknots, and, especially and most typically, garlands created delicate frames for stones that, despite their all-pervasive glitter, were almost completely subordinate to design.

Imagine the Chrysler Building or Rockefeller Center in Manhattan as a brooch or earrings. Surprisingly, architecture works as jewelry, and it worked best in the 1920s, when Art Deco jewelry (the finest of which is now in short supply) was crafted into dazzling, geometric architectonic designs. Art Deco diamond pieces, especially the creations of French jewelers, often incorporated inexpensive colored stones—onyx, agate, and chrysoprase (green agate) with diamonds—or, often, combinations of rubies, sapphires, and carved emeralds, known colloquially as "fruit salad." Such pieces also incorporated cultured pearls, which first appeared on the market in 1921. Among typical Art Deco motifs were diamond baskets brimming with carved and cabochon fruits;

flowers; circles, rectangles, and squares in diamonds; Egyptian figures; and Persian, Indian, and African subjects. Inexpensive Art Deco jewels and both contemporary and modern copies (made from castings in unimaginative styles) usually used rather small stones, and an examination of the backs of such pieces generally reveals crude workmanship.

The 1930s was the era of "white" jewelry—diamonds simply set in platinum without the leavening of the colored stones of the 1920s. Clip fittings first appeared on the backs of earrings in the 1930s, replacing screwbacks or wires. And particularly typical of 1930s style were vaguely triangular pairs of dress clips with spring fasteners at the back, useful on lapels or for emphasizing businesslike and primly décolleté necklines.

By 1937, the platinum fad was over and yellow gold had reappeared. By the 1940s, polished yellow gold jewelry, scrolled and draped in bold, chunky designs and somewhat mechanical in appearance (even when curved), was *de rigueur.* Large, flexible gold links gleamed on every neck and wrist. Semiprecious stones—citrines and clear quartz crystals cut in bold, geometric shapes—became fashionable, due in some measure to wartime shortages of other jewels. Termed "retro" today, such designs, often in pink, green, or white gold (created by the addition of alloying metals) and adorned with colored stones, reflected the industrial might that would win the war.

FOLK JEWELRY

Native American jewelry is today highly collectible, though the trade in jewelry began with simple bartering, when, in the nineteenth century, Mexicans and Navajos traded their jewelry for horses. Bartering turned swiftly into business, however, and by the twentieth century much of the weaving and pottery that had been sold to supplement tribal income was supplanted by the more commercially successful turquoise and silver jewelry.

Navajo jewelry is among the best known of American Indian wares. In 1895, the Navajos were the first tribe to

A silver Hopi bracelet, ornamented with finely worked sun motifs.

Above: A Zuni "petit point" necklace in silver and turquoise with silver pendants. Below: Typically chunky, a turquoise and silver Navajo squash-blossom necklace, c.1908.

Indian wares. In 1895, the Navajos were the first tribe to employ the technique of sandcasting. Most of their very bold pieces were decorated with simple designs worked in silver and decorated with locally mined turquoise. Late-nineteenth-century pieces have filed or chiseled engravings, while pieces from early in the twentieth century incorporate chunky stones and Mexican motifs. Important Navajo squash-blossom necklaces, grand displays of turquoise matrix inlay, are currently quite expensive and desirable, and have been for decades.

Unlike the Najavos, Hopi jewelers use few stones in their creations. Hopi jewelry can be recognized by its characteristic blackened and pitted silver-overlay designs.

Zuni jewelry, which provides much of the modern tribe's income, has rows and/or groups of turquoises, each set in delicately worked silver, or mosaics of turquoise in combination with shell and jet, mother of pearl and coral. Native craftsmen prefer to work with small stones.

FURTHER READING

Bennett, David, and Ascetti, Daniela. *Understanding Jewelry.* Woodbridge, Suffolk, England: Antique Collectors Club, 1996.

Giles, Stephen. *Miller's Jewelry.* London: Reed Consumer Books, 1997.

Lyman, Kennie. *Gems and Precious Stones.* New York: Simon & Schuster, 1986.

Matlins, Antoinette, and Bonnano, A.C. *Gem Identification Made Easy.* Woodstock, VT: GemStone Press, 1997.

Newman, Renee. *Ruby and Sapphire Buying Guide.* Los Angeles: International Jewelry Publications, 1996.

Chapter Six

CLOCKS AND WATCHES

In the long, slow history of the decorative arts, clocks and watches—traditionally a male preserve—are a fairly modern convenience. The first truly useful timepieces date to the sixteenth century. Clocks and watches did not become ornamental objects until some time later.

A dual market then evolved. Clocks and watches could be considered jewelry or furniture, "just another pretty face" (which some collectors prefer), or appreciated as the mechanical marvels they are, featuring "complications" like split-second chronographs, moon phases, and tourbillons (more appealing to mechanism-oriented collectors). "Grandfather" clocks, for instance, known formally as tallcase clocks in America and longcase clocks in Great Britain, can be abundantly decorated in elegant wood, lacquer, or bronze-mounted cases, as can mantel clocks, carriage

This sixteenth-century clock from the infancy of timekeeping looks cumbersome but displays dazzling craftsmanship.

The fine essence of a novelty watch: a jeweled pistol with a watch in its handle.

A highly complex brass and wood clock with four faces, numerous dials, and figuratively, at least, "all the bells and whistles."

clocks, wall clocks, and bracket clocks. Other shapes are housed in gilt bronze, silver, diamonds, or gold. And while any of these might be artistic enough, fine enough, or decorative enough to qualify as valuable decorative art, they might also house boring, but functionally adequate, movements.

Serious timepiece collectors care less for the decorative housing than for the "soul" of a timepiece—its movement, the ingenious arrangements of gears and springs, jewels and rods, that keep the time, and keep it to the neat split-second. In eras when men of mechanical mindset weren't engineering missiles, computers, or automobiles, they were honing their considerable mechanical talents on increasingly sophisticated timepieces: lavishing finely made gears on them; fitting them to keep track of phases of the moon, days, months, years; and often losing their eyesight in the demanding service of ever more accurate time. The place in history of these early clock- and watchmakers, whose inventiveness and craftsmanship still impress us today, is guaranteed because they almost always signed their work.

Pocket watches and wristwatches, like clocks, can be pretty but ordinary, or they can be plain but able to keep the railroad running; they may have a dozen, sometimes noisy complications (including chimes, alarms, and music), or they may be beautiful but "dumb." Watches of gold or silver, set with stones, engraved or enameled, were both status symbols (as they are today) and marvelous, magical toys. Fitted with miniature mechanized scenes of Rebecca hauling water at the well, firemen quenching a fire, or highly explicit erotic tableaux, watches were prized and collected in the eighteenth century. Yet precision of movement, not complicated automation, is and always has been the watchmaker's dream. Watchmakers have always sought the mechanism that could tell the seconds, the date, the time of day in Ireland and Rangoon, and strike the hour, the half-hour, the quarter-hour, and play "Non Piú Andrai"—all within a two-inch case.

Wonderful, functional toys, these watches and clocks. Fragile ones, too, and yet surprisingly sturdy. "My Grandfather's Clock," that dear old song about the clock that "stopped short" on the day its owner died, is poignant but misleading. A timepiece that has seemingly stopped forever is seldom irreparably dead. Sometimes a squirt of oil can get it going again. Other times it may require a lot more (a new hand-cut gear, for instance). But after all, the truly worthwhile in life always requires maintenance. Which is why we wear quartz.

ANATOMY OF A TIMEPIECE

Once upon a time, clocks were as fashionable as the latest-model cars are today and could be purchased, like cars, primarily on the basis of their appearance (the case) or their performance (the movement). There were luxury-model timepieces, available with all the options, and economy models—simple devices that just told time. But the keeping of precise time, with better than hourglass accuracy, was slow in arriving. And, like the car, it required wheels and gears.

All timepieces consist of three parts: the movement, the case, and the dial.

THE MOVEMENT

The movement is the set of mechanical parts that drives the hands around the face of the clock. It is important to know, however, that there are two basic types of clock movement: the spring-driven clock, which is propelled by

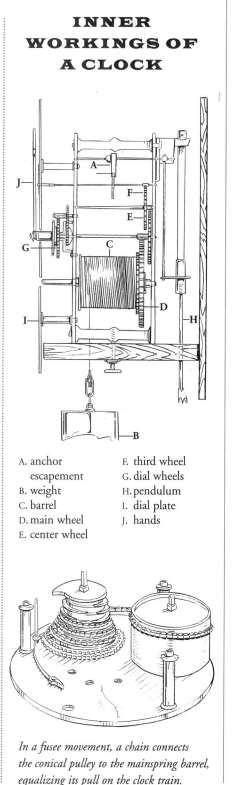

INNER WORKINGS OF A CLOCK

A. anchor escapement
B. weight
C. barrel
D. main wheel
E. center wheel
F. third wheel
G. dial wheels
H. pendulum
I. dial plate
J. hands

In a fusee movement, a chain connects the conical pulley to the mainspring barrel, equalizing its pull on the clock train.

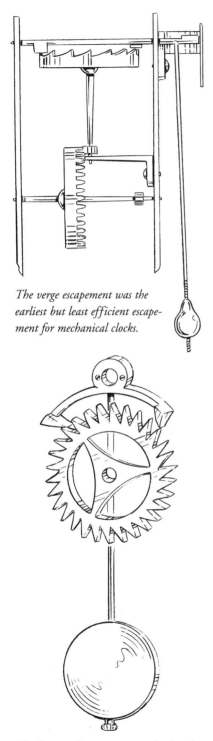

The verge escapement was the earliest but least efficient escapement for mechanical clocks.

The later anchor escapement, developed c. 1650, allowed long pendulums to swing more slowly.

the uncoiling of springs, and the weight-driven clock, which is powered by the dropping of weights. In both movements, a series of intermeshing gears revolves and moves the hands of the clock around the dial at a precisely measured pace. The exactness of this timekeeping is regulated by the escapement, the mechanism that allows the power trapped in the wound spring or the hoisted weights to "escape" in a controlled manner. As the weight drops or the spring unwinds, tension is released. (The movement of the escapement causes that familiar "ticktock" sound.)

Strictly speaking, a clock that only keeps time and does nothing else is referred to as a timepiece, although we'll use the term less rigorously here. A clock that strikes or chimes the hours on a bell or a gong is called a striking clock. In the latter, one weight or spring drives the clockworks and another weight or spring drives the chimes. Until the advent of the battery-driven movement, c. 1900, clocks had to be wound, usually every eight days, although the period could be as little as one day (or thirty hours) or as long as several months to a year. (Collectors prize long-running clocks.)

Before the creation of the spring-driven movement, all clocks were large, awkward, weight-driven devices, with hour hands only. The invention of the spiral spring, or mainspring, finally allowed them to become portable: not quite wristwatches yet, but still timekeepers that one could carry from room to room—for only the wealthy owned more than one or two clocks.

In England, clocks have chimed for centuries. Big Ben's fourteenth-century precursor was a great bell that struck every hour. And its current chime is taken from the fifth bar of Handel's *Messiah*, "I know that my Redeemer liveth." But some clocks don't stop at simple chiming. Some are capable of striking the hours and quarters and minutes on gongs—spiraled metal bands. In the early part of the twentieth century, grandiose clocks were available with elaborate sets of tubular chimes, almost capable of playing the entire *Messiah* from first bar to last.

THE CASE

The case houses the clock movement and protects it from dust and accidents. It was almost never made by the clockmaker. Instead, the clock mechanism would be passed from the "mechanic" (who often inscribed his name on it) to a second craftsman—a cabinetmaker, porcelain manufacturer, or bronze sculptor, often a recognized artist in his field—for whom the clock case, large or small, was a blank canvas awaiting decoration.

Case designs, naturally, tended to closely follow fashions in furniture. Late-eighteenth-century cases were in the Chippendale style, and Empire cases in the Classical style. Most commonly, clock cases were made of wood, an inexpensive and infinitely workable material that lent itself well to almost endless adornment, particularly to being veneered. Veneer could be laid in quarters, its matched grains creating handsome patterns, or elaborately inlaid with floral or geometric shapes and mounted with brass or bronze fittings. Wood cases could be lacquered black, red, green, or yellow, in imitation of exotic and desirable Chinese wares, or painted, gilded, and ebonized. Mantel and table clock cases in dazzling gilt bronze could be embellished in porcelain, brass, or costly silver, paved in Tiffany glass mosaic, and occasionally gold- and diamond-studded.

Even the backs of such clocks were ornamental. The brass backplates of mantel clocks, for instance, which bore the maker's signature, were frequently engraved and luxuriously finished, since the backs might be seen reflected in over-mantel mirrors.

The only thing that kept clock design from running completely rampant was aesthetic restraint: if the case was *too* flamboyant, who could bear to look at it thirty or so times a day? Thus, the truly perfect case became an elegantly beautiful housing for the equally elegant and beautiful mechanism it contained.

A characteristically restrained English marquetry longcase clock of the William and Mary era.

William and Mary brass clock face with applied chapter ring, calendar aperture, subsidiary dial, and applied brass corner spandrels.

Mahogany, poplar, and iron tallcase clock, John Riley, Philadelphia, 1800–1810.

THE DIAL AND HANDS

The dial, or face, of the clock, displays the time. While the simplest eighteenth- and early-nineteenth-century American dials were made of painted wood (inexpensive, but likely to warp or split), painted metal dials were also affordable favorites. Both types could be embellished with painted floral bouquets or scenes of daily life. The all-white enameled dial, though more costly, provided the brightest and easiest-to-read background for the numerals, while the all-brass dial, frequently engraved or finished with a dull-gold matte surface, was the most elaborate and expensive. (High-quality silvered brass dials, incidentally, have often been polished down to the brass base metal and today look like brass.)

We seldom focus on clock hands themselves, but they, too, are delicate works of art. Clock hands were customarily made of blued steel (steel treated with a high-heat process intended to keep them from rusting) and were available in a variety of arrow-like shapes, ranging from exceptionally fanciful examples tipped with curls and arabesques and incorporating pierced designs (on eighteenth-century clocks) to the increasingly minimal, modern, severe, but still arrow-form hands we use today. To some extent, it is possible to date a clock by the hands. Gilt-metal clock hands, for example, became particularly common in the last part of the nineteenth century.

Timepieces with complications often do not have dials like the usual clock or watch. Several things may seem to be happening on the face of a mechanically interesting piece or, conversely, fewer things than one would expect to see.

IS IT OLD?

Determining the age of a timepiece depends a great deal on the type of clock or watch it is. Because different types were made during the same time period, you may see mechanical advances in one type of clock that do not appear in another example of the same age.

Some advancements clearly mark your timepiece as modern: batteries, electric cords, and plastic or celluloid parts, for example. For details on determining age, see the "What to Look For" section for each type of clock discussed.

IS IT VALUABLE?

There are four criteria for determining if a clock or watch has value. While mechanical complexity, the reputation of the maker, and a fine aesthetic all contribute to the value of a timepiece, first and foremost is condition. Collectors want their timepieces to be in original condition and, ideally, to work.

♦ If the movement of a timepiece has been extensively repaired, if crucial mechanical parts are no longer the original ones, or, most disastrously, if case and movement were not born together, value will be significantly diminished.

♦ Often, clocks or watches that strike the hour, the quarter-hour, the minute (in ascending order of value) also play music or incorporate moving figures and are more valuable than any ordinary timepiece. It can be very expensive to repair such timepieces, however, and never easy to find knowledgeable and competent repair persons.

♦ Old clocks that have to be wound daily are not as desirable as eight-day clocks. Although clock winding may have once been a comforting daily ritual, the average modern purchaser of an antique clock can seldom find the time for such routine.

♦ Most clocks—tallcase, bracket, carriage, shelf, and banjo—are signed or labeled by their makers. The signature of the clockmaker will be of only documentary interest, however, unless it is that of an *important*

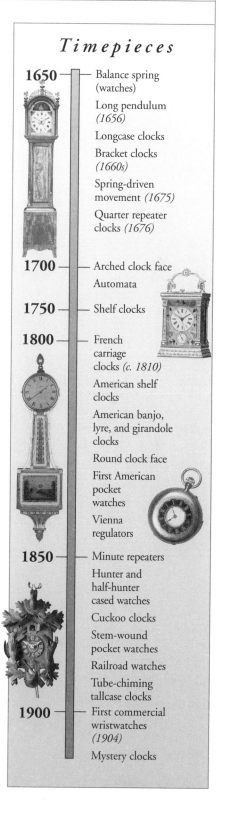

Timepieces

1650 — Balance spring (watches)

Long pendulum *(1656)*

Longcase clocks

Bracket clocks *(1660s)*

Spring-driven movement *(1675)*

Quarter repeater clocks *(1676)*

1700 — Arched clock face

Automata

1750 — Shelf clocks

1800 — French carriage clocks *(c. 1810)*

American shelf clocks

American banjo, lyre, and girandole clocks

Round clock face

First American pocket watches

Vienna regulators

1850 — Minute repeaters

Hunter and half-hunter cased watches

Cuckoo clocks

Stem-wound pocket watches

Railroad watches

Tube-chiming tallcase clocks

1900 — First commercial wristwatches *(1904)*

Mystery clocks

S C O T T I S H
G R A N D F A T H E R
C L O C K

This guest did not believe the story the salesman told her when she bought a grandfather clock in Chicago in 1969: it supposedly had been given to the previous owner by William Randolph Hearst. According to Gordon S. Converse, the signature on the dial, which reads "A W Marshall/Wishaw," identifies it as Scottish, made by the Marshall family of clockmakers between 1820 and 1825.

The spandrels contain portrait miniatures of four Scottish literary figures, including Robert Burns and a scene from his "Cotter's Saturday Night." The gilt hands in the form of a thistle are very Scottish. Although the clock is missing the finial as well as its columns, it is worth $6,000 to $7,000 today.

maker, for only an important maker's name will increase the value of a clock.

♦ Dials should not be crazed or cracked, although replacement hands, if not glaringly obvious (out of scale, out of period), do not seriously affect value.

♦ Any timepiece with a replaced movement, either battery-driven or electric, is worthless as an antique.

CLOCKS

Before the nineteenth century, homeowners certainly might have *liked* to have a clock in every room—at least in the bedroom, the kitchen, and the hall (which is where clocks usually were)—but most didn't. Clocks were expensive, luxury items. Despite this, if you multiply all the homes that might have housed a clock in the last two hundred years by only one or two timepieces, you can easily understand why so many clocks are still in existence. Though each clock in turn was made obsolete by some exciting technological advance—the capacity to track the phases of the moon, for instance, or the advent of the second hand—old-fashioned models were often cherished.

TALLCASE CLOCKS

The turning point in the history of timekeeping came with the invention of the pendulum in the mid-seventeenth century. The short pendulum, combined with a verge escapement, allowed the addition of a minute hand. But short pendulums swung in a wide arc and kept frustratingly imperfect time. The subsequent long pendulum, combined with the anchor escapement, provided the coveted accuracy—allowing seconds hands to be added—yet also required protection from bumps and knocks. Thus the pendulum was enclosed in a tall, narrow case made to stand upright on the floor. (All tallcase clocks must be firmly anchored because the pendulum causes the case to move in sympathy with it, thereby stopping the clock.) Such cases sometimes had to be screwed to the wall through the back of the case, for they could be so top-heavy that when the weights could be fully wound up, the clocks were inclined to topple over.

The longcase English clock, which kept excellent time for eight days before needing to be rewound and tolled the hours on a bell, was unequaled in the late seventeenth to the early eighteenth century. The elaborately inlaid London-made clocks of the early part of this period are enthusiastically collected today, not just for their sophisticated, dependable movements, but also for their perfectly proportioned, coolly elegant form. Longcase clocks continued to be produced in England well into the 1830s and were the most widely produced of English clocks, but craftsmanship was never again as fine as it was in these early models.

The American tallcase clock was produced primarily in Pennsylvania, Connecticut, and Massachusetts. Because brass was scarce in Colonial America, many models were made with wooden movements. (For that same reason, dials on early American tallcase clocks were made of painted metal rather than brass.) These old wooden movements, now somewhat rare, have shrunk, warped, and cracked through the years and no longer keep useful time. But many old clocks keep excellent time. Chippendale and Federal tallcase clocks had English movements, with British place-names on their dials, and it's easy to confuse these with American place-names. Fortunately, as with American furniture, their cases are classifiable by region, for certain construction techniques were characteristic of particular areas. The paper labels often found within American clocks can reveal the history of the clock—the name of the maker, the place and the date it was made—and frequently, information on maintenance and care.

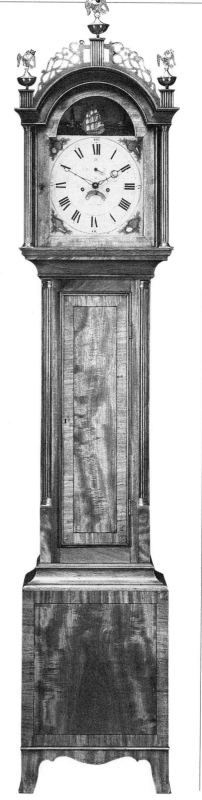

A mahogany tallcase clock with perfect proportions, eagle finials, and, most important, the Willard label.

A fine and typical Dutch burl walnut longcase striking clock; movement by Thomas Monkhouse of London, mid-eighteenth century.

Most American collectors prefer to look for American clocks. One way to distinguish an American tallcase clock from its English counterpart is by the "whale's tails," the carved scrollwork crowning the hood.

Dutch clockmakers were early leaders in the field. The Dutch were among the original inventors, in fact, of both the pendulum and the balance spring. But while Dutch movements were exquisitely complex mechanisms, Dutch longcase clocks were extravaganzas of the casemaker's art: angels trumpeted from their grandiose hoods, doors were decorated with explosions of rococo marquetry, and typically Dutch *bombé* (curved and swelling) bases balanced on animal-paw feet. Highly ornamental and ever popular among collectors, Dutch tallclocks are somehow droll and pompous at once.

TALLCASE CLOCKS: WHAT TO LOOK FOR

The movement of the tallcase clock is often no longer the original one. A new movement may have been put in an old case, an old movement in a new case, or an original movement that was broken or lost may have been replaced by the clockmaker with a similar mechanism he had in stock. You can determine this by carefully removing the hood and looking to see if the clockworks seem to be standing on a block of wood that looks newer or is lighter or darker than the other wood of the interior. The wood block, which makes the works stand a little taller, is a sure sign of a mismatch.

♦ On the front of the clock, gaps between the clock dial and the wooden hood can indicate a change in the movement, for original movements will fit snugly into the surrounding frame.

♦ If the dial has old holes that have been plugged, this can indicate a new dial on the movement.

♦ It is important that the case not be damaged or missing original parts. This means that a tallcase clock should have the feet, hood, and trunk it was "born" with. And if the clock has its original metal or wood finials, that's a distinct plus.

♦ Painted faces depicting moons or rural or maritime scenes are typical of clocks made in the English provinces until the mid-nineteenth century. Although such country clocks can be charming, their movements are seldom technically sophisticated. You are more likely to find a potentially interesting English or Continental movement in a clock that has an elaborately decorated face in brass or silvered brass.

♦ Very tall clocks that don't fit readily into today's rooms are seldom as desirable as clocks under eight feet tall.

BRACKET, SHELF, AND MANTEL CLOCKS

All these spring-driven clocks were designed to sit on a support. In America, they were usually found on a wood shelf or a mantel; on the Continent, they sometimes sat on a bracket, or small ornamental shelf.

EUROPEAN CLOCKS

The European bracket clock, made contemporaneously with the longcase clock (seventeenth and eighteenth centuries), was a miniature version of the latter, with a "hood" section for the movement and dial, and a shortened trunk that housed an abbreviated pendulum. It was intended to stand on a piece of furniture or on a wall bracket that generally matched the clock case. Most such clocks chimed the hour; sometimes, the quarter-hour as well.

English bracket clocks, the most sought-after type, usually had a handle on the top so they could be easily carried from room to room. The sides of the case were frequently inset with a metal grille that allowed the chime to be clearly heard. The door at the back of the case was usually made of glass, and more than a few such clocks

William and Mary quarter-repeating ebonized bracket clock.

Though rarely found together, the wall-mounted bracket and the clock that was meant to rest on it created, en suite, a type of "wall" clock.

Shelf clock by Eli Terry,
mid-nineteenth century.

were fitted with a mysterious cord at one side. A pull on the knob of the cord caused the clock to "repeat," or chime the last hour struck—an invaluable convenience for insomniacs before the era of electric light. Among the most valuable bracket clocks were those made by Thomas Tompion, the greatest of English horologists and clockmakers. Tompion was so celebrated for the superb craftsmanship of his complex clock movements that upon his death in 1713 he was interred in Westminster Abbey.

AMERICAN CLOCKS

The American shelf clock was similar to the bracket clock. Its movement was spring-driven, and it had a short pendulum. The first American shelf clocks were made c. 1800 by Massachusetts clockmaker Simon Willard and his brother Aaron. A much more conveniently sized clock, about half the height of the first Willard models, was eventually patented by Connecticut clockmaker Eli Terry (1772–1852).

Made first with a wood movement and then with brass, the finest of Terry's clocks were the dainty "pillar and scroll" models, perfectly combining accurate timekeeping and versatility of size with elegance of design.

American shelf clocks were fashioned with either thirty-hour or eight-day movements, and they struck the hour on a coiled gong. They are more interesting for their decorative qualities than for their mechanics, but then, America's primary contribution to horology was its mass production techniques rather than its inventive craftsmanship. Such techniques, in fact, were the foundation of Terry's success. The advent of a method for manufacturing inexpensive rolled brass allowed him to make, for the first time, interchangeable clock parts. With their painted-tin or even paper dials, Terry clocks could thus be sold for only a dollar or so, and large numbers—

Perhaps the simplest and most common of American shelf clocks is the clock with the ogee-molded wood frame. If the reverse-painted panel is damaged, the clock is less desirable.

in lyre forms, steeples, and sturdy rectangular forms—were sent abroad. Although Terry's company was the first in America to produce affordable clocks in quantity, its supremacy in the market was eventually superseded by the even less expensive products of Seth Thomas.

Working in Connecticut, Seth Thomas mass-produced sturdy and versatile movements so effectively that his American product eventually ended the English domination of the clock field. Among several Seth Thomas models, the rather graceless ogee clock is the clock most frequently seen. The ogee clock has a wide, simply molded mahogany frame, usually with a single glazed door divided horizontally by a wood strip. Above this divide is the dial; below it, a glazed panel, sometimes reverse-painted on the glass with a landscape, figures, animals, or historic scenes. The movement of the American wall clock is usually labeled by the clockmaker, who also frequently glued his card within the case.

FRENCH CLOCKS

For the French, a clock's primary function was decorative, although precision was also important. Luxurious materials like gilt-bronze, marble, and lacquer suited French taste nicely, and French clockmakers came to specialize in unusual case forms—martial trophy-clocks, for example, or Classical figure- and flower-form clocks, or exotic and amusing elephant- or rhinoceros-shaped clocks. While there are several well-regarded Parisian clockmakers—among them, A.L. Breguet, inventor in 1801 of the sophisticated tourbillon watch movement—French clocks as a group are collectible as much for their elaborate and imaginative cases as for their movements.

In the latter part of the nineteenth century, thousands of the then-fashionable girandole sets—mantel clocks with matching candlesticks—were crafted in France.

This amusingly overwrought French Neoclassical timepiece has Father Time in a swan boat with Cupid, beribboned implements, droll webbed feet, and, incidentally, a clock.

Louis XVI ormolu and Carrara marble mantel clock, c.1785.

With gilt incised designs and a decorative dial, this is a better-than-usual example of the common marble mantel clock.

BRACKET, SHELF, AND MANTEL CLOCKS: WHAT TO LOOK FOR

In the nineteenth century, Tiffany and other American retailers regularly imported English and Continental clocks and stamped the names of their own firms on the dial. In addition to those names, however, movements may be labeled by the actual manufacturer.

♦ There are so many American mantel clocks available to collectors that condition becomes of utmost importance.

♦ Eighteenth- and nineteenth-century English and American bracket clocks were typically made of wood and were most often ebonized (painted black), rather than finished with decorative veneers. American nineteenth-century shelf clocks and banjo clocks will often feature reverse-painted (eglomise) panels.

♦ Look for the clockmaker's signature on the backplate.

♦ Engraved cases and/or backplates are more attractive, and therefore more valuable, than those that have no engraving.

♦ A clock or watch that still has its original key is usually somewhat more valuable.

♦ Highly elaborate German porcelain mantel clocks were made in great quantities at the end of the nineteenth century and are frequently seen today. They may look expensive, but tastes have changed over the past century, so, despite their flamboyance, they are of modest value.

♦ Common in the United States, and thus worth mentioning, was a substantial and ponderous late-nineteenth-century mantel clock made of black Belgian marble or slate, often incised in gold or decorated with colorful marble inserts. Although these clocks tend to look impressive, they were made in great numbers, usually with very inexpensive movements; consequently, though they can be attractive, they are not collectible today.

WALL CLOCKS

In the early nineteenth century, American wall clocks were the special province of the Willard family—Aaron, Simon, and Benjamin. Their famous "banjo" clock had a circular dial and usually a rectangular, reverse-painted, glazed base, the top and bottom connected by a slender throat and the sides outlined in arcs of delicate pierced brass. The banjo clock (named for its shape) is one of only a few truly American clock designs. Ornamental, graceful, and often finely painted and gilded, Willard banjo clocks are still popular among collectors, though they do not usually strike the hour—they "only" keep time.

Regulator clocks are extremely accurate weight-driven wall or floor-standing clocks. In the clockmaker's shop, or in any house with several clocks, the regulator was the precision timekeeper—the clock by which all other clocks were set.

Although regulators were made in several countries, the weight-driven Vienna regulator (made in Vienna between 1800 and 1840) is thought to be the finest ever made. Later clocks, generally termed Vienna regulators, were mass-produced wall clocks and not true regulators. Later copied throughout Germany, precision regulator clocks made in France, England, and eventually America were housed in severe architectonic cases (cases that incorporate architectural elements) usually of mahogany, with glazed doors and sides. The craftsmanship of their dials, their numbers, and even their hands was as superb as their movements.

Above: A regulator clock with a mahogany-and-glass case, Vienna, early nineteenth century.

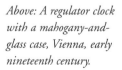

Cuckoo clocks, popular for generations, were frequently purchased as souvenirs.

Diamond-studded numerals and hands with "no visible means of support" characterize this mystery clock.

Because their movements were poor-quality, the "clocks" that enliven the architecture of nineteenth-century painted landscapes are often not working when found.

NOVELTY CLOCKS

In addition to telling time, playing music, and incorporating moving figures—sometimes doing all three things at once—novelty clocks are often interestingly shaped and attention-getting timekeepers. The universally popular cuckoo clock, for instance, which many think of as a Swiss invention, actually originated in the Black Forest area of Germany in the middle of the nineteenth century. (Cuckoo clocks were not made in Switzerland until the twentieth century.) On the hour, a hinged door swings open to reveal a toy cuckoo, whose chirp (created by compressing a small leather bellows) coincides with the striking of the hours. In fine examples, the bird moves its tiny head and opens and closes its beak.

On some clocks, the mechanical figures, or "automata," move in even more elaborate ways. The arms of a figure may lift and fall to strike an hourly bell or swing a scythe to suggest the doleful passage of Father Time. Peasants may dance in and out of double doors while music plays. Although such devices are clever and fun, they have little to do with the fine points of timekeeping.

"Painting" clocks, in which an actual working watch face is set into a (usually) primitively rendered landscape painting—the top of a church steeple, most commonly, or the town hall—are even more gimmicky and far less technically interesting than automata. Collectors, however, love them despite (or even for) their silliness, as they do most novelty timekeepers, particularly pre-1860 examples.

With the advent of the Industrial Revolution, clocks that resembled miniature machines became quite popular; appropriately, their machinery, independent of the mechanism, nicely whirred and turned.

Mystery clocks are perhaps the supreme type of novelty clock. These are precisely crafted, usually expensive clocks with completely concealed (thus, "mysterious") connections between the hands and the mechanism. The hands seem to float in air or water, for example, and appear to work without power or wheels. Cartier was renowned for its elaborate mystery clocks.

CARRIAGE CLOCKS

An earlier style of the portable bronze clock introduced c. 1800 was the *pendule d'officier*, whose name gave rise to the idea that carriage clocks were developed for Napoleon's officers to carry on the march. Although carriage clocks are available in several sizes, they were never very large and were even made in miniature versions. Predominantly French, they invariably had a handle, were glazed on four sides and the top, and came, when new, in a tough, leather carrying case which, over the years, was often lost. Particularly elegant examples from the end of the nineteenth century possess painted or cloisonné enamel panels, front and side, instead of glass, and often elaborately engraved designs on the case.

Early carriage clocks struck the hour on a bell, clearly visible through the glass panel at the back, while later examples struck a gong and often incorporated "repeating" mechanisms, whereby depressing a button on the top of the case caused the last hour struck to be repeated. Even more highly sophisticated models, called *grande sonnerie*, sounded both the hour and the quarter-hour, with, for example, 3:15 being indicated by three single strokes, followed by two strokes on a higher note for the quarter-hour.

CARRIAGE CLOCKS: WHAT TO LOOK FOR

♦ The brass of period (pre-1830) carriage clocks should be of uneven thickness. Modern brass is evenly thick.

♦ If the serial number on the back plate of a carriage clock consists of more than five digits, the clock is

CARTIER TRAVEL CLOCK

This clock's original owner was a woman who traveled frequently. Her granddaughter inherited the clock and brought it to *Roadshow* expert Jonathan Snellenburg, who was able to point out the unmistakable signs of a work by Cartier: first the leather travel case, stamped "Cartier" on the bottom, then the design—a typical Art Deco example of 1920s-style chinoiserie. Small doors on the clock's front open to expose its face in a recognizable (and patented) Cartier design.

Cartier objects, because they are popular, are often faked. But a quick peek behind the rear doors of this clock revealed the French hallmark and the tiny stock number of the authentic piece. Snellenburg appraised the clock at $10,000 to $15,000. Now, that's traveling in style.

Though small and portable, carriage clocks can sometimes have elaborate striking mechanisims.

A pierced cover is often an indication that the watch has a chime or alarm.

modern. If less (and the maker's records are available), the serial number can help determine the date of manufacture.

♦ Finding the maker's name on carriage clocks, can be quite difficult, as the name is often hidden behind the backplate of the mechanism or on its mounting, which only an expert can remove. Almost all, however, were marked.

♦ The name of a well-known retailer on the face of a carriage clock—Tiffany or Cartier, for instance—increases its value.

♦ A button on the top of a carriage clock indicates that it repeats, making it more valuable than a simple timepiece. Carriage clocks that strike the hour on a bell, rather than a gong, are highly collectible.

♦ Between the first and second world wars, there was a renewal of interest in small, portable clocks called boudoir clocks. Often shaped like antique carriage clocks, boudoir clocks were frequently made in costly materials—translucent enamels on silver or gold backgrounds, or brass with porcelain insets.

WATCHES

Personal, portable timekeeping was not really possible until the last quarter of the seventeenth century, when the development of the balance spring or hairspring (which keeps the balance wheel oscillating at a fixed rate) led to a watch capable of counting the minutes as well as the hours. Few very early European watches turn up in the United States—only those that were originally part of watch collections. Early Americans who could afford watches tended to own plain and sturdy English examples. The first American pocket watch, in fact, wasn't made until 1809, and extensive manufacture didn't begin until the 1850s.

The cases of pocket-watch movements were designed to be protective, of course, but they were frequently ornamental. The very oldest watches, those of the seventeenth century, were actually jewelry more than they were precision movements: the movements kept very poor time.

Some early pocket watches had two nested cases, often of differing materials—tough tortoiseshell on the outside, for example, and chased silver within. Alternatively, sometimes the inner case was plain or lightly engraved, while the outer case was highly decorated in *repoussé* or jewels. Having two cases, of course, afforded fragile movements better protection from rain and other damage. Such well-protected watches were known as pair-case watches and were particularly popular in England.

As early as the end of the seventeenth century, pocket watches were capable of striking the hour and the quarter-hour, just as clocks were. A watch with the capacity to strike the hour on demand is termed a repeater if it strikes just the hour; a quarter repeater or minute repeater if it sounds the quarter-hour or the minute. Often the inner case of a pair-case repeater will be pierced around the outside edge so the "repeat" can be heard. This mechanism is initiated either by depressing the stem end of the watch or, in nineteenth-century versions, by sliding a raised thumb piece along the edge of the case.

Since the early seventeenth century, enameled watch cases were a specialty of Geneva watchmakers. In the late eighteenth century, they became the fashionable choice over high-relief (*repoussé*) gold or silver decoration. Enameled watches made of gold and realistically painted in opaque colors with miniatures of Classical figures or landscapes, all surrounded by half-pearls, were popular, and watches were rich showcases for glossily translucent guilloche enamels as well. As was true for clocks, the movements for watches could be manufactured in countries far distant from the makers of the cases that housed them.

The fashion for enameled watches drifted easily into novelty watches, nineteenth-century paragons of both the

Before glass was widely available, the intricacies of early watch movements were often protected with transparent rock crystal covers.

GOLD
POCKET WATCH

While Jonathan Snellenburg took tweezers to the case of a gold-and-silver watch at the Chicago *Antiques Roadshow,* the owner commented that the watch had belonged to her husband's grandfather, a watchmaker in Glasgow, Scotland. The case was round and lined with old, weathered papers. The watch inside was oval and missing a hand.

Snellenburg dated the watch to 1640 and thought it may have been owned by a cardinal. Dials and apertures for the zodiac and hour, days of the week, and phases of the moon revealed that it was an English calendar watch. One of a few made at the time and signed by the clockmaker, Edmund Gilpin of London, it is currently worth $15,000. Snellenburg's opinion: it is very plain—and extremely rare!

jeweler's and the mechanic's art. Tiny gold figures on swings could be made to swoop across the watch face; Moses could strike a rock at the push of a button and unleash twisted glass rods simulating running water; tiny feathered birds could pop up from trapdoors and realistically tweet. The Swiss were masters of these automated watches, along with musical and form watches: whimsical, often jewel-encrusted shapes of pansies, or snuffboxes, or beetles whose spreading wings opened to reveal the dial.

Less spectacular, more affordable, and thus far more common than automated or form watches were eighteenth-century open-face case watches of plain gold or silver with no cover at all over the glass. The backs of such unpretentious timepieces were usually engraved simply or monogrammed, and until the development of the hunter cased (closed-case) watch, they were the commonest pocket watch. The hunter cased watch, with its hinged cover over the dial to protect the glass, was a late-eighteenth-century development and usually unadorned, as was the half-hunting case, invented by either Napoleon or Wellington, depending upon your nationality. Its small glass peephole in the center of the hinged lid and numbers enameled directly on the cover allowed its owner to view the watch hands without snapping open the lid.

POCKET WATCHES

Almost all watches made before the Civil War were wound with a key. Keyless winding became common in the 1860s with machine-made, "stem-wound" watches (wound by twisting a knurled crown). Towns around Boston and Chicago pioneered the mass production of American machine-made watches from the mid-nineteenth century until 1957, ultimately manufacturing thirty-five million inexpensive watches and providing several grades of movement for every kind of case. The Elgin watch company alone produced fifty-five million.

RAILROAD WATCHES

The railroad watch, developed in response to a series of tragic accidents beginning in 1893, set the time by which the railroads ran their trains. Engineers and conductors scheduling runs through several time zones—New York to Chicago, for example—required impeccable timepieces. Because railroad jobs were blue-collar jobs, however, such highly accurate watches also needed to be inexpensive. The result, an affordable triumph of accuracy, was the railroad watch. It was set by pulling a lever out from under the dial (thus users couldn't accidentally reset the watch as it was wound).

By the turn of the nineteenth century and into the twentieth, the railroad watch (like much professional specification equipment today) reached the pockets of the general public. Made by both Waltham and Elgin, among others, its well-known accuracy became an effective selling point, further capitalized upon by having the movement placed in a case embossed with the powerful image of a speeding train. Produced in several qualities, but usually in gold plate or silver plate, a railroad watch could endow the ordinary deskbound fellow with a dependable symbol of adventure and romance.

WRISTWATCHES

The modern wristwatch evolved from the 1890s *montre militaire,* a small pocket watch adapted for wearing on the wrist by artillery officers who needed to time the flight of a shell. Later, during World War I, the convenience of a wristwatch for soldiers became evident, and Rolex produced the first tank watch.

After the war, the wristwatch was disdained as effeminate (women had been dangling tiny watches from their wrists for centuries). Yet something so convenient was far too handy to ignore for long, and eventually, like the carriage

Visible on the edge of this nineteenth-century hunter cased pocket watch (at the right of its stem) is the slide indicating that the watch repeats.

Half-hunter cased pocket watch with Roman numerals standing out in attractive relief against an enameled background.

Cartier curved tank wristwatch: a popular shape.

A white gold and diamond ladies' wristwatch like this one, signed "Ulysse Nardin," has more value as jewelry than as a timekeeper.

Art Deco open-face pocket watch by Patek Philippe & Cie of Geneva, Switzerland.

clock before it, the wristwatch took the postwar world by storm. It was crafted in every conceivable metal, from steel to platinum, and while its small size restricted the size and type of potential embellishment (there was no room for singing birds, for instance), there was still no end, it seemed, to the horological improvements and complications that could be compressed into wristwatch-size movements. Swiss companies like Rolex began to offer refinements in wristwatch timekeeping: automatic or self-winding watches and waterproof watches, split-second chronographs, perpetual calendars, and watches that could track two or more time zones.

Today the wristwatch, one of the few acceptable forms of male jewelry, is a major collecting field. And even wholly modern watches by important makers are eagerly sought after.

WATCHES: WHAT TO LOOK FOR

Ninety-five percent of watches are not valuable. "Almost all the watches ever made still survive," says *Roadshow* clock and watch expert Jonathan Snellenburg. "Have you ever known anyone to throw a watch away?" However, here are a few tips to help you know if you have one of the watches of the lucky 5 percent.

♦ Key-wound pocket watches are usually older than stem-wound watches.

♦ Highly elaborate painted cases, enameled cases, and cases made of gold or set with precious gems are generally more valuable than gold-plated unadorned cases, unless the latter's movement is a fine example by an important maker.

♦ Gold cases, when marked 14K, 18K, or 750 (and be aware that not all are), should be stamped on the inside back cover of the watch. If there is no mark at all, the watch is probably not gold. If the watch is stamped "Guaranteed for [x] years," it is not gold, but gold-plated. The letters GF, anywhere inside a watch case, also indicate that it is gold-filled (i.e., gold-plated).

♦ Nineteenth- and twentieth-century pocket watches are set with jewels (real or synthetic gems set into the movement to facilitate the smooth running of the gears). These watches are more highly crafted and therefore of better quality than those without. A fully jeweled watch train has 17 jewels. Because jewels are harder than brass, they very effectively prevent the wear and elongation of the holes in which the arbor (gear shaft) rides, thereby preserving the watch's accuracy.

♦ Rectangular-shaped wristwatches were fashionable at the close of the twentieth century and more desirable than round ones.

♦ Many American jewelry stores used to put their names on watch dials. Look at the movement, however, for the name of the actual manufacturer. A fine man's watch from the 1930s, for instance, might be marked Tiffany on the dial, and Patek Philippe on the movement.

♦ Because they are considered to be jewelry, ladies' watches seldom bring the prices that men's watches do.

♦ An original gold or platinum watchband increases a watch's desirability.

♦ The heaviness of a pocket watch may indicate that it has a sophisticated movement or a case of solid gold. The heavy watch is always worth a second look.

♦ The subsidiary paraphernalia of watch collecting constitutes a collecting field in itself. For ladies' watches, chatelaines (decorative belt attachments for a matching watch, its key, and a seal, among other things), watch chains, chain slides, and watch pins to secure watches to dresses are all in demand. Collectors of men's watches are often keenly interested in watch

LADIES' WATCHES

Ladies' watches were made throughout the eighteenth and nineteenth centuries and were more elaborate—though less likely to have mechanical complications—than men's watches. Today, for the most part, ladies' watches are collected as antique jewelry. If the movement of a ladies' watch is the work of a highly respected maker or if the watch was originally retailed by a very fine jewelry store, it will be somewhat more collectible than an ordinary example. The thousands of ladies' lapel watches made by Elgin or Waltham in America around 1900—small and often delicately enameled watches attached to a matching pin (a fleur-de-lis or flower shape were frequently used)—are far too common to be valuable. They are usually worth only what the metal they're made from would sell for as scrap.

A lapel watch and pin. In a better example, the watch and pin would be stylistically related to each other.

holders (which stand on night tables to display and support the watch), fobs, seals, chains, and keys, for all such items can be both ornamental and utilitarian.

FURTHER READING

Britten, F.J. *Old Clocks and Watches and Their Makers.* New York: Bonanza Books, 1955.

Bruton, Eric. *Antique Clocks and Clock Collecting.* London: Hamlyn, 1974.

———. *Dictionary of Clocks and Watches.* New York: Bonanza Books, 1963.

Camerer Cuss, T.P., et al. *The Camerer Cuss Book of Antique Watches.* Woodbridge, Suffolk, England: Antique Collectors Club, 1995.

Pearsall, Ronald. *Connoisseur's Guide to Antique Clocks and Watches.* New York: Smithmark, 1998.

Schwartz, D. Marvin. *Collectors' Guide to Antique American Clocks.* Garden City, NJ: Doubleday, 1975.

Shugart, Cooksey. *The Complete Price Guide to Watches.* Paducah, KY: Collectors Books, 1998.

An accessory for the pocket watch: a men's watch fob and seal in Egyptian style, Carter, Yough & Co., 1890s.

Chapter Seven

METALWORK

With the exception of bronze, most of the metals we find in our attics or basements are far from glamorous. Few early craftsmen sculpted iron into marvelous statues or gilded homely gray pewter. Both iron and pewter, in fact, were used for the humblest of objects—hinges, dishes, trivets, and mugs.

This was true not just in America but also in Europe, where, from the dawn of man, weapons along with lighting and kitchen utensils were fashioned from the "base" (common) metals: iron, pewter, copper, and brass. And it was particularly true in Colonial America, where trade with the British was uniquely one-sided: the Crown expected its colonies to ship raw metals to England, then buy back the finished objects. The British encouraged the search for iron ores, but frowned on Colonial products being made from them. And if enough desirable metals couldn't be found in America, England would send them in costly sheet form.

So completely subject to British regulations were the colonies that even had the talent and opportunity existed, metals were simply too precious for Americans to justify using them for such splendors as the intricate brass chandeliers being made in Holland, or the fine iron caskets and locks fashioned in Germany and France.

A pewter porringer fashioned by Paul Revere, c. 1760–1790.

APPLE BUTTER COPPER KETTLE

A copper kettle, used for making apple butter, was the first antique that the guests ever purchased together, and they've had it for the twenty-eight years they've been married. Appraiser Wendell Garrett was excited by it, as it "speaks Pennsylvania in both construction and use." Kettles like it were used for boiling, stewing, and roasting, and were made from sheets of copper imported from England that were put together using dovetailed joints exactly like those in furniture.

While the kettle was typical in every way, it did have one unique feature: the maker's mark stamped on the lip, which made the piece of copper, originally purchased for $30, worth over $2,000 today. Garrett emphasized that it was the craftsman's mark that made it a real treasure and strongly suggested that, since wood dents copper, the owner stop using it to store firewood.

In the 1730s, American metal foundries (some of them, surprisingly, owned by women) advertised that not only did they sell and repair metals, both imported and locally made, but they would buy anything available in old copper, brass, pewter, lead, and iron. Used metals were even taken in trade for services. And they were constantly refashioned and repaired by men who were uniquely capable of working with them all. The patriot Paul Revere is a fine example of the versatility of America's master craftsmen. In his famous portrait, Revere is seen proudly displaying a sample of silver work, his specialty. But he also retailed copper, supervised the casting of iron cannons for the war, made official seals in bronze and brass, engraved the brass plates for the first Continental currency, and cast bronze bells. His fellow metalworkers were equally multifaceted—because they had to be. The objects they created out of metal may have been homelier and plainer than those of their European counterparts, and for the most part more provincial, but their product was ultimately and distinctively American.

Many antique metal objects can still be found today, for they are, of course, durable. But if we arrange the metals in descending order of value—bronze at the top, followed by brass, copper, pewter, and iron—our "finds" will be bottom-heavy. For there is plenty of iron still extant, but little American bronze. And this is an inequity we should surely redress by taking a long and, necessarily, hard look at its statuesque and noble past.

BRONZE

Princely bronze was far too expensive for settlers and pioneers. Consequently, it wasn't until the end of the nineteenth century that American sculptors could begin to work seriously in bronze—when new American wealth commissioned it. The country's best sculptors, Frederic Remington and Augustus Saint-Gaudens, may not have been Michelangelo and Donatello, but the former turn up in America's attics now and then, and the latter don't.

Bronze (an alloy of copper and tin) is the most splendid of the base metals. And while we value it and collect it today, perhaps the Native Americans of the Colonial era valued it most appropriately. Contemporary sources recorded that, in the eighteenth century, they so treasured the large bronze European kettles traded by settlers that they not only broke them up to make implements and weapons, but even buried them with their dead.

Bronze is both harder and more durable than copper, and yet it is highly workable—capable of being hammered, melted, drawn into rods or wire, beaten, chiseled, engraved, gilded, and, most notably, cast. In its natural state, bronze is a warm shade of brownish yellow, though it is distinctly cold to the touch. It resists corrosion and can be given an artificial patina that imitates the effects of oxidation. Yet when it ages naturally, bronze acquires particularly rich patinas of strong, lustrous brown, or brilliant lapis lazuli blue, or sharp, distinctive turquoise-green.

Bronze is also heavy. It is serious, sober, and grave, and thus ideal for statuary. The Greeks and Romans recognized labor-intensive bronze as the appropriate medium for honoring gods, warriors, and legends. They cast bronze from molds, painstakingly chased or engraved it after the cast (called "cold-working" themetal), and sometimes plated it with gold, embellished it with silver, painted it, and inlaid it with stone or glass fingernails, lips, and eyes. Greek images of deities were intended for permanence; their makers knew that bronze would last.

An authentic casting of Remington's The Bronco Buster *will be marked with the foundry mark "Roman Bronze Works, N.Y." and will have a casting number inscribed into the underside of the base. The woolly chaps on the rider will be crisp and rough. The underside of the base will have sockets and bronze pins to hold the figure. Later bronze copies will be both smaller and lighter in weight than the original.*

FREDERIC REMINGTON

In a letter to a friend in 1895, Frederic Remington wrote, "Did I tell you I was about to become a great sculptor—if not—well damn my modesty—it is so." And it was. Remington's dynamic renderings of what, in the 1890s, was fast becoming the Old West coincided with the era's interest in bronze sculpture. His heroic frontier images are exercises in technical virtuosity. In one of his best-known images, *Coming Through the Rye,* four carousing cowboys sit astride four galloping horses, but only five of the sixteen legs touch the base— a breathtaking feat of metal craft.

Remington's works are widely known, especially the famous casts *The Bronco Buster, The Rattlesnake,* and *The Cheyenne.* Authorized castings of Remington's bronzes ceased in 1919, but thousands of surmoulages (casts taken from a cast) exist to confuse the unwary.

Lost-Wax Casting

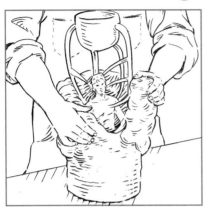

The wax sculpture is enveloped in clay. Steam vents are added.

After the wax has been melted away, the hollow mold is filled with molten bronze.

The clay is smashed to reveal the bronze sculpture. The clay mold is lost, along with the original wax sculpture.

CASTING BRONZE

One method of casting bronze dates from antiquity. A wax sculpture is formed on a clay core and surrounded by a clay envelope with vents. The wax is melted away, the heat and moisture escape through the vents, and all that remains is the clay mold. The mold is then refilled with molten bronze, and when this is cool, the clay is broken away. The result is a perfect replica of the original wax sculpture, though with some detail lost. All that remains is to chisel that detail by hand and polish the bronze.

This technique is referred to as *cire perdue,* or the "lost wax" process, and it has been the method of choice for complicated bronze work since ancient times. Another early method of working bronze horses and small bronze animal groups involved crafting them from hammered bronze strips welded together, but during the Middle Ages this technique was forgotten. In the Renaissance, the heirs of the ancient sculptors, such as the Florentine Donatello, began to cast monumental sculptures and, using the lost-wax process, were able to fabricate huge, free-standing figures in bronze, a great technical feat. Men of taste and power commissioned such tributes, while both scholarly humanists and princes ordered, from local talents like Pietro Bonalcosi and Andrea Briosco, small statuettes of gods—in the manner of classical bronzes—to decorate their homes.

During that time, imitations of ancient bronzes were cast in the thousands. There were favorite subjects, like *Youth Removing a Thorn from His Foot* (after the original in Rome) and *Hercules Resting on His Club,* after a monumental statue in the museum at Naples. These images are familiar to us even today, because they have been so frequently recast over the intervening centuries that it's hard to tell a Roman bronze from the Renaissance copy from the modern "authorized museum copy." Today, large and small reproductions of works of colossal scale replicating the powerful modeling of Michelangelo, the genius of bronze, can be bought in resinous "bronze."

GILT BRONZE

Not all bronze is statuesque and somber—especially not when it's gilded. Gilding was the specialty of the sophisticated, flamboyant eighteenth-century French and, embraced with a passion when the fashion for ormolu and gilt (doré) bronze swept the court, leaving lavish mounts (decorative trim), radiant candelabra, and suffering craftsmen in its gleaming wake. Suffering because, until the nineteenth century, a highly dangerous gilding technique, which involved painting bronze with a mercury-gold amalgam, then burning the mercury off, was the only known method for creating gilt bronze. Mercury poisoning was endemic among gilders, and it wasn't until the nineteenth century and the development of electroplating, a technique initially developed to make silver plate, that bronze could be clad in gold with no danger to the craftsman.

Gilt bronze objects, luxurious and expensive, perfectly reflected the glittering reigns of the French kings. Scrolling Rococo furniture clocks in ormolu, as well as candlesticks, chandeliers, and all types of otherwise utilitarian objects that the bourgeois could afford only in pewter and iron, were made for the courts in bronze. Portrait busts, inkstands, andirons, and innumerable frolicking cupids adorned luxurious palaces.

In the Neoclassical style: a masterful gilt-bronze centerpiece by Thomire.

An Art Deco gilt-bronze sconce, by French designer Jules Leleu, with faceted crystal fittings.

PIERRE PHILIPPE THOMIRE

Thomire gilt bronze may be the finest ever made. The founder of the French bronze workshop Thomire-Dutherne et Cie was Pierre Philippe Thomire, son of a bronze sculptor and student of the great French sculptor Houdon. Born in 1751, he began his career making bronze mounts for court furniture and ultimately established a huge workshop, with perhaps eight hundred employees who produced impressive and elegant centerpieces, candelabra, and wall lights, many of which incorporated finely cast and detailed Classical figures. In 1785, the city of Paris commissioned him to make the candelabra celebrating the Declaration of Independence for presentation to General Lafayette. The firm also accepted special commissions for Napoleon. Many Thomire bronzes are stamped, but even when they're not, the superb quality of their casting and sculpting is their distinguishing characteristic.

Diana, *by Augustus Saint-Gaudens, sculpted for the top of the old Madison Square Garden in New York City, c. 1892–1894.*

Roger and Angelica: *flow and drama in a Barye bronze.*

ANIMALIER BRONZES

The French love of objects in bronze continued well into the nineteenth century, when thousands of bronzes were cast for middle-class *maisons* by the large and successful French foundry of F.K. Barbedienne. Innumerable clock sets, enameled and alabaster candlesticks, tazzas (shallow cups on pedestals), and urns were manufactured by this large firm, which also cast reproductions of celebrated Renaissance bronzes, including the *David* of Michelangelo.

In addition, Barbedienne produced "animalier" bronzes: individual animals or groups of animals intended to decorate tabletops and mantels. These sculptures met with immediate success, especially Antoine-Louis Barye's dramatic and vigorous depictions of animal groups. His subjects are considered somewhat insensitive today—lions devouring their prey and pythons strangling crocodiles were typical—but their highly realistic modeling and the strength and balance of their composition brought Barye fame. Perhaps his best-known sculpture is *The Turkish Horse,* a powerful rendering of a rearing horse that was so popular it was cast again and again for fifty years. Barye's models were made in plaster, which could be coated repeatedly with wax, allowing the sculptor to rework the fine detail for each cast and guaranteeing that the last sculpture out of the mold would be as crisp as the first.

Animalier sculptures were the first bronzes, in fact, to be cast more than two or three times from the original mold. Barye's models were ultimately cast in as many as six sizes. Before 1830, bronzes were always individually commissioned and were usually one of a kind. Now, for the first time, it was possible to own an original work of art that was not unique. There would be several—identical—other works, known as "multiples." Today, multiple casting simply seems efficient, but in the 1840s it was revolutionary, and because of it, critics of both Barye and the products of the Barbedienne foundry termed their work "furniture"—not art. But if it was "furniture," it was bold and glittery furniture, the type the French had always loved. The popularity of Barye's animal bronzes paved the way for a small group of talented imitators such as Moigniez, Mène, and Isidore Bonheur. And the proliferation of their accessible and popular small works in bronze created a very large market for imitations in white metal, also known as spelter.

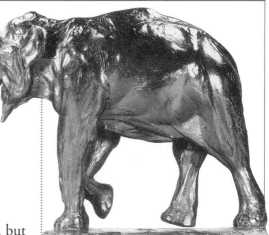

King-size poetry in motion, as interpreted by Rembrandt Bugatti (1885–1916).

WHITE METAL/ SPELTER

A typical Barye subject: the bronze Tiger Devouring an Antelope.

White metal is an inexpensive alloy of zinc, lead, and tin, silver or blue-white in color and rather good for imitating bronzes both large and small. It was particularly convincing because hollow white metal sculptures could be made to feel as heavy as bronze by being loaded with plaster, and fitted with a piece of felt on the bottom to hide the plaster filling. Adding even more weight, white metal imitations could be affixed to a marble or wood base, usually labeled with an engraved metal plaque indicating the title and the sculptor of the original bronze statue.

Sculptors of Bronze

Little Bull, *a wax model by Antoine Barye.*

ANTOINE-LOUIS BARYE *(1796–1875)*

FRENCH Barye was the pioneer of animalier bronze sculptures. His style is dramatic and his subjects seem ennobled, despite being frequently engaged in unattractive activities such as attacking or devouring prey. Barye incised his signature (most often in all capitals) on the model, not the mold, and his sculptures are numbered.

PIERRE JULES MÈNE *(1810–1879)*

FRENCH Mène is famous for gentle images of anatomically accurate animal groups in which dogs play with balls and horses nuzzle one another. His mounted jockeys and whippet sculptures are perennially popular, and—beware—extensively reproduced. Genuine Mène horses exhibit a rectangular outline beneath their bellies.

Stag and deer with fawns by Rembrandt Bugatti.

JULES MOIGNIEZ *(1835–1894)*

FRENCH Highly detailed birds with carefully defined plumage, often in aggressive poses, are the specialty of Moigniez, whose work is always signed.

AUGUSTUS SAINT-GAUDENS *(1848–1907)*

AMERICAN Trained in his youth as a cameo cutter, Saint-Gaudens went on to become the most cosmopolitan of American sculptors, creating major monuments like the Lincoln memorial in Chicago, works of elegant simplicity like *The Puritan* and *Diana of the Tower,* and portrait busts and numerous bas-reliefs of contemporary figures, Robert Louis Stevenson among them. Individual sculptures exist in sizes from monumental to less than a foot tall.

ROSA AND ISIDORE BONHEUR *(fl. 1850–1899)*

FRENCH Although Rosa Bonheur is well known, and perhaps best known as a painter, both she and her brother Isidore also sculpted domestic animals. Bulls by Isidore Bonheur are generally dramatic, always signed, and bear the foundry stamp of Hippolyte Peyrol. (A genuine Bonheur bull was brought to the *Roadshow* and valued at $6,000. Its lucky owner found it in the town dump.)

REMBRANDT BUGATTI *(1885–1916)*

ITALIAN Bugatti, younger brother of the automobile designer, sculpted for only fifteen years, producing bold, unusual, and stylized animal bronzes. He observed his subjects over a length of time, then sculpted his clay model quickly, sometimes within an hour. His animals are considerably less realistic than those of his colleagues, but he succeeds remarkably in capturing their essence. Only small numbers of each cast exist, ten on average. His work is of particular interest to collectors of Impressionist art.

DEMETRE CHIPARUS *(Romanian)*
FERDINAND PREISS *(German)*
CLARE-JEANNE-ROBERT COLINET *(Belgian)* *(fl. 1920–1935)*

Known for their work in chryselephantine, a combination of bronze and ivory, Chiparus, Preiss, and Colinet are among the best of the Art Deco sculptors, fashioning playful figures of costumed women in particularly theatrical attitudes. These artists produced commercially successful, often exotic bronzes with unusual patinations and elaborately worked gilt or silver embellishments. Occasionally the figures are painted, and they are often mounted on geometric bases of onyx and alabaster. This type of bronze has been widely reproduced.

White metal can be recognized in several ways. It is never cold to the touch, like bronze. Its "patina" will have been painted on, for white metal only pits and corrodes with age, never developing a patina of its own. Spelter never has the hand-filing marks associated with hand-finished bronze, either, for it is not hand-finished. To determine if a piece is bronze or spelter, make a small scratch in an inconspicuous spot. If it is spelter, the scratch will appear to be a silver or pewter-gray color, not the bright gold of genuine bronze. Animal bronzes most commonly reproduced in white metal include Mène's *L'Accolade*—an equestrian group depicting a stallion nuzzling a mare—and delicate greyhounds and whippets, alone or in groups.

IS IT OLD?

Determining the date of a sculpture's casting is generally problematic, since the dates that appear on sculptures are usually the dates when the original work was executed. However, in examining a bronze, keep in mind:

♦ Signing bronzes did not become common until the mid-nineteenth century. Bronzes made before that date are often unsigned.

♦ Patina can be either natural or artificial. Formulas for successful or particularly beautiful artificial patinations were considered precious trade secrets by sculptors and founders.

IS IT VALUABLE?

The most important criterion for determining the value of bronze is authenticity. Other metals can look like bronze, but even if a sculpture *is* bronze, it should not be a copy of a one-of-a-kind piece.

♦ Many bronze sculptures from the last century are being cast today directly from nineteenth-century

The naturalistic shape of a thistle-form bronze goblet, created by Tiffany c. 1907, exemplifies the essence of Art Nouveau style.

TIPS
from the experts

Eric Silver offers a few observations on metals and on methods for examining bronze:

A bronze reduction and enlargement device invented by Collas enabled bronze foundries to create several sizes of the same bronze.

Patina can be created on bronzes by combining heat with chemicals and working the color into the surface. You can chip off a painted "patina" with your nail.

The metal bronze is not expensive in itself. It is the high degree of finishing required—equal to that of silversmithing—that makes bronzes expensive.

If fingers look like stripes rather than real fingers, and hair, eyes, and toes are poorly defined, the bronze is a reproduction.

In eighteenth- and nineteenth-century Russia, brass samovars were as ubiquitous as toasters in twentieth-century America. They were all marked with "medals of merit," and every family had one. They may have sentimental or decorative value, but they have little or no value as collectibles.

Karl Kipp, a top workman at Roycroft who worked in copper, sometimes marked his wares, and these are more than ordinarily valuable.

Don't polish bronze. You'll destroy the patination.

casts. Such reproductions are known as surmoulages. They can be recognized because they always lack the sharp definition of the original and authentic bronze, and they always differ somewhat in size.

♦ The genuine bronze exhibits clear, sharp detail in every feature—hands, face, ears, texture of fur, feathers, or cloth. If fingers are crudely executed, if the hair seems smooth and sketchily finished, the sculpture is likely to be a reproduction of an older cast.

♦ A genuine bronze always shows the marks of the finishing file.

♦ Some imitation bronzes are actually just a thin sheet of copper over a base of porcelain or plaster. Tap various areas of the sculpture to listen for the "hollow" sound that might identify a spot where the metal skin is not attached. Or scrape the metal in an inconspicuous spot; if it shows the reddish gleam of copper, it cannot be bronze. Bronze is always golden.

♦ Crispness and refinement of detail and, naturally, attractiveness of subject determine the value of a bronze. Size is also important. Usually, the larger the casting, the more expensive the piece will be. The quality of the patina is also a determinant of value. Rubbed or worn patina is disadvantageous.

♦ Signatures on bronzes are often incised into the original sculpture ("signed in the cast") and thus cast into all multiples. They usually appear on the base of the sculpture itself.

♦ The mark of the bronze foundry may also appear on the base of the statue, so don't be confused if there seem to be two names. Certain foundries are associated with particular artists: the Roman Bronze Works with Frederic Remington, for example, and Barbedienne with Barye.

♦ Marble bases, while impressive and heavy, account for very little of a sculpture's value. They are often added to spelter to make the piece look more like genuine bronze.

♦ The animalier sculptors liked to finish their bronzes with a rich, deep brown patina.

♦ Iron rusts. Bronze neither rusts nor pits. If exposed to weather, it turns a crusty blue-green. If you are in doubt as to whether a heavy sculpture is bronze, try holding a magnet to it. If it sticks, the piece is cast iron. You can also check for traces of rust underneath the base, particularly around the nuts and bolts that hold the figure to the base.

♦ Gilding (ormolu) adds value to bronze for collectors who enjoy gilt bronze. Some bronze enthusiasts, however, consider it garish.

♦ A bronze that has lost its original gilding is diminished in value.

♦ Groups of figures are generally more valuable than solitary figures.

♦ Art Deco bronze-and-ivory (chryselephantine) figures should have subtly toned painted faces that exhibit signs of age. The details of the bronze elements should be sharp, while all ivory parts should show a distinct grain. Many of these sculptures are attached to their bases with wing nuts, rather than ordinary nuts. All should be signed.

♦ Bird groups tend to be unpopular with collectors and less valuable than the ferocious animal groups.

BRASS

Brass was rare and costly in early Colonial America. There were few domestic mines of copper and zinc, the metals from which the alloy brass is made, so raw material had to be imported from Great Britain.

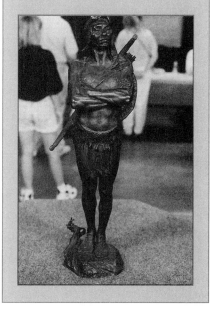

ANTIQUES DISCOVERY ROADSHOW

H.A. MACNEIL BRONZE SCULPTURE

The guest's grandfather bought this sculpture in Southampton, New York, after his wife joked that it looked like him, and it has remained in the family since. H.A. MacNeil (1866–1947) was an important American artist, but more important is the inscription: Roman Bronze Works. According to appraiser Lawrence DuMouchelle, this New York company made the finest bronze sculptures.

Dated 1907, the piece depicts an American Indian. In the words of DuMouchelle, you can always tell a good jeweler by the attention to detail, and this sculpture has a lot of it! He estimated its worth at $25,000.

Considering its early date, c. 1724, this brass tobacco box is in superb condition. On many such pieces, the engraving has been polished into illegibility.

A great rarity in American brass: an engraved sundial by Isaac Johnson, made in New York and dated 1731.

Consequently, metalworkers often took scrap in payment for their services; even clockworks at one time had to be made of wood, for lack of brass. Much foundry effort was expended in repairing metals of all sorts, but by 1783, due to the easing of trade restrictions, brass had become less expensive in New York and Philadelphia than it was in London.

In 1788, in Philadelphia's Independence Day parade, the city's braziers (brass founders and workmen) marched behind a float representing their profession, their proud banner announcing to spectators "In Vain the Earth Her Treasure Hides." And though, strictly speaking, brass is not mined, their pride in their work was understandable. Colonial and Federal artisans, after all, were heirs to an ancient and honorable craft, and their own neatly wrought and graceful wares maintained that long tradition.

Brass is the color of molten gold and burnishes to a honeyed gleam. It is harder than copper, generally its prime component, and also tarnishes less readily and is not as brittle. Because brass is free-flowing when molten, it is ideal for making complicated shapes such as candlesticks. But to be formed into these indispensable and ubiquitous objects it must be extensively worked, and the process— casting, filing, chasing, stamping, soldering, screwing, pickling, turning, burnishing, and lacquering—was obviously no small effort for such humble items.

Somewhere along the line, brass was often ornamented with the same type of chasing and engraving found, at the time, on silver. It might be embellished as well with small round beading called pearlwork or with gadrooned edges (also seen on silverwork), especially popular in the latter part of the eighteenth century. Like silver, brass could be easily hammered into *repoussé* flora and fauna, or bosses (domes). Unless it was handled constantly, however, brass tarnished quickly. While plating with gold (ormolu) or silver (French plate) kept it from tarnishing, lacquer—a mixture of alcohol and seed-lac (the sap of the *Rhus vernicitera* tree)—was usually used to coat brass in the eighteenth century, just as it is today.

CASTING BRASS

The key was in the casting. Large items were usually cast below ground level, so the molten metal could pour directly from the furnace down into the molds. But smaller, everyday objects were cast in a box filled with very fine sand that had been tamped around a basic pattern. (The sand used for early wares was finer than that used today, creating sharper detail.) Hollow objects were cast in parts and joined. The pattern was then carefully removed, and molten brass was poured into the void that remained in the sand. But brass, being expensive, was sold by weight, so the careful brass manufacturer cast his wares as thin as he dared and, wherever possible, made them hollow to keep their weight and cost down.

After casting, the metal was finished—filed down and subjected to the remainder of the aforementioned processes. The locales of brass foundries came to be called, in fact, Battery Works (or sometimes, the Battery), and the products made there were often superb.

AMERICAN BRASS

Although brass had once been scarce, Americans of the eighteenth and nineteenth centuries owned a great deal of it. They wore buttons and belt buckles of brass and owned a variety of surprisingly handsome brass kitchen utensils—chafing dishes, toasting forks, and ladles. Furniture hardware, and "vehicular" hardware in the form of horse brasses, were functional but always decorative additions to the home and stable.

Sand Casting

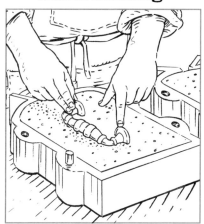

Creating the mold.

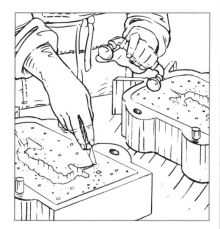

Adding vents.

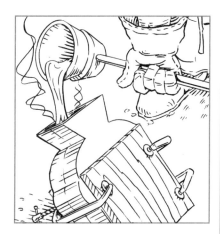

Pouring the liquid brass.

Delicately scalloped brass and iron candlesticks by George Grove were made in Birmingham, England, c. 1758.

Although it looks very French, this unusual brass candelabra with painted sheet-iron shade was made in Philadelphia in the mid-1870s by Baker, Arnold & Company.

Certainly the most frequently found form of brass was the candlestick. Every room required one, and usually more than one, and shapely pairs of brass candlesticks were often among a housewife's most prized possessions, although chambersticks, with their short nozzles set on large pans (to catch the inevitable hot wax drippings as the chambersticks were borne from room to room), may have been used more.

Lighting forms show off brass to best advantage. The warm and brilliant glow of brass sconces, lanterns, and tapersticks was not, somehow, superseded by the table lamps produced in great numbers by the second decade of the nineteenth century. Candlelight, however, was made obsolete by the introduction of oil and gas lighting, and American lamp and chandelier manufacturers like Henry N. Hooper of Boston and the Cornelius firm of Philadelphia produced quantities of good oil lighting in argand, sinumbra, and solar lamps, each an improvement on the one before.

But while more and better light was being brought to American parlors, the heat provided by a well-fed fire in a good-size fireplace meant home, and despite the growing use of the Franklin stove, fireplaces remained the primary source of heat well into the nineteenth century.

American brass fireplace furnishings—andirons, fenders, fireplace implements, and the myriad arm's-length gadgets that enabled cooks to work in open hearths—are among the most splendid of American brass objects. Among them, andirons are a particularly fine form and highly collectible as well. If American metalwork ever approached the beauty of its Continental counterparts, it came closest with andirons. Their makers certainly considered them art, for they signed them, an unusual thing in the utilitarian metals trade.

Most brass andirons of the eighteenth and nineteenth centuries were manufactured in the same way. The parts were sand-cast: the ball- or urn-form top, the shaft, and the base of the shaft (or plinth) were cast in two parts and brazed together. The curved, arched legs were of solid brass. The legs formed a tripod with the iron, wood-supporting member at the back, providing stability. (In Boston, the backs of these curved legs were hollow-cast, to save on metal.) A threaded iron rod ran top to bottom, internally, to screw the parts together. Cabriole legs, with ball-and-claw or pad feet, reflected the furniture styles of the era—first the Chippendale style and, later, Classical styles, and were designed to complement room decor.

Sizable andirons were made for use in family rooms, which usually had good-size fireplaces, but in bedrooms both the andirons and fireplaces were smaller. They were a household necessity throughout the era, and andirons sold for less than $10 a pair. Fireplace fenders, equally ubiquitous, could be modest and plain or elaborately pierced and chased, and quite beautiful. They were always fashioned of fretted brass or openwork wire to allow heat from the fire to reach the feet of the room's occupants.

For around two hundred years, the warming pan was a comfort in winter. Attached to a long lathe-turned wood handle, a round box made of pierced brass or copper with a hinged lid held hot coals from the fireplace. The box could be slid between cold sheets to warm an icy bed. Despite exhortations from experts that the lids on the pans should be of solid brass in order to retain heat, makers preferred to pierce that top and embellish it with often whimsical punchwork. Warming pans are attractive and not especially expensive, and occasionally a warming pan is signed.

In addition to the countless domestic objects made in brass, there was also, until modern times, a busy trade in scientific instruments, frequently small works of art in themselves. Brass measures, sundials, and sextants, hallmarked much like silver, could be beautifully engraved and finished like the technical jewels they actually were. And the best-quality medical kits were fitted with exquisitely machined brass tools—finer, in every way, than the medicine of the time. The passage of years has lent luster and a silky burnish to all such early brass.

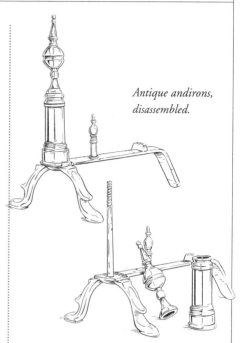

Antique andirons, disassembled.

A superior pair of brass and iron andirons, probably made in New York City c. 1760–1780, combine swirled and faceted elements with well-defined ball-and-claw feet.

IS IT OLD?

There are numerous collectors of brass candlesticks and tobacco boxes but, for obvious reasons, not many collectors of andirons or fenders. Small bits of finely crafted brass, however, may be unique among antiques in being valued as much for the genuine tactile pleasure they provide their owners as for their age, condition, and rarity.

A Parisian telescope, c. 1875.

An 1825 brass telescope made in London.

♦ The shaft and base of an antique brass candlestick was cast in three parts: a two-piece shaft and the base. Sophisticated artisans took care to hide the seam with decoration or a flange at this joint. (A visible seam would suggest that the candlestick may have been the work of a provincial craftsman.)

♦ The undersides of eighteenth- and early-nineteenth-century candlesticks were generally skimmed on a lathe, to clean away burrs and roughness left after the casting process. After about 1890, these were left unfinished. As a result, the undersides of candlesticks of more modern manufacture will appear roughened, as if they had been rubbed with a cloth while still somewhat molten.

♦ Both the presence of repairs and a smooth, worn finish can be evidences of age.

♦ No examples of signed eighteenth-century American candlesticks are known.

♦ Chamfered ball-and-flame andiron finials are an eighteenth-century form.

♦ Finials in the form of acorns are rare on eighteenth-century andirons.

♦ In the Federal era, two urns, one smaller than the other, were a popular shape for American andiron finials.

IS IT VALUABLE?

Fine craftsmanship and sophisticated design are the hallmarks of valuable metalwork. ("Signed" pieces are rare, but a signature is not necessarily an indication of unusual value. Very ordinary objects can be signed and be of primarily documentary interest.)

♦ American andirons were not infrequently signed to inform customers that a maker guaranteed his work. Signed andirons command a premium today.

♦ Chamfered ball-and-flame finials on andirons are more sophisticated and therefore more valuable than ball finials, which are far more common and were in use for generations. Because the ball-top andiron is a common form in both England and America, it is difficult to determine the country of origin unless the andirons are signed. This is also true of fenders, although these are less frequently marked than andirons.

♦ Wire fenders with brass trim or finials are considered more desirable than plain wire fenders.

♦ The serpentine fender with pierced fretwork and elaborate chasing, made c. 1800, is among the most sought-after of antique brass fenders.

COPPER

Copper is wonderfully malleable. It is also rust-resistant and a good conductor of heat (think of French copperware and copper-clad stainless steel), and its color is a distinctive and rich, tawny red. The metal can be worked using a variety of methods, and hammering, particularly, strengthens it. Because copper is soft, it is often combined with other metals to make bronze, brass, or pewter. Copper imparts a metallic flavor to food,

---

ANTIQUES DISCOVERY ROADSHOW

TIFFANY CANDLESTICK

Viewers know that not all *Roadshow* stories have happy endings. The owner of this delicate Tiffany candlestick received it as a gift from her grandmother on her twenty-first birthday because she had always admired it. The candlestick was dark when she received it, so she polished it in an attempt to restore some of its original beauty. Unfortunately, as appraiser Barbara Deisroth explained, that was just the wrong thing to do. Polishing the candlestick removed all of its original patination, leaving only the copper sheathing, and lowered the value by 80 percent or so. Rather than being worth $1,000 to $1,500, this signed Tiffany candlestick was evaluated at no more than $200. While the owner was clearly disappointed, she was quick to remind Deisroth of one thing: you can't put a price on sentimental value.

COPPER TEA KETTLE

Gregory A. Kuharic was intrigued upon hearing that this modern-looking teapot belonged to the owner's grandparents when they were homesteaders in South Dakota, as the piece was rather sophisticated for that time and place. Kuharic noted that the design of the kettle had been popular in Austria and Germany in the early 1900s. Thanks to the mark on the bottom (an ostrich running inside a diamond), Kuharic identified the pot as being a product of the WMF Metal Company and manufactured in Germany in 1911.

Though well-used, the teapot was very close to being in original condition. Even knowing that, the owner was completely surprised to learn that this family heirloom had a value of $800 to $1,200.

however, and is thought to be potentially poisonous, which is why the interior of otherwise handsome and useful copper cookware is always coated with tin. Of all the base metals, copper is least collectible and has least value.

During the Renaissance and Baroque eras, copper was fashioned into the same types of elaborate objects as silver and gold. But by the eighteenth century, it had become primarily a utilitarian material, suitable mainly for kettles and pots, dry and liquid measures, and stills—an essential copper product for spirited and spirit-imbibing Americans. Abstemious housewives, on the other hand, were content just to own one good copper kettle large enough to withstand the constant and hard use it would be given. This, along with a few saucepans (in the Colonial era, pots with narrow openings) and stew pans (straight-sided, flat-bottomed pots with handles), was the extent of the average home's copper needs. Favorite cookware would often be repaired and retinned when the tin wore through.

Copper was also used in plumbing, as it still is today. A Boston manufacturer of weights and measures fitted out the USS *Constitution* with the copper tubes the ship used for its "necessary." And the astonishingly entrepreneurial Paul Revere provided rolled copper sheathing for the *Constitution,* as well as the material for the copper dome on the Boston State House.

ROYCROFT COPPER: AN AMERICAN ORIGINAL

In America, the Arts and Crafts movement, taking its cue from the movement's British founders, sought to reverse the trend toward machine-made objects and to return the decorative arts to an idyllic, preindustrial age: one in which the handmade object—clearly created by the human hand—could be made available to everyone. Reacting against the perceived over-ornamentation of

American Arts and Crafts Metalworkers

A Dirk Van Erp copper vase.

DIRK VAN ERP
(1860–1953)

The talented Dirk Van Erp was the son of a coppersmith; born in Holland, he emigrated to the United States in 1886. His work was influenced by the Arts and Crafts movement and especially by the Mission style, an American offshoot of England's Arts and Crafts movement. In 1908, he opened his first copper shop in Oakland, California, retailing patinated, red-brown, hammered copper bowls and vases. When he moved to San Francisco two years later, he expanded his line into desk sets and vases, but he is particularly known today for his Japonesque table lamps. His lamps have conical shades paneled in sheets of mottled, buff-tone mica. The bases tend to be simple bullet shapes or tapered cones. Van Erp also manufactured electrified floor lamps, ceiling fixtures, and wall lights. His conspicuously handworked copper wares, often patinated in red, brown, green, and purple, have visible rivets and seams.

ROBERT JARVIE
(fl. 1900–1917)

An Arts and Crafts acolyte, Robert Jarvie produced metal wares in copper, brass, pewter, bronze, and silver. Jarvie made bookends, trays, desk sets, lanterns, and sconces, but he is best-known today for his elegant, acid-finished candlesticks.

KARL KIPP
(fl. 1912–1915)

Having begun life as a banker, Kipp found his calling as a designer of metal wares for Roycroft. In 1912, he left to open his own firm, the Tookay Shop. His work often employed combinations of brass and copper in logical geometric motifs, typical of the Vienna Secessionist style.

LILLIAN PALMER
(fl. 1900–1910)

Self-trained metalworker Lillian Palmer, working in San Jose, created *repoussé* hammered copper objects. She also worked in lead, setting beach pebbles into the metal, much as Renaissance metalworkers set their far more precious metals with colored stones.

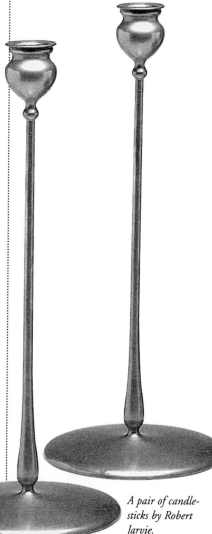

A pair of candlesticks by Robert Jarvie.

DIRK VAN ERP LAMP

Dirk Van Erp of Oakland, California, has always been the acknowledged king of Arts and Crafts lighting, its earliest and best practitioner. This 1920 copper lamp with a thick mica shade is a prime example of his artistry. The market for Dirk Van Erp lamps has exploded recently, and that's good news for the lamp's owner, who found it in the rafters of a garage many years ago. She took it home and cleaned it up. And that's bad news.

"The key thing is always the patina," explained Michael Flanigan. Given the lamp's condition, Flanigan appraised the piece in the current market at $20,000 to $30,000. If the owner hadn't cleaned it, he confessed, it would have brought $60,000 to $80,000.

Victorian art, the proponents of this movement decided to create objects with simple lines, made of inexpensive and natural materials, crafted by hand.

American Elbert Hubbard was converted to the Arts and Crafts brotherhood on a trip to England in 1895 and founded the creative community "Roycroft" in East Aurora, New York. Here, furniture, lighting devices, and textiles were all made in the pure, understated style of the Arts and Crafts movement. Household items were crafted from several metals, but mainly from copper. Copper was easy to work with and, in keeping with the goal of providing handsome objects for ordinary people, inexpensive as well. The Roycrofters, often amateurs new to the craft, learned to fashion metals into boxes, vases, lamp bases, and many other useful and decorative objects. The business Hubbard founded remained commercially successful throughout the course of almost fifty years.

Although the community's first objects were made of iron and unmarked, the work with which the Roycrofters are most commonly identified is a deep red, unpatinated, hammered copper ware. The din made by scores of artisans pounding away at their copper (collegially termed their "anvil chorus") met with much success. By 1910, their vases, bowls, plates, candlesticks, humidors, and chandeliers, often embellished with geometrical patterns in other metals or inset stones, and always with the hammer's dimples—"like lines of experience on the thoughtful face," said a commentator—were being retailed from Providence to Los Angeles.

As the years passed and styles changed, Roycroft metal wares became increasingly sophisticated. Decorative rivets and brass mountings were added, and after World War I colored copper—with blue, silver, and even green finishes on a subtly hammered base—was employed. These later Roycroft copper objects are always marked, most often with an orb and cross (a logo so much like the Nabisco baker's logo that the firm brought suit).

PEWTER

Humble gray pewter is made predominantly of tin, with a moderate seasoning of copper and lead. (The more lead it contains, the softer the metal and the darker the gray.) From the time of the Renaissance, pewter was the material used most for everyday eating and drinking utensils and for lighting devices. Before glass, ceramics, stainless steel, and aluminum were available, pewter was known as "the poor man's silver." An apt analogy might be to modern plastics, for pewter was both ubiquitous and utilitarian—though, fortunately, not instantly disposable.

Pewter is made by being heated and cast in molds, and while the metal itself was inexpensive, the manufacture of pewter was very expensive because the molds were made of costly brass or bronze and every object required its own mold. For economy's sake, therefore, molds had to be versatile. The body of a teapot and a pitcher might be cast from the indentical mold, while the distinguishing characteristics—the spout or lip—would be added later. After casting, the rough edges and seams of the object would be smoothed on a lathe, then strengthened and given an attractive silvery gleam with a light hammering, administered by the aristocrats of the craft, the hammermen.

Like brass, pewter imitated the forms of silver and was polished to increase the resemblance. Like silver, it tarnished. But it was far softer, and it dented and scratched more readily. It could also be chased or engraved with initials, although American pewter tended to be plain, unpretentious, and without ornament. Not infrequently, it was painted, usually in gold on black, but also in other colors.

A handsome pewter flagon, made by Boardman and Company in New York, c. 1825, with a particularly vigorous handle.

More useful than beautiful: a late-eighteenth-century English pewter standish for desk accessories.

Pewter flasks: one from Lancaster, Pennsylvania c. 1776, in the traditional, conveniently carried "Pilgrim" shape; the other, larger one made in eighteenth-century Germany or America.

Pewter candlesticks by Archibald Cox for Liberty & Co., c. 1900–1905.

Early colonists owned minimal pewter ware, only what was necessary, because no tin was mined in America and pewter was costly. Eventually, it became the most common metal for dozens of household items, from tablewares and desk accessories to lighting devices. Pewter was imported from England in great quantity. It is known that pewter objects worth almost 80,000 pounds sterling were shipped to America just before the Revolutionary War.

Until the early nineteenth century, American pewterers could make a decent living simply by repairing and refashioning old wares. But the arrival, c. 1785, of the more attractive and more affordable silver plate cut into the American market for pewter. Despite the pewterers' stopgap technique of making their wares look more silvery by adding antimony to the mixture, (see "Britannia Metal," page 224), they couldn't halt the tide of fashion. Within fifty years, pewter was rarely found in homes.

Still, in the last years of the nineteenth century, especially in England and Germany, a renewal of interest in base metals produced a flurry of decorative Art Nouveau pewter. Liberty and Company in London manufactured a type of Art Nouveau pewter called Tudric, and Liberty pewter, strongly Celtic in design, is collected today, mainly in England. In Germany, Kayserzinn produced its own version of "art" pewter, strongly Art Nouveau in style, which can be identified by the Kayserzinn embossed oval applied on the bottom.

THE USES OF PEWTER

Early American and English pewterers used the term "sadware" for their plates, dishes, and chargers, or large serving plates. Pitchers, pots, tankards, mugs, and other vessels were called holloware. Perhaps the most popular pewter product, and the best-known today, was the porringer, a multipurpose bowl five or six inches in diameter with a tab handle and a slightly domed bottom. The porringer could be used for either solid foods or liquids. Only the porringer handle, formed into flower shapes, dolphins, or pierced geometric designs, allowed the craftsman an outlet for his individuality and also distinguished one porringer from another. Long after the porringer form became extinct in England, the source of the prototype, Americans continued to use it, making it problematical to determine the country of origin and the date of an unmarked porringer.

After porringers, teapots were perhaps the most common type of American pewter holloware. The most collectible form, however, is the tankard, which, like its silver counterparts, dates from the eighteenth century. Pewter tankards copy silver forms, but, of necessity, they are simpler (although now and then a tankard handle will break out into a lone bit of scrollwork). Touchmarks—the maker's marks or emblems—can usually be found inside the bottom of pewter tankards.

Most of the pewter we find today is in the form of plates, ranging from six to twenty inches in diameter. After spoons, plates were by far the most common object made of pewter, manufactured by the tens of thousands over a period of two hundred years. Of course, countless plates were made in every country, but American examples can often be distinguished from foreign plates by the molded edge around the plate rim. When American pewter plates are marked at all, they will be stamped on the underside of the well (the deep section of the plate).

Though commonplace, domestic pewter had its own elegance, as in this matched set of five nineteenth-century English pewter half-pint measures and three pewter plates by Yates & Birch and James Yates, Birmingham, England.

A pewter communion service, attributed to Timothy Brigden, 1774–1819.

BRITANNIA METAL

In 1732, Thomas Boulsover in England developed a technique for silverplating copper, and the public, which couldn't afford sterling silver, was delighted to be able to replace common pewter household articles with this convincing and affordable silver look-alike. Spurred by this competition, British pewter manufacturers developed a lightweight, silver-colored, easily worked metal alloy which, with chauvinistic pride, they named Britannia metal. Britannia could be used as a base for silver plate instead of copper, which eventually showed through. James Dixon in Sheffield produced much silverplated Britannia, and much was also sent to America.

IS IT OLD?

Pre-nineteenth-century American pewter is quite rare, and because it is frequently marked, it has attracted groups of dedicated collectors who particularly appreciate its gentle presence in period kitchens and dining rooms.

♦ Antique porringers do not have the folded-over rim that appears on twentieth-century copies. Period porringers also have thicker walls.

♦ When early pewterers attached the handle to the side of the porringer bowl, they often grasped the bowl with a piece of cloth, leaving the imprint of its weave and texture on the side. Such an impression is one excellent indication of age.

♦ The handles of eighteenth-century pewter tea- and coffeepots are made of wood.

♦ Hammer marks all over a pewter object indicate handmade ware and usually suggest age.

♦ Despite hearsay, it is not true that all unmarked pewter is American. Pre-revolutionary American pewter marks often capitalized on Great Britain's reputation for quality goods. An American maker's name, for instance, might be placed beside a Tudor rose and a crown or even adjoining the words "London" or "From Old England." After the Revolution, however, pewter was often marked with the American eagle or the word "Liberty."

IS IT VALUABLE?

The collecting of pewter goes in and out of fashion, and it is not usually among the most valuable of collectible metals—even when, periodically, it *is* fashionable. Its subtle allure, however, consistently attracts fairly sophisticated collectors, and there is always a market for fine pewter.

♦ Unmarked old pewter is fairly common and is worth perhaps half as much as marked pewter.

♦ Period pewter should be unpitted and without dents or missing pieces. The particularly rare object, as with every antique, is permitted some flaws.

♦ Early painted pewter is quite rare. Any paint remaining on a pewter object should be left untouched.

♦ Pewter coffeepots are rare and valuable, even when unmarked. If they are marked and also elaborately decorated, they can be worth twenty to thirty times the value of an unmarked pot. Lighthouse-shaped coffeepots can be distinguished from teapots of the same shape by the presence of a strainer where the teapot's spout attaches to the body.

♦ Sadware pieces (plates, dishes, and chargers) tend to look very much alike. Collectors distinguish pieces by the importance of their makers or by the region of the country where they were made.

Eighteenth- and nineteenth-century American pewter porringers exhibit their individuality only in the scroll-work of their more or less elaborate tab handles.

Single-reed pewter plate, Richard Lee, Vermont, c. 1790–1816.

Deep pewter dish with double-reeded rim, Thomas D. Boardman, Hartford, Connecticut c. 1805–1820.

◆ Midwestern and Southern pewter is rarer than that made in Boston or New York and is therefore more valuable. Any dish attributable to a Georgia pewterer, for instance, would surpass its northern counterpart in monetary value.

◆ On early New York and Pennsylvania pewter, the maker's mark is often accompanied by a crowned X.

◆ Attributions can sometimes be made based on similarities in castings from the same mold, but attributed pieces are always worth less than actual, marked examples.

◆ After the turn of the nineteenth century, pewterers' marks became quite businesslike, exhibiting just the maker's name or initials within curved or rectangular frames.

IRON

The blacksmith led a hellish life. All day, he stood before a raging fire, thrusting heavy tools into the heat. Striking (literally) while the iron was hot, he hammered at his forge unceasingly, fashioning and repairing hardware, kitchen utensils, swords, axes, and ultimately, when machines began to compete for his trade, just horseshoes. Worst of all, as one sixteenth-century observer commented, "the unhappy workmen are never able to enjoy any quiet except in the evening, when they are exhausted by the laborious and long day that began for them with the crowing of the cock."

Cast-iron owl andirons, c. 1920, Rostand Manufacturing Company, Milford, Connecticut.

WROUGHT IRON

In eighteenth- and early-nineteenth-century America, the blacksmith worked primarily with wrought (hand-forged) iron. Wrought-iron hinges and door hardware, candlestands and axes—all the functional and homely essentials of daily life—were made at his forge.

Iron, of course, could be used for almost everything that didn't get wet, and it was in plentiful supply. Prosaic and functional, it could also occasionally be made into art by imaginative and talented village blacksmiths who couldn't resist making the functional beautiful. Thus, they wrought their iron into whimsical trivet shapes or wove it into lacy fender wire. Sometimes they fashioned iron andirons into human or animal shapes. And when they took sheet iron, dipped it in tin, and fashioned it into handsome chandeliers and spice sets, modest householders no longer needed to covet silver.

The blacksmith worked in an ancient tradition, often with designs basically unchanged since the Middle Ages, and left us little record of himself. Only among fireplace and kitchen equipment, the largest and most varied group of wrought-iron objects, are there any signed or dated iron pieces. Yet no community was without its blacksmith. And his work was evidently expensive, for the colonists complained about his prices.

The American style in ironwork is unostentatious and lacking in unnecessary ornament. It emphasizes pure utility. While an iron strongbox made by a European smith might be embellished with elaborate applied scrolls and even paint, the American version was a simple box, at most touched with brass or copper. The English or German lock might be chiseled, gilt, or damascened, but the Colonial lock was foursquare and plain. Every so often, costly brass was used to ornament sober iron pieces. Tall, tapered wrought-iron pot stands with open

Although this Liberty weathervane has lost the American flag once held in the left hand, the figure is still imposing.

Nineteenth-century American paint-decorated sheet-metal pig weathervane.

INSURE THYSELF, OR ELSE . . .

The Great Fire of London in 1666 inspired the growth of fire insurance companies whose fire brigades would fight a fire if the house owner had bought insurance from the company and marked his home with its "fire mark," a cast-iron emblem. (If these firemen saw no fire mark, or the mark of a rival firm, they just stood and watched the house burn or simply went home.) American fire brigades, first organized by Benjamin Franklin in 1736, fought any fire, and fire marks in the colonies were mainly used as a form of advertising for American insurance companies. With the growth of professional municipal firefighting units toward the close of the nineteenth century, the fire mark fell into disuse.

An American fire mark.

Nineteenth-century tinned sheet-metal wrigglework coffeepot, stamped "W. Shade" and made in Pennsylvania.

shelves could be capped in brass, and lanky wrought-iron candle stands could be treated to shiny brass drip pans; even iron fire tools and, often, fenders were tipped with brass. But trivets, or any utensils intended to be used directly in the fire, were made wholly of wrought iron since brass embellishments wouldn't stand up to the heat. As the nineteenth century progressed, wrought iron began to find an application both for garden furniture and for inexpensive brass-ornamented iron beds, and these became widely fashionable.

ROLLED AND TINNED IRON

Both blacksmiths and tinsmiths worked in rolled and tinned iron, an eighteenth-century discovery that was welcomed in Colonial America. Formed by dipping sheet iron in tin, this material combined the best qualities of both metals. It was rigid and strong like iron, but rust-proof, solderable, and shiny like tin. Products sold in rolled-tin containers could be reused. The amalgam could be fashioned into candle molds, hatboxes, measures, and, most successfully, chandeliers and wall lights, with the shiny surface of the tin very effectively reflecting the light of the candles they held. It was most widely used, however, to make large, inexpensive coffeepots.

CAST IRON

Not blacksmiths but iron foundries manufactured large cast-iron items like cannonballs, architectural elements, and even, in the eighteenth century, the homely fireback—a rectangle of metal placed at the rear of the firebox to protect the brick from excessive heat and reflect that heat back into the room. The fireback is one of the earliest types of decorative American cast iron. It was frequently impressed with portraits or designs depicting heroes of the French and Indian War (like General Wolfe) or with the typical sentimental tulips and hearts of Pennsylvania German decoration.

It required an enormous amount of charcoal to heat the furnaces that melted iron, so iron foundries, often owned by the same families for generations, sprang up in parts of the country with much natural woodland. With the spread of the railroad, the foundries expanded into making railroad tracks and locomotives. Wars, naturally, required cannon, and the Civil War put American foundries to the test, which they met all too admirably. But when peace returned, bringing with it a demand for cast-iron garden ornaments and household objects, wartime foundries quickly converted from making guns to making birdhouses, letter holders, and doorstops. Cast-iron garden furnishings, including urns, chairs, settees, fountains, and life-size animals, were manufactured by American firms like Wood and Perot in Philadelphia, the J.W. Fiske Works in New York City, and the Miller Iron Company in Providence, Rhode Island.

Pennsylvania punch-decorated tinned sheet-metal coffeepot, c. 1848.

American eighteenth-century cast-iron fireback impressed with the figure of a heraldic lion.

IS IT OLD?

There is much less collector interest in iron hardware and cooking utensils than there is, particularly in recent years, in cast-iron garden ornaments. Early American wrought-iron lighting, however, is always highly desirable, as are fine firebacks.

♦ The iron cook-spit did not change in design from medieval times until the middle of the nineteenth century. Thus, the dating and attribution of this form are extremely difficult.

♦ Antique cast-iron garden ornaments can be distinguished from modern aluminum copies by testing them with a magnet, which will adhere to the iron.

JOSIAH HARRISON WEATHERVANE

Josiah Harrison flourished in Vermont from 1868 to 1880, making, among other things, weathervanes.

This example was snatched up by the owner for $700 at an antiques show almost before it had been unloaded from the truck. Depicting a horse and carriage, complete with driver, it is unfortunately in very poor condition: originally gilded, it is now coated with gold radiator paint. The horse and driver are original, but the entire piece has undergone substantial restoration, not all of it acceptable. Even the maker's mark is difficult to see.

But there was good news here, too. Because weathervanes of this type are very rare and the piece does have the Harrison signature, however faint, Wayne Pratt appraised it at $6,000 to $8,000. With a tenfold return on his investment, this pleased owner might be tempted to add, "Condition *isn't* everything."

IS IT VALUABLE?

Least expensive among iron fireplace fenders, when new, was the fender with perfectly straight parallel wires and an iron frame. Each refinement or addition of brass ornament added value. Similarly, iron andirons with brass decorations were generally more costly than their all-iron counterparts. The values are comparable today.

♦ Wrought iron is almost never signed and is only infrequently dated.

♦ Labeled cast-iron furniture and garden ornaments are more valuable than unlabeled pieces.

♦ Iron hardware can reveal regional characteristics and thereby becomes more valuable when it is still attached, as it often is, to recognizably regional architectural elements such as doors.

♦ Ornamental wrought iron, particularly that on gates, was expensive, custom-made work, and it is correspondingly valuable today (although, due to size, this market is frequently limited).

♦ Art Deco wrought-iron firescreens and sculptures by the American craftsman Hunt Deidrich have become quite costly. They often depict stylized animals or birds in flight.

FOLK ART

Quite a lot of metal qualifies as folk art. Painted tin plate, made by "whitesmiths" (as opposed to blacksmiths) but stenciled or painted at home, plus gaily colored coffeepots and boxes of all sizes in decorated tinware, are highly sought after by folk art enthusiasts. Shop signs in the shape of eyeglasses or pointing fingers were just as handsome in cut tin or molded metal as they were in wood, and shop signs became virtual works of art when curled into delicate tendrils of finely wrought iron. Even tin candle sconces and the homeliest of lamps and pot hooks sometimes possess the naïve artistry that turns the ordinary object into folk art. But undoubtedly the best-known and most popular of metal folk-art objects is the weathervane.

In the eighteenth and nineteenth centuries, the lives of both seafarers and farmers were governed by the weather, thus making the weathervane more practical than ornamental. Which is not to say it could not also be whimsical. Colonial weathervanes were most often shaped like fish, Indians, and arrows, and designs eventually came to include birds of all types, fire engines, and Gabriel blowing his trumpet: all idiosyncratically wrought, and all in silhouette, for when viewed from afar (as they usually are) subjects had to be strong in profile.

Weathervanes were frequently made by amateurs from any number of metals and whatever was handy—iron or sheet tin. One-of-a-kind exercises in metalworking whimsy and skill, they depict their themes with varying degrees of artistic success. But when crafted by professionals, they were handsome and sturdy, most often made of copper hammered over a carved wooden mold made in two parts and then seamed together. (More complicated forms might be made in several pieces.) Weathervanes were also manufactured of cast iron. Eventually, they came to be produced by firms specializing in certain designs, like the famous "Columbia" weathervane patented in 1868 by Cushing and White of Waltham, Massachusetts. A three-dimensional trotting stallion—a handsome rendering of the champion trotter Black Hawk—was a widely popular form, produced originally by the J.W. Fiske Works of New York City in 1875. The more successful of these metalcrafters sold their products in catalogs and hardware stores, and their vanes could

The full-bodied figure of a copper horse and driver decorates a late-nineteenth-century weathervane created by L.W. Cushing & Co. of Waltham, Massachusetts.

be gilt or painted or, if copper, left to turn a handsome gray-green. Weathervanes that retain their original surface and are not severely weathered (or shot full of holes) are highly desirable.

———

FURTHER READING

Drury, Elizabeth. *Antiques, Traditional Techniques, etc.* New York: Doubleday, 1986.

Fennimore, Donald. *Metalwork in Early America.* Delaware: Winterthur/Antique Collectors Club, 1996.

McNerney, Kathryn. *Antique Iron.* Paducah, KY: Collector Books, 1996.

Schiffer, Herbert, Peter, and Nancy. *Antique Iron.* Atglen, PA: Schiffer Publishing Limited, 1979.

———. *The Brass Book.* Atglen, PA: Schiffer Publishing Limited, 1978.

Shapiro, Michael. *Cast and Recast.* Washington, D.C.: The Smithsonian Institution Press, 1981.

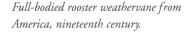

Full-bodied rooster weathervane from America, nineteenth century.

Chapter Eight

RUGS, QUILTS, AND SAMPLERS

H andmade—in the schoolroom, the farmhouse kitchen, the tent—is what collectible textiles ought to be. Most of our quilts, samplers, and tribal rugs are true and literal "folk" art, combining beauty with utility, freshness, originality, and, most important, the sweetly awkward touch of the human hand. For, despite claims to true perfection, no machined textile has ever been, or will ever be, valuable.

Being folk art, most handmade soft goods are humble, but a few are legendary. Say "carpet," for instance, and most of us think "Persian," because early Persian weavings were of such high quality that seventeenth-century traders paid fortunes for large extravaganzas of silk, wool, and silver thread. Consequently, exquisite Persian workmanship became the standard by which other rugs were judged. Yet India, Ottoman Turkey, and Central Asia produced rugs of equal quality. Nomads, living hard lives in humble tents,

Like all handmade rugs, this geometric Gendje contains noticeable variations in weave, color, and design.

wove, too: saddlebags, mats, and camel trappings, which, along with their innumerable sturdy rugs, displayed such bold, stylized figures and imaginative color combinations that some wily collectors today would trade ten Persian rugs and three small goats for one fine Caucasian weaving.

Sadly, machine-made rugs, purchased from furniture and department stores, are the kind most often found in our attics. Throughout the twentieth century, stacks of these harshly colored woven clones were churned out to satisfy the demands of the traditional decorating trade, as well as for the modern homeowner.

The use of geometric patterns is as common to most native weaving as the mark of the human hand. In places as distant as Turkey, the Caucasus, Ohio, and Massachusetts, generations of weavers and quilters independently discovered that it was far easier to pattern their textiles in straight-line designs than in rounded ones, which is why cotton quilts, silk rugs, and woolen bedcovers and blankets all over the world share sometimes identical linear motifs.

They share another trait as well. In that chilly time before central heating, soft goods (except the samplers, of course) were made to keep the makers and their families warm—to protect them from hard, cold earth and chilly air. But cotton, silk, and wool are fragile. Lay any textile on the floor, after all, and it will wear out if it's walked on for a hundred years or so. Wash a quilt too much (as thorough housekeepers are inclined to do), and eventually it will fall to shreds. Hang a sampler on a wall for fifty, twenty, or even ten years, and it will fade in the light. Moths eat wool. Silk threads rot. We're lucky, come to think of it, to be able to include a chapter on textiles at all.

A trio of handmade carpets from the East. Top to bottom: geometrically patterned Luri rug from southwestern Persia; antique prayer rug woven with silk and metal threads and centered with a flowering mosque lamp; a Turkoman Saryk Engsi, or door rug.

RUGS

Oriental carpets are exceptionally heavy textiles with highly romantic associations. Handmade, sometimes on small portable looms, they were once used, we're told, to waft mythical heroes through the clouds and to gift-wrap ancient Egyptian queens. But the oldest carpet on earth was discovered just a few decades ago in Siberia, in an ancient Scythian tomb that first flooded, then froze. The frigid Siberian climate kept the tomb and all its contents fresh from the fifth century until 1949, when the pile carpet, depicting elk and processions of men on horseback, emerged from cold storage, fresh as the day it was made.

Today, the term "carpet" is used to describe weavings larger than 9' x 6'. Anything smaller is a rug. (In this chapter, we'll use the terms interchangeably.) Rugs can be made with either a pile or a flat surface, like tapestry: most flat-surface rugs are the work of tribes from the Middle East and the Caucasus. Pile rugs are more difficult to make and thus more expensive when new. The very large and elaborately designed pile carpets—the famous "Persians"—are from urban looms.

The rug market in the United States is not very old. Its heyday didn't even begin until 1890, because before the mid-nineteenth century few American families could afford to have Oriental rugs on their floors. In fact, if they owned a "Turkey carpitt," it was more than likely to have been used on a tabletop, like a tablecloth. Today, with vacuum cleaners and synthetic underlayments, we can afford to be casual about our rugs, to consider and divide them into two separate groups: collectible rugs and decorative floor coverings.

Collectible rugs are those that are scarce, that are of an unusually early date, or that exemplify a particular style or design. Because earlier examples are rare, this is a market mainly for eighteenth-, nineteenth-, and twentieth-century carpets.

ANTIQUES DISCOVERY ROADSHOW

PERSIAN QASHQA'I BAG FACES

Mark Topalian showed the owner of these textiles how village weavings were made for the weavers' personal use. Originally, these pile weavings had a flat, or kilim, backing that made each one a bag. Slits along the top edge allowed insertion of a strap so that the bag could be hung and used for storage.

From southern Persia, these turn-of-the-century textiles feature a pattern that incorporates goats and flowers, and they make great pillows! Topalian appraised them at $1,500 to $2,000 each.

Flat-weave rugs, like the antique Kilim above, are not as durable as pile rugs. Below, a boldly patterned Kazakh typifies the geometric rugs made in village workshops.

"Decorative" rugs tend to match the color of the sofa and neatly fit the room. When decorating magazines and designers decree that muted shades are fashionable this year or that scatter rugs are passé, they directly affect the decorative rug market. But collectible rugs are not generally subject to the vagaries of fashion.

ORIENTAL RUGS

Oriental rugs are made predominantly of wool pile on a cotton foundation. Many exceptions exist, among them silk rugs, which have excellent color retention. Because silk fibers dry out easily, however, they rot and crack. It's rare, too, to find antique silk rugs in large sizes. Turkey produced inexpensive silk rugs in the twentieth century, but in general their fragility makes silk rugs better for wall display than for being walked upon. Goat hair yarns instead of cotton are sometimes used as the warp (the vertical thread) for wool rugs. Perhaps this is because of the persistent myth that snakes won't venture onto goat hair.

Rugs are commonly identified by the village or town in which they are manufactured or by the name of the tribe that manufactures them. All the exotic names you've ever read about—Kazakh, Isfahan, Heriz, Daghestan—are place-names, the Eastern equivalents of Missouri or Pittsburgh.

NOMADIC RUGS

Made by nomads for their own use, rugs, storage bags, and camel trappings were meant to be used until they wore out. Consequently, very few pre-eighteenth-century provincial tribal weavings survive to the present day.

VILLAGE WORKSHOP RUGS

Rugs manufactured in village workshops were produced specifically for sale and not for use within the tribe. Like the designs of nomadic rugs, those created by village workshops are abstract, stylized, and bold. Typical workshop-made rugs are Kazakh, Shiraz, and Kuba.

TRIBAL PATTERNS

Both village and nomadic rugs are woven in geometric patterns that are generally nondirectional; that is, they look the same when viewed from either end. (Carpets with central medallions are also nondirectional, though the medallion, which creates a definite center in the rug, makes them more challenging to place in a room.)

Prayer rugs, made in tribes and villages throughout the Islamic world, have a niche design at the center of the weaving. At one end, this niche (or *mihrab*) is either triangular or centered by a square open to the niche at one end. This end of the rug (and the head of the supplicant) faces east, toward Mecca, during prayer. When not in use, prayer rugs were rolled up to keep them clean.

The niche, or mihrab, *at one end is the identifying characteristic of a prayer rug.*

City-made Persian carpets display curvilinear patterns and sophisticated designs.

URBAN RUGS

Urban-made Persian carpets have always been coveted because their curved, nondirectional designs of stylized flowers, animals, and birds are more graceful and, perhaps, more versatile than tribal examples. Often, they were woven on ivory or pastel grounds, resulting in rugs that were subtle, soft, and effective with any decor. Certain urban-made designs, in fact, were created only for export. Because Persian carpet weavers are required to follow tribal patterns exactly and are allowed no individual touches, their beautiful, always formal rugs can seem somewhat stiff and mechanical.

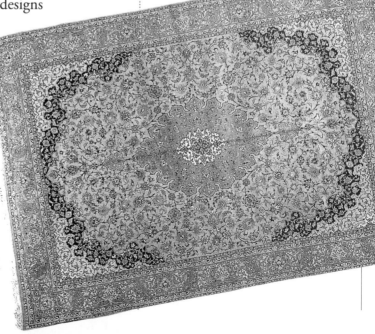

CHINESE RUGS

Chinese rugs are in a different category from Orientals. Their distinctive palette—blue, yellow, ivory, black, and brown—makes them subtler than Middle Eastern varieties, as do their fretwork or floral borders and the spaciousness, or "air," between their restrained dragon, basket, and lotus designs. These rugs were especially popular in the 1920s and 1930s, when they particularly complemented the Art Deco aesthetic, but they went out of fashion thereafter. Because it is difficult to match their wools and dyes, they are the hardest of rugs to restore.

IS IT OLD?

*Above:
A few widely scattered motifs on a solid-color ground create serenity and restraint in Chinese rugs.*

Right: The band of lighter color, an accident of weave called abrash, *interrupts the dark background of this Kuba.*

Age is perhaps less important in rugs than are rarity, design, and condition (in that order). Rug age is classified according to the scales in the chart on the facing page. Below are some tips on evaluating a rug's age.

♦ Truly old rugs, those made before the discovery of inexpensive synthetic dyes in the 1860s, are uncommon—especially old rugs in good condition.

♦ Look for the dyes in genuinely old rugs to shade—to change in intensity from dark to medium blue, for instance—often in the middle of a design. Such shading, called *abrash,* is not a flaw. The weaver might simply have had to change yarns at an inconvenient spot, and that *abrash* is the result of color inconsistencies in different dye batches of wool yarns. (Sometimes, weavers created *abrash* intentionally, as a sign of authenticity.) *Abrash* in a rug that appears to be old in other respects is an indication of age. Machine-made carpets from the first three-quarters of the twentieth century are generally uniform in color throughout.

Rug Age
Retail Trade

ANTIQUE RUGS *(50 or more years old)*

SEMI-ANTIQUE RUGS *(30–99 years old)*

OLD RUGS *(20–99 years old)*

SEMI-OLD RUGS *(10–50 years old)*

USED RUGS *(10–50 years old)*

NEW RUGS *(1–10 years old)*

0   10   20   30   40   50   60   70   80   90   100   +
YEARS

Rug Age
Experts and Connoisseurs

ANTIQUE RUGS *(100 or more years old)*

OLD RUGS *(40–99 years old)*

SEMI-OLD RUGS *(20–39 years old)*

NEW RUGS *(1–19 years old)*

0   10   20   30   40   50   60   70   80   90   100   +
YEARS

(Note that experts seem to be more demanding.)

ANTIQUES DISCOVERY ROADSHOW

SHIRVAN RUG

The owner had coveted this rug ever since he saw it as a college student in 1942. Eventually it became his, and he's treasured it ever since.

And that's good, said expert Elisabeth Poole—the decades were kind to the rug, since it spent them hanging on a wall instead of being underfoot. This Caucasian geometric from Shirvan (a village in northern Persia on the coast of the Caspian Sea) is in great condition.

Although the late-nineteenth-century rug was woven in prayer-rug format, with a niche at one end, it was probably never used as one. As with many handmade textiles, you can see the traces of the human maker—or makers, in this case, as the rug was probably made by two weavers working side by side. The pattern clearly differs from the left side to the right side as you scan it from bottom to top.

Caucasian rug patterns are very popular now. Elisabeth Poole estimates a value of $3,000 to $5,000.

KIRMAN CARPET

This large Kirman carpet, the owner explained, has really been lived on. Purchased by his great-grandparents around the turn of the century, the rug has seen eighty years of everything from bachelor parties to sick babies.

According to appraiser Mark A. Topalian, the bright colors of this rug, made in southeast Persia and woven in a "garden design," indicate it was produced after the introduction of chemical dyes, which dates it to around 1910. An interesting detail is a light blue strip that runs across the center, seemingly a flaw in

the design. Such variations are thought by some to have been purposefully woven into rugs by Persian weavers who believed only Muhammad was capable of true perfection. Others think they were caused by the uneven aging of different types of wool used in the creation of this large piece. Regardless, this carpet, in remarkably good condition considering its age, has a value of $25,000 to $35,000.

♦ You can easily distinguish a machine-made carpet from a handmade carpet: in the handmade example, the design will be equally clear on both sides. (If you are doubtful, you can bend the pile backward to expose its "roots." A handmade rug will have a knot on the front surface at the foot of the pile.)

♦ Because wool reacts differently to different dyes, some rug colors will have faded or worn more than others. The dark blues, dyed with indigo, will still be vivid, for instance, when the reds and yellows have paled.

♦ Old rugs rarely come in exact 9' x 12' and 12' x 15' sizes, or even in handy 6' x 9' or 8' x 10' sizes. Most native looms produced rugs that were 5' x 10', 6' x 12', or 10' x 18'—long and rather narrow.

♦ After years of being trod upon, old rugs have smooth, flattened knots on the back.

♦ Carefully pick one knot out of the back of a rug. Smooth it straight, and see how quickly it recurls. If it snaps right back, the rug has age.

IS IT VALUABLE?

In valuing an Oriental rug, the most important criterion is that it be handmade. Machine-made rugs, no matter how large, how beautiful or perfect, are of little value in the rug market.

Generally speaking, when comparing two rugs of the same type (Tabriz to Tabriz, or Kazakh to Kazakh), the more knots you can count on the back, the finer the weaving and the better the rug. (This makes sense, for fewer knots per inch create a loose weave, and the looser the weave, the faster a rug will wear.) If the average Tabriz has 150 knots per square inch, the top-quality example will have 500 or more.

Of course, the knot count is only one factor in determining quality.

CONDITION

Because carpets are functional as well as beautiful, they are particularly desirable when they're in good condition. But moths love wool carpets and even exhibit distinct color preferences. Hold an old carpet up to the light. You shouldn't be able to see through it. The more light you see, the happier the moths have been or the more worn the rug. And the more worn the rug (especially the more unevenly worn), the less anyone else will want to buy it. In fact, a rug with no warp threads visible on the front (they look like white patches) can bring three times the price of a worn rug.

♦ Put your ear to an old carpet and gently roll it between both hands. Does it sound crunchy? Feel dry? That means it's rotten and, no matter how attractive, can't be walked on. A good rug has soft wool and a full pile. Silk, especially, should be smooth and soft to the touch.

♦ The back of a rug can tell you whether or not it's been repaired. Scars that indicate the rug has been slit, perhaps to accommodate an electrical cord, are not as damning as those indicating that it's been "reduced"—altered in size. Very large rugs may once have had several rows of borders, but entire borders can be removed to make a "fit." Carpets have been cavalierly cut to go around hearths, as it is all too easy, unfortunately, to slice off a foot or two of a too-big rug to make it fit the niches of a small room. So check all four sides. If a pattern seems to end abruptly or if one border seems different from the others, the rug may have been cut down.

♦ The fringes at the two ends of a rug are the warp threads that remain after the rug has been cut off the loom. These threads should be intact. If the fringe is no longer there, the possibility arises that one or more rows of design have unraveled from the edge.

KAZAKH RUG

This colorful rug was purchased in Oklahoma during the oil boom, and its owner had been hounded for years by a dealer who wanted to buy it. According to Mary Jo Otsea, it is a Kazakh rug made in the southern Caucasus by nomadic weavers. A type of rug usually used on divans, beds, and floors, it is fashioned of thick, coarsely knotted wool with a geometric design in primary colors. Dating to the 1880s, the rug is in good condition and has a value of $8,000 to $12,000. Since the dealer had offered much less, the guest was happy she hadn't sold it.

♦ Reweaving on sixteenth- and seventeenth-century carpets is not as serious a fault as it is on more recent examples. Collectors find so few genuinely rare rugs that they seldom expect perfection. Very few carpets this old, however, are found in the United States.

♦ Stains, especially hard-to-remove dog stains, are, needless to say, a drawback.

COLORS

The colors of antique and semi-antique rugs are more vivid than those of modern rugs—unless they've faded, which they often have. General, allover fading is not unattractive, but many carpets fade spottily because some dyes disappear faster than others. (The first aniline dyes, made from coal tar rather than vegetable matter, eroded wool cruelly.) Such fading has often been touched up and sometimes even completely "painted" by rug dealers, a treatment that considerably diminishes value. If you want to test a rug for this kind of repair, just moisten a white cloth with saliva and rub each color vigorously. If no color comes off, the dye is original, although some vegetable dyes might leave the slightest stain. (Dampened aniline dyes, by the way, have an unpleasant smell.)

♦ Rugs in rare and hard-to-find colors—like green—always bring a premium.

♦ In the 1920s, many rugs were given a chemical wash to soften their colors for American tastes. If the reverse of a rug is brighter than the front, and if you've broken open the pile to view the knots and found that their color is brighter than the pile's surface, the rug is likely to have had a chemical wash. Unfortunately, although it gives you some indication of the rug's age, the wash has also harmed the fiber and the value.

The evaluation of antique rugs, surprisingly, has much more to do with decorating trends than does the evaluation of most other antiques. At the end of the twentieth century, for instance, pale rugs with allover designs were favorites of the design community, which made them expensive, but in the 1970s pale shades were disdained and not valuable at all. In the 1980s, when homeowners coveted flat-weaves and strong geometric designs, prices soared, but "scatter" rugs lost the favor they had enjoyed for decades and sales languished.

FOLK RUGS

Rag rugs were the earliest American rugs, simple cloth strips woven together. In the 1830s and 1840s, shirred rugs—lightweight, flexible, and ultimately faded to soft tones—were quite common, though they're seldom found today. By the end of the nineteenth century, however, the rugs in most American homes, if they were not Orientals, were braided or hooked. Braided rugs are easy to make: simply stitch cotton or wool strips into tubes, braid them together, coil them round and round, and sew the plaits to each other.

Hooked rugs, thought by many experts to be one of the few indigenous American arts, aren't quite that easy to make. Their patterns were drawn by hand or traced onto a linen, hemp, or homespun backing, and a special hooked tool was used to pull loops of wool or cotton fabrics through it. The earliest hooked rugs, beginning about 1830, employed the same sorts of geometric patterns found in quilts, and these wholly original patterns and color combinations were charming and naïve.

Halfway through the nineteenth century, burlap, a soft, inexpensive backing, became commercially available at about the same time as printed hooked rug patterns. Together, they fueled a craze for rugmaking in America. At last, one didn't have to be able to draw to create an attractive hooked rug. But predrawn patterns (easily recognizable by

For centuries, rugs have been made from braided strips of cloth. This wool example is from New England, c. 1900.

Jumbo trumpets happily on a whimsical hooked rug from the 1920s.

Idiosyncratic designs are particularly desirable in a hooked rug.

their symmetry and stiffness) also succeeded in taking the spontaneity out of the craft. Though replete with flowers, borders, animals, and scrolls, the rugs had lost the quirkiness and personality of the older, home-drawn sorts. Today, knowledgeable collectors ignore these extremely complicated, three-dimensional predrawn designs, preferring rugs from about 1825 to 1840, with their individualistic designs and unusual color schemes.

In the early part of the twentieth century, handicrafts cooperatives, which made hooked rugs for sale, existed throughout Appalachia and New England. The work produced there often had sprightly and highly inventive pictorial designs, and some of this output is highly collectible.

Yarn-sewn rugs, their design composed of clipped loops of two-ply yarn, are rather old (perhaps 1750 to 1825) and rare, as very few such rugs seem to have been made. Sometimes rug designs combine yarn-sewing with shirred chenille.

Late-nineteenth-century Shaker braided rugs are quite collectible. They were made both for use in the home and for sale in shops run by the Shaker community. Shaker rugs can usually be identified by the concentric rings of colors radiating out from the center to several rows of braided borders at the edge. The Shakers also made colorful shag rugs and woven rag rugs. Like all carefully crafted Shaker furnishings, the rugs wore like iron.

IS IT OLD?

Hooked rugs are still being made, of course, and because many of the old designs are still in use, it can be hard to tell them from the originals. Modern rugs, however, can be distinguished from older examples by their too-strong, too-fresh colors. Check the back of the rug to

A handsome braided rug reveals the highly developed Shaker sense of design.

see if the color remaining there is more intense than on the front—a sign of age.

Modern rugs are also characterized by the evenness of their pile, which will be perfectly uniform in height. Old pile should be soft and unevenly worn down. Dates incorporated into rug designs, by the way, should not necessarily be taken at face value. As with samplers, these might commemorate earlier events.

Naïve and somewhat ineptly drawn designs can indicate early manufacture. Irregularities in design are also indications of age.

Flower designs on hooked rugs became more realistic in the Victorian era.

Woven and embroidered with wool yarns, c. 1800, this cheerful textile was used as a table mat.

IS IT VALUABLE?

The size of most hooked rugs is 3' x 5'. A rug that is either smaller or larger than this standard size will be more expensive.

As with most folk art, the rug of eccentric design (in not-too-worn and not-too-faded condition) is the most sought-after.

Brilliantly colored rugs, and those with freely interpreted floral forms, are desirable, as are those with figures and animals.

AMERICAN INDIAN RUGS

Some experts consider Navajo weavings to be among the finest textiles made in the twentieth century. Navajo women (and almost all the weavers were women) were wonderfully accomplished long before American independence was declared, so it's hardly surprising that by the nineteenth century a single Navajo blanket might be traded for as

Above: Unraveled strips of cloth were used for weaving a Ganado rug.

Left: A typical Two Gray Hills rug, distinguished by its camel color and the absence of the color red.

Quite simple geometric patterns were typical of Ganado rugs, as was the use of rich, ruby red.

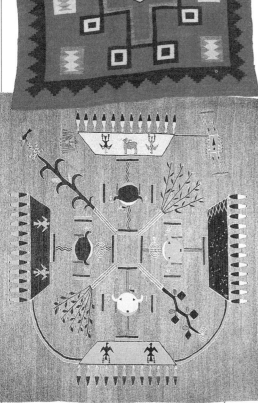

Ceremonial sandpaintings, made to be destroyed, were usually copied from memory for Navajo sandpainting rugs.

many as ten buffalo robes. And today, when Navajo weavings have been hotly collected for a century and more, a mere ten buffalo robes wouldn't begin to buy the best tribal work.

In the late nineteenth century, various traders living near Navajo communities in Arizona and New Mexico commissioned native designs that they thought might be commercially successful. Such styles as Ganado and Two Gray Hills, a complex geometric pattern, were named for their locales. Ganado, in fact, is an Arizona trading post that published mail-order catalogs of rugs. Its catalogs offered buyers not only various sizes, colors, and patterns, but also several qualities of weaving.

GEOMETRIC

Navajo women worked geometric patterns in natural shades—earth tones, often accented by strong reds. Their geometric rugs are sometimes so complex that they might be mistaken for Oriental rugs.

PICTORIAL

"Sandpainting" rugs, woven reproductions of the Navajo sandpaintings in which tribal legends and powerful spiritual beings were depicted in colored sand, were initially the work of an eccentric medicine man, Hosteen Klah, who worked in western New Mexico in the early twentieth century. Later, other members of the Navajo tribe produced pictorials, too. These rugs, whose designs included cornstalks, birds, deities, and words, were extremely expensive. They were produced mainly between 1919 and 1936.

VEGETAL

The "vegetal" rugs of the 1920s, crafted at first with vegetable dyes but eventually with virtually identical synthetics, were woven in pale pinks, grays, and tans. They were sold extensively from a Boston shop established by a patroness of Navajo weavings.

QUILTS

We may never know for certain whether quilts with designs originated from pure necessity or as a bed-size showcase for a housewife's skill with needle and thread. Fortunately for us, a century of harsh American winters bred a bumper crop of quilts and imaginative quilting.

In the vastness of pioneer America, quiltmaking was often a cooperative effort (remember the quilting bee?), although it certainly could be a solitary pursuit. An Ohio woman, for example, ruefully noted: "It took me more than twenty years, nearly twenty-five, in the evening after supper when the children were all put to bed, to make that quilt. My whole life is in that quilt—all my joys and all my sorrows." Her wistful comment sums up what we intuit in the best work today, both collective and individual—the presence of the artist's heart. That explains as well why American artists Grant Wood and Charles Sheeler collected quilts and why, in 1971, the Whitney Museum chose to mount a quilt exhibit. American quilts are arresting, internationally admired, and extensively collected. In other words, Art.

Labor of love: a star-pattern quilt assembled from two fairly simple designs.

TECHNIQUES AND TYPES

There are three basic quilted bedcovers—the appliquéd quilt, the pieced quilt, and the whole-cloth quilt. Appliquéd quilts are the earliest type. Before America began to manufacture its own printed textiles, it imported English and East Indian fabrics, both far too costly to be used for bedcoverings. So thrifty quilters purchased small amounts of these pricey goods, cut out the prettiest motifs—baskets of flowers and bouquets—and then stitched (appliquéd) them to a foundation cloth.

In the border of an album quilt: a cluster of American emblems, carefully stitched.

Below: Although cotton crazy quilts were usually pieced together from scraps, velvet-and-silk crazy quilts like this one were made from kits.

Bottom: A "log cabin" quilt in the Courthouse Steps pattern.

From the 1840s on, however, most American quilts were of the pieced variety, constructed block by block from an assemblage of fabric scraps. The blocks could be worked on anywhere, as they were just 10 to 20 inches square, and portable. While some quiltmakers saved all their sewing scraps, sometimes for years, others bought brand-new fabrics.

Quiltmaking was time-consuming. Each bit of fabric had to be cut against a template to the desired shape, with just enough left to fold over for seams, and quilters sometimes left their newspaper or cardboard templates in the finished quilt for extra insulation. Next, they stitched the pieces together, and when the top of the quilt was complete, they layered cotton batting on it and backed it with another piece of fabric. Then they brought out the collapsible quilting frame (most households had one) and stretched the quilt on it. The quilting pattern was traced on the fabric with chalk or pencil (the marks disappeared with laundering) or the design was pricked on the surface with a needle, and this three-piece "sandwich" was stitched, or quilted, together with wonderfully decorative stitch patterns, or with several patterns, each a superb display of sewing skill. Whole-cloth quilts, which showcased the intricate, finely executed stitching patterns that became the quilt's only decoration, used a single piece of fabric for the top—often of tightly woven, solid white or ivory cotton. The finest needlewomen (as many as twelve might work on a quilt at once) were able to sew a remarkable fourteen stitches to the inch. Once a quilt was completed, its edges were bound or hemmed.

Though quiltmaking can be a demanding craft, children (who sometimes had to complete their daily allotment of quilting before they were allowed out to play) learned to do it. Even young boys—Dwight Eisenhower, for one—were taught to piece quilts together. Most quilters were women, however, for whom the work was a welcome creative outlet and a justifiable source of pride.

MATERIALS

Usually, quilts were made of wool or cotton fabrics. The earliest examples, made in the eighteenth century, were dyed with homemade, highly unstable colors, several of which ultimately caused these quilts to deteriorate over time. But wool and cotton are durable, and numbers of such quilts have survived in decent condition, along with all-silk quilts made for "show" (never used) and late-nineteenth-century "crazy quilts," composed of velvet and silk scraps. (Crazy quilts were actually tufted rather than quilted. In tufting, or tacking, several lengths of thread are pulled through the quilt "sandwich" at regular intervals; then each one is tied off in a knot.)

PATTERNS

There are innumerable quilt patterns, some of which have been popular for two centuries. Many have picturesque names—Goose in the Pond, Courthouse Steps, Barn-Raising, Star of Bethlehem, Drunkard's Path, Kansas Troubles. Several of these patterns can be found in a variety of sizes. Among the most collectible, because they are so well suited to framing and particularly, to hanging on apartment walls, are crib quilts and pillow shams, as well as the so-called "hired-hand" quilts made in single-bed sizes.

Quilts with geometric designs are especially common because they're among the easiest to execute. The most popular of the geometrics is the "log cabin" quilt, named for the logs, or long, narrow strips of cloth, that form the designs. When the logs are pieced together the repeating blocks of darks and lights in the completed quilt create riveting, illusionist patterns.

BALTIMORE ALBUM QUILT

This lovely quilt really made Leslie Keno's day. And no wonder! Made in 1850 and in superb condition, its patchwork depicts fruit, leaves, and stylized rifles, all in brilliant reds and greens. Quilts like this are typical of the Baltimore area and are quite rare.

According to Keno, the quilt is unusually elaborate and its large size makes it especially desirable. In addition, elements like the watermelon and knife on a compote provide a unique folk element. With an appraisal of $50,000, Keno clearly made the owner's day, too!

AMERICAN QUILT

Appraiser Leslie Keno was very impressed by an extremely well-preserved American mid-nineteenth-century appliquéd quilt that belonged to the owner's great-great-grandmother. Because the quilt had been hidden away in a cedar trunk, the strikingly deep, rich reds and greens used in the center pin-wheel design, the flowers at the top and bottom, and the peacocks and flying doves in the corners have not been faded by sunlight.

Also impressive are the many hours of work apparent in the tightly woven plumes of flowers that form a circular pattern, fanning out into pineapple motifs in the background. The combination of color and design makes this a powerful example of American folk art.

Keno valued this treasured family heirloom, inscribed to the owner's grandmother, at $12,000 to $15,000.

Bridal quilts were elaborate, all-white "show" quilts, also known as whitework. In some parts of the country, before a woman married, she was expected to make thirteen quilts—twelve pieces for everyday use and one, her bridal quilt, simply for display. (Bridal quilts often incorporated quilted heart motifs, which were considered to be extremely unlucky to use on any other quilt.) Whitework was not just quilted; it was sometimes stuffed as well, using a technique that required carefully pushing aside the threads of the quilt's cloth backing and inserting small pieces of cotton through the tiny opening. This painstaking process created subtly raised designs called trapunto on the surface—without question some of the finest needlework ever produced in this country. (It was, legend has it, considered bad luck by some needlewomen to make a perfect quilt. Amish quilters, for example, firmly believed that only God could create perfection. Intentional mistakes, therefore, were stitched into otherwise flawless work.)

The album quilt, a group effort, was usually made as a parting gift for a friend or a minister, but it could also commemorate a birth or wedding. Each square, a different design from every other, was appliquéd by the friend or congregant and usually signed by its maker in embroidery or pen-and-ink. In addition, the designs might be embroidered or stuffed. The famous Baltimore album quilts of the mid-nineteenth century were made by an unknown but talented group of needlewomen and professional quiltmakers who worked in the environs of Baltimore. Their quilts are generally considered to be among the most beautiful and historic of American examples.

The unique quilts made between 1890 and 1940 by the Amish in Lancaster County, Pennsylvania, are among the most collectible today. The Amish (known as "plain folk") crafted wool quilts with a firm, squarish central focus and employed only deep, bold colors—for their religion prohibited them from using patterns. Such restrictions, however, hardly hampered the brilliant Amish quilters, who stitched quilts that resemble twentieth-century contemporary paintings. With distinctively wide, finely quilted borders, often incorporating a typically Amish feather pattern, they were executed with consummate skill.

Mennonite quilts are handsome and can be distinguished from those of the Amish by their particularly intricate quilting patterns, including tulips, baskets, and wreaths, their printed fabrics, and their machine-stitched piecing. Later Mennonite quilts are occasionally abstract.

Quilts with star designs are quite common. The Star of Bethlehem quilt, with its typical red center, is among the most well-known, and patriotic quilts, incorporating images of flags, eagles, and, sometimes, portraits of American presidents, are in great demand.

Although interest in quilting declined after 1890, it drifted back on the cold winds of the Depression, when popular quilting kits, usually containing fabrics in pastel shades on pale grounds, allowed housewives to be both creative and frugal at the same time. And while they were once disdained by collectors, today Depression quilts have become desirable. Interestingly, in the 1970s, as a corollary to the Peace Movement and the celebration of America's Bicentennial, quilting became popular once more.

A good example of a common type of "log cabin" quilt.

IS IT OLD?

Almost unique among antiques, the field of quilts is one in which age is deemed less important than beauty. Amish quilts made of natural textiles were fabricated until the mid-twentieth century, but due to the strength, clarity, and color combinations of the Amish designs, they appeal to art collectors and textile connoisseurs alike and are now among the most expensive American textiles. Pictorial quilts, depicting

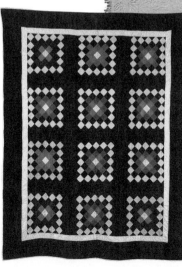

Above: This whitework quilt exhibits both virtuosic stitchery and trapunto.

Left: A typically bold Amish cotton-and-wool quilted coverlet, Holmes County, Ohio, c. 1930.

Intricate, inventive stitchery is dazzling on a pieced and appliquéd Ohio quilt, 1920.

The "Star of Bethlehem" on a Colonial-era quilt made in New Jersey.

whimsical and naïve figures, farm animals, or both, are highly valued, even when they're relatively new: fine craftsmanship, interesting composition, and pleasing colors outrank age.

Some types of quilts, however, like album quilts and particularly the more ordinary geometrics, are more desirable if they have some age. Luckily, there are several ways to determine the age of a quilt.

♦ Look at the threads used for stitching. Very early threads were three-ply, while six-ply threads indicate later manufacture.

♦ Look for machine-stitching. When the sewing machine first became widely available, around 1850, women who had previously stitched their quilt blocks together by hand—the most tedious, least creative part of quilting—welcomed it with gratitude. And who could blame them? We certainly don't, for their machine-stitched straight work isn't even considered a drawback today. It's simply one more convenient tool for dating quilts: an indication that a piece must have been made after the mid-nineteenth century.

♦ American collectors prefer quilts of American fabrics, although it takes special expertise to be able to distinguish these from the many imported textiles. Fabric dating, too, is the province of the specialist, for quilt fabrics were often collected over many years, even generations. Therefore, experts leave a ten-year leeway for dating a quilt by its fabric patterns. (By the same token, dated newspaper templates left inside a quilt were sometimes printed long before its actual fabrication, since they were often saved but not used until years later.)

Unfortunately, all those whimsically named quilt patterns are virtually useless for dating, as many were popular for generations and are still in use today. Amish patterns are an exception: a central block surrounded by a wide border is a fairly accurate indication that the quilt was made before 1850.

Perhaps the surest guarantee of quilt age is the fineness of the needlework. In the nineteenth century, the golden age of the American quilt, truly elegant needlework was as highly regarded a female skill as excellence at litigation is at the end of the twentieth century.

IS IT VALUABLE?

In general, the most desirable quilts are not faded. Their colors are as vibrant and bold as the year they were made, and the quilts themselves are thoughtfully designed, with careful attention given to juxtapositions of color and choices of quilting patterns. Valuable quilts shouldn't be worn or cut down to smaller sizes, of course. But after all these considerations, the very best quilts are always precision-cut and pieced, reveal very fine needlework, and, of course, display virtuosic quilting execution and design.

♦ Knowing the maker's name, particularly if it's that of a well-known quilter or some person of historical importance, will add to the value.

♦ Increasingly rare, but always desirable, are quilts incorporating the American flag and patriotic designs.

♦ Any circular-patterned geometric quilt, such as Star of Bethlehem or Mariner's Compass, will be costly because it is so difficult to piece those patterns accurately.

♦ Quilts depicting African-American themes, or those made by African-Americans, command a premium.

♦ In "log cabin" patterns, collectors look for drama—quilts with optic glamour.

♦ Amish work is exceptionally valuable, but only when it's made of all-natural fabric. In the twentieth century, the Amish sometimes used synthetics, which collectors dislike because they pill.

The American flag stands out on this collaborative album quilt in which no two squares are alike.

A rare African-American quilt, incorporating characteristic motifs.

Some thoughts on quilts from expert Nancy Druckman:

The *perfect* quilt would be sensationally graphic: teeming with figures and flowers, and so fresh that it would virtually crackle when opened.

Because there are thousands and thousands of old quilts in existence, no "buts" about quilts are acceptable ("but it's really old," "but it was well-used," etc.). Excellent condition is paramount, and any soil, stain, fading, or tattered fabric immediately diminishes value.

The quilt market is somewhat regional. In the East, for instance, and particularly in New York, pink and green quilts are not as popular as the deep olives, rusts, and blacks of Amish quilts.

Left: Two layers of cloth add warmth to a double-weave coverlet. The dark side is considered the front; the light side, the back.

Below: An overshot coverlet might have been made at home or by professional weavers.

♦ Baltimore album quilts are almost unbuyable today, as are many of the finest nineteenth-century quilts. The few excellent examples that come on the market are quite costly.

COVERLETS

Woven coverlets (or bedcovers) were, as might be expected, exceptionally common. They were often made by itinerant weavers, who provided their customers with four basic types of design in cotton and wool: the Overshot, the Double-Weave, the Summer and Winter, and the Jacquard, all in shades of blue, cream, red, and black. Three of these types have geometric patterns.

The **Overshot** coverlet, made in the eighteenth century in striped, diamond, and square patterns, was among the earliest. Thick but quite loosely woven, it was fashioned on narrow looms that necessarily created a bedcover made in two pieces and seamed down the middle.

In the reversible **Double-Weave,** which generally dates from the nineteenth century, the front and the back of the coverlet can actually be pulled apart.

The **Summer and Winter** coverlet, first woven in Pennsylvania, was also reversible, but it was all of one piece and could not be pulled apart. It was dark on one side (Winter) and light on the reverse (Summer).

Jacquard coverlets, the type most frequently seen, were woven on a special loom attachment that allowed the weaver to create repeating curvilinear patterns—birds, flowers, and even railroad trains. Often woven into a corner was the weaver's name, the town, and the date, along with the name of the person for whom it was made.

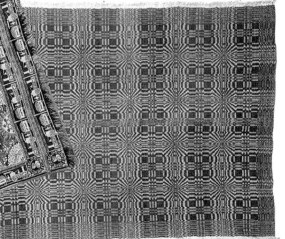

While reproduction coverlets are still being made, these can be distinguished from the old because they feel somewhat stiff and "crisp."

Old examples will always show some wear and be soft to the touch. Fringes on coverlets (three sides only) should be original, not later add-ons.

SAMPLERS

A long time ago, the well-educated woman knew how to play the piano, sing a little, paint a bit, and do fine—often exquisite—needlework. Male sentiments regarding any additional female education seem neatly expressed by the following lines of verse:

> *One did commend me to A Wife both fair*
> *and Young*
> *Who had French, Spanish and Italian tongue.*
> *I thanked him kindly, and told him I loved*
> *none such,*
> *For I thought one tongue For A Wife too much.*
> *What, love ye not the learned? Yes, as my life*
> *A Learned Scholar, but not A Learned Wife*

Although needlework was a dull necessity of daily life, girls whose parents could afford it were sent to ladies' seminaries to learn how to sew—not just curtains, but a truly fine seam—and how to do that beautifully. They learned this on "samplers."

The original purpose of the samplers they stitched was simply to preserve and hand down old and intricate patterns in a convenient form, thereby ensuring that future generations of schoolgirls would continue to sit and practice needlework, instead of conjugating Latin verbs or writing multiplication tables. (Of course, the samplers did offer lessons in numbers or the alphabet.) Thousands of samplers still exist to tell us much about the times, the values, and, perhaps too rarely, the gratifyingly independent views of

Samplers often displayed their maker's talents at stitching the alphabet, a verse, and a decorative panel.

A nicely worked—if not altogether correct —map of Europe and North Africa.

An American family tree sampler with neatly labeled "fruit" and pinked edges.

"Nancy Forrest's sampler wrought in the fourteenth year of her age, 1811": silk on linen with a solidly worked background.

the girls who made them, like this far-from-tender sentiment on an early-nineteenth-century example: "Patty Polk did this and she hated every stitch in it. She loves to read much more."

Most little girls were less outspoken. Although their average age was eleven and they surely must have preferred play (or reading) to needlework, many of them dutifully worked neatly stitched renderings of the patterns—drawn by themselves if they were artistic, or by their schoolmistresses. Not infrequently, professionally drawn, rented patterns were used. And often the designs were copied from well-known engravings.

TYPES OF SAMPLERS

Alphabet samplers were the most common. These would present, in a variety of stitches, the alphabet, punctuation marks, and a series of numbers, along with instructive little verses. When a sampler was finished, the proud (and probably relieved) seamstress usually stitched her name and the completion date on it, although in her later years she might pick out the threads of the date to protect the secret of her age.

Schoolgirls also stitched **maps**, which taught them a bit about geography, though a style of geography that makes us smile today since the maps were often comically inaccurate. Map samplers were more common in England than they were in the United States. The dozen or so known American examples include maps of New Jersey, Maryland, and Massachusetts.

Exceptionally fashionable during the nineteenth century was a particularly American specialty—family record samplers, or **genealogies**. Composed in somber colors, these samplers recorded family births, deaths, marriage dates, and quite literal family "trees." Mourning pictures, which came into vogue around 1800 and which contained elements of the family records, also incorporated tombstones, mourners, and, more often than not, at least one of the period's omnipresent weeping willows. Pictorial mourning embroideries, related to samplers, were often worked on silk and included painted elements and printed inscriptions. These embroideries were especially popular in America around the time of the death of George Washington in 1799.

Presentation samplers, made by fond children as gifts for proud parents, were often handsomely framed by the doting recipients.

Pictorial samplers, a common form, have very little lettering, unlike the preceding types. Their stitching is often a tour de force of animals, people, and buildings, combined with decorative embellishments like borders, flowers, and scattered butterflies.

MATERIALS

Some seventeenth- and eighteenth-century samplers were stitched on a linen ground, but the majority were worked on either cotton canvas or wool. All-cotton samplers—cotton thread on cotton canvas—tended to be somewhat crude, while wool, though an excellent ground material to stitch upon, was also subject to galloping moth damage. A type of wool called tammy, imported from England until about 1825 (identifiable by its edges, which incorporate thin blue lines) was a frequent ground for American samplers. The finest samplers, however, were worked on bolting cloth, a highly transparent wool used in the flour industry. Satin was saved for mourning pictures, because its shiny surface was the ideal background on which to paint the mourners' faces and clothes as well as the lettering on the tombstones. Samplers worked on colored grounds are rare, but a green linsey-woolsey was in use between 1790 and 1825 in New England.

The threads used for samplers were of linen, cotton, wool, or silk, and their colors were home-dyed. The finest threads, of course, were silk, but over the centuries some silken greens have turned to blue, and blacks, which were dyed with iron

TIPS
from the experts

Nancy Druckman discusses what to look for in samplers:

To have a hope of being valuable, samplers must be perfect. Only a real rarity, like Martha Washington's very own sampler, would be acceptable in less than perfect condition.

The usual conditional problems include water stains, faded colors, and discolorations.

Although American samplers are sought after, some English samplers, especially those with interesting documentation, can be quite valuable.

English samplers are always busier and more ornate than American samplers. The stitching is tighter and harder, and the background canvas is more tightly woven.

American samplers sometimes contract words to make them fit on a line.

Mourning pictures, commonly worked on satin, often depicted a tomb, topped by draped urns and flanked by mourners.

PENNSYLVANIA SAMPLER

According to the guest, this sampler has been in the family for four generations. That would be hard to tell, though, considering its excellent condition. It depicts a child in front of her house with a tree in the background and, as shown, was made in Monture County, Pennsylvania, in 1838. It is a great piece of folk art, and due to its superb condition and wonderful color, Peter Curran estimates its value at $40,000 to $50,000.

rust, have rotted. The reds, purples, and yellows faded first, however, which means that only the rare sampler will come down to us in its original brilliant hues.

In addition to simple stitchery, samplers were often embellished with beads, ribbons, appliqué work, rosettes, and watercolor painting, to which chenille might be added.

IS IT OLD?

The delightful thing about samplers is that, unlike rugs and quilts, they can be dated with a fair degree of accuracy. Several elements are helpful here: not least, of course, is the actual date, stitched in. But beyond such simple and satisfying documentation, we know, for instance, the precise years when certain designs were first used, and we even know *where* they were used. Thanks to specific regional characteristics and techniques, we can also occasionally attribute samplers to particular schools or at least to regions of the country where they were made.

Seventeenth-century American samplers are uncommon (the earliest-known examples were made in Massachusetts in 1630), but they share certain motifs: the tree-of-life design, the fleur-de-lis, and the pineapple. Very early works were usually sewn on long, narrow linen. As the eighteenth century progressed, the fabric canvas became more square.

Here are some reference points for dating eighteenth- and nineteenth-century samplers:

♦ Stylized borders used as frames for samplers are an early-eighteenth-century convention. Also during this period, samplers were often sewn to the pine backing board.

♦ The eagle first appeared on a sampler in 1756.

♦ Any sampler stitched with a vine and berries was made after 1760.

♦ A house is first found stitched on a sampler in 1766.

♦ Figures of men date from 1775.

♦ In the 1760s, the Providence (Rhode Island) State House became the first public building to appear on a sampler.

♦ Samplers including grapevine, strawberry, rosebud, morning glory, and rose motifs were made after 1800.

♦ No Kentucky sampler has been found that dates before 1800, and none from Ohio before 1807.

When attempting to date a sampler, bear in mind the following:

♦ A death date on a sampler should not necessarily be considered the date of the sampler itself. Mourning pictures were frequently created a long time after the event.

♦ When the place of death appears on the epitaph inscribed on a tomb, it's usually safe to assume that the deceased actually died in that place. It would be a mistake, however, to take it for granted that the sampler was made there.

♦ By the mid-nineteenth century, sampler patterns, like quilt patterns, began to appear in ladies' magazines and also to be printed on canvas. Such patterns were termed "Berlin" work, after the European city of their origin. Eventually, the convenience of printed art replaced the earlier handiwork. Usually incorporating floral and biblical motifs and executed in tent or cross-stitch, Berlin work was frequently done with very brightly colored wool.

Some collectors enjoy being able to identify a sampler's origin. Here are some keys to regional styles (keep in mind that some homesick girls stitched their own hometowns on their efforts, regardless of where they attended school).

♦ A pattern called the "Boston band," with a hexagonal border around the sampler, was used in that city until the 1820s.

A neat Quaker sampler with embroidery, stitched in 1829.

A needlework sampler made in Warren, Rhode Island, probably under the tutelage of schoolmistress Martha Pease Davis. It shows the strong influence of the Polly Balch School in nearby Providence.

Two examples of early American needle-work: above, a silk-on-linen sampler created by Desire Demmen in 1804; below, a sampler depicting the Garden of Eden, stitched in silk by Susan Rabson in 1789.

♦ Before the Revolution, New England samplers, usually pastoral in design, often included a fishing female figure called the "Fishing Lady."

♦ The major motifs of some New Hampshire designs are outlined in black.

♦ Polly Balch ran a famous school in Providence, Rhode Island, and her pupils' work is so remarkable that even before the 1920s, when Americana first began to attract collectors' attention, samplers from this school were eagerly sought.

♦ Quaker women taught sewing everywhere, from New England to Virginia, and their easily recognizable Quaker alphabet appears up and down the East Coast. In this alphabet, so revealing of its English antecedents, the bottom-most, pointed sections of the letters M and N descend right to the base line, and the J and Q extend below it. Punctuation marks, as part of the alphabet, are often found on Quaker samplers. The inclusion of cross-stitched floral motifs and swans indicates Quaker instruction.

IS IT VALUABLE?

Since many samplers repeat the same designs, any departure from the ordinary adds value, and it's a plus for a sampler to contain unusual motifs. A recognizable building, for instance, makes a sampler more valuable. If a sampler contains figures, collectors especially like to see them wearing clothing other than typical white dresses or black suits. A striped frock can add unexpected dimension to the conventional mourning picture.

♦ Southern examples are rather rare, so a documented Southern provenance for a sampler would be highly desirable.

♦ It's a definite advantage to find a sampler still in its original frame.

American vs. English

Many English samplers hang on American walls, placed there both by tourism and by inheritance. American specimens, of course, will always be valuable to American collectors, so it's important to be able to distinguish them from English-made samplers.

♦ Although English and American samplers look much alike (especially in versions from the seventeenth and eighteenth centuries), one interesting distinction between the two is that American teachers seem to have been endearingly tolerant of pupils whose skills were not up to par. Samplers made in America have more stitching and spelling mistakes in them than do English examples.

♦ All-American motifs are always giveaways, of course. Eagles, for instance, flocked onto samplers in the Federal era, as did flags and fond references to the Father of Our Country.

♦ English samplers are often brighter than American examples, since English students and their teachers had access to better dyes. These samplers also feature decidedly more formal, symmetrical compositions.

♦ It's easy to be confused by town names. There are Plymouths, Portsmouths, and Bostons on both sides of the Atlantic.

♦ American girls seldom included allusions to Shakespeare in their needlework, but English girls often did so.

♦ American schoolgirls were much given to working a view of Mount Vernon, taken from a well-known print, into the backgrounds of their samplers.

Condition

Moth-eaten backgrounds and faded colors diminish value. Unfortunately, numerous samplers, framed by proud families, were allowed to hang on sunlit walls,

One of a special group of samplers from Marblehead, Massachusetts, c. 1788.

An English silk-embroidered needlework picture, c. 1760.

and far too many of these have faded to pale shadows of their former vivid selves. Turn your stitchery over and examine its back if you want to see the true, original colors. (It's a bittersweet paradox that those families who perhaps couldn't afford to frame their children's work actually conserved it best; these stored samplers, for the most part, still retain their original brilliance.)

Finally, remember that the sampler with the finest needlework is always the most valuable. What was true two hundred years ago is still true today.

FURTHER READING

Bishop, Robert. *The Knopf Collectors' Guides to American Antiques: Quilts, with Coverlets, Rugs & Samplers.* New York: Alfred A. Knopf, 1982.

Bolton, Ethel, and Coe, Eva. *American Samplers.* New York: Dover, 1973.

Bonsib, Sandy. *Folk Art Quilts: A Fresh Look.* Bothell, WA: Martingale, & Co., 1998.

Bosly, Caroline. *Rugs to Riches.* New York: Pantheon, 1980.

Lipman, Jean, and Winchester, Alice. *The Flowering of American Folk Art.* New York: Viking, 1974.

Middleton, Andrew. *Rugs and Carpets.* London: Mitchell Beazley, 1996.

Milanesi, Enza. *The Bulfinch Guide to Carpets.* Boston: Little, Brown, 1992.

Peck, Amelia. *American Quilts and Coverlets in The Metropolitan Museum of Art.* New York: Dutton Studio Books, 1990.

Penney, David, and Longfish, George. *Native American Art.* Southport, CT: Hugh Lauter Levin Associates, 1994.

Ring, Betty. *American Needlework Treasures.* New York: Dutton, 1987.

Chapter Nine

TOYS, DOLLS, AND COLLECTIBLES

This chapter is about serious nostalgia, about tracking down and recapturing, if not our youth, then at least the toys we played with—the cars, dolls, teddy bears, Donald Ducks, Robbie the Robots, Captain Midnight decoder rings—and all those beloved stars and images like Elvis, Bogie, Joltin' Joe, Coca-Cola, Snow White, King Kong, Harley Davidson, and that dazzling Texaco star.

Bisque-head "Gretchen": a character doll made by Kämmer & Reinhardt, Germany, 1909.

From the collector's viewpoint, great age is not important for toys, dolls, and collectibles. Toys made before World War II, for instance, are considered "antique," while toys made after the war are "modern." Most of the toys still in existence were created after 1880, in fact, but many of the most desirable are only a few decades old, and it's surprising that there are as many toys and dolls of collectible quality as there are. Toys, if they were good, were played with and led hard

NOAH'S ARKS

The Schoenhut firm produced a Noah's Ark set with numerous pairs of wooden animals, the ark itself, and appropriate human companions. Toys with such biblical associations were often designated "Sunday toys"; that is, toys that could be played with only on Sundays. (Similarly, expensive, elaborately dressed dolls were frequently "Sunday toys.") Folk-art toy collectors are particularly drawn to the many carved wood representations of Noah's Ark that were fashioned by untrained American artists, as well as all sorts of wooden folk pull toys and games.

Not surprisingly, some of the animals are no longer two-by-two on this carved and painted Noah's Ark, a "Sunday toy" from Germany.

lives, which was why playthings had to be made of sturdy materials. Toys for boys were usually made of tough substances—wood, tinplate, and iron. Girls, who presumably were more gentle in their play, were entrusted with much more fragile toys like real porcelain dolls. Most toys were not expected to last as long as they have.

Collectibles are not dissimilar, although there are many more of them—simply because almost anything that more than two people want seems to become a collectible. A thing doesn't have to be old, useful, attractive, or rare to be collectible. Scholarship accrues to items as different as barbed wire and Barbie dolls almost before the former rusts and the latter changes her hair style, as long as a few people collect them. But the most desirable objects, the ones that survive the vagaries of fashion and the passing years, appeal to innumerable enthusiasts. Which is why, if it smacks of speed, Hollywood, baseball, or popular music, Americans collect it.

TOYS

Toys and dolls are a particularly well-researched field, with well-established guidelines as to which are common examples and which are rare. This is also a well-labeled field, with hundreds of documented makers and marks. There is little guesswork involved in identifying toys (a feature collectors appreciate), for most are clearly marked in accessible (though sometimes obscure) spots. Condition is more important to toys than any other attribute, and formulas have been devised to grade their condition and rarity (see "Is It Valuable?" page 271). Consequently, toy connoisseurship is gratifyingly direct and straightforward.

WOODEN TOYS

Some of our oldest manufactured playthings are wooden toys, mass-produced in America since the mid-1850s. And though fond fathers of every era and country have carved wooden animals or pull toys for their children, Germany, home to fine wood-carvers for centuries, had established its own very large and very successful toy-making industry by the nineteenth century. Thousands of individual craftsmen carved toys to order at home, while the city of Nuremburg developed into a great center of the craft. Germany's products, cunningly designed and carefully wrought, influenced other toy manufacturers throughout the world.

In America, the best-known manufacturer of wooden toys was the Schoenhut Company of Philadelphia, founded by Albert Schoenhut, a German immigrant. The Schoenhut firm made fine-quality wooden figures with jointed limbs and was especially noted for its multipiece sets of animals and dolls comprising circuses and bands. Schoenhut toys can be recognized by the fact that they are strung with elastic, and therefore movable, and by the two holes in the base of the dolls' feet, which allowed them to be mounted on a stand.

Carved rocking horses may date back to the earliest civilizations and were, in fact, mentioned in medieval manuscripts. By the seventeenth century, the two-dimensional rocking horse, having board sides rather than legs, was in common use, and by the mid-nineteenth century the rocking horse as we know it today was widely available. Homemade hand-carved horses, lovingly fitted with horsehair manes and tails, were widespread in rural America. Often, these steeds are so inventive and well-carved that, along with their nostalgic associations, they are appreciated and collected as folk sculptures in themselves.

A printed paper-on-wood clock-work whirligig merry-go-round.

Not an old-fashioned rocking horse, but a sophisticated descendant. The legs move and the head nods as the wheels move forward.

Complete with African backdrop, a wooden Schoenhut diorama showcases Teddy Roosevelt on safari.

"Woman's Rights": an American clockwork toy with unusual sociological significance.

The hobbyhorse (or rocking horse) may have been the most popular of children's amusements and a paragon of the wood-carving art, but in Pennsylvania the talented descendants of German toymakers were also creating simple and elegant carved wood toys such as ninepins, dolls, and animals for their own children. And because children love movement, entertaining "action" toys with windmilling arms, called "whirligigs," were devised for them along with pairs of wood acrobats that twirled around a bar, miniature merry-go-rounds, and circus wagons full of exotic animals. All these wooden toys constitute a bonanza of carved naïveté for folk enthusiasts.

TINPLATE TOYS

Toys fashioned of metal are the largest group of toy collectibles, and a significant number of them are tinplate, constructed initially from thin sheets of steel coated with tin—inexpensive, lightweight, readily milled, and therefore matchless for toymaking. Yet the process was inefficient at first, for tin toys were initially soldered together and hand-painted. The finishing coat of paint effectively protected the metal (except, of course, on boats and steam engines, which were constantly exposed to water and required, instead, a coat of rustproof nickel plate). Eventually, manufacturers learned not to solder, but to fasten the toys with neat preformed tabs on one section fitting into slots on the opposing section, a much more efficient process. In addition, with the discovery of the offset color lithography process, it was no longer necessary to hand-paint the toys. They could be shipped from the factory coated with cheerful, realistic, color-lithographed detail.

MECHANICAL TOYS

Toys that have motion (as opposed to "still" toys, which simply sit still) are considered "mechanical," and mechanical tinplate toys first appeared in America in the mid-nineteenth century. Fortunate children of that era could choose among pull toys (fire engines or horse-drawn carts), bell toys (fitted with a bell that rang as the toy was pulled), and clockwork toys, activated by actual clock mechanisms manufactured in New England. Given a good clock movement, a skeleton could dance and a hoop toy could roll on its own across the floor. (Numbers of clockwork toys, once they were wound, could roll or dance for half an hour.)

After 1880, competitive European toymakers began to market mechanical toys with stamped tinplate gears, considerably lighter and less expensive than the American prototypes, and by 1900 fully one-third of the tinplate toys made in Germany were being sold in the United States. American metal toys of this era were often more whimsical than their German counterparts; while the great German toy manufacturers were producing stolid battleships and self-important floor trains, most American makers were opting for gentler animal and people toys.

WHEELED VEHICLES

Americans liked any and all types of speedy vehicles, and cars in particular. The hand-enameled, spring-driven cars of the German firm of Georges Carette were perhaps the finest and most accurate reproductions of full-size luxury autos ever made, and while several models of these appealing and popular cars were retailed in America and England, Carette autos and other tinplate vehicle toys were ultimately supplanted by cars, trucks, and buses in cast iron. Smaller than earlier toy vehicles, and sturdier, by the 1930s European and American cast-iron cars were perfect miniatures of the automobiles then on the road.

TRAINS

Toy trains were popular throughout the nineteenth and early twentieth centuries, when the locomotive, epitomizing power and speed, captured the imagination of generations of children, and adults as well. The first toy trains were floor

The George Brown tinplate "Charles" hose reel, c. 1875, is probably the rarest early American tin toy known to exist.

With luggage, carriage lamps, elegant coach work, and chauffeur, this Carette car was top-of-the-line: a plaything for a privileged child.

Two-car Carette tinplate electric tram car set.

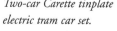

B U D D Y L T O Y C A R S

I t's hard for a child to be given a toy and not be allowed to play with it. But when the toy is an eighty-year-old Model T Roadster in excellent condition, it becomes a valuable antique.

Expert Noel Barrett identified the owner's two cars as having been made by the famous Buddy L company c. 1919 or 1920—the red and gold Buddy L decal on the bottom is authentic. The "flivver" series, according to Barrett, included the Flat-Top Roadster and the Roadster Pickup Truck—both shown here.

The owner, who was given the cars as a child, guessed their worth at about $100 for the pair. Barrett, noting the rarity of the pickup truck, the acknowledged superiority of Buddy L toys, and the excellent condition of both cars, appraised the flat-top at $1,000 and the pickup at $1,600 to $1,700.

The owner plans to give the cars to his grandson. And he won't let him play with them.

toys (to be pushed by their owners) or toys operated by simple spring mechanisms or clockworks. After the mid-nineteenth century, some actually ran on live steam. Eventually succumbing to the fate of similar vehicles, tinplate trains were replaced by cast-iron models, to be replaced again by lithographed tinplate in the late nineteenth century. (Trains that ran on sectional tracks, incidentally, were not invented until 1891, by the Märklin Company in Germany.) The heyday of the electric train was 1920 to 1950, and while pre–World War II trains have been collected for years, post–World War II train sets and accessories are increasing in popularity.

B O A T S

Toymakers also manufactured toy boats, but not in great numbers. Many vintage boats on wheels to be pulled along the ground still exist, yet the best boats were those that could float on water. Such seaworthy tinplate toy boats are rare today—perhaps because they were quite expensive, or because they could be played with only in warm weather, or because they had an unfortunate tendency to sink. (Early toy planes and dirigibles are rare for a similarly obvious reason: what goes up comes down—often too hard.) Still, a rare few have stayed afloat through the years, probably because their owners, generally the children of wealthy families, played with them under a nanny's supervision.

CAST-IRON TOYS

C ast-iron toys were made by pouring molten iron into molds of very fine sand. Thousands of cars, cows, or soldiers could be cast at once in this way, and inexpensively. These low-technology cast-iron toys were a purely American phenomenon, perhaps because of the country's natural resources or its large, unskilled work force. Whatever the reason, throughout the first half of the twentieth century America excelled at cast-iron toys. And fortunately for enthusiasts, cast iron has survived the ravages of childhood and time far better than perishable tinplate.

BELL TOYS

Bell toys were cast-iron toys consisting of an animal or figure, mounted between two rolling wheels, that rang a little bell as it was pulled across the floor. While vehicles and banks were enthusiastically played with, bell toys were also popular, and unquestionably the last word in bell toys was the cast-iron fire engine.

BANKS

The ordinary bank is a "still" bank—drop a coin in the slot and it disappears. The piggy bank is a still bank, and many early cast-iron banks, in fact, were formed as pigs and other animals. Many more, however, were cast to resemble impressive institutional architecture and bore the name of a real bank. The earliest examples of still banks are painted in several colors and are crisply detailed.

The mechanical bank—the bank that performs an often complicated and/or amusing action as it takes your coin—is a purely American invention. The oldest example of the mechanical bank is Hall's Excelsior, an 1869 model designed by John Hall of Watertown, Massachusetts, for the Stevens Company. The Excelsior is shaped like a small building, and when its doorbell is pulled, a monkey labeled "Cashier" emerges from the dome. Place a penny on the table in front of the monkey, and the dome closes, the monkey disappears, and the coin disappears with it. The Excelsior was perforated, so that small investors could enjoy watching their wealth accumulate, and its success prompted a deluge of cast-iron imitators. Today more than 400 types of banks are known. Among the curiosities of the era were the X-ray bank, which employed mirrors to simulate an X-ray machine; the working merry-go-round bank; and the elaborate fowler bank, on which a hunter brings down a soaring game bird with a gun that shoots caps. There were also banks with rare

Britain's Ltd: A rare early set of the 3rd Hussars (The King's Own), c. 1940, with original box, plus an early prewar set of the Horse Guard (The Blues), c. 1930s.

It's important to have the original passengers for toy automobiles. This early cast-iron model had three, and an interesting hand brake.

A dentist yanks his patient's tooth on a mechanical bank of cast iron.

At the turn of the century, many high-quality toy banks were made. It's not always easy, however, to tell the difference between an original and a fake. An original toy bank has high sheen. A reproduction looks grainy and is actually not smooth, and its pieces do not fit perfectly together.

According to Noel Barrett, the definitive answer lies at the bottom of the bank. Most crucially, reproduction banks have circular indentations on the bottom. And this, according to Noel, is "the real bottom line," differentiating a $75 toy bank from a $4,000 one!

A cast-iron mechanical "Magic" bank in excellent condition. Made by J&E Stevens, c. 1880.

religious subjects, like Jonah and the Whale—the drop of the coin causes the whale to deposit Jonah on land. There were banks for little girls, like the Speaking Dog (1885), Confectionery (1881), and the Girl Skipping Rope (1890), which factory workmen deemed the most difficult bank to cast and thus cost more to sell—too much more, in fact, for people to pay, so existing examples are rare. Banks with political themes were popular and more affordable, although an unfortunate strain of prejudice was evident in several bank subjects, with minorities, foreigners, and blacks being rudely caricatured by manufacturers.

The inventiveness expended between 1869 and 1910 by American toy firms trying to jolly children into saving their pennies by buying cast-iron banks will probably never be surpassed.

IS IT OLD?

In accordance with the McKinley Tariff Act of 1890, imported toys made from that year on must be marked with their country of origin. Thus, they will be marked Germany, England, or France, for example. ("Made in U.S. Zone Germany" or "Made in Occupied Japan" indicates a date from 1945 to 1952.)

Because the majority of toys were mass-produced, they can usually be dated by their maker's marks, by marks denoting their country of origin, and by their patent numbers. Conveniently for the collector, American toys manufactured after 1870 were often patented. For a small fee, toys with printed, stenciled, or embossed patent numbers can be submitted to the United States Patent Office for the name of the maker and the date of the original patent application. Unmarked twentieth-century toys can sometimes be identified by the original firm (if it is still in existence) if the toy bears its earmarks.

The following pointers can also be helpful in dating the vintage toy.

♦ Authentic chronology isn't necessarily an indicator of age: long after actual horse-drawn fire engines were obsolete, they continued to be the model for fire engine toys.

♦ On tinplate toys fastened together with tabs, empty slots usually indicate missing pieces.

♦ European toys made before the invention of color offset lithography were painted in several colors with great attention to detail. American toys of the same era had a single thin coat of paint with stenciled details and decorations.

♦ Toys were first decorated with applications of lithographed paper in the 1880s.

♦ Unlike other collectibles, even ten-year-old toys, if they were originally produced in limited quantities, can be highly collectible.

IS IT VALUABLE?

The most important factor in evaluating any toy is condition. Expert Noel Barrett observes that "nineteenth-century toys in exceptional, unplayed-with condition are almost 'freakish' in their rarity and thus *very* valuable."

CONDITION

Four quality levels are used to indicate condition:

To be termed **mint,** a toy must be like-new and in its original packaging (which should also be like-new).

A toy in **very good condition** may be slightly worn or exhibit *light* fading or damage to the finish. It may or may not have original packaging.

A toy in **good condition** is intact but exhibits wear. It lacks its original packaging.

The **play-worn** toy, unless it is a great rarity, has little value.

GAMES

Carved and painted wooden game boards for Parcheesi, backgammon, and checkers are collected for their decorative, austere beauty, and folk-art collectors display them like the abstract works of art they are. Scrabble and Monopoly, however, are collected for the pleasures inherent in the games themselves.

Designed by the unemployed Charles Darrow in the depths of the Depression and patented in 1935 by Parker Brothers, the game of Monopoly has sold 80 million sets over the years. (Appropriately, Darrow used his earnings from the sales of his creation to speculate successfully in the real estate market.) Expect the buildings of the earliest sets to include stained wood pieces and metal markers.

Only these earliest editions, in like-new condition, have value. Since 1945, the game has had plastic pieces.

The most collectible of American games are actually the beautifully lithographed yachting and football games of the McLaughlin firm.

Opponents choose the "night" or "day" end of this boldly painted checkerboard.

SCHOENHUT ROLY DOLLY

When appraiser Leila Dunbar saw the bright colors on this Santa, she was almost certain, before looking at it closely, that it had been repainted. She was happily surprised to learn she was wrong. In brand-new condition, this Santa Roly Dolly, known today as a Roly Poly, was inherited by the owner's wife from a great-uncle, who was such an avid collector that he actually needed to buy the house next door to his own in order to store all his collectibles.

Produced in the early 1900s, it was manufactured by Schoenhut, the Philadelphia toy-maker. In addition to its fine original paint, it still has its original label on the bottom. Morever, it is not only a toy, but also a Christmas collectible, which gives it additional value and great crossover appeal for two different segments of collectors. Based on these considerations, Dunbar valued this piece at $2,000 to $3,000.

RARITY

There are also four levels for judging rarity:

A **rare** toy can be one that had a low survival rate (like boats and airplanes, which often succumbed to overenthusiastic play) or that was originally—perhaps because it was costly to produce or not well-received—made in limited quantities.

The **scarce** toy is seen infrequently and is thus highly sought after.

Of **limited rarity** is the toy that isn't seen often, but can still be found.

The **common** toy is the toy often seen in dealers' shops.

More specific markers for valuing old toys include the following:

♦ The most valuable toy is the toy that's never been played with.

♦ The more complex a toy, the less likely it is that many were made or are still in existence.

♦ Repairs, no matter how skillfully done, negatively affect value, as does any repainting on an old toy. On very rare toys, however, some fading or crazing is considered acceptable, as is the replacement of (very) minor interior parts.

♦ Although a toy may be in otherwise perfect condition, missing elements—the driver and passengers of an automobile, for example, or a lost headlight—will decrease its value.

♦ The name of the manufacturer, especially if it's a well-known and desirable manufacturer, increases a toy's value, as does any original labeling or accompanying printed material.

♦ Even single wood figures by Schoenhut are costly, especially the glass-eyed animals and figures with ceramic heads. Complete sets, like the popular "Circus," can be quite expensive.

Toy Manufacturers

IVES, BLAKESLEE & CO.

"Ives Toys Make Happy Boys" proclaimed advertisements, and throughout its sixty-year history this Connecticut company made cast-iron cars, tinplate and dancing clockwork figures, and, most successfully, wind-up and electrified trains. Its seven name-changes (always including Ives) included these marks:

HUBLEY

Hubley was known for its cast-iron toys. The two most popular models were the Royal Circus Giraffe Cage, considered highly collectible, and the Farmer's Van, also very scarce. The most sought-after Hubley toys in today's market are the 1930s motorcycles.

J.&E. STEVENS

Noted for its mass-produced cast-iron toys, including toy cannons, tools, and stoves, Stevens was best known for its cast-iron mechanical banks. The Connecticut firm eventually merged with that of George W. Brown.

BUDDY L

An Illinois firm, Buddy L made the most expensive and finest American pressed-steel toys from automotive-grade steel. Buddy L toys were frequently purchased by America's wealthiest families.

JAMES FALLOWS & SON

An Englishman, James Fallows founded his own tinware company in 1874 in Philadelphia, and manufactured riverboats, horse-drawn wheeled vehicles, and trains. His toys are marked IXL, which has been interpreted to be Fallows' slogan, "I excel."

ALTHOF BERGMANN

Four partners—L. Althof and three Bergmann brothers—manufactured tinplate toys and were quite successful with both floor trains and painted tinplate clockwork toys, particularly hoop toys. The New York firm also made dollhouse furniture and kitchens.

A Hubley Santa sleigh pulled by two reindeer, 1880s–1890s.

GEORGE W. BROWN & CO.

The first of the American manufacturers to put clockwork mechanisms in toys, this Connecticut firm is best known for its horse-drawn carts, dancing figures, and hoop bell toys.

CARETTE; BING; MÄRKLIN

These were three  German manufacturers, famous for fine craftsmanship. After 1890, German toys may be marked with patent and copyright marks such as D.R.G.M., D.R.P., or Ges. Gesch.

MARX

Marx sold its products, which included every type of toy with the exception of dolls, through mail-order and variety stores. Before World War II this American firm made novelty toys, and in the 1930s specialized in science-fiction toys. After the war, it produced plastic toys.

ROSSIGNOL

This French company made elegant touring cars in the 1920s and 1930s.

"Li'l Abner's Dogpatch Band."

A Märklin hand-drawn live-steam fire pumper, c. 1890s, in particularly fine condition.

This Märklin tinplate toy is desirable because it's an aviation toy and a rare form—a zeppelin.

♦ Large-size toys, because fewer were manufactured, are found infrequently and are usually more valuable than standard sizes.

♦ Blocks decorated with lithographed colored paper are highly popular with collectors. Because the lithography tends to fade, these very seldom appear in good condition.

♦ Painted tinplate toys have a tendency to flake since no primer was used before the paint was applied. Flaking paint, of course, always diminishes the value of painted toys.

♦ An original box can double or even triple a toy's value.

♦ Large ships by Märklin, particularly those that are labeled, are extremely valuable.

♦ Toy soldiers fabricated by Britain's Ltd. of London are highly collectible today. Sets should be in their original boxes.

♦ Among collectors of toy soldiers, cavalry is more valuable than foot soldiers.

♦ J.&E. Stevens Company cap guns and cannon are quite collectible.

♦ Japanese toys manufactured after World War II are labeled "Japan" or "Occupied Japan." Prewar Japanese toys were seldom marked and today are scarce and valuable.

♦ Old glass and ceramic banks, because they were customarily smashed to retrieve the contents, are rather rare but not especially collectible.

♦ Old tinplate banks are common.

♦ Some of the least valuable toys are scooters, die-cast miniatures, construction kits (Lincoln Logs), and chemistry sets.

CARS

Original metallic paint—silver is the color most often seen—adds value to tinplate cars from the 1920s. Red metallic paint is uncommon, but blue metallic paint is very unusual and therefore most valuable.

Race cars (especially Ferraris and similar exotic cars) are highly collectible, as are vehicles that display advertising, along with large and realistic cars from the 1930s with working headlights. Toy cars of actual models in all materials are desirable.

Buddy L toys, like this pressed-steel bus, were substantial and exceptionally well crafted.

TRAINS

The age of an electric train can usually be determined by the width of its tracks—the "gauge"—which is measured between the inner edges of the rails. Although the first Ives American trains ran on 1 gauge tracks, it was usually the European trains that employed gauges 1 to 4. As of the early twentieth century, trains in the United States employed standard-gauge tracks of 2⅛". When this large size became prohibitively expensive during the Depression, American trains ran on 1¼" tracks (0 gauge) thereafter.

DOLLS

Most adults in childhood had a teddy bear, so it may come as a surprise to learn that those traditional teddies weren't actually "invented" until 1903. Dolls, on the other hand, have a long, long history—probably prehistoric—and exist in every culture. European, Native American, and American-made dolls, however, are those we're most likely to find.

Above: The doll dressed by Marie Antoinette as she awaited execution.

Left: German peg wooden doll, c. 1820, in period clothing.

AUTOMATA

Automata are mechanical dolls—dolls with clockwork interiors that imitate human movement. They were exceptionally well-dressed, terribly fragile, and made to appeal to adults, perhaps, more than to children, because they were rather expensive and definitely didn't lend themselves to being played with. Made in France, Germany, and America, automata are judged by the condition and elaborateness of their clothing, by the complexity of the movements they make, and by the appeal of the doll's face. The most complex, and most desirable, are the French automata, which are often richly dressed, and those that have marvelously intricate movements, dolls like the seated Lady with a Bird who holds a caged bird that revolves and sings while the lady turns her head from side to side and shakes her finger at the cat lying at her feet.

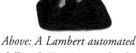

Above: A Lambert automated doll with Tête Jumeau head, c. 1890–1900.

Right: German character doll by Kämmer and Reinhardt, c. 1909.

TYPES OF DOLLS

Considering that dolls are usually associated with the adorable and the childlike, it seems too brusquely scientific that collectors classify them by the material from which their heads are made. But this has been the doll fanciers' choice, perhaps because doll heads were created from so many and such diversified substances: china, wood, bisque (unglazed porcelain), rubber, papier-mâché, wax, cloth, vinyl, and plastic, among others. The best doll heads have always been made of the most lifelike materials available at the time—wax and bisque, for example—and the most expensive dolls when new have always been European.

EIGHTEENTH-CENTURY DOLLS

The first dolls, as you might expect, were made of wood, and dolls with wooden heads are often quite old. Despite their humble derivation, they can still be finely carved and painted. Many such dolls were exported to America to become the cherished playthings of Colonial children. (A well-preserved doll still exists that once belonged to William Penn's daughter.) The invisible parts of such dolls could be quite crudely fashioned, however, and also underdressed: until 1800 or so, women did not wear drawers (which, being a men's garment, were considered to be risqué) and dolls didn't, either.

Very early eighteenth-century dolls are recognizable by their wide-spaced dark eyes, conical bodies, shoulders set in almost military posture, and high bosoms. Their late-eighteenth-century descendants had more relaxed postures. Most of the doll bodies have kid or wooden arms and wooden legs and torsos. Late-eighteenth-century wood dolls were much cruder. Many so-called Queen Anne wooden dolls were produced as late as the 1840s, often with blue eyes.

PEG DOLLS (PEG WOODENS)

Early-nineteenth-century German peg woodens had movable peg and socket joints. Although they resemble the dolls of the preceding century, they are prettier and have smaller, more delicate faces. Made between 1800 and 1850, peg woodens have wispy painted hair, nicely parted in the middle, and dainty feet—which, unlike later models with simple leg-ends dipped in pink or red paint—were realistically shaped, with painted black, green, yellow, red, or blue flat-heeled shoes.

WAX DOLLS

In the nineteenth century, wax must have seemed the ideal material for dolls. Warm to the touch and as close to the appearance of skin as it was then possible to be, wax could also be beautifully sculpted, having in fact been used to make preliminary models for sculptures for centuries. Unfortunately for doll collectors today, wax was also fragile. Cold cracks it, and heat, of course, softens it. Nonetheless, in their prime, wax dolls were the most lifelike and costly of dolls.

English wax dolls are noted for their hair, which is inserted strand by strand into the head. Their eyes are blown glass, usually either brown or blue. Germany produced wax and wax-over-papier-mâché dolls to compete with the English wax dolls. Most German waxes were produced in the 1840s through the 1890s.

French fashion dolls, some with bisque swivel heads, the latest and most elegant frocks, hair combs, little hatboxes, or visiting cards, might have been used either as playthings (very carefully) or as models of the latest in Parisian fashion for adult fans of French couture.

ANTIQUES DISCOVERY ROADSHOW

DOLL COLLECTION

"Our great-grandmother bought the dolls for her daughter, our great-aunt, between 1910 and 1917. She was a much-loved child, and she took good care of her dolls."

The current owner of this collection of forty-four dolls showed a picture of her great-aunt as a child surrounded by her doll family; the dolls are in the same fine condition they were in more than eighty years earlier.

Expert Richard Wright identified the four dolls the owner had brought in as an original Raggedy Ann, an

excellent example in perfect condition, valued at $3,000 to $4,000; a Simon & Halbig black doll, model 1348, valued at $10,000 to $12,000; and two Kewpie dolls (a "merry widow" with a Los Angeles hairdresser's stamp on the bottom, valued at $400 to $500, and a small, jointed Kewpie valued at $600 to $800).

According to Wright, the entire collection might bring $50,000 to $100,000.

Doll Makers and Their Marks

LUDWIG GREINER
(1850s–1870s)

A German immigrant working in Philadelphia in the mid-nineteenth century, Greiner was America's first doll maker. His papier-mâché doll heads almost always had painted eyes (unlike German dolls of the period, which had glass eyes). Molded Greiner heads were made with either black or blond hair and could be purchased in sizes to fit bodies from 13" to 36" tall. Greiner dolls are stamped "Patent Head" or "Greiner's Patent Heads." Their bodies are made of cloth, with leather arms.

GEBRÜDER HEUBACH
(1910–1930)

Heubach was originally founded as a porcelain factory in Germany, but eventually it turned to making "character" dolls—bisque-head dolls with exaggerated facial expressions. Gebrüder Heubach dolls wear amusing, but not always cheerful expressions, and their eyes are molded, with an indented iris and pupil. Sometimes a white dot has been added to the iris to enliven it.

KEWPIE DOLLS

Created in 1913, Kewpie dolls were supposed to be angels guarding small children. Based on pictures by book illustrator Rose O'Neill, they often have a heart-shaped or circular label on their chest or back, and starfish-shaped hands. Kewpie dolls were made in composition, celluloid, rubber, and bisque, the most desirable material.

MONTANARI (1850–1880)

Manufactured in England, Montanari wax dolls were very expensive when new. They often had brown, blue, or green glass eyes, and their human or mohair hair was usually brown, seemingly "rooted" into the scalp. These dolls were seldom signed, although occasionally the signature of Madame Montanari can be found scrawled across the body in brown ink.

PIEROTTI (1790–1930s)

Pierotti made English wax dolls, with a tilt to the head and thick, blond hair, sometimes with an incised signature behind the head. These dolls tend to be somewhat less plump than Montanari dolls.

Pierotti

ARMAND MARSEILLE
(1885–1930)

A.M.

Marseille was a prolific German factory that made millions of dolls. As a result, the Armand Marseille is the most common early doll. The firm's Model 390 was perhaps the most popular doll ever produced.

SIMON & HALBIG
(1869–1930)

Among the earliest and most productive of the German doll makers, by 1895 this firm was producing dolls with "sleeping" eyes that closed when the doll was lying down, and genuine hair eyelashes. The majority of Simon & Halbig dolls have a mold number by which they can be identified.

BRU JNE ET CIE
(1866–1899)

The most famous of the French bisque doll manufacturers, Bru made three types of dolls (few of which were imported to America): the famous *bébé*, with a kid body and carefully molded hands; the Bru doll, with a composition and wood body; and the Fashion doll.

BRU Jᴺᴱ R

JOHANNES DANIEL KESTNER (1816–1930s)

J. D. K   made in Germany
2 4 3
J. D. K.

Kestner fashioned Parian (unglazed white porcelain) dolls with elaborate molded hair styles.

JUMEAU (1873–1899)

The French firm founded by Pierre Jumeau is known for its exquisite and valuable *bébés*, with tenderly rendered faces, often portraits of real children or women. Jumeau dolls are bisque-head dolls with large paperweight eyes topped by strong eyebrows that almost meet over the nose. Jumeau doll markings are varied. "Portrait" and "premier" Jumeaus are unmarked. The most common mark is a printed "Tête Jumeau." A portrait Jumeau *bébé*'s body bears the blue stamp "Jumeau/Medaille D'or/Paris." The head is marked with a size number.

BÉBÉ JUMEAU

DÉPOSE
E. 7 J.

PAPIER-MÂCHÉ DOLLS

Papier-mâché dolls were produced in Europe, mainly in Germany, and in America from 1800 to 1890. Most German papier-mâché dolls have eyes painted brown or blue (though rare dolls may feature glass eyes), and with inset hair or applied wigs. From 1820 to 1850, many of these dolls came with kid bodies and wooden limbs. Older papier-mâché dolls are sometimes found on homemade cloth bodies. Hair is usually molded in black or brown, though some later models have blond or red hair.

CERAMIC DOLLS

Doll heads and limbs were frequently made of porcelain, either glazed, in which case the head is shiny (china-head dolls); or Parian, a matte porcelain; or bisque, a delicate, pink-tinted porcelain. The very best dolls had fine bisque heads, carefully modeled and painted.

Most china-head dolls, despite being termed "French" china dolls, were made predominantly in Nuremberg, Germany, between 1840 and 1920. Their heads and bodies could be purchased separately, in any of several sizes—a particular convenience when heads broke. The hair of china dolls was molded and painted on the head. The most common late-nineteenth-century hair style was the self-explanatory "wavy low brow," but dolls also came with upsweeps or buns. A dependable and interesting indication of the age of china-head dolls is often the poor quality of the porcelain used, which invariably incorporated tiny black specks—called "peppering." The Sèvres, Royal Copenhagen, and Meissen factories, however, made fine-quality porcelain doll heads. Many china dolls were fashioned after celebrities or well-known characters in literature, such as Jenny Lind, Mary Todd Lincoln, and Alice in Wonderland.

BISQUE DOLLS

Bisque doll heads were produced in Europe and the United States from 1850 through 1940. Before 1890, they were pressed from matte porcelain tinted a pale pink. The finest

DOLL HEADS

There were different methods of constructing doll heads, and these are an aid to identification.

The typical French and German type was the socket-head doll, with its neck resting in a cup-shaped socket.

Shoulder-head dolls were among the earliest kinds. The head, neck, and shoulders were all of a single piece. With early porcelain models, the shoulder-head could be purchased separately and sewn onto a soft, homemade or purchased leather or cloth body. The lower front and back edge of the shoulder area was perforated for stitching.

Swivel-heads were set into the shoulder of the doll, and the cup in which the neck sits was lined with leather, allowing the head to turn easily.

Wigs were either affixed to the doll's head with glue or attached with string to holes in the head.

The Bru bébé doll comes in several models. Among the most valuable are the circle-dot bébé, *which has a cork pate and is marked with a dot within a circle, and the Bru Jeune* bébé (below, marked "bru jne9") *with a cork pate.*

Googly-eyed dolls (and bears) are those with eyes swiveled to the side. The term possibly derives from the German guck augen, *meaning "eyes that stare flirtatiously to one side." Above: An example of a mask face googly (left) and a Kämmer & Reinhardt googly.*

and most valuable bisque dolls, often considered works of art, are the French fashion dolls made in the last decades of the nineteenth century. These are typified by the creations of Emile Jumeau, whose dolls had jointed composition or wooden bodies, and painted faces that were remarkably lifelike.

After the 1880s the child doll, rather than the adult, became popular. Firms such as Bru, Jumeau, and Steiner also began producing fine-quality child dolls for the luxury market. The child doll remained popular until the baby doll, first introduced by Kämmer & Reinhardt in 1909, gradually replaced it in popularity. Baby dolls remained the most popular doll until the advent of Barbie dolls in the 1960s.

Unusual and rare bisque dolls of the late nineteenth and early twentieth centuries were made from black and Asian heads produced both in France and Germany by firms such as Simon & Halbig, Kestner, Jumeau, Bru, and Steiner.

CLOTH DOLLS

American cloth dolls were first manufactured in Rhode Island in 1850 by Izannah Walker, who received an 1873 patent for a doll made of stockinette, a knitted elastic fabric. They ranged in size from 10" to 22". Izannah Walker dolls in good condition are especially hard to find.

Another American cloth doll maker, more prolific than Walker, was Martha Chase, whose late-nineteenth-century dolls had jointed knees and hips, shoulders and elbows. Like Walker dolls, Chase dolls have oil-painted heads, hands, and feet, and stuffed cloth bodies. Chase dolls were manufactured well into the 1930s. In 1911, they sold for more than twice the price of the most expensive bisque-head dolls. Large numbers of these dolls still exist today.

In Germany, from 1910 until World War II, Käthe Kruse produced very high-quality, realistic dolls made of waterproof muslin, a unique and attractive feature that allowed them to be bathed. These dolls are considered by many to be the queens of the cloth doll market.

An Izannah Walker cloth doll, c. 1860.

Raggedy Ann dolls are among the most beloved of American cloth dolls. Although Raggedy Ann, who debuted in 1915, eventually became a redhead with tin or plastic eyes, she began her lengthy career with brown yarn hair and black shoe-button eyes. A "candy heart" made of brass, and eventually of plastic, was affixed to her chest.

FOLK DOLLS

Folk dolls were often made at home with leftover sewing scraps and household objects. In the rural South and Appalachia, such dolls were frequently the product of cottage industries, while in seaside areas, as in Maine or Florida, they might be sold as souvenirs.

Homemade folk dolls often are ingeniously crafted of painted nut shells, seashells, carved wood, fruits, and even corn husks—anything that a doting parent could stitch or pin together to make a figure—and dressed in any small pieces of cotton or silk available. There are black dolls, soldier dolls, clown dolls, and Indian dolls. Unsurprisingly, but sadly, in periods when children were dressed and treated as little adults, the doll the child was least likely to own was a baby doll.

Kachina dolls (the name means "ancestral spirit") were crafted by Arizona's Hopi Indians. As Hopi ritual involves wearing the costumes of ancient ancestral spirits (kachinas) each of which has its own distinctive markings, clothing, and headdresses, the Hopi created dolls dressed in miniature kachina costumes to teach their children tribal lore. There are 250 kinds of kachina dolls, each wearing some combination of shells, feathers, roots, husks, beads, and skins.

IS IT OLD?

Because the most popular dolls were made for years, dating them can often pose problems. Although doll styles changed sufficiently from the late eighteenth to the mid-nineteenth century that it becomes clear from style

A Raggedy Ann by Voland, c. 1915–1918.

Kachinas, the spirits the Hopi left in the Underworld, are impersonated yearly in tribal dances. Until the beginning of the twentieth century, kachina dolls (small versions made for Hopi children) were never sold to outsiders.

FRENCH FASHION DOLL

For every treasure discovered at the *Roadshow,* there are twice as many frauds. This French fashion doll was purchased by the owner at an auction. Made to look like the dolls produced by François Gaultier between the 1860s and the 1880s, it sports the mark FG beneath the wig. Unfortunately, appraiser Richard Wright easily recognized this as one of many counterfeit dolls produced in the 1960s.

Wright's advice: when purchasing collectibles, be sure to deal with only reputable dealers and auction houses. Had this been a true FG fashion doll, the few hundred dollars the owner spent would have bought a treasure worth $1,800 to $2,500. Made in the 1960s instead of the 1860s, however, the doll's value is $100 to $200. That hundred years makes all the difference.

and method of manufacture which dolls fall into the earliest category, from 1850 on, dating requires detective work.

MARKS

The heads of both German and French bisque dolls from the 1850s to the 1940s were usually marked with initials, names, or numbers, and these are found on the back of a shoulder-plate or under a wig. Other markings can be found on German and French bisque-head dolls on torsos, on the bottoms of feet, or affixed to labels or ribbons original to the dolls.

The oldest bisque dolls occasionally had model numbers molded on the inside of the arm where it joined the body.

Trademarks were not used until the end of the nineteenth century.

PHYSICAL CHARACTERISTICS

♦ Hair styles can be a clue to age. Until around 1875, all doll hair was dark; the bun worn by Queen Victoria was popular in the 1830s and 1840s; in the 1850s, hair was parted in the center, sometimes caught up with a snood; the succeeding Civil War style was a wrapped braid; in the latter part of the century, dolls with blond hair began to be produced.

♦ German dolls had a cardboard or plaster pate (the top part of the head, always covered by a wig). French dolls usually had cork pates and are also distinguishable by their eyes, which seem to move; by the delicacy of their complexions; by their hand-painted eyebrows and eyelashes; and by their pierced ears.

♦ Before 1850, the painted shoes on bisque dolls were flat. After 1850, following fashion, their shoes had heels.

♦ Old china-head dolls often have a red line above the eyes.

◆ Late in the nineteenth century, bisque dolls acquired "sleeping" eyes that closed when the doll was laid on its back.

IS IT VALUABLE?

Condition is all when valuing dolls. Rarity is a close second. More specific rules of thumb follow.

◆ Composition (made either of boiled and formed waste rags or, later, of pulp) or papier-mâché dolls in perfect condition are exceptionally rare and command a premium.

◆ Signs of aging, like crackled eyes or craze lines, are considered acceptable on valuable composition dolls.

◆ Replaced heads or limbs are acceptable if they are of the same vintage as the originals.

◆ Even if an original wig is matted, it is still more desirable than a replacement wig or no wig.

◆ Closed-mouth bisque-head dolls can be twice as valuable as comparable open-mouth dolls.

◆ Dolls with original clothing, and especially those with well-preserved wardrobes and accessories, are always more costly.

◆ Dolls should be appropriately dressed; that is, they should be wearing the clothes of the era in which they were made.

◆ Folk dolls with a known provenance can be valuable, as can Indian dolls made before World War II.

◆ A black doll will be more valuable than the identical white doll.

◆ Greiner's smaller dolls are preferred to the large dolls.

◆ Bru dolls are more valuable in America than Jumeau dolls, perhaps because there are fewer of them in the U.S.

OLD NEWS

Some dolls were so popular when new that they overpopulate the *Roadshow* in their old age. Sorry to say, the years have not been kind to the following types:

◆ Magic Skin baby dolls, like "Sparkle Plenty" (the bodies are usually falling to pieces)

◆ Dirty Barbies

◆ American composition dolls

A Jumeau porcelain doll, c. 1900, with typically strong eyebrows, blue paperweight eyes, and pierced ears.

"Drawing the line in Mississippi," by American cartoonist Clifford Berryman, 1902. The invention of the "Teddy Bear" was inspired by Theodore Roosevelt's refusal to shoot a cub while on a Mississippi bear hunt.

Teddy Roosevelt's own bear.

TEDDY BEARS

The origin of the teddy bear throws an interesting light on both the political and politically incorrect psychology of early-twentieth-century America. In 1902, President Theodore Roosevelt went bear-hunting in Mississippi. When no ferocious bear conveniently turned up, his companions captured a bear cub, tied it to a tree, and suggested that he shoot at that. Roosevelt—ever the sportsman—refused to take the shot and this rather dismal incident was turned into a famous cartoon titled "Drawing the Line in Mississippi." Inspired by the event, a Russian immigrant in Brooklyn manufactured a furry stuffed toy that he called "Teddy's Bear." And, suddenly, bears became a craze, with thousands of bears almost instantly being manufactured worldwide—particularly in the United States, but also in England (where, even today, they love their bears) and Germany. Currently, collecting old teddy bears is still an international passion. Collectors term themselves "arctophiles" (after the Great Bear constellation, whose brightest star is Arcturus) and, unlike Teddy, hunt their bears with well-stuffed wallets.

STEIFF BEARS

Among the best-known teddy bears are those made by Steiff, a German firm. The first Steiff bear—the Bär 55 PB—was made in 1902, and in Steiff's early years of manufacture every seventh bear had a seam down the center of its head, to economize on fabric. In 1905, Steiff patented its trademark, a button in the bear's ear with the firm name on it, and by 1907, when the bear craze hit its peak, Steiff stuffed bears had become so popular that the factory produced 974,000 bears a year. Although most Steiff bears are collectible today, a few of them—the Dolly Bear, made in red, white, and blue (and given away during Roosevelt's unsuccessful reelection campaign of

1912), and Elliott, a rare blue bear—are hotly pursued by collectors. In 1908, the firm created a collectible tumbling teddy bear. The arms acted as a "key," and when they were wound backward, the bear somersaulted forward. Steiff ear-buttons and labels changed frequently. The earliest, and rarest, was the "elephant" button, depicting an elephant with an upraised, s-shaped trunk (1904–05), followed by a blank button (1905–09), and then by variations on STEIFF, with the F underscored (1905–1950).

PETSY BEARS

Available in ten sizes, the Petsy bear, made of white mohair tipped with red-brown, debuted in 1928 and was made just for a short while. It had a pink nose, blue googly eyes, and a seam running down the front and back of its head and across its ears. The ears were wired to make them movable, and the bear had a voice box.

BING BEARS

Bing bears are German and were first manufactured by Gebrüder Bing in 1907, in the midst of the teddy bear fad. The company is most famous for its mechanical bears: a skating bear and a tumbling bear are among the most collectible. Bing bears are identified by their shaved snouts and wide smiles. When they have lost their arrow-shaped ear tags or their under-the-arm labels (which they often have), they can sometimes be identified by their orange-and-black glass eyes.

J.K. FARNELL

Legend has it that Harrods department store in London sold Christopher Robin the Farnell bear that became Winnie the Pooh. It's a fact, however, that initially the Farnell firm had to export almost all its bears to America, South Africa, and Germany, because British consumers were not the least bit taken with the idea of teddy bears. Yet Farnell's bears, with their long silky mohair coats, shaved

TEDDY BEARS

Timothy Luke identified the smaller of these two bears as a mass-produced brown Steiff, valued around $2,500, but the larger one was quite a different story. First, Luke pointed out the nose, made of sealing wax (rather than stitching), which dates the bear to around the turn of the century. More important is the white (rather than typical brown) fur. But the most intriguing feature was discovered in X rays provided by the owner, which reveal it to be a rod bear (with small rods connecting the joints), produced only between 1904 and 1905.

The owner, a collector of bears, knew the rod bear was valuable, but she had no idea what a treasure she had stumbled upon. Despite a missing ear tag and a bit of wear on the mohair, its limited production, unusual color, and the rare rod construction give this bear a value of $20,000.

Slender cinnamon-color bear, manufactured by Ideal c. 1911–1912.

Gold mohair bear with button eyes, felt pads, and squeaker, made by Bing c. 1910.

muzzles, prominent back humps, and long plump arms eventually won over all doubters. Farnell patented its "Alpha" trademark in 1928, and the large Farnell Alphas are most desirable today.

THE IDEAL NOVELTY AND TOY COMPANY

This is the firm founded by Rose and Morris Michtom, the immigrant Brooklyn couple who made the first teddy bear, and naturally their 6" googly-eyed bear (mimicking the cub in the cartoon) is exceptionally valuable. Early Ideal bears can be recognized by their black boot-button (not shoe-button) eyes, their short mohair fur, and the pads on their feet, which taper to a point.

AETNA TOY ANIMAL COMPANY

Because Aetna was in business for only two years (1906–1908), its bears are very rare. They can be identified by the printed oval trademark "Aetna" across the center of the left foot.

IS IT OLD?

No teddy bear is older than 1903, a fact that comfortably narrows the field for dating. Knowing some details of materials and manufacturing makes the detection of early bears easier.

♦ Vintage bears were generally made of wool mohair.

♦ Bears made before World War I had boot-button eyes. Glass eyes were used from the 1920s (as early as 1912 in Britain), and plastic eyes date from the 1950s.

♦ Each manufacturer developed its own technique for stitching noses, and some (like the *Antiques Roadshow* discovery on page 285) used sealing wax. Learning the various techniques can be of help in identifying makers.

Vintage bear noses were usually sewn with silk thread.

♦ On vintage bears, the paw pads were generally made of old felt.

♦ Early bears were stuffed with kapok (the hairs from the seed of the silk-cotton tree) and wool. (In lean times, bears were often stuffed with factory waste.)

♦ Early in the century, bears resembled real bears and were less lovable-looking than they later became. They had long muzzles, long arms, and a distinctly humped back.

♦ In the 1930s, velvet was a frequent choice for foot pads, while later bears may have pads made of leather or plush. In the 1950s plastic was used.

♦ Artificial silk plush dates from around 1930, and cotton plush is post–World War II. Nylon plush and other synthetics were not introduced until the 1950s.

♦ Bears made after World War II have shorter arms and flat faces.

♦ In the 1930s, there was a trend toward pink, green, and blue teddy bears.

♦ The panda bear became a popular stuffed toy in the 1930s when pandas first appeared in British and American zoos.

Steiff purse bear.

TIPS *from the experts*

Richard Wright has some advice on dolls and teddy bears for grown-ups.

Examine a doll for identifying marks by lifting the hair on the back of its head and looking for a name, initials, or a number. (If the wig is glued down, you can very carefully pry it up.)

Check what marks you find (if you find any) in Colman's *Encyclopedia of Dolls.*

The worst damage that can befall a good doll is a cracked head. Under no circumstances, however, should you try to have this repaired. Attempts at repair only compound the problem.

The bodies of some bisque-head dolls have come unstrung, but that does not mean they're broken. (And even when they *are* broken, the head can still have value.)

Character dolls are preferable to "girlie-face" dolls.

Steiff black Teddys are the rarest bears, followed by cinnamon and white bears.

Bears that actually look like bears, with hump backs, pointy snouts, and long arms, are most desirable.

The Steiff Dicky bear, with printed paws, is a great rarity.

The white Steiff tag says this blond mohair bear was "Made in U.S.-Zone Germany," which dates it to the late 1940s. Bear labels are fabric or metal tags attached in the ear and on or under the arm.

"Alfonzo": a rare red plush teddy by Steiff, 1906–1909. Although this bear is dressed, for some collectors the only acceptable bear is the bear in its natural state.

A rare 1914 Boston Braves pennant.

Babe Ruth card: originally a "prize" in a package of chewing gum.

IS IT VALUABLE?

As with toys and dolls, condition and rarity rule. Specific to teddy bears are the following details:

♦ Unusual vintage bears, like black bears and white bears, are highly sought after.

♦ The gray teddy bear first designed by Richard Steiff, nephew of the founder of the firm, is a great rarity.

♦ Bing bears are rarer than Steiff bears, but Steiff bears are market favorites.

♦ Value will be seriously affected by threadbare or moth-eaten fur.

♦ Cinnamon-color bears, especially Steiff bears, are rare because the color fades easily.

♦ "Dual" plush, or tipped mohair, is unusual. The tipped effect is created by lightly brushing the surface of the mohair with a darker dye.

♦ American bears are very collectible, especially early examples and those by Ideal.

♦ Some bears are valuable because of their provenance. Well-documented, famous bears are very collectible, as are vintage pocketbooks in the shape of teddy bears.

♦ Hot-water bottle bears by Steiff are very rare. Only ninety were made between 1907 and 1914.

COLLECTIBLES

Genuine collectibles are accidental by nature. They were not made in the thousands. They are not numbered. They make no claims to being rare or to being art. They were created, actually, to be used and discarded, although obviously they were saved. Consequently, they sell today for much more than they were ever worth new. The fact that some people have decided to rescue them from history's landfill within years of their manufacture is a novel, strictly twentieth-century idea.

The field of collectibles is huge, encompassing pocket knives, oyster-related objects, wax paper, radio and television premiums (those Captain Midnight decoder rings), UFO/alien items, calf weaners, sandpaper, fast food–associated items, hangers, and pedal cars. The choicest collectible will still be in its original box—if there was a box—and as close to "untouched" as its years and function allow. Almost all of the detritus of American society might be collectible, it seems, and will find a buyer somewhere. But out of this vastness of choice, space constraints have forced us to focus on just these few: sports, Rock and Roll, advertising, movies, and ephemera.

The good thing to know about the collectible market is that everyone can play, and, more than in any other field, the rule to remember is—Condition Is All.

SPORTS

The center of the huge sports market, and the passion of possibly 95 percent of all collectors of sports memorabilia, is baseball. And among the many baseball-related collectible objects—cards, uniforms, scorecards, caps, gloves, autographs, and spikes—the pinnacle of the baseball collector's aspirations is the Signed Ball. That's why a dozen or so signed balls turn up at every *Roadshow* event. But knowledgeable collectors know that the ball has to have been signed by a deceased Hall of Famer in the days before the era of baseball-card show signings—someone like Lou Gehrig or Babe Ruth. This means that most signed balls, especially those signed by marginally well-known players or current players (except for Mark McGwire), have little or no value. Big Game balls, signed by the team, can be good, of course, although some corroborative evidence as to provenance is considered a definite plus. And finally, whatever a ball may have written

SIGNATURE BASEBALLS

Only one man in the history of baseball pitched a perfect game in a World Series—New York Yankee Don Larsen, in 1956.

The first-base umpire for that game was Hank Soar, who had the foresight to gather a group of signature balls: 1) the ball Larsen pitched for the next-to-last out of the game; 2) another ball used in the game and signed by Soar; 3) a team ball signed by all the Dodgers; and 4) a team ball signed by only nineteen of the Yankees, but with Mickey Mantle's signature on the sweet spot.

The collection came to a friend of Soar's, who told his son, "Hang on to these." At the Richmond *Roadshow,* expert Leila Dunbar noted that the accompanying letter of authenticity from Hank Soar was a welcome sight in a category filled with fakes. She appraised some of the collection at moderate prices—$200 for the Soar ball and $600 for the incomplete Yankee team ball. The Dodger team ball got on base with $2,000 to $3,000, but the Don Larsen ball, even though unsigned, was the real home run: $15,000 to $18,000.

HONUS WAGNER CARD

Early in the twentieth century, Honus Wagner played shortstop for the Pittsburgh Pirates for twenty-one years. Unlike other ballplayers of his day, he neither smoked nor chewed tobacco, and when, to his dismay, he found his image on a tobacco company–sponsored baseball card, he insisted it be taken off the market and never be printed again. Only eight of these now-famous Honus Wagner cards, therefore, are known to exist, the last example to come on the market selling for $640,000. But be warned: there are numerous reproductions of this card around. They can be recognized by the fact that they are larger than the original and printed on thinner paper.

WAGNER, PITTSBURG

The rare and valuable Honus Wagner tobacco card, c. 1910.

upon it, that ball should be white (*never* shellacked) and have a clear signature; if there is only one signature, it should be written right on the sweet spot. With every one of these points in place, you *might* own a valuable baseball. Without them *all,* sorry to say, you're out.

Baseball cards are a separate and special field. Card enthusiasts have something in common with stamp collectors, who also seek rare images on small squares of paper. And as with stamps, the vintage baseball card will have unusual value only when it's in perfect condition, when the image on it is perfectly centered on the cardboard (not lopsided in any way), and when the colors are strong and bright. A good card shouldn't be scuffed or dog-eared, either.

There *is* collectible life beyond the baseball stadium, however. Just try to buy inexpensive golf items, for example, a field of burgeoning interest in which thousands of collectors vie for tees, old golf balls, wood and iron clubs, and golfing prints. In the fishing category, there's little discussion of the one that got away, for nothing gets away from enthusiasts collecting decorative old creels, early-twentieth-century wood lures, fine rods, and rare and increasingly costly reels. Football cards attract as many collectors as can fit into the Super Bowl stadium, and even gamblers seem to retain enough of their winnings to acquire the artifacts of their "sport."

ROCK AND ROLL

Rock and Roll is among the youngest of all collectibles. Even the term "rock and roll" was invented only in 1951 by a Cleveland disk jockey who combined the two slang terms most frequently heard in black rhythm and blues. Favorites among vintage R&R collectibles today are magazines, posters, artifacts, and, chiefly, recordings.

By 1954, Elvis Presley had succeeded in melding black rhythm and blues with country music in suggestively masculine style and ascended permanently to the empyrean of

Rockdom. Today, his cars, his motorcycles, and his costumes still bring six-digit sums. Not one of the popular music artists of the early 1960s has ever outshone Elvis, nor has the 1963 British invasion by the shockingly long-haired Beatles affected his supremacy. The Rock and Roll era itself, however, culminated at Woodstock in upstate New York in 1969, when a half-million overly long-haired fans gathered for the three-day concert that many buyers of early Rock and Roll memorabilia consider their collecting cutoff point.

MUSIC

Enthusiasts are not particularly interested in 78 rpm records by their favorites, however. What they really want are 45 rpm singles—those seven-inch disks, introduced in 1949, with silver-dollar-size holes for the thick spindle and one tune on each side. This preference is so entrenched that, if the same song is available on both 78 and 45 rpm, the 45 rpm will bring twice as much. And collectors are far less concerned with the individual recording than with the rarity of the disk. If a recording did poorly its first time out, for example, but was reissued after becoming popular, collectors will pay five times as much for that earlier, rarer version. The center labels are important, too. When, in 1955, Duotone originally released the Penguins' "Earth Angel," the recording was so successful that the record-pressing plants ran out of the original red label and shipped succeeding versions with labels of maroon, blue, and black. Of these, the first label, the red one, is most valuable.

Other desirable R&R disks are those specially made for disk jockey use and those made by famous performers before they were famous, such as the disk Elvis cut for Sun Records in 1954 of "That's All Right," which is hard to find today. To be *really* valuable, however, a disk will have never been played and will still be in its original sleeve—preferably unopened.

Essence of an era:
a Janis Joplin concert poster.

WOODSTOCK NATION

Woodstock was the apotheosis of Rock and Roll concerts, and while one might assume that tickets to that watershed event would be rare, there are actually thousands of Woodstock tickets still around. The reason is that the huge and unwieldy crowd of concertgoers never actually purchased tickets. Instead, it stormed the gates, and the promoters found themselves with 500,000 unsold tickets, which they promptly sold to mail-order houses. As a result, souvenirs are worth only about $20 today.

A dime a dozen: a ticket from the original Woodstock concert.

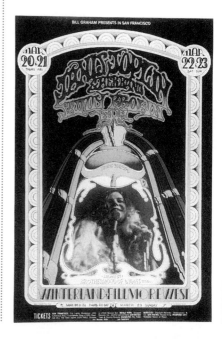

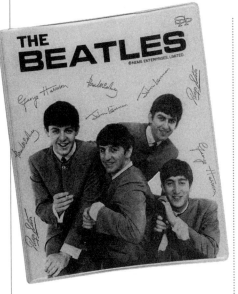

All types of Beatles memorabilia are collected, even school notebook covers.

In his bell-bottom jump-suit studded with silver, a quasi-squash blossom neck-lace, and sand-painting figures, Elvis took countless worshipful "scalps."

PERSONALITIES

Collectors of R&R items look for concert posters of their favorite performers and posters with particularly good graphics, along with costumes worn by celebrities like Madonna and the Rolling Stones. Most desirable are Rock and Roll guitars.

Of course, Elvis memorabilia is a field unto itself. There are Elvis T-shirts, plaster statues, jewelry, purses, and a porkpie hat with the titles of Elvis' hits on the hatband—far more valuable, by the way, if its tag is still attached. (Incidentally, Elvis gave out so many autographs that they are not as scarce as might be supposed.)

The Beatles were a phenomenon from the moment they appeared in the United States. Enthusiasts don't have to be able to buy John Lennon's Rolls-Royce, however (which brought $2.9 million in 1990), when they can look for cels from the animated film *Yellow Submarine* or, remarkably, buy Beatles wigs, quite valuable in themselves. The recordings, of course, are still to be found. "She Loves You," the essential early Beatles tune, was first issued on a white Swan label and then on a black Swan label. Collectors covet the white one.

Elvis and the Beatles top the field today, but as is true in every one of the collectibles markets, Rock and Roll collecting is solely dependent on its enthusiasts' "collective memories." For keep in mind that, as Beatles and Elvis fans age, their favorites will inevitably be supplanted by newer stars, their children's stars. The direction the market takes, like the celebrities the public loves, is wholly generation-driven.

ADVERTISING

With the invention of color offset lithography in the 1870s, that quiet time before radio and television, the field of advertising flourished. Abetted by the rise of a middle class with discretionary income as well as a system of railroads that networked the country, American firms found themselves suddenly capable of distinguishing their own products from their competitors'. Now, instead of ambling into the local soda fountain and asking for a soda pop, consumers nationwide seemed ready to be convinced that what they really thirsted for was a Coke.

They could, in fact, be deluged with tin signs, serving trays, calendars, containers, and all sorts of intended-to-be-disposable objects decorated with powerfully painted images (not photographed, as they are today) by more-than-competent artists like J.C. Leyendecker, who painted the ads for Arrow Shirts; precision surrealist Maxfield Parrish, who depicted Mazda Edison Lamps; and talented women like Maud Humphrey, mother of Humphrey Bogart, who painted the ads for Ivory Soap. In the Golden Age of American advertising (between the 1880s and World War II), all lent their talents to creating the indelible images with which America truly grew up. For what, in fact, is more American than advertising? Those iconic images—Elsie the Borden Cow, the Red Goose of Red Goose shoes, Jack on the Cracker Jack box—epitomize America's childhood. Its youth, however, came to be symbolized by exemplars of speed.

Motorcycle and automotive advertising objects are a collectible category all their own, a powerful by-product of America's love affair with the road. Harley Davidson was founded in 1903, and Oldsmobile made the first mass-produced vehicles in the U.S. in 1904. Early Harley ads are worth their weight in rubber, and vintage automobilia (if such a word exists) has extensive crossover interest with toy collectors and poster collectors as well. An offshoot of this interest is oil and gas advertising (a.k.a. petroliana), an area that flourished, enthusiasts believe, in the first decades of the twentieth century. (The Texaco company was the first such company to use nationally branded advertising.)

Within the first quarter of the twentieth century, vehicular and associated advertising co-opted every emblem of speed imaginable, from the winged foot of Mercury (Goodyear tires) to the winged helmet of the Valkyrie (Chrysler cars)

From 1917: the gentle persuasion of an advertisement for 99⁴⁴/₁₀₀% pure Ivory soap.

A quietly tasteful tin sign from the 1920s.

Both famous film and attractive image: The Kid, *starring Charlie Chaplin, 1921.*

Expert Brian Witherell has dubbed this print "the greatest Western image": a semi-clad Indian riding a buffalo bareback through a horseshoe in the sky.

Actually, the picture is from a calendar, created in 1901 for the Buffalo Brewing Company of Sacramento, California. It combines all the qualities one could hope for in top-tier advertising memorabilia—excellent lithography, colorful design using iconic images, and the sponsor's name in very large letters across the top. Not to mention the fact that there are only about eleven known examples. That combination prompted Witherell to appraise this piece of advertising at $20,000.

to the winged Pegasus of Mobil. America, judging by its advertising, was in full, four-wheeled flight.

MOVIE MEMORABILIA

Hollywood collectibles really need no introduction. There's probably no one who doesn't understand the enormous allure of its mythology and idols, and probably no one who wouldn't like to buy—or, failing that, to steal—a flame or two from that dazzling, pseudo-Olympian fire. Which is why posters, clothing, photos of the stars, and ruby slippers go for huge sums. In a Hollywood-style cliché: "What price, after all, our dreams?"

POSTERS

Unlike many other collectibles, posters were never intended to be sold to consumers, and surprisingly, London—not Los Angeles or New York—seems to be the movie poster capital of the world. The three most popular subjects for movie posters worldwide are Horror, Science Fiction, and Classics.

Interestingly, horror films, in their day, were the equivalent of our X-rated films. Some theaters refused to screen them, a reluctance explaining why posters advertising horror titles are so rare. That also accounts for the premium prices being paid for classic horror posters like *Frankenstein* and *The Mummy,* with Boris Karloff.

Science-fiction posters are second to horror films in popularity, causing us to conjecture that collectors value violence and thrills, fear and awe, rather more than they do the gentler emotions like love; for romantic classics like *Casablanca* and *Gone with the Wind* come in third.

The term "poster" actually encompasses all printed displays from the 14" x 11" lobby card to the billboard-size six-sheet. In between are one-sheets (27" x 41"), the most common size and the size used in most theater display cases, and three-sheets (40" x 80"), which, along with the six-sheet, are most rare. Although the earliest movie posters were reproduced by expensive copper or wood engraving, the Golden Age of the poster coincided with the use of stone lithography and ended with its discontinuation in the mid-1930s. Developed by the same firms that produced circus posters, among them the Morgan Lithography Company of Cleveland, the technique of stone lithography allowed the poster artist's work to be reproduced in fine detail less expensively than the earlier engraving process. Film posters from the period before 1935 are desirable and rare, but numerous collectors prefer the work of particular poster artists like Thomas Hart Benton, who painted the original of the poster for *The Grapes of Wrath,* and Norman Rockwell, who illustrated *The Razor's Edge.* Sometimes, two versions of a poster were printed for two distinct markets. Northerners would be treated to the poster of Greta Garbo passionately entwined in the arms of her leading man in *Flesh and the Devil,* while the Bible Belt was shipped a poster portraying Garbo as a solemn penitent, remorseful and alone. Both posters are collectible today, but to be particularly desirable a fine poster must always be—and here is the key to collecting movie posters—of large size and of iconic stars in well-known films. And, of course, they must be in pristine condition, not scuffed, torn, or water-stained. Among our favorites are Marilyn Monroe, naturally, Humphrey Bogart, Charlie Chaplin, and the charismatic, short-lived James Dean.

In horror films, the big one: a poster of the original King Kong, *released in 1933.*

Poster from the Twentieth Century–Fox movie The Day the Earth Stood Still.

ANIMATION CELS

Cels from Walt Disney animated films are a popular collectible. Because every motion in every Disney cartoon had to be hand-painted by an artist on a piece of celluloid, called a "cel," there are thousands of cels available. In the 1930s, Walt Disney sold several thousand old production cels from his films to the Courvoisier Company, which paid him $5 each. After matting and framing, these were offered at the I. Magnin department store in San Francisco and elsewhere for $25.00 each.

A Warner Bros. classic—and perhaps the iconic movie poster.

TITANIC
LUNCHEON MENU

Appraiser Rudy Franchi said this oil painting of the *Titanic* was not even bad enough to be interesting. The owner spotted the picture on the floor, against a wall, under a table in an antique shop in England in 1971, and decided he liked it. His bad taste paid off. On the back of the painting was a luncheon menu from the day the ship went down, April 14, 1912. Menus were printed on board each day, and this is the only intact menu known to have survived.

Franchi explained that, while the value of *Titanic* memorabilia has certainly increased due to the popularity of the movie, this menu is valuable regardless. Based on his experience as a dealer and as a member of the Titanic Historical Society Inc., Franchi evaluated this treasure at $75,000 to $100,000.

Disney was a fast learner and a superb businessman, of course, so when he opened Disneyland in 1955, he made back his investment by selling many more thousands of cels. There is a great deal of animation art still in existence, primarily in cels that depict individual figures, the most common and least valuable kind. Rarer are production cels with backgrounds called set-ups. Not surprisingly, the more beloved or iconic the subject, the more expensive the cel. For example, the Prince awakening Snow White with a kiss against a background, or Bambi and his father standing among the forest ruins, would inevitably be more highly sought after and more valuable than Sneezy in the dwarfs' cottage or Thumper on some grass.

Mickey Mouse, the all-time most popular Disney character, has spawned a closetful of collectibles. In animated form, in the Mickey Mouse Club, at Walt Disney World Resort, Mickey is ubiquitous and beloved. (Some of his animated pals, however, like Goofy and Donald Duck, have considerably smaller fan clubs.) There are Disney tie-ins to other fields as well: with tin windup toys and porcelain figures, and with the cloth Disney character dolls like Snow White, Mickey Mouse, Donald Duck, and Jiminy Cricket, all created by the Knickerbocker doll and toy company of New York. Curiously, the Seven Dwarf dolls don't bring as much as the others, for the value of Disneyana is determined by the popularity of the character. Prices for all Disneyana, incidentally, tend to be higher on the east and west coasts than they are in the center of the country.

EPHEMERA

Because it consists of things that should have been thrown away, the field of ephemera is enormous. It also has innumerable categories, because anything at all that was short-lived or of short-term usefulness is, technically speaking, classed as ephemera. For that very reason, however, ephemera can present us with some scraps of history that are particularly revealing of the tenor of their times. Ephemera incorporate all unbound printed paper material, such as calendars, playing cards, bookplates, advertising cards, posters, transportation timetables, newspapers, stock certificates, valentines, tickets to ballgames, dance programs, and so on. Ephemera also are those comic books your mother threw away, which weren't valuable anyway because you were guilty, from the comic book collector's point of view, of the cardinal sin . . . *reading* them. Carefully preserved postcard albums—your family's souvenirs of long-gone railroad stations or amusement parks—if they are still bright and still unthumbed, can be a source of unexpected treasure. And every now and then a magic piece of printed paper turns up. (See the *Antiques Roadshow* discovery on the facing page.)

Though ephemera are not just paper goods: they're pinback buttons and straw hats, Brownie pins, and souvenir spittoons. Naturally, just *because* they're disposable, the condition of ephemera is of paramount importance. So many, after all, are made of fragile paper. But ephemera offer a historical record of the country's culture and are widely collected.

On the cover of the Harrison-Tyler almanac, the successful campaigners serve hard cider as someone "endeavors to stop the supply" with a syphon hose.

POLITICAL EPHEMERA

By far the most popular kind of ephemera is political, for political souvenirs are both historically relevant and fun.

Collectors often concentrate on a particular presidential campaign, focusing on the colorful ribbon badges stamped with candidates' names, for instance, or on the associated banners, posters, and other campaign giveaways, like walking sticks. After the 1840 presidential election, American political campaigns erupted in floods of souvenirs—beanies, straw skimmers with printed hatbands, and neckties. Today, such "party favors" constitute the bulk of campaign memorabilia.

Naturally, the ephemera of certain campaigns are more desirable than others. Among the most collectible campaigns are Harrison vs. Van Buren (1840), McKinley

Despite their awkward slogans, these Truman campaign buttons did the trick.

The oldest souvenirs—among them this campaign ribbon for William Henry Harrison, the hero of Tippecanoe—date from 1840.

vs. Bryan (1896), and McKinley vs. Bryan (1900). The campaign that pitted William Henry Harrison against Martin Van Buren was the first to produce a significant number of souvenirs. Van Buren, the incumbent, was accused of having lavish and luxurious tastes, while Harrison was touted as a humble frontiersman. Harrison's "log cabin, hard cider" campaign distributed "Log Cabin" whiskey gimcracks and "Log Cabin" almanacs to supporters. Among the many giveaways from this election were metal tokens, small disks with the candidate's image impressed on them. (Metal election tokens are actually quite common, and are not very valuable despite their age.) Later in the century, campaign badges were distributed to followers, embellished with elaborate frames into which actual photographs of the candidates were laboriously hand-fitted. Such badges, quite collectible today, are precursors of perhaps the most popular of political souvenirs, the familiar pin-back button. First used in the William McKinley vs. William Jennings Bryan election of 1896, these early pin-backs featured pictures of the candidates printed on paper and backed by metal beneath a clear celluloid protective cover. (Because of this, pin-back buttons of all kinds are still called celluloids.) By 1920, candidates' portraits were being lithographed directly onto the metal, so there was no longer any need for the celluloid cover.

A rare campaign button for Teddy Roosevelt depicted T.R. sharing a drink with Booker T. Washington.

After pin-back buttons, other favorite political souvenirs are items made of cloth: flags, kerchiefs, and banners. The skimmers and beanies that even today are part of the paraphernalia of American elections were originally not just decorative, but also functional. During the era of the torchlight parade, the hats protected marchers' heads from being burned by hot oil dripping from the "torchlights"—lanterns on poles.

A Republican campaign token for the presidential campaign of 1900.

IS IT VALUABLE?

Rarity is the most important determinant of value in political memorabilia. For example, a famous president's image doesn't automatically command a premium among campaign-button collectors. In some instances, the loser's button is rarer and worth far more.

♦ Ulysses S. Grant's 1872 campaign produced fragile paper lanterns that are scarce today.

♦ One particularly droll and quite valuable license-plate attachment is a souvenir of Prohibition. On it, the portraits of Franklin Delano Roosevelt and his running mate, John Nance Garner, flank a glass of beer, symbolizing their proposal for repeal of Prohibition in 1932.

♦ Very few buttons were issued for Democratic candidates James Cox in 1920 and John Davis in 1924; they are therefore highly sought after.

♦ A button that pictures the presidential and vice presidential candidates together is called a jugate (from the Latin word for "yoke"). One exceptionally collectible jugate depicts James Cox with his running mate, Franklin Delano Roosevelt, in 1920. Only fifty are known to exist. (The team had so little confidence in their ability to defeat Harding that they distributed a minimum of campaign material.)

♦ A very rare 1904 button shows Theodore Roosevelt dining with black educator Booker T. Washington.

♦ Cartoon buttons, even those of fairly recent origin (like the 1972 caricature of an elephant and Nixon), can be collectible.

♦ Nineteenth-century souvenir campaign hats are rare, but twentieth-century hats are fairly common. One exception is the derby given away during the unsuccessful 1928 race of Democrat Al Smith, whose trademark was his cocked brown derby.

TIPS *from the experts*

Noel Barrett, Leila Dunbar, Rudy Franchi, and Kathleen Guzman have seen it all—and then some.

Barrett's Law and Corollary: The one you have is not the one they want. Things are considered rare (and valuable) because they *are* rare.

Advertisements are valuable when they have great graphics, like the Mobil logo in which the flying horse is "bursting" through its tin sign. —L.D.

Look for character-related advertising: Howdy Doody items, or Mighty Mouse.—R.F.

Don't "invest" in collectibles. You should only buy if you love something.—R.F.

Advertising art was never put on belt buckles. If you see one, it's a 1950s fake.—R.F.

Don't worry about the stack of baseball cards that your mother threw away. In handling them as you traded them, you devalued them long before Mom sent them out with the trash. —K.G.

World's fair memorabilia is not valuable.—K.G.

Prices do not automatically go up. —N.B.

O·L·D N·E·W·S

All of the following are perhaps lovable but, sadly, of modest commercial value.

♦ Tupperware

♦ Eyeglasses

♦ Stereopticon cards

♦ 99.9 percent of political buttons

♦ Most records, especially those of Caruso, and almost all used (opened and played) disks of the 1960s and 1970s.

♦ Carved pipes

♦ Gold-colored pens with retractable nibs—they are all worth $35

♦ Advertising belt buckles

♦ Hummels

♦ Lladro ceramics

♦ Collectors' plates

♦ Any religious memorabilia

♦ Cameras

♦ Typewriters

♦ Definitely, Mah Jongg sets

♦ Marbles (even if there were a few good ones, they've been banging around against each other in your jar for years, and can't be in perfect condition)

♦ Most signed baseballs

♦ Radio Flyer sleds and, in fact, most old sleds

♦ Tricycles

♦ Any campaign hat is more valuable when pinned with a jugate.

♦ Campaign buttons with photos lithographed directly on their metal surfaces were produced in enormous quantity and consequently are less desirable than celluloids.

♦ Any souvenir with the candidate's likeness upon it is more valuable than one without.

♦ "Coattail" materials put out by local (rather than presidential) candidates to link their names with the men on the national ticket are valuable only if the local candidates went on to become famous (like candidates for the Senate who went on to become president).

FURTHER READING

Goodrum, Charles, and Dalrymple, Helen. *Advertising in America*. New York: Harry N. Abrams, 1990.

Herlocher, Dawn. *200 Years of Dolls*. Dubuque, IA: Antique Trader Books, 1996.

Kerr, Lisa. *American Tin-Litho Toys*. Portland, OR: Collectors Press, 1995.

Mullins, Linda. *American Teddy Bear Encyclopedia*. Grantsville, MD: Hobby House Press, 1995.

1999 Sports Collectors Almanac. Edited by Sports Collectors Digest, 1999.

Warda, Mark. *100 Years of Political Campaign Collectibles*. Clearwater, FL: Galt Press, 1996.

Whitton, Blair. *Toys*. New York: Alfred A. Knopf, 1984.

Chapter Ten

BOOKS AND MANUSCRIPTS

This chapter is about nothing less than the accumulated intellectual and political history of mankind, but don't let that intimidate you. It's in collectible form, of course, which makes it palatable, accessible, and even—trust me, now—fun.

And as with all the excellent objects in this volume, you'll discover in this chapter that the closer your books and documents have been to those who possess genius, courage, and power, the rarer, more interesting, and collectible they become.

Take books, for example. Victorian critic John Ruskin wrote, "All books are divisible into two classes, the books of the hour and the books of all time." And though he made this statement in 1865, the modern world of book collecting is, in fact, still conveniently divided into Ruskin's two categories: antique books and modern first editions. There is a third and extensive category of entirely noncollectible books, however, called "reading copies." These are the

Original score of Handel's Messiah.

BOOK PRINTED BY BENJAMIN FRANKLIN

It's not often that we hear about the printer of a book, let alone a well-known printer like Benjamin Franklin. This book was printed by Franklin in America in 1734 (as indicated in the book). At that time, he was twenty-eight years old and had been a printer for only five years.

This eighteenth-century text, a religious sermon, retains its original calf binding. Appraiser Francis Wahlgren was amazed at its excellent condition, since most books this old have not stood the test of time well and tend to have browned pages. Thanks to its wonderful condition and history, he estimated its value at $3,000 to $4,000.

beach books, nightstand books, and bathtub books that are bought for no other reason than to be read.

The antique books are Ruskin's "books of all time"—the Dantes, Shakespeares, Spensers, Keatses, and Melvilles of literature, the Darwins, Vesaliuses, Ben Franklins, and Captain Cooks of science and exploration. This field embraces works by Jane Austen, Umberto Eco, Mark Twain, and James Joyce (for "classics" needn't be from antiquity) and the world of children's books. Treasures such as *The Wind in the Willows, Treasure Island,* and *Winnie-the-Pooh* actually touch on a second dimension of books. For not only is the text of the book an integral part of our universal and individual consciousness; the book itself is also often a beautiful object. Its covers and narratives may be exquisitely illustrated. Its pages can be handsomely bound in morocco leather and gold leaf. Its paper may be handmade. Its binding can be set with precious gems or clasped in gold. All of this, from the collectibles standpoint, potentially makes books doubly valuable: precious as objects and as repositories of human wisdom.

Modern first editions can be both beautiful objects and literary treasures, despite the fact that they are merely popular books—"books of the hour"—whose ascendancy to "classic" heights is still in doubt if even possible. It's rather unlikely that anyone will ever regard the 1993 first edition of John Grisham's first book, *A Time to Kill* (published by Wynwood) as a literary classic, but it did bring four figures at auction recently. On the other hand, F. Scott Fitzgerald's *The Great Gatsby,* John Updike's *Rabbit, Run,* and Patrick O'Brien's *Master and Commander* are far more likely to last beyond the current "hour." With this in mind, collectors of modern first editions mine our very recent past and bet, a bit, on the future.

Manuscripts are a more spontaneous record and far more revealing than most books. The most popular type of manuscript is the handwritten letter, through which we can gain insight into the thought processes and personalities of famous people—just the kind of thing devotees of

Lincoln, Napoleon, or Mozart hunger for. While today we can document our geniuses on videotape—study every nuance of facial expression, hear the timbre of their voices, note the color of their eyes—all we will ever have to hint at the most private thoughts of the legendary men and women who changed and made our world is their letters. Other types of documents, such as deeds, wills, and records of court proceedings, are also manuscripts, which illuminate history in less personal but often surprisingly revealing ways. But, even if we can't truly know a man or his era, in compiling a paper trail we can still begin to puzzle out our past. It wasn't until the twentieth century, after all, that print technology and photography combined to give us comprehensive and reliable historical documents. Despite these undeniable advantages—our videotapes and scanners—we certainly won't see *ourselves* clearly until much more time has passed.

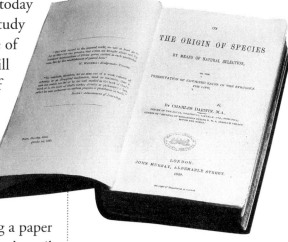

Title page of The Origin of Species *by Charles Darwin, first edition, published by John Murray, 1859.*

BOOKS

I t is true of all antiques and collectibles, but most definitely true of books, that the fewer there are of a very desirable object, the more valuable that object becomes. Recently, for example, a children's book sold for $1.5 million, establishing an auction record for any children's book published since Shakespeare's time. This record-shattering volume was the perennially charming Victorian fantasy *Alice's Adventures in Wonderland* by Lewis Carroll. Here's how it was evaluated:

It was unique. *Alice* is undoubtedly among the best-known and most beloved children's books ever written. It may, in fact, stand alone as a classic of children's literature, and it is still read today, for it has not been out of print since it was originally published in 1865. This means that there are hundreds of thousands of copies of *Alice* out

The last page of Lewis Carroll's holograph manuscript of Alice's Adventures Under Ground, *onto which Carroll pasted his 1859 photo of Alice Liddell at age seven.*

TIPS
from the
experts

Roadshow experts Selby Kiffer and Jerry Patterson explain how *not* to judge a book by its cover.

Look for famous early editions or books that have primacy in their field, particularly in subjects such as science or medicine.—S.K.

A very rare book may not leap out of the bookcase at you. An early-eighteenth-century volume of Americana, for example, will certainly be bound in the simplest of bindings or may not be bound at all. The typical early American binding was undecorated sheep- or calfskin affixed to thin wooden boards.—S.K.

A good provenance, such as inclusion in a well-known collector's library, can increase the value of a book. A bookplate can be a fairly dependable form of provenance.—J.P.

In the nineteenth century, the art of the facsimile signature was highly advanced. Be warned: Ulysses S. Grant's autobiography and books by Mark Twain often contain very convincing facsimiles of the authors' signatures.—J.P.

The more famous the book, the more likely it is to have been reprinted and the less likely it is that the one you own is a first edition.—S.K.

---

there. But of the mere twenty-three copies that are known to have survived from the first printing, this one is unique because it is believed to have belonged to the author himself. Consequently, it has associative value (and is, in fact, termed an association copy).

It was a withdrawn first edition. In other words, it was printed from the first setting-in-type of the author's longhand manuscript, but was withdrawn after having been run off the presses because Carroll was dissatisfied with the quality of the printing of the accompanying illustrations.

It was annotated in purple ink. Experts assume that the author himself made the notes in the margin from the fact that purple ink was the color used for grading papers at Oxford, where Carroll taught mathematics at the time.

The pages were untrimmed. In other words, the rough edges of the pages had not yet been trimmed by the binder. In Lewis' era, books were sold as loose pages in cardboard or paper covers, being bound together only after purchase. This book, therefore, is one small but significant step closer, in book collecting's quite precise hierarchy of value, to being in original condition.

Ten original drawings were tipped in (added later). Not only does this little volume contain the memorable and celebrated engravings with which Sir John Tenniel illustrated *Alice's Adventures in Wonderland,* but it also includes the artist's actual drawings for what would later become those engravings. In other words, it contains ten pages of genuine and unique art. Now fanciers of Lewis Carroll and his Alice would certainly look a long time for a book that could bring them closer than this to the hand and mind of genius. It is a book that has everything.

Most of us have a general sense that books by important authors are valuable. For example, we would certainly know we'd stumbled on something of potential value if we found a 1623 First Folio edition of Shakespeare's works: not the rarest book in existence, perhaps, but certainly the heart's desire of thousands of Shakespeare zealots willing to go into debt for a copy. We might also recognize the potential value in an 1892 edition of Arthur Conan Doyle's *Adventures of Sherlock Holmes* (with its dust jacket). We might even look twice at a first edition of *Carrie* by Stephen King. (It was his first book, after all, published when he was just another unknown author, and today, not surprisingly, it is a prize among King collectors.) "First edition" is the key word in all of the above and in the ranks of collectible books. A first edition, simply put, is all of the copies of a book that are printed from the first setting-up of the type. But here a short digression is required.

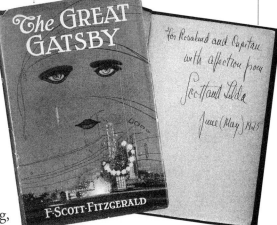

First collected edition of William Shakespeare's poems, illustrated by William Marshall, London, 1640.

First edition, first printing, of The Great Gatsby *by F. Scott Fitzgerald, Scribner's, 1925, with an inscription by the author to Zelda's sister Rosalind and her husband, Newman Smith.*

Gutenberg Bible, illuminated by Johannes Gutenberg.

FIRST EDITIONS

The printed word began with Johannes Gutenberg, who invented movable type in Germany in 1455 and printed the famous Gutenberg Bible, of which, amazingly, fifty copies still exist. (J.P. Morgan owned three of them.) Before Gutenberg, what books that did exist had been painstakingly lettered by hand or fashioned by a laborious process in which every page was carefully hand-carved into a block of wood, then stamped onto paper or parchment. Within fifty years of Gutenberg's marvelous invention, approximately forty thousand books were printed, a group of works known collectively today as *incunabula* (Latin for "things in their cradle").

As time went on, movable type proved to have some inherent disadvantages, chief among them the fact that the pages of each book published had to be typeset, printed, and then dismantled when printing was completed. In an era when labor was inexpensive, as it remained for generations, this was not considered overly cumbersome—at least not until a book found an audience. Then, if its delighted

Endpapers, inside the covers, can be plain (as above), decorative (below, left), or marbled (below right). Pasted onto the endpaper at right is a bookplate.

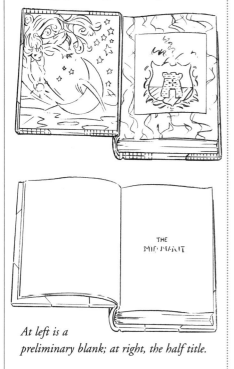

At left is a preliminary blank; at right, the half title.

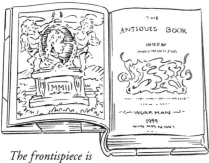

The frontispiece is at left; the title page, at right.

publisher wanted to print more copies, all the pages of his suddenly desirable product would have to be completely reset in movable type for its second edition. Invariably, there would be small, occasionally meaningful variations between the first edition and the second edition of the same work, for typesetters were only human and mistakes were inevitably made. (Variants within editions are referred to as *points* and also include alterations in text, title page, paper, illustrations, or binding.) After 1800, however, as more and more of the general population became literate, publishers began to request that printers leave a book's type set up for a time, in case it was needed again. If a book did get another printing from that original, preserved typesetting, this second printing came to be called the *second impression* and was, technically, part of the first edition. But more editions down the road could still require resetting, and typesetters, as we've noted, are only human. Each time type had to be changed, there was more than a distinct possibility that the accumulated mistakes would appear in the text, and this is one of the reasons book collectors prefer first editions. It often happened that the farther an edition was removed from the author's original manuscript—to the third, fourth, fifth edition, and so on—the more likely that the original errors would compound, rather like a printer's version of the whispering game "telephone."

COLOPHONS AND TITLE PAGES

Because first editions are so important to book enthusiasts, the very first thing you will need to know is how to find out if the book you're holding is a first edition. The edition number is usually in a highly visible location: on the back of the title page. If a book is a first edition, however, it won't necessarily have a publisher's statement to that effect. (After all, a publisher might not assume there will be other editions, so why mark this one "first"?) But the absence of such clear-cut information is part of what makes book collecting so challenging to enthusiasts. They have even compiled reference books listing each publisher's method of indicating dates. If only the date of a book's publication appears, for instance, you can consult these lists—bibliographies of books as physical objects—to learn if the date is the date of the first (or second or third) edition. In some cases, you can turn to the back of the book, where the date of publication can sometimes be found in the *colophon,* an informational statement that might also contain any of the following: the name of the work, its author, its printer, and its place of printing. After that, if no information has been forthcoming, you must continue to hit the books. Edition identification is very labor-intensive and can easily frustrate the novice.

POINTS

After establishing which edition of a book you have, you might also like to discover something about the small distinctions, or points, within editions. These are the incorrect spellings, missing commas, and other typographical errors by which the more—or less—valuable editions of the same book can be recognized. For example, in the first edition of the 1861 novel *The Cloister and the Hearth* by Charles Reade, there is this droll error: "she threw her head over her apron." Naturally, this is the edition that collectors want to own, since the mistake was speedily corrected in later printings. It is the differences—between their covers, their errors, the quality of the paper used—that make one edition distinguishable from another. In modern first editions, the edition with the misspelled word can be worth four times as much as the one that is word-perfect.

Many American book collectors collect first editions of books by modern American authors such as Fitzgerald, Hemingway, and Faulkner. (There are experts who believe that Hemingway's current status as perhaps the most politically incorrect author who has ever lived in America actually *adds* to the value of his first editions.) And the first editions of a few other writers, like Margaret Mitchell, have armies of highly romantic fans. Books signed by the

LOOKING AT BOOKS

There is an art to identifying a potentially valuable book. *Roadshow* expert Selby Kiffer describes his method.

FIRST, look at the title page bearing the author's name and the title of the book. If the title isn't familiar, is the author's name one you recognize? Check the date of publication. Is it an early book, or is it early for its location? (For example, 1783 isn't early for an English book, but it would be very early for a book printed in Kentucky.) Don't depend on the information printed on the front cover or the spine of the book. There may not have been room on the spine, for instance, to include the book's full title.

NEXT, look at the condition of the book. Examine the exterior for bumped corners, scuffs to a leather binding, water stains, and tears.

LEAF through its pages for illustrations, maps, or plates.

LOOK for an inscription in the front of the book.

CHECK the last pages to see if a colophon indicates that the book was a special printing.

Back cover (left), spine (center), and highly ornamental front cover (right).

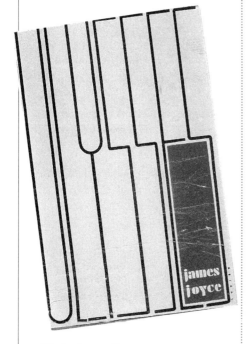

The book cover for James Joyce's novel Ulysses, *illustrated by Henri Matisse, 1922.*

Title page for Last of the Mohicans *by James Fenimore Cooper with illustrations by Felix O.C. Darley, 1872 edition.*

author are doubly attractive, and a first edition of *Gone with the Wind,* even in a pristine dust jacket, is worth almost twice as much if Mitchell signed it. Yet, while any book signed by its author does command a premium, the rarity of that signature is also key to value. The signature of an author who inscribed hundreds of his books is much less desirable than that of Charles Dickens, for example, who was frequently asked to sign his work but intensely disliked doing so and avoided it whenever he could. Quite naturally, this makes a signed volume by Dickens uncommon today and consequently valuable.

In a special category are limited signed first editions, first seen in the 1920s. These were books printed by small private presses with more stringent aesthetic standards than those employed by the publishers of mass editions. Printed on high-quality paper with fine bindings, often protected by a slipcase, and sold predominantly by subscription, the volumes printed by these elite presses offered a limited but appreciative public great talents like Melville, Shakespeare, and Dante, along with contemporary novelists like Steinbeck or Updike, in special editions that were wholly integrated works of art. Often, such editions are dazzlingly illustrated by contemporary artists. The Limited Edition Club's version of *Ulysses* by James Joyce, for example, was illustrated by no less a master than Matisse. Joyce signed 250 copies of this edition, and Matisse signed every one of them.

ILLUSTRATED BOOKS

Illustrated books are perennially popular, for when the eyes weary of print, nothing is so pleasant as the artful, illustrative picture. In the early days of printing, the only type of book illustration was the woodcut. By the eighteenth century, engraved illustrations, full of shadow and detail, prevailed. (In America, silversmith Paul Revere not only engraved the plates for the new republic's currency, fashioned fine silver, and sounded alarms; he also illustrated books.) Engraved book illustrations were, however beautiful, still limited to shades of black and white. They were colorless, moody, and often ill-suited to cheerful tales. The only way to color them was by hand, a highly labor-intensive process.

Twenty years after Bass Otis published the first American lithograph in 1819, color lithography finally arrived to lessen the expense of color book illustration and make it feasible on a large scale. At last, the natural history books, the volumes of flowering plants, colorful fish, and tropical birds that proliferated in the nineteenth century, along with children's fairy tales and the travel and topography books that the public loved, could all be illustrated in vivid and realistic color (although the best were illustrated by hand).

Eventually, even the marvels of color lithography were made obsolete by the spread of photography. But there did emerge from this era an impressive list of famous illustrators: Felix O.C. Darley, who collaborated with Washington Irving in the 1840s; the late-nineteenth-century sculptor Frederic Remington, who illustrated books about the Old West; Arthur Rackham, famous for his romantic and fantastical illustrations of fairy tales; and N.C. Wyeth, who brought classics to life for Scribner's. Among the hundreds of acclaimed illustrators of this era, which lasted well into the twentieth century, were Howard Pyle, Beatrix Potter, Maxfield Parrish, Howard Chandler Christy, Rockwell Kent, and Norman Rockwell.

BINDINGS

The bindings of books—the hard covers that protect the pages and hold them together—represent a category of collecting quite distinct from those that focus on content. The collector of book bindings is interested primarily in the covers of the book and only tangentially in what exists

FRENCH FLORA

This large book of botanical illustrations was given to the owner's great-grandfather, the first secretary of agriculture in California, and was presented to him by the French

government for his help in fighting a livestock disease then sweeping through Europe. Appraiser Jerry E. Patterson observed that the two-volume set chronicles Empress Josephine's garden at Malmaison, her house outside Paris, and was among the greatest works of the French artist Redouté.

Patterson explained that since most of the plants at Malmaison are long gone, the guest's book is now one of the few surviving records of Josephine's garden. Because the book is also in good condition, and a personal letter to the owner's great-grandfather is attached, Patterson valued it at $75,000.

BOOK ON NORTH AMERICAN INDIANS

The North American Indian was the culmination of a twenty-year project by Edward S. Curtis to document the tribes of America before they vanished. Published from 1907 to 1930, the set of twenty bound books and twenty portfolios presented the exquisite photogravures and text of this controversial American photographer.

Here, in the hands of expert Selby Kiffer, was Volume 1, covering the Apache and Navajo tribes. From set #455 (out of a planned 500 sets in the edition), it includes the signature of Curtis himself. Kiffer explained that the value of these hard-to-find sets has risen dramatically: if the complete forty-piece set were available, it might fetch as much as $400,000 at auction.

Even this single volume, in its handsome original binding and very fine condition, with Curtis' signature, could be valued at $8,000 to $10,000. The owner had called it his "treasure," and it's easy to see why.

between them. Occasionally bindings themselves reflect the nature of the contents, however; a book of natural history may be tooled with floral designs, or the binding of a military history will bristle with trophies of war.

Within this field are three subdivisions: the historically significant binding, the specially commissioned fine binding, and the decorative binding, which tends to be a commercial binding. All these can be beautiful and valuable on their own, with no reference at all to the text of the book, or they can more than suggest the pleasures within.

The historical binding documents the history of bookbinding and is primarily of interest to the student of that field. The commissioned binding was custom-made. It was very frequently monogrammed, embellished with silver or gold, or set with jewels. Ordered by European nobles or men of learning for their libraries, books might feature gold-tooled, morocco leather covers with highly ornamental renderings of family coats of arms or splendid family devices (emblems). Queen Elizabeth I, who could have encrusted all her books in pearls if she so desired, had a preference for embroidered bindings.

The decorative binding dates from the third quarter of the nineteenth century. It was usually, as befits that particularly flamboyant era, a tour de force of extravagant pictorialism, often set with ivory miniatures or jewels. A magnificent *Rubáiyat of Omar Khayyám,* for example, bound by the renowned firm of Sangorski and Sutcliffe and set with over a thousand jewels, went down with the *Titanic.*

DUST JACKETS

There is currently something of a fetish in the book-collecting world about dust jackets. Certainly, there is little to distinguish between various editions of the majority of mass-produced modern first editions except for the presence or absence of, and the condition of, their dust jackets. Dust jackets were not even standard until c. 1910, and then they were intended to be disposable. In fact, one prominent *Antiques Roadshow* book expert recalls that, whenever his mother brought home a new book, she immediately stripped off its jacket and threw it away. The dust jackets of F. Scott Fitzgerald's books (who, along with Hemingway and Faulkner, is the most highly collected of pre–World War II American authors) have all crumbled to dust, not because they were shoddily made, but because they were considered, even by their makers, to be disposable. This very fact, however, has produced a fifteen-fold increase in the price of a *Great Gatsby* with its dust jacket over the identical book without it. Understandably, then, some collectors have been treating the dust jacket as a form of cash—which, in a way, it has become. Without their dust jackets, most of the famous books printed since 1950 are relatively worthless and considered mere "reading copies."

Before the turn of the nineteenth century, almost all books were issued without dust jackets, among them, the first edition of Mark Twain's *Life on the Mississippi,* printed in 1883 and bound in decorated cloth. (Twain's works, incidentally, were collected within his own lifetime, a rarity in that era.) Needless to say, there is no dust jacket on another uncommonly rare and valuable piece of printed Americana published in Barcelona in 1493. This very small book—only four leaves—contains Christopher Columbus' letter to the treasurer of King Ferdinand and Queen Isabella of Spain, reporting on his first discoveries.

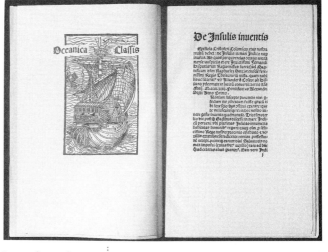

Opening pages of the first printed and illustrated account of "The Discovery of the New World," Christopher Columbus' letter to Gabriel Sanchez, 1493.

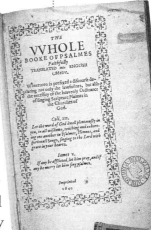

Left: Title page of The Bay Psalm Book, *Cambridge, Massachusetts, 1640.*

Below: Adventures of Huckleberry Finn *by Mark Twain, first American edition, 1885.*

IS IT OLD?

Old books don't interest antique book collectors unless they are *really* old, even if they're leather-bound and the pages are brown at the edges. Antique European books, unless they are specialist or illustrated books, have to have

been printed before 1525 or written by noted authors.
American books must have been published before 1800.
Even very old books are not necessarily valuable. Much
depends on the market for their particular subjects.

♦ Until relatively recently, c. 1830, books were sold
"loose," their pages held together by flimsy cardboard
or paper covers. Customers selected their own bindings, depending on their tastes and pocketbook.

♦ The mass-produced book, uniformly produced,
printed, and bound, first appeared around the time of
the Civil War.

♦ The term *incunabula* is frequently used to describe
the early books of any given area or historical period,
not just the books published in the fifty-year period
right after Gutenberg's invention. The category of
American incunabula, for example, includes any
books printed in America before 1701.

♦ Modern books printed in small editions may be
considerably more collectible than old books printed
in large numbers.

♦ Educated guesses are possible, even with no special
knowledge of book collecting. For instance, a book
dated 1814 will *not* be a first edition of Shakespeare.

IS IT VALUABLE?

The issue of greatest importance to the book enthusiast
is condition. No matter how old the book, remember
this: its condition will be compared with that of brand-
new books today. No allowance can be made for age. This
means that a modern first edition should be close to perfect, and a hundred-year-old first edition should be—well,
pretty much perfect, too. There is *some* leeway. Children's
books, for instance, like an early *Alice's Adventures in
Wonderland,* can't be held to such high standards. Neither
can cookbooks. *The Joy of Cooking* has usually been read—
and probably spattered on.

Damage isn't only caused by thoughtless readers. Paper has a few natural enemies—among them, the ravenous book worm. Yes, there are real book worms: fly or moth larvae that feed on paper (and don't object, on the whole, to leather-bound hors d'oeuvres). They tunnel through a book's pages, leaving small holes behind. Beetles can be destructive, too. Some have been known to chew straight lines through twenty volumes. Also common is foxing. Caused by traces of iron or fungus in the paper, foxing leaves disfiguring rust-brown sprinklings on the page, and its presence in old books is deemed a serious flaw by collectors. Finally, paper just naturally ages, turning yellow, brown, dry, and crumbly. And every evidence of human, invertebrate, or fungal misuse compromises a book's condition and diminishes its value.

CONDITION

♦ Foxed pages reduce the value of a book dramatically.

♦ *Ex-library* copies, or books that have been "removed" from libraries and other institutions, are recognizable by call numbers on their spines, paper card pockets on the flyleaves, and stamped identification on title pages or plates. These generally have no value at all.

♦ Taping dust jackets to books utterly destroys their value.

♦ Wide paper margins surrounding the print of antique books are considered an advantage. They indicate that the pages have not been trimmed by later binders and that the volume is closer to its original condition.

FIRST EDITIONS

♦ A modern first edition in good condition and *with* its dust jacket is worth at least five to ten times the price of the same book without. A first edition of Hemingway's *For Whom the Bell Tolls* in very fine

JUDGING THE BOOK AND ITS COVER

There is a convenient scale for grading book condition:

The Very Fine Book is the book in perfect condition. No page corners have been turned down or torn out. It has not been underlined. All the illustrations and foldout maps are exactly where they ought to be and are undamaged. The spine is not broken. The hinges are perfect. The dust jacket, if it has one, is without a crease, chip, or tear. (What we're describing, you've gathered by now, is the book that hasn't been read.) When it's the right title by the right author in the right edition and is in mint condition, this is the collector's dream-come-true.

The Fine Book rates just below the Very Fine. This book has been read, but has been handled with care. A few minor indications of use—a small scuff on a leather cover, perhaps, or the smallest drop of venison stew on an 1864 volume of *The Art and Mystery of Curing, Preserving, and Potting All Kinds of Meats, Game, and Fish*—are considered acceptable.

The Very Good Book has visible flaws. Its value has been lessened by the unhappy fact that a few corners have been carelessly turned down or the book's price has been clipped from the dust jacket.

The Fair Book is a book of no value to anyone. This category includes former library books, water-damaged books, and book-club books.

Two children's classics by Beatrix Potter, privately printed, 1901 and 1902, London.

condition, for instance, is worth 200 times more with its dust jacket than without it.

♦ Quite rare and costly is Edgar Allan Poe's first book of poetry, *Tamerlane* (1827). Poe's name is not on the cover; rather, according to the cover, the book was authored "by a Bostonian." *Tamerlane* is rare because Poe published it as a vanity book and couldn't pay his printer, who angrily destroyed most of the copies.

♦ When first published in America, Mark Twain's *Adventures of Huckleberry Finn* was bound in both blue and green cloth. In London, however, it first appeared in a red cloth binding. Even though *Huckleberry Finn* appeared first in London (for copyright reasons), American collectors prefer the first American edition in the scarcer blue cloth.

♦ The first printing of a first edition has more value than later printings.

♦ Well-known books by well-known authors, when printed close to the time of their writing, have the best chance of being valuable.

SIGNED BOOKS

♦ The value of a book is increased if the author inscribed it to a member of his or her family or to someone with a personal connection. This makes the book a *presentation copy*—that is, a copy of a book given by, or at the behest of, its author. Those who stand in line waiting for authors' signatures should be aware that books signed at the request of the book's owner, called *inscribed copies*, have less value to collectors than do presentation copies.

♦ A *dedication copy*, the copy presented by the author to the individual to whom the book is dedicated, is

Letter from Samuel Langhorne Clemens, written in 1863 in San Francisco and bearing the earliest Mark Twain signature in existence.

highly desirable. If the author has signed it with a nickname or a well-known pseudonym, the book will command a premium.

CHILDREN'S BOOKS

♦ The first editions of children's books illustrated by Arthur Rackham (illustrator of Hans Christian Andersen's *Fairy Tales* and *Peter Pan in Kensington Gardens*) can be exceptionally valuable.

♦ When a book contains colored illustrations, the illustrations must be bright, not faded.

♦ More important than the age of a children's book is its status among the classics of children's literature. To be of value, it must be a title that continues to be read and loved.

MANUSCRIPTS

The word "manuscript" defines itself, for manuscript means, literally, written by hand. The handwritten letter and the signed document are the most popular manuscript forms today, and, fortunately for collectors, vast amounts of handwritten material are extant. Included in this category are letters, deeds, speeches, wills, and every other type of written communication that marked all formal connection between human beings before the advent of the typewriter.

LETTERS

Letters between talented, powerful, and infamous people from all eras and all countries revive and enliven our past. The poet John Donne observed that "more than kisses, letters mingle souls." And it's true. For what

TIPS *from the experts*

Roadshow expert Chris Coover observes that because every document has its own unique combination of age, condition, content, and autograph, there can be no hard-and-fast rules concerning value. He offers some useful criteria.

Order of value of presidential autograph material:

♦ A handwritten, signed letter from the White House

♦ A short, signed note from the White House

♦ A typewritten document, signed

♦ A typewritten document, signed by a secretary

Content:
 A Washington letter discussing the crossing of the Delaware will be much more valuable than a Washington letter discussing growing wheat on the north forty.

 Because modern presidents handwrite so few letters, they are the rarest form of modern presidential manuscript.

 Letters written by Lincoln, Andrew Jackson, and Robert E. Lee are widely collected.

 Civil War diaries and letters written in pen are preferred to those written in pencil.

A RUEFUL POSTSCRIPT

Much to the horror of today's collectors, autograph albums filled with "clipped" signatures were a prominent feature of the nineteenth-century middle-class parlor. Displayed on the usual center table, one might have seen the autograph of the revered President Lincoln, recently clipped from the bottom of a letter and glued into the family album. The rest of his letter, of course, was thrown away.

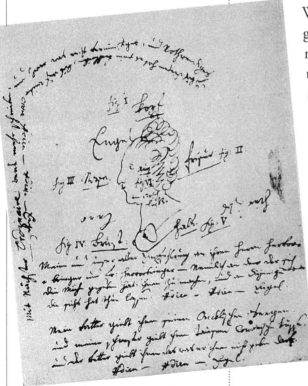

Excerpt of a letter written by Wolfgang Amadeus Mozart from Salzburg on May 10, 1779, to his cousin Maria Anna Thekla Mozart in Ausburg. He addressed her as Basle (a pun on the word Baschen), *which means "little cousin" or "little bass (cello)."*

Napoleon collector, for instance, wouldn't like to own one of the passionate love letters from the emperor to Josephine in which he waxes rhapsodic about her hygienic deficiencies? And who wouldn't laugh—aloud—while perusing the letter in which Lord Chesterfield informs his son, "In my mind, there is nothing so illiberal and so ill-bred, as audible laughter"? Collectible manuscript material even includes letters from children, among them the famous "Is there a Santa Claus?" letter.

Broadsides and posters seeking recruits, soliciting supplies for hungry troops, or patriotically depicting the buxom and beautiful young Columbia exhorting troops in "the spirit of '61" captured the tenor of the Civil War, as did the many enormously crowded lithographs of furious battles and heroic charges. But nothing brought the war home so completely as the letters and diaries of the participants themselves. Aware even then that they were living in a historic moment, Americans saved souvenirs and correspondence from sons, sweethearts, and fathers. In the long history of American warfare, this was the first conflict in which most of the soldiers could read and write. Having little to do on the campgrounds but make entries in diaries and write letters home, they did both, prolifically.

There are thousands of Civil War diaries and letters still in existence that, to their descendants, are equally fascinating, dull, and all-important. Letters, often with drawings and amusing descriptions, detailed the boredom and terror of homesick young men. (One such touching letter recounted a story of dueling bands on the Rappahannock: one playing "Dixie," the other responding with "The Star-Spangled Banner.") Their poems and prayers—even more than their uniforms, carbines, and swords—today make the soldiers' grand, innocent, and awful Civil War come alive. Nonetheless, only those writings that describe important battles, such as Gettysburg, or the firing on Fort Sumter, or watershed moments like the surrender at Appomattox, have unusual monetary value.

AUTOGRAPHS

There is an undoubted fascination in the handwritten documents of the famous. Not only are they a valuable cultural and historical record, but they also can be scrutinized for insights into their writers' minds—for revealing moments of hesitation in the flow of the pen, or for decisive strokes or the firmness of the hand itself. Also collectible are early drafts of literary works, along with essays, poems, and musical notations signed by their authors or composers. Signatures of wartime figures are abidingly popular, although, unsurprisingly, their value depends upon the war. Americans have their favorite wars: the Spanish-American War and World War I inspire little collector interest, for example, but Civil War material, especially when it touches on the events that defined the conflict, has been sought after since the years of the war itself.

Through their manuscripts, we can approach the private emotions of people of genius, celebrity, or power, although, for some collectors, the thrill is in the mere physical contact with the page—the tangible reality of the very note or sheet of paper that the hand of Lincoln, Mozart, or Elvis touched.

CONTEMPORARY REPRODUCTIONS AND FAKES

Fortunately, there are several ways to confirm real age. The paper of eighteenth-century documents, for instance, was produced by the ancient papermaking technique of suspending macerated rags and cloth in water, then gathering this mixture, called slurry, on the top of a rectangular screen before drying it. This created a product that was

ABRAHAM LINCOLN LETTER

This rare piece of Americana, a letter from Abraham Lincoln to the guest's great-great-grandfather, Andrew McCormick, concerns William Walter, who was up for reelection in 1841. In the letter, Lincoln seems appalled that his friend McCormick would vote for Walter rather than Lincoln's friend, Simeon Francis.

Appraiser Marsha Malinowski claimed that this is one of the most emotional Lincoln letters she has ever seen. The president doesn't use his full name when signing (he signs it "Lincoln"), which indicates that he was writing to a dear friend. Probably written around January 1841, the letter is in pristine condition, still with its crisp, original folds. Malinowski estimates that it is worth $75,000 to $125,000.

SHIP'S PASSPORTS

They look like a sea of old parchment, but each piece carries an impressive signature and tells a story of adventure from the age of sail.

The papers come from New Bedford, Massachusetts, the heart of America's nineteenth-century whaling industry. Inherited by the present owner from a great-uncle who ran the largest whaling fleet in the country, these papers are actually ship's passports—letters of safe passage in an age of rampant piracy on the high seas. Each parchment document carries an official seal and is signed by the then-current president of the United States: John Quincy Adams, Martin Van Buren, James Monroe, and Andrew Jackson, among others.

The most valuable passport in the collection is signed both by President Thomas Jefferson and by his secretary of state, James Madison. Expert Christopher Coover appraised the Jefferson passport at $4,000 to $5,000, and each document in the rest of the collection at somewhat less. Altogether, it's a collection of great historical interest as well as value.

chemically quite different from modern wood-pulp paper, which wasn't developed until the middle of the nineteenth century. Rag paper also ages differently, for wood-pulp paper oxidizes faster, turning yellow and then brown around the edges (just the color, in fact, of all those souvenir copies of the Declaration of Independence).

Not infrequently, the wire screen on which that wet paper slurry was collected was cleverly interwoven with its maker's name, monogram, or logo, so the resulting paper would incorporate a watermark. Watermarks, visible when a piece of paper is held to the light (seen on some modern papers as well), can be an aid to dating and therefore to authenticating a document. The inks used are also helpful in dating documents, since early inks were produced from gallic acid and tannic acid, which oxidize in an entirely different fashion from modern, synthetically manufactured inks. Documents of George Washington's time, for example, can be verifiably dated to the eighteenth century with handmade papers, eighteenth-century watermarks, antique inks, and obviously eighteenth-century handwriting and still be imitations, for it was common in the eighteenth century for presidents to have secretarial copies made of all their important papers, to be kept on file. The secretary would copy out the documents in his own handwriting, sign the president's name, and, below that signature, sign his own. This accounts for the "G. Washington" signatures on genuine period manuscripts—honestly and scrupulously marked as file copies.

Also bewildering are "Lincoln-signed" land grants. Land grants during Lincoln's presidency were so numerous that land agents were given the authority to sign for the president. They dutifully noted this by signing their own names beneath his (e.g., A. Lincoln by John Smith). In the period between the Jackson and Lincoln administrations, many documents were signed by proxy, for the technology for creating facsimile signatures was highly advanced. In the twentieth century, too, from the Eisenhower era of the 1950s until today, presidential signatures have been reproduced using the autopen, an ingenious mechanical pen that can make perfect facsimile signatures. (The Pope's signature is often reproduced by autopen.) Assistants to Presidents Harding, Taft, and Franklin Roosevelt commonly signed by hand for their busy employers, especially their more ordinary typewritten correspondence. President Kennedy's secretaries were also empowered to sign less important documents, and some of them achieved a wonderfully convincing imitation of his signature.

FAMOUS SIGNATURES

Our generation will not be adding much to this treasure-trove of collectibles. The Palmer Method is no longer taught in schools, and the art of the beautiful longhand is lost. Most of today's schoolchildren don't write in script at all, let alone in a hand as elegant, idiosyncratic, and legible as John Hancock's, perhaps the most recognizable of all American signatures. Samuel Houston's robust flourish is close to three inches long—and the largest of autographs (not unexpected for a founding Texan). The rarest American signature of a sitting president belongs to our ninth president, William Henry Harrison, who caught cold at his own inauguration and died within the month. Only several dozen or so documents and a handful of letters are known to have been signed by Harrison, who, remarkably, did manage to conduct some business in his very short term.

A genuine Abraham Lincoln signature is always worth owning, and Washington's signature runs a close second. Recently, a letter written by the Father of Our Country to his brother-in-law, penned twenty-seven years before he became president and, significantly, descended in the family of his sister, sold for a considerable sum. There is consistent demand for both Washington's and Lincoln's signatures, although neither could be considered rare—or at least, not as rare as the signature of one signer of the Declaration of Independence, Button Gwinnett. The autograph of this Georgia politician is something of a manuscript "grail," for

CARNEGIE AUTOGRAPH BOOK

Handed down through this guest's husband's family was this little autograph book in its seventeenth-century Dutch silver binding, weighty with illustrious names.

Its original owner was Louise Whitfield Carnegie, wife of Andrew Carnegie. The Carnegies enjoyed the Victorian fashion of autograph collecting, but, because of their prominence, the autographs were of the era's notables: Mark Twain (who also signed his real name, Samuel Clemens), Rudyard Kipling, John Hay (Lincoln's private secretary and McKinley's and Roosevelt's secretary of state), and General William T. Sherman, as well as Tchaikovsky (who included a musical signature) and Paderewski (who jotted a musical notation).

Expert Peter Kraus, noting the album's nice clean signatures and the celebrity of its signers, appraised the book at $10,000. (Which, for the Carnegies, of course, would be small change.)

The following books and documents appear often at the *Roadshow* and, being more common than most of us suppose, are of negligible value:

♦ Little Leather Library books— miniature books of the classics (like Shakespeare's works) published in the 1920s and 1930s

♦ Nineteenth-century books with frontispiece portraits of their authors

♦ Encyclopedias, textbooks, and dictionaries

♦ Clothbound sets of collected works by standard authors—i.e., Scott, Thackeray, Dickens, Hardy, and Kipling

♦ Paperback books

♦ Children's books in very poor condition

♦ Famous documents like the Declaration of Independence and the Gettysburg Address printed on crinkly brown paper

he rarely signed his name at all and was killed in a duel shortly after signing the declaration.

But the most sought-after of all American manuscripts might be a draft of the Gettysburg Address. While Lincoln is supposed to have written a draft of the speech on the back of an envelope en route to the battlefield, it is known that he made at least five copies of the speech after the event. That sixth one may just be tucked in a book somewhere, waiting to be unfolded.

Happily, the autograph field is large and varied, encompassing programs signed by basketball players and rock musicians as well as notes jotted by the original signers of the Declaration of Independence and, naturally, the signatures of movie stars. There are thousands of eight-by-ten glossy still photographs of film personalities in circulation, some actually signed by the celebrity pictured. (Most, of course, were signed by the battalions of women hired to do nothing but sign photos for fan clubs.) A genuine Marilyn is desirable. A genuine Bogie is desirable. A genuine Dan Duryea is just a photograph on shiny paper.

FURTHER READING

Carter, John. *ABC for Book Collectors*. Delaware: Oak Knoll Press, 1997.

Ellis, Ian C. *Book Finds*. New York: Berkley Publishing Group, 1996.

Porter, Katherine. *Miller's Collecting Books*. London: Reed Consumer Books, 1995.

Autographed note from President Lincoln to General Hitchcock, Washington, September 30, 1864, written on the front of a blank envelope.

GLOSSARY

AESTHETIC MOVEMENT: a late-nine-teenth-century trend that sought to reform and simplify household decoration.

ALABASTER: a smooth, white, some-what soft stone (gypsum), often used in place of costly marble.

ALLOY: a mixture of two or more metals; for example, brass is an alloy of copper and zinc.

AMBROTYPE: a photographic image printed on glass.

ANIMALIER BRONZE: a sculpture of an animal or group of animals.

ANTIQUE: in the United States, legally, any object 100 years old or older.

APPLIQUÉ: an ornament that is glued, stitched, or otherwise fastened to a surface.

ARMOIRE: a large, usually tall, free-standing wooden closet or cupboard; originally used for storing armor.

ART NOUVEAU: late-nineteenth-century decorative art movement; designs are curvilinear and based on natural forms.

ARTS AND CRAFTS: a nineteenth-century movement emulating earlier ideals of craftsmanship as a reaction to industrialization.

BAIZE: cotton or woolen felt-like fabric, usually dyed green.

BAROQUE: highly decorated style, with extravagant ornamentation, developed in the seventeenth century.

BASE METALS: nonprecious metals.

BAS-RELIEF (OR LOW-RELIEF): sculpture and architecture in which figures project only slightly from the background.

BEAUX-ARTS: from the French École des Beaux-Arts; an eclectic, academic style of the nineteenth and twentieth centuries.

BÉBÉ: nineteenth-century French doll modeled as an eight-to-twelve-year-old child.

BELLE ÉPOQUE (1900–1910): the American and French term for the Edwardian period in England.

BISQUE (OR BISCUIT): fired but unglazed porcelain with a matte surface; first made in eighteenth-century France.

BLOOM: the frosted or matte surface on many types of gold jewelry, especially in Victorian jewelry designs.

BLUE-AND-WHITE: popular porcelain and pottery decoration of cobalt blue on a white ground.

BOMBÉ: literally, bomb-shaped; describing the bulging curve on the front of furniture (often seen on bureaus and commodes).

BOSS: rounded protuberances; design term used predominantly in silver and metalwork.

BRAZE: to join metals by partial fusion with a layer of soldering alloy.

BRIGHT-CUT: a metal-engraving technique created by chiseling light-reflecting facets; a design that stands out brilliantly on the metal's surface.

BRITANNIA METAL: a form of pewter, used as a base for silver-plated wares in the nineteenth century.

BROWN WOOD: informal term for mediocre furniture.

CABOCHON: a gemstone cut that is unfaceted, dome-shaped, and highly polished.

CABRIOLE LEG: an S-curved, tapering leg terminating in an ornamental foot, most characteristic of Chippendale and Queen Anne furniture.

CANN: A word used to describe an American straight-sided mug.

CASED (OR OVERLAY) GLASS: layered colors of glass, often cut through the copper layer to the base; a technique first used in ancient Rome and rediscovered in the nineteenth century.

CASE FURNITURE: items intended as receptacles, e.g., a chest of drawers.

CAST: formed with a mold. Bronze and iron are often cast, as is glass.

CATALOGUE RAISONNÉ: a list of all the known works of a particular painter.

CERAMIC: general term for items made of clay and fired in a kiln.

CHAMFER: *in furniture,* an angled oblique corner, made by beveling.

CHASING: a technique of tooling metal by removing small imperfections and adding detail.

CHINOISERIE: decorative objects in the Chinese style.

CLOISONNÉ: a decorative enamel technique; the pattern is outlined by metal wire on a gold, brass, or copper setting, and each section is filled in with colored enamel.

COLLET: in a jewelry setting, the metal band or crown-shaped claw that holds the stone.

COLONIAL REVIVAL: a late Victorian style popularized by the American Centennial in 1876.

COMMODE: a low chest of drawers or cabinet.

CRAQUELURE: the all-over crazing frequently seen on the surface of oil paintings.

CRAZING: minute cracks in varnish or paint (see CRAQUELURE).

DELFTWARE (OR DELFT): seventeenth- and eighteenth-century tin-glazed earthenware, often decorated in cobalt blue.

DORÉ BRONZE (OR BRONZE DORÉ): gilt-bronze.

EARTHENWARE: pottery made from porous clay, requiring glaze as a sealant (unlike stoneware or porcelain).

EBONIZE: to stain wood black (to the color of ebony).

ELECTROPLATE: to cover one metal (often nickel or brass) electrolytically with a thin coating of another, less corrosive one, such as silver or gold; a modern silver-plating technique.

EMBOSSING (OR REPOUSSÉ): a method of ornamenting metal by hammering, producing designs in relief.

ENAMEL: *in metalwork,* a method of coating an object with brightly colored, molten glass; *in pottery,* a decorative colored glaze used on top of the glaze; *in glass,* glass powder mixed with oil and used as a decorative paint.

EN GRISAILLE (OR GRISAILLE): a painting done entirely in shades of gray, perhaps with black and white, or other neutral, grayish colors.

EN TREMBLANT: a French term describing jewelry with spring-mounted elements—usually flowers—that "tremble."

EPNS (ELECTROPLATED NICKEL SILVER): silver-coated nickel.

ESCUTCHEON: the brass plate that surrounds and protects the edges of a keyhole.

FAIENCE: tin-glazed earthenware, similar to majolica but made in France and Germany.

FAMILLE ROSE: predominantly rose-hued enamel decoration on eighteenth- and nineteenth-century Oriental export porcelain.

FAMILLE VERTE: predominantly green-hued enamel decoration (see FAMILLE ROSE).

FILIGREE: delicate ornamental work in silver or gold wire.

FINIAL: the ornament that tops a piece of furniture, or the cover of a vessel.

FLATWARE: eating utensils, cutlery, and serving pieces; knives, forks, ladles, and spoons of all types.

FLEUR-DE-LIS: a stylized three-petal design representing a lily.

FOLIATE BAND: a border design incorporating leaves.

FOOT RING: the rim on which a plate, saucer, cup, or bowl rests.

FOXING: spots of discoloration on paper.

FRENCH PLATE: silver plate over brass.

GADROON: a decorative, lobed ornamental border on furniture and metalwork.

GERMAN SILVER (OR NICKEL SILVER): an alloy of copper, nickel, and zinc developed in mid-nineteenth-century England.

GLAZE: *in pottery,* the glassy coating that prevents ceramics from absorbing liquids; (can also serve as colored, translucent, or opaque decoration); *in painting,* a transparent layer of paint over another layer; also, to fill a window with panes of glass.

GOTHIC: originally an architectural style characterized by the pointed arch, rib vault, and flying buttress; flourished from the eleventh to the fifteenth centuries, revived in the eighteenth and nineteenth centuries in furniture design.

GOUACHE: opaque watercolor.

GUILLOCHE: enameling in which a metal surface is first engraved, then coated with translucent enamel that allows the pattern beneath to be seen.

HALLMARK: a punch or stamp on precious metals that indicates purity and/or genuineness.

HEPPLEWHITE: an English furniture style characterized by graceful curves and light woods; named for George Hepplewhite, its creator.

HIGHBOY: a tall chest of drawers, usually in two sections; the lower section is a stand with drawers.

HIGH-RELIEF: sculptured or carved work that stands out sharply from its background.

HOLLOWARE: vessels such as silver and silverplate bowls, vases, and pitchers.

INCUNABULA: the earliest printed materials of any art or area (especially books published before 1500).

INLAY: decorative pattern made by inserting one material, such as ivory, gold, or wood, into another.

JAPONESQUE: in the Japanese manner.

KILN: an oven in which pottery and porcelain are fired.

LACQUER: a mixture of alcohol and seed-lac used to coat and protect brass or silver; varnish for furniture (see ORIENTAL LACQUER) made of resin dissolved in a solvent.

LATHE: a machine for shaping or boring wood or metal items.

LEAF: a very thin sheet of metal, often gold, used decoratively.

LIMNER: early term for the professional portrait painter.

LOUPE: a small magnifying lens used by jewelers and watchmakers.

LOWBOY: a dressing table with drawers, sometimes made together with an upper chest of drawers and then called a highboy.

MAIOLICA: tin-glazed earthenware made in Renaissance Italy, Spain, and Portugal.

MARK (OR MAKER'S MARK): a factory name, pattern name, country name, or maker's name or symbol.

MARQUETRY: decorative patterns of veneer and inlay.

MARRIAGE: an unauthentic combination of unrelated furniture parts.

MARTELÉ: a line of silver products made between 1891 and 1910 by Gorham & Company.

MEDIUM: a material, or combination of materials, used to create an artistic work.

MICROMOSAIC: A nineteenth-century Italian technique featuring tiny mosaics of colored glass that often depicted ancient ruins, local landscapes, or figures in national dress; became inexpensive souvenir objects of the grand tours.

MULTIPLES: mass-produced works of art.

OBJETS DE VERTU: small decorative pieces, usually made of precious metals.

ORIENTAL LACQUER: a decorative finish made of hard, waterproof varnish; can be built up in layers and carved.

ORMOLU: gilt metal.

PARIAN: A semi-matte biscuit porcelain often used to imitate marble statuary in the nineteenth century.

PATINA: any pleasing alteration to a surface, caused by age and/or long handling; on bronze, the effect of natural oxidation or a green finish applied to simulate aging.

PEARL WORK: small, round ornamental beading.

PEDESTAL: a base or support.

PERIOD: made in the era when a given design was initially popular and new.

PIERCED: having openwork designs.

PILGRIM FURNITURE (1620–1670): Technically, American Jacobean furniture of the Pilgrim period.

PITCH: a thick, black distillation of tar, used for weighting candlesticks and other hollow-cast silver or metal items.

PLIQUE-À-JOUR: enameling technique in which transparent, colored enamel is suspended within metal frames.

POD FINIAL: a finial formed like a seedpod.

PORCELAIN: a hard, translucent white ceramic made from china clay (kaolin) and chinastone (petuntse), and, in England, bone ash; and fired at a high temperature.

PORRINGER: a small, shallow bowl with slightly domed bottom and tab handle.

POTTERY: wares made from fired clay (except porcelain and bone china).

PRECIOUS METALS: gold, silver, and platinum; relatively rare, desirable, and therefore expensive metals.

PRECIOUS STONES: diamonds, rubies, emeralds, and sapphires; rare, desirable, and thus expensive gemstones.

PRESENTATION SILVER: silver holloware made for presentation, e.g., a trophy.

PROVENANCE: the record of all previous ownership of an antique object.

PUNCH: the impression of a stamp in metal (see also HALLMARK).

QUATREFOIL: an architectural ornament with four lobes or petals.

RECAMIER: an early nineteenth-century couch with a shaped back and backrest at one end, made in imitation of ancient Greek furniture.

REPOUSSÉ. See EMBOSSING.

ROCOCO: a highly decorative, elegant style characterized by asymmetry and depictions of foliage, rocks, shells, and scrolls; popular expecially in the eighteenth century.

RUNCIBLE SPOON: a fork with two broad tines and one with a curved, sharp edge (also called an ice-cream fork).

SALVER: a silver tray form without handles, often on feet.

SAND-CAST: to make an object by pouring metal into a mold formed in sand.

SCOTTISH PEBBLE JEWELRY: Popular nineteenth-century jewelry made of native agate, frequently of silver.

SEMIPRECIOUS STONES: the non-precious gemstones, such as amethyst, topaz, turquoise, opal, jade, tourmaline, and garnet.

SHEFFIELD PLATE (OR FUSED PLATE): thin sheets of silver fused over copper, dating from the mid-eighteenth century.

SHELLAC: a common early furniture finish; a type of lacquer made from secretions of the lac insect.

SIDEBOARD: a piece of furniture with drawers, cupboards, and shelves for use in a dining room.

SPELTER (OR WHITE METAL): an inexpensive alloy of zinc, lead, and tin that is silver or blue-white in color; often used for imitating bronze sculptures.

STANDISH: a stand for inks, pens, and other writing materials.

STERLING: an alloy containing no less than 925 parts silver in 1,000 parts of the metal, or 925 parts silver to 75 parts copper (included to harden the silver).

STILES: the vertical parts of a framework, especially on chair backs.

STONEWARE: a durable, nonporous ceramicware of clay and sand or flint.

TANKARD: a large drinking vessel with a handle and hinged lid.

TINPLATE: thin sheets of steel coated with tin, commonly used for toys and household articles.

TINTYPE: a photo on a tin backing.

TOURBILLON: A watch movement in which the escapement is mounted on a revolving carriage; invented in 1801.

TOWN MARK: a hallmark representing the town of origin of a piece of silver.

TUREEN: a large, covered, footed bowl, usually with handles.

VENEER: a thin sheet of wood laid over an inexpensive wood surface, often having ornamental wood grain.

WHATNOT (ÉTAGERE): a mobile stand with multiple open shelves for holding ornamental objects.

WHITE METALS: see SPELTER.

WRIGGLEWORK: any sinuous cut or carved decorative pattern.

SUGGESTED READING

Bly, John. *The Confident Collector.* New York: Prentice-Hall, 1986.

Burke, Freedman, et al. *In Pursuit of Beauty.* New York: Metropolitan Museum of Art/Rizzoli, 1986.

Clark, Robert Judson. *The Arts and Crafts Movement in America, 1876–1916.* Princeton, NJ: Princeton University Press, 1972.

The Complete Encyclopedia of Antiques. New York: Hawthorn Books, 1965.

Duncan, Alastair. *Art Deco.* London: Thames and Hudson, 1988.

Garrett, Wendell. *Classic America: The Federal Style & Beyond.* New York: Rizzoli International, 1992.

———. *Victorian America: Classical Romanticism to Gilded Opulence.* New York: Universe Publishing, 1996.

Garrett, Wendell, and David Larkin. *American Colonial: Puritan Simplicity to Georgian Grace.* New York: Monacelli Press, 1998.

Hornung, Clarence. *Treasury of American Design and Antiques.* New York: Harrison House/Harry N. Abrams, 1986.

Knowles, Eric. *Discovering Antiques.* London: De Agostini Editions, 1996.

———. *Miller's Victoriana to Art Deco.* London: Reed Consumer Books, 1993.

Mallalieu, Huon. *The Illustrated History of Antiques.* Philadelphia: Running Press, 1993.

Miller, Judith and Martin. *Miller's Pocket Antique Fact File.* New York: Viking, 1988.

———. *Understanding Antiques.* London: Reed Consumer Books, 1998.

———. *Understanding Antiques.* London: Mitchell Beazley Publishers, 1989.

Miller, R. Craig. *Modern Design, 1890–1990.* New York: Metropolitan Museum of Art/Harry N. Abrams, 1990.

Oxford Illustrated Encyclopedia of the Arts. New York: Oxford University Press, 1990.

Rago, David. *American Art Pottery.* Edison, NJ: Knickerbocker Press, 1997.

Sack, Albert. *The New Fine Points of Furniture: Early American/ Good, Better, Best, Superior, Masterpiece.* New York: Crown Publishing Group, 1993.

The Thames and Hudson Dictionary of Art Terms. London: Thames and Hudson Limited, 1984.

Vaughan, William. *Arts of the 19th Century,* Vol I. New York: Harry N. Abrams, 1998.

RESOURCES

Telepraisal, Inc.
P.O. Box 20686
New York, NY 10009
Tel. 1-800-645-6002 or
(212) 614-9090
Telepraisal, an art research service, maintains a database listing of how works by more than 130,000 artists have sold at auction. Reports can be ordered via the 800 number or on the Internet: telepraisal.com.

Many antiques books may be out of print or hard to find, yet are still great resources to have on hand. Bibliofind.com is a book-selling site that will search for your rare, hard-to-find, and out-of-print books for free. This service offers nine million used and rare books, periodicals, and ephemera from thousands of booksellers worldwide.

FINDING AN APPRAISER

Most towns have at least one lawyer, doctor, and banker. Unfortunately, most don't have an antiques appraiser. So if you are in possession of a potentially valuable object (and if *Antiques Roadshow* isn't coming your way soon), you'll want to know how to find a good appraiser, and most particularly, an appraiser who is knowledgeable about your category of objects. Some appraisers are generalists in antiques, while others have specialties such as jewelry or toys.

A formal appraisal—one in which your item or items are thoroughly described as to age, condition, and weight (for silver)—is also an inventory of your personal property, i.e., a written, notarized document accompanied by a signed statement detailing the purpose of the appraisal (estate, fair market value, or insurance—each is different) and the evaluation, accompanied by documentation, where necessary, explaining the derivation of the estimate. Naturally, appraisers charge for these services, either by the hour or with a flat fee. Ethical appraisers never base their fee on a percentage of the total appraisal. And while most appraisers are thoroughly ethical, the appraisal community itself is not regulated in any way. No license or any type of certification is required for those wishing to be appraisers, so it's a good idea to hire an appraiser who is a member of one of the well-known appraisal associations or organizations, or to contact an established auction house, which employs appraisers who work in all fields. The appraiser you hire will review the extent of the job with you, estimate his or her charges, and examine the objects. The most effective way is to examine them on-site. If that is impossible, the job can be done through photos, but this will result in a tentative and qualified evaluation.

Expert Barbara Deisroth appraising a Tiffany lamp for guests in College Park, Maryland.

A reliable way to locate a qualified appraiser is to phone the appraisal departments of those auction houses listed on the following pages, or contact the offices of one of three national organizations: the American Society of Appraisers, the Appraisers Association of America, and the International Society of Appraisers. Such associations keep databases of members throughout the country and their specialties, and are happy to refer you to someone in your immediate area.

AUCTION HOUSES

Frank Boos Gallery
420 Enterprise Court
Bloomfield Hills, MI 48013
Tel. (248) 332-1500

Christie's
20 Rockefeller Plaza
New York, NY 10020
Tel. (212) 636-2000
Fax (212) 636-2399

David Rago Auctions, Ltd.
333 N. Main Street
Lambertville, NJ 08530
Tel. (609) 397-9374

Northeast Auctions
P.O. Box 363
Hampton, NH 03801
Tel. (800) 260-0230 or
(603) 433-8400
Fax (603) 433-0415

**Phillips Fine Art Auctioneers
& Appraisers**
406 East 79th Street
New York, NY 10021
Tel. (212) 570-4830
Fax (212) 570-2207

**Phillips-Selkirk Fine Art
Auctioneers & Appraisers**
7447 Forsyth Boulevard
Clayton, MO 63105
Tel. (314) 726-5515
Fax (314) 726-9908

Skinner, Inc.
357 Main Street
Bolton, MA 01740
Tel. (978) 779-6241
Fax (978) 779-5144

63 Park Plaza
Boston, MA 02116
Tel. (617) 350-5400
Fax (617) 350-5429

Sotheby's
1334 York Avenue
New York, NY 10021
Tel. (212) 606-7000
Fax (212) 606-7107

Swann Galleries
104 East 25th Street
New York , NY 10010
Tel. (212) 254-4710
Fax (212) 979-1017

**Weschler's Auctioneers
and Appraisers**
905 E Street
Washington, DC 20004
Tel. (212) 628-1281

William Doyle Galleries
175 East 87th Street
New York, NY 10021
Tel. (212) 427-2730
Fax (212) 369-0892

Witherell's Americana Auctions
9290 Yorkship Court
Elk Grove, CA 95758
Tel. and Fax (916) 683-3266

APPRAISAL ORGANIZATIONS

**American Society
of Appraisers**
60 East 42nd Street
New York, NY 10165
Tel. (212) 953-7272

**Appraisers Association of
America, Inc.**
386 Park Avenue South, Suite 2000
New York, NY 10016
Tel. (212) 889-5404
Fax (212) 889-5503

**International Society
of Appraisers**
16040 Christensen Road, Suite 102
Seattle, WA 98188
Tel. (206) 241-0359 or
(888) 472-5587

ANTIQUES ROADSHOW™ APPRAISERS

Susan Abeles
Christie's
20 Rockefeller Plaza
New York, NY 10020

Eric Alberta
Sotheby's
1334 York Avenue
New York, NY 10021

Sally Ambrose
Ambrose Appraisal Service
P.O. Box 536
Leavenworth, WA 98826-0536

Alexander Anthony
Adobe Gallery
413 Romero NW
Albuquerque, NM 87104

Gillian Arthur
Sotheby's
1334 York Avenue
New York, NY 10021

Caroline Ashleigh
Caroline Ashleigh Associates
800 East Lincoln
Birmingham, MI 48009

Richard Austin
Christie's East
219 East 67th Street
New York, NY 10021

Kathy Bailey
160 Gilman Boulevard, NW
Issaquah, WA 89027

Noel Barrett
Noel Barrett Antiques & Auctions Ltd.
Carversville, PA 18913

Dianne Lewis Batista
J. Mavec & Co.
946 Madison Avenue
New York, NY 10021

C. Jeannene Bell
Jewelry Box Antiques
7325 Quivira Road, Suite 238
Shawnee, KS 66216

Max Bernheimer
Christie's
20 Rockefeller Plaza
New York, NY 10020

Bill Bertoia
Bill Bertoia Auctions
1881 Spring Road
Vineland, NJ 08361

Nancy Bialler
Sotheby's
1334 York Avenue
New York, NY 10021

David Bonsey
Skinner, Inc.
63 Park Plaza
Boston, MA 02116

Frank Boos
Frank H. Boos Gallery
420 Enterprise Court
Bloomfield Hills, MI 48013

Ron Bourgeault
Northeast Auctions
Treadwell House
93 Pleasant Street
Portsmouth, NH 03801

Mollie Burns
Christie's
360 North Camden Drive
Beverly Hills, CA 90210

John A. Buxton
International Society of Appraisers
6717 Spring Valley Road
Dallas, TX 75240

Jim Callahan
Skinner, Inc.
63 Park Plaza
Boston, MA 02116

Judy L. Campbell
5500 Summerset Drive
Midland MI 48640

Frank Castle
Castle Fine Arts
454 Sutter Street
San Francisco, CA 94108

Andrew Cheney
Martlesham, Berry Lane
Littlehampton
West Sussex BN17 5HD
United Kingdom

Nan Chisholm
Sotheby's
1334 York Avenue
New York, NY 10021

Gordon Converse
Gordon S. Converse & Co.
Spread Eagle Village
503 West Lancaster Avenue
Strafford, PA 19087

Chris Coover
Christie's
20 Rockefeller Plaza
New York, NY 10020

C. Wesley Cowan
Historic Americana
747 Park Avenue
Terrace Park, OH 45174

John T. Crabtree
3443 Mahanna Street #2106
Dallas, TX 75209

Donald Cresswell
Philadelphia Print Shop
8441 Germantown Ave
Philadelphia, PA 19118

Carl Crossman
Northeast Auctions
Treadwell House
93 Pleasant St
Portsmouth NH 03801

John Culme
8427 East Palm Lane
Scottsdale, AZ 85257

Peter Curran
Peter Curran Antiques & Appraisals
444 Danbury Road
P.O. Box 7395
Wilton, CT 06897

Suzanne Davis
Christie's
170 Bloor Street
Toronto, ONT M5S 1T9

Nicholas Dawes
67 East 11th Street
New York, NY 10003

Linda Dawson
Dawson's Auctioneers & Appraisers
128 American Road
Morris Plains, NJ 07950

Doug Deihl
Skinner, Inc.
63 Park Plaza
Boston, MA 02116

Barbara Deisroth
Sotheby's
1334 York Avenue
New York, NY 10021

Antoine de Vermoutier
392 Central Park West
Apt. 10-Y
New York, NY 10025

Linda Donahue
William Doyle Galleries
175 East 87th Street
New York, NY 10021

Nancy Druckman
Sotheby's
1334 York Avenue
New York, NY 10021

Ernest DuMouchelle
Lawrence DuMouchelle
Robert DuMouchelle
DuMouchelle Gallery
409 East Jefferson Avenue
Detroit, MI 48226

Leila Dunbar
Sotheby's
1334 York Avenue
New York, NY 10021

Ronald Dupuis
Dupuis Jewellery Auctioneers
94 Cumberland Street
Toronto, ONT M5R 1A3

Linda Dyer
P.O. Box 1104
Franklin, TN 37065-1104

Ian Ehling
Christie's East
219 East 67th Street
New York, NY 10021

Rochelle Eisenberg
Art Directives
P.O. Box 173
Ambler, PA 19002

Donald Ellis
Donald Ellis Gallery
1002 Mineral Springs Road
RR#3
Dundas, ONT L9H 5E3

Mildred Ewing
Skinner, Inc.
63 Park Plaza
Boston, MA 02116

Dean Failey
Christie's
20 Rockefeller Plaza
New York, NY 10020

Peter Fairbanks
Montgomery Gallery
353 Sutter Street
San Francisco, CA 94108

Ken Farmer
Ken Farmer Auction, LLC
105A Harrison Street
Radford, VA 24141

Virginia Farrell
12 Chestnut Street
Westfield, MA 01085

Alan Fausel
William Doyle Galleries
175 East 87th Street
New York, NY 10021

Rupert Fennell
P.O. Box 171
Spencertown, NY 12165

Colleene Fesko
Skinner, Inc.
63 Park Plaza
Boston, MA 02116

James Ffrench
12 East 86th Street
Apt. 736
New York, NY 10028

Tara Ana Finley
Christie's East
219 East 67th Street
New York, NY 10021

Conor Fitzgerald
Christie's East
219 East 67th Street
New York, NY 10021

Andrea Fiuczynski
Christie's
360 North Camden Drive
Beverly Hills, CA 90210

J. Michael Flanigan
J.M. Flanigan American Antiques
1607 Park Avenue
Baltimore, MD 21217

Stephen Fletcher
Skinner, Inc.
63 Park Plaza
Boston, MA 02116

Susan Florence
Christie's
216 Newbury Street
Boston, MA 02116

Debra J. Force
Debra Force Fine Art, Inc.
14 East 73rd Street
New York, NY 10021

Rudy Franchi
Barbara Franchi
Regina Franchi
The Nostalgia Factory
51 North Margin Street
Boston, MA 02113

Constantine Frangos
Christie's
20 Rockefeller Plaza
New York, NY 10020

Hadley Freeman
Christie's East
219 East 67th Street
New York, NY 10021

Andrea Blunck Frost
William Doyle Galleries
175 East 87th Street
New York, NY 10021

Masatoshi Fukumaru
Japanese Antiques
8700 Commerce Park Drive
Houston, TX 77036

Melissa Gagen
Christie's
20 Rockefeller Plaza
New York, NY 10020

David Gallager
William Doyle Galleries
175 East 87th Street
New York, NY 10021

Christopher Galliard
Christie's
20 Rockefeller Plaza
New York, NY 10020

Wendell Garrett
Sotheby's
1334 York Avenue
New York, NY 10021

Mona Gavigan
Gallery Africa
2010 R Street, NW
Washington, DC 20009

Peggy Gilges
Christie's
20 Rockefeller Plaza
New York, NY 10020

Claire Givens
Andrew Dipper
Givens Violins
1004 Marquette Avenue
Suite 205
Minneapolis MN 55403

George Glastris
Skinner, Inc.
63 Park Plaza
Boston, MA 02116

Elizabeth Goldberg
Sotheby's
1334 York Avenue
New York, NY 10021

Bernardo Gutterman
Bernardo Gutterman Violins
200 South State Street
Chicago, IL 60604

Kathleen Guzman
200 East End Avenue
New York, NY 10128

Reyne Haines
Just Glass Auctions
405 Lafayette Avenue
Cincinnati, OH 45220

Ted Hake
Hake's Americana & Collectibles
P.O. Box 1444
York, PA 17405

Titi Halle
Cora Ginsburg, Inc. 1
19 East 74th Street
New York, NY 10021

Martha Hamilton
Skinner, Inc.
63 Park Plaza
Boston, MA 02116

Roy Harrell
American Indian Antiques
12251 Manor Road
Glen Arm, MD 21057

Jerry M. Hart
Hart Galleries
2301 South Voss Road
Houston, TX 77057

Christopher Hartop
P.O. Box 282
Spring Glen, NY 12483

Kathleen Harwood
Harwood Fine Arts, Inc.
P.O. Box 219
Maplewood, NJ 07040

Dana Hawkes
Sotheby's
1334 York Avenue
New York, NY 10021

Ann G. Hays
Ken Hays
Kenneth S. Hays Associates, Inc.
120 South Spring Street
Louisville, KY 40206

John Hays
Christie's
20 Rockefeller Plaza
New York, NY 10020

Gertraud Hechl
Weschler's Auctioneers
  and Appraisers
905-909 E Street, NW
Washington, DC 20004

Vivian Highberg
1741 Partridge Run Road
Pittsburgh, PA 15241

Jeffrey Holmes
Shar Fine Instruments
2645 South Industrial Way
Ann Arbor, MI 48104

Mark O. Howald
Phillips-Selkirk
7447 Forsythe Boulevard
St. Louis, MO 63105

Michael Hughes
Christie's
20 Rockefeller Plaza
New York, NY 10020

Riley Humler
Cincinnati Art Galleries
225 6th Street
Cincinnati, OH 45202

Anne Igelbrink
William Doyle Galleries
175 East 87th Street
New York, NY 10021

Don Jensen
7216 Soundview Drive
Edmonds, WA 98026

Harmer Johnson
146 East 84th Street
New York, NY 10028

Joyce Jonas
215 East 80th Street
New York NY 10021

George Juno
American Soldier
1125 North St. Elmo Street
Allentown, PA 18104

Alan Kaplan
Leo Kaplan, Ltd.
967 Madison Avenue
New York, NY 10021

Daile Kaplan
Swann Galleries
104 East 25th Street
New York, NY 10010

Karen Keane
Skinner, Inc.
63 Park Plaza
Boston, MA 02116

Kerry Keane
Christie's East
219 East 67th Street
New York, NY 10021

Leigh Keno
Leigh Keno American Antiques
980 Madison Avenue
New York, NY 10021

Leslie Keno
Sotheby's
1334 York Avenue
New York, NY 10021

Selby Kiffer
Sotheby's
1334 York Avenue
New York, NY 10021

Evelyn Kraus
Peter Kraus
Ursus Books, Ltd.
981 Madison Avenue
New York NY 10021

Jo Kris
Skinner, Inc.
63 Park Plaza
Boston, MA 02116

Greg Kuharic
Sotheby's
1334 York Avenue
New York, NY 10021

David Lackey
David Lackey Antiques
Antique Pavilion
2311 Westheimer
Houston, TX 77098

Christopher Lane
Philadelphia Print Shop
8441 Germantown Avenue
Philadelphia, PA 19118

Julianna Lang
Monte Cristo's
445 Daniels Street
Raleigh, NC 27605

Thomas Lecky
Christie's East
219 East 67th Street
New York, NY 10021

Catherine Leonhard
Christie's
360 North Camden Drive
Beverly Hills, CA 90210

Gloria Lieberman
Skinner, Inc.
63 Park Plaza
Boston, MA 02116

Daphne Lingon
Christie's
20 Rockefeller Plaza
New York, NY 10020

Deedy Loftus
540 16th Street
Paso Robles, CA 93446

Martin Lorber
William Doyle Galleries
175 East 87th Street
New York, NY 10021

Karen Lorene
Facere Jewelry
1420 Fifth Avenue #108
Seattle, WA 98101

Nicholas Lowry
Swann Galleries, Inc.
104 East 25th Street
New York, NY 10010

Timothy Luke
Tim's Toy Times
6270-3 Riverwalk Lane
Jupiter, FL 33458

Louise Luther
Skinner, Inc.
63 Park Plaza
Boston, MA 02116

Becky MacGuire
Christie's
20 Rockefeller Plaza
New York, NY 10020

A. Duncan MacLean
Waddington's
111 Bathurst Street
Toronto, ONT M5V 2R1

Nick Maclean
Christie's
20 Rockefeller Plaza
New York, NY 10020

Richard J.B. Madley
Phillips Fine Art Auctioneers
    & Appraisers
406 East 79th Street
New York, NY 10021

Marsha Malinowski
Sotheby's
1334 York Avenue
New York, NY 10021

Lark Mason
Sotheby's
1334 York Avenue
New York, NY 10021

Stephen Massey
108 East 81st Street
New York, NY 10028

Elyse Luray Marx
Christie's East
219 East 67th Street
New York, NY 10021

David McCarron
Frank H. Boos Gallery
420 Enterprise Court
Bloomfield Hills, MI 48013

Nancy McClelland
Christie's
20 Rockefeller Plaza
New York, NY 10020

Milly McGehee
P.O. Box 666
Riderwood, MD 21139

Philip Merrill
Nanny Jack & Co., Inc.
5005 Edmondson Avenue
Baltimore, MD 21229

Michael Millea
Dawson's
44 Coconut Row
Palm Beach, FL 33480

Stephen Milne
Stephen Milne Collections
45 Tudor City Place
New York, NY 10017

Gregory L. Minuskin
Time On Your Hands
P.O. Box 538
Tustin, CA 92781

Chris Mitchell
c/o American Soldier
1125 North St. Elmo Street
Allentown, PA 18104

Alasdair Nichol
Freeman Fine Arts
1808 Chestnut Street
Philadelphia, PA 19103

Juliet Nusser
P.O. Box 282
Spring Glen, NY 12483

Brett O'Connor
Sotheby's
9665 Wilshire Boulevard
Los Angeles, CA 90212

Christina Orobetz
Sotheby's
9 Hazelton Avenue
Toronto ONT M5R 2E1

Fred Oster
Christie's
1529 Pine Street
Philadelphia, PA 19102

Mary Jo Otsea
Sotheby's
1334 York Avenue
New York, NY 10021

Peter Pap
Peter Pap Oriental Rugs
Box 286
Dublin, NH 03444

Adam Patrick
A La Vieille Russie
781 Fifth Avenue
New York, NY 10022

Jerry Patterson
William Doyle Galleries
175 East 87th Street
New York, NY 10021

Suzanne Perrault
Perrault-Rago Gallery
17 South Main Street
Lambertville, NJ 08530

Elisabeth Poole
Christie's
20 Rockefeller Plaza
New York, NY 10020

Wayne Pratt
Wayne Pratt & Company
346 Main Street South
Woodbury, CT 06798

Jane Prentiss
Skinner, Inc.
63 Park Plaza
Boston, MA 02116

Russ Pritchard
American Military Antiques
    & Fine Art, Ltd.
311 Millbank Road
Bryn Mawr, PA 19010

Paul Provost
Christie's
20 Rockefeller Plaza
New York, NY 10020

Marley Rabstenek
Christie's East
219 East 67th Street
New York, NY 10021

David Rago
David Rago Auctions, Ltd.
333 North Main Street
Lambertville, NJ 08530

Carolyn Remmey
Remmey Galleries
4 Lake Trail
West Harding Township, NJ 07960

Jonathan Rendell
Christie's
20 Rockefeller Plaza
New York, NY 10020

Lee Richmond
The Best Things
12640 Magna Carta Road
Herndon, VA 20171

Letitia Roberts
Sotheby's
1334 York Avenue
New York, NY 10021

Eve Reppen Rogers
Sotheby's
215 West Ohio Street
Chicago, IL 60610

Christie Romero
P.O. Box 42
Anaheim, CA 92815

Trudy Rosato
William Doyle Galleries
175 East 87th Street
New York, NY 10021

Andrew Rose
Christie's
20 Rockefeller Plaza
New York, NY 10020

Jennifer Roth
Sotheby's
1334 York Avenue
New York, NY 10021

Paul Royka
Design20c
147 Hemlock Drive
Lunenberg MA 01462

Charles Rudig
5970 Crabtree Lane
Cincinnati, OH 45243

Albert Sack
Israel Sack, Inc.
730 Fifth Avenue
New York, NY 10019

Virginia Salem
Phillips Fine Art Auctioneers
    & Appraisers
406 East 79th Street
New York, NY 10021

Randy Sandler
Cincinnati Art Galleries
225 6th Street
Cincinnati, OH 45202

Polly Sartori
Christie's
20 Rockefeller Plaza
New York, NY 10020

Rosalie Sayyah
"Rhinestone Rosie"
606 West Crockett
Seattle, WA 98119

Peter L. Schaffer
Mark Schaffer
A La Vieille Russie
781 Fifth Avenue
New York NY 10022

John E. Schulman
Caliban Books
410 South Craig Street
Pittsburgh, PA 15213

John Sexton
Stone Mountain Relics
968 Main Street
Stone Mountain, GA 30083

Bruce Shackelford
23221 South Fork
P.O. Box 15707
San Antonio, TX 78255

Peter W. Shaw
2315 University Boulevard
Houston, TX 77005

Sig Shonholtz
Second Time Around
8840 Beverly Boulevard
West Hollywood, CA 90048

Kerry Shrives
Skinner, Inc.
63 Park Plaza
Boston, MA 02116

Eric Silver
William Doyle Galleries
175 East 87th Street
New York, NY 10021

Leonard Sipiora
Leonard Sipiora Fine Art
   & Antiques
1012 Blanchard Street
El Paso, TX 79902

Larry Sirolli
Sotheby's
215 West Ohio Street
Chicago, IL 60610

Stuart Slavid
Skinner, Inc.
63 Park Plaza
Boston, MA 02116

Jeanne Sloane
Christie's
20 Rockefeller Plaza
New York, NY 10020

Jonathan Snellenburg
Jonathan Snellenburg Antiques, Inc.
154 West 57th Street
Studio 90
New York, NY 10019

Gary Sohmers
"Wex Rex" Collectibles
P.O. Box 702
Hudson, MA 01749

Marvin Sokolow
425 West Fairy Chasm Road
Bayside, WI 53217

Daniel B. Soules
Frank H. Boos Gallery
420 Enterprise Court
Bloomfield Hills, MI 48013

Anne Spink
Christie's
20 Rockefeller Plaza
New York, NY 10020

Gary Stradling
1225 Park Avenue, Penthouse E
New York, NY 10128

Usha Subramaniam
icon20.com
515 West 20th Street, Suite 5-W
New York, NY 10001

Arlie Sulka
Lillian Nassau Ltd.
220 East 57th Street
New York, NY 10022

Beth Szescila
9546 Enstone Circle
Spring, TX 77379

Riya Takaya
Christie's
20 Rockefeller Plaza
New York, NY 10020

Martha Tips
David Tips
7012 Blackwood Drive
Dallas, TX 75231

Gerald Tomlin
Joanne Tomlin
6148 Crestmont Drive
Dallas TX 75214

Mark Topalian
William Doyle Galleries
175 East 87th Street
New York, NY 10021

Suzanne Torrey
Sotheby's
9 Hazelton Avenue
Toronto ONT M5R 2E1

Kelly Troester
Christie's
20 Rockefeller Plaza
New York, NY 10020

August Uribe
Sotheby's
9665 Wilshire Boulevard
Los Angeles, CA 90212

Anthony Victoria
Frederick P. Victoria & Sons
400 West End Avenue, 15-B
New York, NY 10024

Michael Vinson
P.O. Box 142147
Austin, TX 78714

Francis Wahlgren
Christie's
20 Rockefeller Plaza
New York, NY 10020

Joan Walker
DuMouchelle Gallery
409 East Jefferson Avenue
Detroit, MI 48226

Barry Weber
Edith Weber
Edith Weber & Associates
994 Madison Avenue
New York, NY 10021

John S. Weschler
William P. Weschler
Weschler's Auctioneers
   and Appraisers
905 E Street NW
Washington, DC 20004

Rick Wester
Christie's
20 Rockefeller Plaza
New York, NY 10020

Todd D. Weyman
Swann Galleries, Inc.
104 East 25th Street
New York, NY 10010

Stuart Whitehurst
Skinner, Inc.
63 Park Plaza
Boston, MA 02116

Laura Whitman
Christie's
20 Rockefeller Plaza
New York, NY 10020

Jody Wilkie
Christie's
20 Rockefeller Plaza
New York, NY 10020

Brad Witherell
Brian Witherell
Witherell's Americana Auctions
9290 Yorkship Court
Elk Grove, CA 95758

Richard Wright
Glenn Stevens
P.O. Box 227
Flowing Springs and Hollow Roads
Birchrunville, PA 19421

Berj Zavian
William Doyle Galleries
175 East 87th Street
New York, NY 10021

Kevin Zavian
125 West 45th Street
New York, NY 10036

PHOTO CREDITS

COLOR

CHAPTER 1

page 1: *top left,* Winterthur Museum; *top right,* Henry Francis Dupont Winterthur Museum, Delaware, USA/Bridgeman Art Library, London/NY; *center left,* Winterthur Museum; *center right,* ©The Metropolitan Museum of Art, Purchase, Mrs. Paul Moore, Gift, 1965. (65.167.6). Photograph ©1996 The Metropolitan Museum of Art; *middle,* Christie's Images; *bottom left,* Winterthur Museum; *bottom right,* Winterthur Museum.

page 2: *top left,* Christie's Images; *top right,* Winterthur Museum; *center left,* Purchased with the help of the Seminarians, A Friend of the Department, the William N. Banks Foundation, Dr. and Mrs. J.W. McMeel and Anonymous Gift. ©Museum of Fine Arts, Boston; *bottom left,* Christie's Images; *bottom right,* ©The Museum of Fine Arts, Houston; Museum purchase.

page 3: *top left,* Christie's Images; *top right,* Christie's Images; *center right,* Shelburne Museum; *center middle,* Christie's Images; *bottom left,* Christie's Images; *bottom right;* Courtesy of William Doyle Galleries.

page 4: *top left,* Christie's Images; *top right,* Cooper-Hewitt Museum, Smithsonian Institution/Art Resource, NY; *center left,* Wallace Collection, London, UK/Bridgeman Art Library, London/NY; *center right,* Christie's Images; *bottom left,* Christie's Images; *bottom right,* Christie's Images.

CHAPTER 2

page 5: *top left,* Christie's Images; *top right,* Winterthur Museum; *center left,* Christie's Images; *center right,* Courtesy of Sotheby's; *center middle,* The Newark Museum/Art Resource, NY; *bottom left,* Winterthur Museum; *bottom middle,* Christie's Images; *bottom right,* Winterthur Museum.

page 6: *top left,* Winterthur Museum; *top center,* Winterthur Museum; *top right,* Christie's Images; *center left,* Christie's Images; *center right,* The Newark Museum/Art Resource, NY; *bottom left,* Christie's Images; *bottom middle,* Christie's Images; *bottom right,* Christie's Images.

page 7: *top left,* Christie's Images; *top middle,* Christie's Images; *top right,* Courtesy of Skinner, Inc.; *bottom left,* Courtesy of William Doyle Galleries; *bottom middle,* Christie's Images; *bottom right,* The Newark Museum/Art Resource, NY.

CHAPTER 3

page 8: *top,* Private Collection/ Bridgeman Art Library, London/NY; *center middle,* Christie's Images; *center right,* Christie's Images; *center left, top,* Christie's Images; *center left, bottom,* Private Collection/Paul Freeman/Bridgeman Art Library, London/NY; *bottom left,* Courtesy of Skinner, Inc.; *bottom middle,* Christie's Images; *bottom right,* Christie's Images.

page 9: *top left,* Christie's Images; *top right,* Aldo Tutino/Art Resource, NY; *center left, top,* Courtesy of Sotheby's; *center left, bottom,* Fitzwilliam Museum, University of Cambridge, UK/Bridgeman Art Library, London/NY; *center right, top,* Private Collection/ Bridgeman Art Library, London/NY; *center right, bottom,* Christie's Images; *bottom left,* Courtesy of Skinner, Inc.; *bottom middle,* Shelburne Museum; *bottom right,* Courtesy of Skinner, Inc.

page 10: *top left,* Winterthur Museum;

top left, middle, Courtesy of Skinner, Inc.; *top right,* Private Collection/Bridgeman Art Library, London/NY; *top right, middle,* Kremlin Museums, Moscow, Russia/Bridgeman Art Library, London/NY; *center left,* Bonhams, London, UK/Bridgeman Art Library, London/NY; *center left, middle,* Apsley House, The Wellington Museum, London, UK/Topham Picturepoint/Bridgeman Art Library, London/NY; *center right,* Christie's Images; *center right, middle,* Aldo Tutino/Art Resource, NY; *bottom left,* Cheltenham Art Gallery & Museums, Gloucestershire, UK/Bridgeman Art Library, London/NY; *bottom left, middle,* The Newark Museum/Art Resource, NY; *bottom right, middle,* Collection of the Museum of American Folk Art, NY; Museum of American Folk Art Purchase; *bottom right,* Aldo Tutino/Art Resource, NY.

page 11: *top left,* Courtesy of Skinner, Inc.; *top middle,* Winterthur Museum; *top right,* Art Resource, NY; *center left,* Christie's Images; *center left, middle,* The Corning Museum of Glass, Corning, NY; *center, middle,* Torre Abbey, Torquay, Devon, UK/Bridgeman Art Library, London/NY; *center right,* Aldo Tutino/Art Resource, NY; *bottom left,* Courtesy of Skinner, Inc.; *bottom middle,* Giraudon/Art Resource, NY; *bottom right,* Cooper-Hewitt Museum, Smithsonian Institution/Art Resource, NY.

CHAPTER 4

page 12: *top left,* Christie's Images; *center right,* Art Resource, NY; *bottom left,* Giraudon/Art Resource, NY.; *bottom right,* Erich Lessing/Art Resource, NY.

page 13: *top right,* National Museum of American Art, Washington,

D.C./Art Resource, NY; *center left,* Nimatallah/Art Resource, NY; *center middle,* Giraudon/Art Resource, NY; *center right,* National Museum of American Art, Washington, D.C./Art Resource, NY; *bottom left,* The Bridgeman Art Library, London/NY; *bottom right,* The Bridgeman Art Library, London/NY.

page 14: *top left,* Christie's Images; *top right,* Private Collection/Christie's Images/Bridgeman Art Library, London/NY; *center left,* Christie's Images; *center middle,* Giraudon/Art Resource, NY; *bottom left,* Christie's Images; *bottom right,* Christie's Images.

page 15: *top left,* The Granger Collection; *top right,* Christie's Images; *center left,* Bonhams, London, UK/Bridgeman Art Library, London/NY; *center right,* Christie's Images; *bottom left,* Bonhams, London, UK/Bridgeman Art Library, London/ NY; *bottom right,* Christie's Images.

CHAPTER 5

page16: *top left,* Christie's Images; *left column,* Diamond; Robert Weldon/© GIA, Courtesy of Stone Collection #16237; *left column,* Zircon: Robert Weldon/© GIA, Courtesy of The Natural History Museum of L.A.; *left column,* Ruby; Tino Hammid/ © GIA and Tino Hammid; *left column,* Citrine; © GIA; *left column,* Sapphire; © GIA; *left column,* Star Sapphire; Tino Hammid/© GIA and Tino Hammid, Courtesy of Benjamin Zucker; *left column,* Emerald; © GIA; *left column,* Aquamarine; Robert Weldon/© GIA, Courtesy of M. Chung Gemstones and Fine Jewelry Co.; *left column,* Topaz; Mike Havstad/© GIA; *left column,* Pearl; © GIA; *left column,*

Almandine Garnet; Robert Weldon/© GIA; *left column,* Demantoid Garnet; Tino Hammid/© GIA; *left column,* Turquoise; © GIA; *left column,* Nephrite; Mike Havstad/© GIA; *left column,* Opal; Robert Weldon/© GIA, Courtesy of Stone Collection #13350; *left column,* Amber; © GIA; *left column,* Jadeite; Nicholas DelRe/© GIA; *center left, top,* Christie's Images; *center middle, top & bottom,* Christie's Images; *center right,* Christie's Images; *center right, bottom,* Christie's Images; *bottom left,* Courtesy of Sotheby's; *bottom right,* Christie's Images.

page 17: *top left,* Christie's Images; *top middle,* Christie's Images; *top right,* Christie's Images; *center left,* Christie's Images; *center left, middle,* Christie's Images; *center right, top,* Christie's Images; *center right, middle,* Christie's Images; *center right, bottom,* Christie's Images; *bottom left,* Courtesy of Sotheby's; *bottom right,* Christie's Images.

page 18: *top left,* Christie's Images; *top left middle,* Christie's Images; *top right middle (bottom),* Courtesy of Sotheby's; *top right,* Christie's Images; *center left,* Christie's Images; *center left middle,* Christie's Images; *center right middle,* Christie's Images; *center right,* Christie's Images; *bottom left,* Christie's Images; *bottom middle,* Christie's Images; *bottom right,* Christie's Images.

CHAPTER 6

page 19: *top left,* Victoria & Albert Museum, London, UK/Bridgeman Art Library, London/NY; *top right,* Christie's Images; *left,* Courtesy of Skinner, Inc.; *center left,* Christie's Images; *center right,* Art Resource, NY; *bottom right top,* Courtesy of Skinner, Inc.; *bottom right,* Courtesy of Skinner, Inc.

page 20: *top left,* Courtesy of Skinner, Inc.; *top right,* Christie's Images; *center left,* Aldo Tutino/Art Resource, NY; *center middle,* Christie's Images; *center right,* Christie's Images; *bottom left,* Christie's Images, London, UK/ Bridgeman Art Library, London/NY; *bottom middle,* Christie's Images; *bottom right,* Christie's Images.

CHAPTER 7

page 21: *top left,* Christie's Images; *top middle,* Winterthur Museum; *center left,* Christie's Images; *center middle,* Christie's Images; *center right,* Philadelphia Museum of Art: purchased Temple Fund; *bottom left,* Buffalo Bill Historical Center, Cody, WY., Gift of Barbara S. Leggett; *bottom right,* Winterthur Museum.

page 22: *top left,* Courtesy of Skinner, Inc.; *top right,* Christie's Images; *center left,* Courtesy of Skinner, Inc.; *center middle,* Christie's Images; *center right, top,* Courtesy of Sotheby's; *center right, bottom,* Winterthur Museum; *bottom left,* Winterthur Museum; *bottom middle,* Christie's Images; *bottom right,* Winterthur Museum.

page 23: *top left,* Courtesy of Sotheby's; *top right,* Courtesy of Skinner, Inc.; *center left, top,* Courtesy of Sotheby's; *center left, bottom,* Courtesy of Sotheby's; *center right,* Courtesy of Skinner, Inc.; *bottom left,* Courtesy of Skinner, Inc.; *bottom right,* Courtesy of Skinner, Inc.

CHAPTER 8

page 24: *top left,* Courtesy of James A. Ffrench; *center left,* Dreweatt Neate Fine Art Auctioneers, Newbury, Berkshire, UK/Bridgeman Art Library, London/NY; *center middle,* Christie's Images; *center right, top,* Winterthur

Museum; *center right; bottom,* Christie's Images; *bottom left,* Courtesy of Skinner, Inc.; *bottom middle,* Art Resource, NY; *bottom right,* Christie's Images.

page 25: *top left,* Courtesy of Sotheby's; *top middle,* Christie's Images; *top right,* Christie's Images; *center left,* Collection of the Museum of American Folk Art, NY; Gift of a Museum friend; *bottom left,* Christie's Images; *bottom right,* The Newark Museum/Art Resource, NY.

page 26: *top left,* Christie's Images; *top middle,* Christie's Images; *top right,* Collection of the Museum of American Folk Art, NY; Gift of Ralph Esmerian; *center left,* Christie's Images; *bottom left,* Christie's Images; *bottom middle,* Courtesy of Skinner, Inc.; *bottom right,* Collection of Museum of American Folk Art, NY; Eva and Morris Feld Folk Art Acquisition Fund.

CHAPTER 9

page 27: *top right,* Christie's Images; *center left, top,* Christie's Images; *center left, bottom,* Christie's Images; *center right,* Christie's Images; *bottom left,* Christie's Images; *bottom right,* Christie's Images.

page 28: *top left,* Christie's Images; *top right,* Courtesy of Noel Barrett Antiques & Auctions, Ltd.; *center left, top,* Courtesy of Sotheby's; *center left, bottom,* Christie's Images; *center right, top,* Christie's Images; *center right, bottom,* Christie's Images; *bottom left,* Courtesy of Noel Barrett Antiques & Auctions, Ltd.; *bottom right,* Christie's Images.

page 29: *top left,* In the collection of Richard Wright; photography by Anne Jackson; *top left, middle,* In the collection of Richard Wright;

photography by Anne Jackson; *top right, middle,* Provided by Richard Wright Antiques; photography by Anne Jackson; *top right,* Provided by Richard Wright Antiques; photography by Anne Jackson; *center left,* Provided by Richard Wright Antiques; photography by Anne Jackson; *center right,* Provided by Richard Wright Antiques; photography by Anne Jackson; *bottom left,* Collection of the Museum of American Folk Art, NY; Gift of Ann Baxter; *bottom middle,* Provided by Richard Wright Antiques; photography by Anne Jackson; *bottom right,* In the collection of Richard Wright Antiques; photography by Anne Jackson.

page 30: *top left,* Courtesy of Hake's Americana & Collectibles, York, PA; *top left, middle,* The Granger Collection; *top right,* The Granger Collection; *center left top,* The Granger Collection; *center left, middle (top),* Milo Stewart Jr./National Baseball Hall of Fame, Cooperstown, NY; *center left, middle,* The Granger Collection; *center left, middle (bottom),* Milo Stewart Jr./National Baseball Hall of Fame, Cooperstown, NY; *center left, bottom,* The Granger Collection; *center middle, top,* Courtesy of Dunbar's Gallery; *center middle, bottom,* The Granger Collection; *center right, bottom,* The Granger Collection; *center bottom left,* ARS; *center right, top,* Courtesy of Dunbar's Gallery; *bottom left,* Courtesy of Dunbar's Gallery; *bottom middle,* Courtesy of Hake's Americana & Collectibles, York, PA; *bottom right,* ©Disney Enterprises, Inc.

CHAPTER 10

page 31: *top right,* Christie's Images; *center left,* Christie's Images; *center* *middle,* The Granger Collection; *center right,* The Granger Collection; *bottom left,* Christie's Images; *bottom right,* Courtesy of Sotheby's.

page 32: *top middle,* Christie's Images; *top right,* Swann Galleries, Inc.; *top right,* Christie's Images; *center left,* The Granger Collection; *center left, top,* Fitzwilliam Museum, University of Cambridge/The Bridgeman Art Library, London/NY; *center left, bottom,* The Granger Collection; *center middle,* Christie's Images; *center right, top,* Christie's Images; *center right, bottom,* Christie's Images; *bottom left,* Private Collection/The Bridgeman Art Library, London/NY; *bottom middle,* The Granger Collection; *bottom right,* Christie's Images.

B L A C K
A N D   W H I T E

CHAPTER 1

page 1: *top,* Jeffrey Dunn, Jan Preus/ARS.

page 2: *top,* Christie's Images.

page 3: *bottom,* Jeffrey Dunn, Jan Preus/ARS.

page 4: *top left,* ©Chun Y. Lai/Esto; *top right,* Christie's Images; *center right,* Christie's Images; *bottom,* Archivio Cameraphoto Venezia/Art Resource, NY.

page 5: *top,* ©Chun Y. Lai/Esto; *center left,* Osterley Park, Middlesex, UK/Bridgeman Art Library, London/NY; *center,* Stourhead, Wiltshire, UK/Bridgeman Art Library, London/NY; *center right,* Christie's Images; *bottom,* Erich Lessing/Art Resource, NY.

page 6: *bottom,* Jeffrey Dunn/ARS.

page 7: *top,* Shelburne Museum.

page 8: *top right,* ©Chun Y. Lai/Esto; *center left,* Christie's Images; *center right,* ©Chun Y. Lai/Esto; *bottom left,* ©The Museum of Fine Arts, Houston; Museum purchase with funds provided by the Alice Pratt Brown Museum Fund.

page 9: *top left,* ©Chun Y. Lai/Esto; *top center left,* American Museum, Bath, Avon, UK/Bridgeman Art Library, London/NY; *right,* The Newark Museum/Art Resource, NY; *bottom left,* ©Chun Y. Lai/Esto; *bottom center left,* ©Chun Y. Lai/Esto; *bottom center right,* Courtesy of Skinner, Inc.

page 10: *bottom,* Christie's Images.

page 11: *top,* Christie's Images; *center,* ©Chun Y. Lai/Esto; *bottom,* Winterthur Museum.

page 14: *top,* Shelburne Museum; *center,* Corning Museum of Glass; *bottom,* ©Chun Y. Lai/Esto.

page 15: *top,* ©Chun Y. Lai/Esto; *bottom,* ©Chun Y. Lai/Esto.

page 16: *bottom,* Jeffrey Dunn/ARS.

page 17: *top,* Shelburne Museum; *center,* Henry Francis Dupont Winterthur Museum, Delaware, USA/Bridgeman Art Library, London/NY; *bottom,* Christie's Images.

page 18: *top,* ©Chun Y. Lai/Esto; *center,* Winterthur Museum; *bottom,* ©Chun Y. Lai/Esto.

page 19: *top,* Christie's Images; *center,* Courtesy of Skinner, Inc.; *bottom,* Courtesy of Skinner, Inc.

page 20: *top,* Courtesy of Skinner, Inc.; *bottom,* Christie's Images.

page 21: *top,* Shelburne Museum;

bottom, National Museum of American Art, Washington, D.C./Art Resource, NY.

page 22: *top & bottom,* Jim Sully/ARS.

page 23: *top,* The Newark Museum/Art Resource, NY; *center,* ©Chun Y. Lai/Esto; *bottom,* ©Chun Y. Lai/Esto.

page 26: *top left,* Christie's Images; *center right,* Christie's Images; *bottom left,* Winterthur Museum.

page 27: *top center,* Christie's Images; *center right,* ©The Museum of Fine Arts, Houston; Museum purchase with funds provided by the Alice Pratt Brown Museum Fund; *bottom left,* The Newark Museum/ Art Resource, NY; *bottom center,* Christie's Images.

page 28: *top,* ©Chun Y. Lai/Esto; *bottom,* ©Winterthur Museum.

page 29: *top,* Christie's Images; *bottom,* Christie's Images.

page 30: *top,* ©Chun Y. Lai/Esto; *bottom left,* ©Chun Y. Lai/Esto; *bottom right,* ©Chun Y. Lai/Esto.

page 31: *top,* Stourhead, Wiltshire, UK/Bridgeman Art Library, London/NY; *bottom,* Private Collection/Bridgeman Art Library, London/NY.

page 32: *bottom,* Osterley Park, Middlesex, UK/Bridgeman Art Library, London/NY.

page 33: *bottom,* Mallett & Son Antiques, Ltd., London, UK/Bridgeman Art Library, London/NY.

page 34: *top,* Erich Lessing/Art Resource, NY; *bottom,* Christie's Images.

page 35: *top,* Art Resource, NY.

page 36: *bottom left,* Erich Lessing/Art Resource, NY.

page 37: *top,* Christie's Images; *bottom,* Giraudon/Art Resource, NY.

page 39: *top,* Christie's Images; *bottom,* Christie's Images.

page 40: *left,* ©Winterthur Museum; *right,* Christie's Images.

page 41: *left,* Shelburne Museum; *center,* Shelburne Museum; *right,* ©Chun Y. Lai/Esto.

page 42: *top,* Christie's Images; *center left,* Courtesy of Sotheby's; *center right,* Courtesy of Skinner, Inc.; *bottom,* ©The Museum of Fine Arts, Houston; Museum purchase with funds provided by Anaruth and Aron S. Gordon.

page 43: *top,* ©Chun Y. Lai/Esto; *bottom,* Christie's Images.

page 44: *bottom,* ©Chun Y. Lai/Esto.

CHAPTER 2

page 45: *top center,* Christie's Images; *bottom right,* Christie's Images.

page 46: *bottom,* Chris Ayers/ARS.

page 47: *top,* Beniaminson/Art Resource, NY; *bottom,* Christie's Images.

page 48: *top,* Jeffrey Dunn/ARS.

page 49: *bottom,* The Newark Museum/Art Resource, NY.

page 50: *top,* Christie's Images; *center,* Christie's Images; *bottom,* Courtesy of Sotheby's.

page 51: *top,* Christie's Images; *bottom,* Courtesy of Skinner, Inc.

page 52: *top,* Courtesy of Skinner, Inc.

page 53: *top,* Courtesy of Skinner, Inc.; *bottom,* Christie's Images.

page 54: *bottom,* Sheffield City Museum, South Yorkshire, UK/Bridgeman Art Library, London/NY.

page 55: *top,* Courtesy of Skinner, Inc.; *bottom,* Courtesy of Skinner, Inc.

page 56: *bottom,* Courtesy of Skinner, Inc.

page 58: *top,* Winterthur Museum; *bottom,* Courtesy of Skinner, Inc.

page 59: *top,* Winterthur Museum; *bottom,* Christie's Images.

page 60: *bottom,* Jeffrey Dunn, Jan Preus/ARS.

page 61: *top,* Christie's Images; *center,* Christie's Images; *bottom,* Winterthur Museum.

page 62: *top,* Courtesy of Sotheby's; *bottom,* Christie's Images.

page 63: *bottom,* Jeffrey Dunn/ARS.

page 64: *top & bottom,* Christie's Images.

page 66: *top,* Christie's Images; *bottom,* The Newark Museum/Art Resource, NY.

page 67: *top,* Courtesy of Skinner, Inc.; *bottom,* Courtesy of Skinner, Inc.

page 68: *center,* Dean Stevenson/ARS.

page 69: *top,* Courtesy of Skinner, Inc.; *bottom,* Courtesy of Skinner, Inc.

page 70: *top,* Courtesy of Skinner, Inc.; *bottom,* Courtesy of Skinner, Inc.

page 71: *top,* Courtesy of Skinner, Inc.; *bottom,* Courtesy of William Doyle Galleries.

page 72: *top,* Courtesy of A La Vieille Russie; *bottom,* S.J. Phillips, London, UK/Bridgeman Art Library, London/NY.

page 73: *bottom,* Jeffrey Dunn/ARS.

page 75: *top,* Christie's Images; *bottom,* Winterthur Museum.

page 76: *bottom,* Beniaminson/Art Resource, NY.

page 77: *top,* Christie's Images; *bottom,* Christie's Images.

page 78: *bottom,* Christie's Images.

CHAPTER 3

page 79: *top,* Christie's Images; *bottom,* The Corning Museum of Glass, Corning, NY.

page 80: *top,* Oriental Museum, Durham University, UK/Bridgeman Art Library, London/NY; *bottom,* The Newark Museum/ Art Resource, NY.

page 81: *top,* Winterthur Museum; *bottom,* New Jersey State Museum Collection; Gift of Cybis.

page 82: *top,* Christie's Images; *bottom,* Courtesy of Skinner, Inc.

page 83: *bottom,* Courtesy of Skinner, Inc.

page 84: *top,* Courtesy of Skinner, Inc.; *center,* Courtesy of Skinner, Inc.; *bottom,* Courtesy of Skinner, Inc.

page 85: *top left,* Courtesy of Skinner, Inc.

page 86: *bottom,* Christie's Images.

page 87: *top,* Dreweatt Neate Fine Art Auctioneers, Newbury, Berkshire, UK/Bridgeman Art Library, London/NY; *center,* Courtesy of Skinner, Inc.; *bottom,* Christie's Images.

page 88: *bottom,* Christie's Images.

page 89: *top,* Christie's Images; *center,* The Newark Museum/Art Resource, NY; *bottom,* Christie's Images.

page 90: *top,* Victoria & Albert Museum, London/Art Resource, NY; *bottom,* Christie's Images.

page 91: *top center,* Courtesy of Skinner, Inc.

page 92: *bottom center,* Courtesy of Skinner, Inc.

page 93: *top,* Christie's Images; *bottom,* Christie's Images.

page 94: *bottom center,* Collection of the Museum of American Folk Art, NY; Gift of Rufus and Joan Foshee.

page 95: *center,* Dean Stevenson/ARS.

page 97: *bottom,* Jeffrey Dunn, Jan Preus/ARS.

page 98: *top,* Christie's Images; *center,* Addison Doty, Sante Fe, NM; *bottom,* Addison Doty, Sante Fe, NM.

page 99: *bottom,* Victoria & Albert Museum, London, UK/Bridgeman Art Library, London/NY.

page 100: *top,* Winterthur Museum; *center,* Winterthur Museum; *bottom,* Courtesy of Skinner, Inc.

page 101: *top,* Gift of Miss Elizabeth Wistar, The Corning Museum of Glass, Corning, NY; *center,* Collection of The Juliette K. and Leonard S. Rakow Research Library of The Corning Museum of Glass; *bottom,* Collection of The Juliette K. and Leonard S. Rakow Research Library of The Corning Museum of Glass.

page 102: *top right,* Collection of The Juliette K. and Leonard S. Rakow Research Library of The Corning Museum of Glass; *bottom left,* Courtesy of Skinner, Inc.

page 103: *top,* mold Gift of Gladys W. Richards and Paul C. Richards, The Corning Museum of Glass, Corning, NY; *bottom,* Courtesy of Skinner, Inc.

page 104: *top,* The Corning Museum of Glass, Corning, NY; *center,* The Corning Museum of Glass, Corning, NY; *bottom,* Bethnal Green Museum, London, UK/Bridgeman Art Library, London/NY.

page 105: *top,* Steve Foxall/ARS; *bottom,* Courtesy of Skinner, Inc.

page 106: *top,* The Newark Museum/ Art Resource, NY; *center,* Winterthur Museum; *bottom,* Winterthur Museum.

page 107: *top,* Courtesy of Skinner, Inc.; *bottom,* Winterthur Museum.

page 108: *bottom,* Steve Foxall/ARS.

page 109: *top,* Courtesy of Skinner, Inc.; *center,* Courtesy of Skinner, Inc.; *bottom,* Courtesy of Skinner, Inc.

page 110: *top,* Courtesy of Skinner, Inc.; *center,* Courtesy of Skinner, Inc.; *bottom,* Winterthur Museum.

page 111: *bottom,* ARS.

page 113: *bottom,* Courtesy of Skinner, Inc.

page 114: *top,* Courtesy of Skinner, Inc.; *bottom,* Winterthur Museum.

CHAPTER 4

page 115: *top center,* Christie's Images; *bottom right,* Christie's Images.

page 116: *top left,* Christie's Images; *bottom left,* Christie's Images.

page 118: *top left,* Art Resource, NY; *bottom left,* Art Resource, NY.

page 119: *bottom right,* Jeffrey Dunn/ARS.

page 122: *bottom left,* Jeffrey Dunn, Jan Preus/ARS.

page 123: *lower right,* The Granger Collection.

page 124: *bottom left,* Christie's Images.

page 125: *bottom right,* Jeffrey Dunn, Larry McCormick/ARS.

page 126: *top left,* Christie's Images; *bottom left,* Erich Lessing/Art Resource, NY.

page 127: *top right,* The Newark Museum/Art Resource, NY; *center right,* The Granger Collection; *bottom right,* Christie's Images.

page 128: *top right,* Giraudon/Art Resource, NY; *bottom left,* Scala/Art Resource, NY.

page 129: *bottom right,* Corcoran Gallery of Art, Washington, D.C./ The Bridgeman Art Library, London/NY.

page 130: *bottom left,* Jeffrey Dunn, Jan Preus/ARS.

page 131: *top right,* Christie's Images.

page 132: *top left,* Art Resource, NY; *bottom left,* Private Collection/The Bridgeman Art Library, London/NY.

page 133: *bottom right,* Jeffrey Dunn, Jan Preus/ARS.

page 134: *top right,* Museo Lazaro Galdiano, Madrid/The Bridgeman Art Library, London/NY; *bottom left,* The Granger Collection.

page 135: *top right,* Roy Miles Esq./The Bridgeman Art Library, London/NY; *bottom right,* Erich Lessing/Art Resource, NY.

page 136: *top left,* The Granger Collection; *bottom left,* The Granger Collection.

page 137: *top right,* Christie's Images; *bottom right,* The Granger Collection.

page 138: *top left,* Christie's Images; *bottom left,* Private Collection/The Bridgeman Art Library, London/NY.

page 139: *bottom right,* Jeffrey Dunn, Jan Preus/ARS.

page 140: *top left,* The Granger Collection; *bottom left,* Private Collection/Christie's Images/ Bridgeman Art Library, London/NY.

page 141: *bottom right,* Jeffrey Dunn/ARS.

page 142: *bottom left,* Ken Balzar/ARS.

page 143: *top right,* The Newark Museum/Art Resource, NY; *bottom right,* National Museum of American Art/Hemphill Collection/Art Resource, NY.

page 144: *top left,* The Granger Collection; *bottom left,* The Granger Collection.

page 145: *bottom right,* Christie's Images.

page 146: *center left,* Erich Lessing/Art Resource, NY.

CHAPTER 5

page 147: *top center,* Christie's Images; *left bottom,* Christie's Images.

page 148: *top left,* Christie's Images; *center left,* Christie's Images; *bottom left,* Christie's Images.

page 149: *bottom right,* Ken Balzar/ARS.

page 150: *top left,* Christie's Images; *center left,* Christie's Images; *bottom left,* Christie's Images.

page 151: *bottom left,* Christie's Images.

page 153: *top right,* Christie's Images; *center right,* Christie's Images; *bottom right,* Art Resource, NY.

page 154: *left,* Christie's Images.

page 155: *bottom right,* ARS.

page 156: *top left,* Christie's Images; *center left,* Christie's Images; *bottom left,* Christie's Images.

page 157: *bottom right,* Christie's Images.

page 159: *top right,* Christie's Images; *center right,* Aldo Tutino/Art Resource, NY; *bottom right,* Christie's Images.

page 160: *top left,* Christie's Images; *center left,* Christie's Images.

page 161: *bottom right,* Christie's Images.

page 162: *bottom left,* Christie's Images.

page 163: *top right,* Christie's Images; *bottom right,* Art Resource, NY.

page 164: *top left,* Christie's Images; *bottom left,* Christie's Images.

page 165: *bottom right,* Christie's Images.

page 166: *bottom left,* ARS.

page 167: *top right,* Christie's Images; *center right,* Christie's Images; *bottom right,* Christie's Images.

page 168: *left,* Christie's Images.

page 169: *bottom right,* Christie's Images.

page 170: *top left,* Christie's Images; *bottom right,* Courtesy of Sotheby's.

page 171: *bottom right,* ARS.

page 172: *top left,* Christie's Images; *center left,* Christie's Images; *bottom right,* Christie's Images.

page 174: *bottom left,* ARS.

page 175: *bottom right,* Christie's Images.

page 176: *right top, bottom,* Christie's Images.

CHAPTER 6

page 177: *top left,* Jeffrey Dunn/ARS; *bottom right,* Philadelphia Museum of Art: Purchased from the Charles F. Williams Collection with Museum and subscription funds.

page 178: *top,* Art Resource, NY; *bottom,* Christie's Images.

page 181: *right,* Christie's Images.

page 182: *top,* Christie's Images; *bottom,* Philadelphia Museum of Art: Gift of Martha W. Shinn in memory of Hoover B. and Hannah S. Rutty. Photo by Graydon Wood, 1997.

page 183: *top left,* Christie's Images; *top right,* Christie's Images; *center left,* Courtesy of Skinner, Inc.; *center right,* Christie's Images, London, UK/Bridgeman Art Library, London/NY; *bottom left,* ©Michael Nelson/FPG.

page 184: *center,* Jim Scully/ARS.

page 185: *right,* Christie's Images.

page 186: *top,* Christie's Images; *bottom,* Courtesy of Israel Sack, Inc.

page 187: *top,* Christie's Images; *bottom,* Christie's Images.

page 188: *top,* Courtesy of Skinner, Inc.; *bottom,* Strike One, London, UK/Bridgeman Art Library, London/NY.

page 189: *top,* Courtesy of Skinner, Inc.; *bottom,* Philadelphia Museum of Art. Photo by Graydon Wood, 1995.

page 190: *top,* Christie's Images; *bottom,* Courtesy of Skinner, Inc.

page 191: *top,* Frank Partridge Ltd., London, UK/Bridgeman Art Library London/NY; *bottom,* ©Michael Nelson/FPG.

page 192: *top,* Christie's Images, London, UK/Bridgeman Art Library, London/NY; *bottom,* Strike One, London, UK/Bridgeman Art Library, London/NY.

page 193: *bottom,* Jeffrey Dunn/ARS.

page 194: *top,* Christie's Images; *center,* Christie's Images; bottom, Art Resource, NY.

page 195: *right,* Art Resource, NY.

page 197: *top,* Christie's Images; *bottom,* Christie's Images, London, UK/Bridgeman Art Library, London/NY.

page 198: *top left,* Christie's Images; *top right,* Christie's Images; *bottom,* Courtesy of Skinner, Inc.

page 199: *bottom,* Courtesy of Skinner, Inc.

page 200: *left,* The Newark Museum/Art Resource, NY.

CHAPTER 7

page 201: *top center,* Museum of American Folk Art, NY; *bottom right,* Christie's Images.

page 203: *bottom right,* Art Resource, NY.

page 205: *top right,* Victoria & Albert Museum/Art Resource, NY; *bottom right,* Christie's Images.

page 206: *top left,* Gift of the New York Life Insurance Company/ Philadelphia Museum of Art; *bottom left,* Giraudon/Art Resource, NY.

page 207: *top right,* Private Collection/The Bridgeman Art Library, London/NY; *bottom right,* Purchased W. P. Wilstach Collection/ Philadelphia Museum of Art.

page 208: *top center,* Giraudon/Art Resource, NY; *bottom left,* Private Collection/The Bridgeman Art Library, London/NY.

page 209: *bottom right,* Newark Museum/Art Resource, NY.

page 211: *bottom right,* Jim Scully/ARS.

page 212: *top left,* Winterthur Museum; *bottom left,* Christie's Images.

page 214: *top left,* Winterthur Museum; *bottom left,* Winterthur Museum.

page 215: *bottom right,* Winterthur Museum.

page 216: *top left and bottom left,* Courtesy of Skinner, Inc.

page 217: *bottom right,* Chris Ayers/ARS.

page 218: *bottom left,* Jeffrey Dunn, Jan Preus/ARS.

page 219: *both,* Christie's Images.

page 220: *bottom left,* Jeffrey Dunn/ARS.

page 221: *top right,* Christie's Images; *bottom left,* Christie's Images.

page 222: *top left,* Christie's Images; *bottom left,* Christie's Images.

page 223: *right (all),* Christie's Images.

page 224: *left (all),* Christie's Images.

page 225: *right (all),* Christie's Images.

page 226: *top left,* Shelburne Museum; *center left,* Shelburne Museum; *bottom left,* Christie's Images.

page 227: *top right,* Shelburne Museum; *bottom right,* Courtesy of Skinner, Inc.

page 228: *center left,* Shelburne Museum; *bottom left,* Christie's Images.

page 229: *top right,* Christie's Images; *bottom right,* Courtesy of Skinner, Inc.

page 230: *bottom left,* Jeffrey Dunn, Jan Preus/ARS.

page 231: *bottom right,* Courtesy of Skinner, Inc.

page 232: *bottom left,* Courtesy of Skinner, Inc.

CHAPTER 8

page 233: *top,* Christie's Images; *bottom,* Christie's Images.

page 234: *top,* Courtesy of Skinner,

Inc.; *center,* Christie's Images; *bottom,* Art Resource, NY.

page 235: *bottom,* Jeffrey Dunn/ARS.

page 236: *top,* Art Resource, NY; *bottom,* Christie's Images.

page 237: *top,* Erich Lessing/Museum fuer Angewandte Kunst, Vienna, Austria/Art Resource, NY; *bottom,* Private Collection/Bridgeman Art Library, London/NY.

page 238: *top,* Art Resource, NY; *bottom,* Courtesy of Sotheby's.

page 239: *top,* Jeffrey Dunn/ARS.

page 240: *center,* Jeffrey Dunn/ARS.

page 242: *bottom,* Jeffrey Dunn, Jan Preus/ARS.

page 243: *top,* Shelburne Museum; *bottom,* Shelburne Museum.

page 244: *top,* Philadelphia Museum of Art. Photo by Graydon Wood, 1991; *bottom,* Braided & Knit Rug, Unidentified Shaker, c. late 19th century. Collection of the Museum of American Folk Art, NY; Gift of Robert Bishop.

page 245: *top,* Shelburne Museum; *center,* Addison Doty, Santa Fe, NM; *bottom,* Christie's Images.

page 246: *top,* Christie's Images; *bottom,* Courtesy of Skinner, Inc.

page 247: *top,* The Newark Museum/Art Resource, NY; *bottom,* Christie's Images.

page 248: *top,* Christie's Images; *bottom,* Collection of the Museum of American Folk Art, NY; Gift of Cyril L. Nelson.

page 249: *center,* Jeffrey Dunn, Jan Preus/ARS.

page 250: *bottom,* Jeffrey Dunn/ARS.

page 251: *top,* Christie's Images;

center, Courtesy of Sotheby's; *bottom,* Christie's Images; *bottom,* The Newark Museum/Art Resource, NY.

page 252: *top,* Christie's Images.

page 253: *top,* The Newark Museum/Art Resource, NY; *bottom,* Shelburne Museum.

page 254: *bottom left,* Collection of the Museum of American Folk Art, NY; Gift of Stephen L. Snow; *bottom right,* Collection of the Museum of American Folk Art, NY; Gift of Cyril Irwin Nelson.

page 255: *top,* Christie's Images; *bottom,* Fitzwilliam Museum, University of Cambridge, UK/Bridgeman Art Library, London/NY.

page 256: *top,* Winterthur Museum; *bottom,* Courtesy of Skinner, Inc.

page 257: *bottom,* Courtesy of Skinner, Inc.

page 258: *bottom,* Steve Foxall/ARS.

page 259: *top,* Philadelphia Museum of Art: Whitman Sampler Collection. Given by Pet Incorporated. Photo by Graydon Wood, 1994; *bottom,* Courtesy of Skinner, Inc.

page 260: *top,* Christie's Images; *bottom,* Christie's Images.

page 261: *bottom,* Courtesy of Skinner, Inc.

page 262: *top,* Christie's Images.

CHAPTER 9

page 263: *top,* Christie's Images; *bottom,* Courtesy of Skinner, Inc.

page 264: *bottom,* Courtesy of the Bob & Marrianne Schneiders, Lancaster, PA; provided by Noel Barrett Antiques & Auctions, Ltd.

page 265: *top,* Courtesy of Noel

Barrett Antiques & Auctions, Ltd.; *center,* Courtesy of Noel Barrett Antiques & Auctions, Ltd.; *bottom,* Courtesy of Noel Barrett Antiques & Auctions, Ltd.

page 266: *bottom,* Courtesy of Noel Barrett Antiques & Auctions, Ltd.

page 267: *top,* Christie's Images; *center,* Courtesy of Noel Barrett Antiques & Auctions, Ltd.; *bottom,* Christie's Images.

page 268: *center,* Jeffrey Dunn/ARS.

page 269: *top,* Courtesy of William Doyle Galleries; *center,* Courtesy of Noel Barrett Antiques & Auctions, Ltd.; *bottom,* Christie's Images.

page 270: *bottom,* Courtesy of Dunbar's Gallery.

page 271: *bottom,* Collection of the Museum of American Folk Art, NY; Promised Gift of Patty Gagarin.

page 272: *bottom,* Jeffrey Dunn/ARS.

page 273: *top,* Christie's Images; *bottom,* Courtesy of Dunbar's Gallery.

page 274: *top,* Christie's Images; *center,* Christie's Images.

page 275: *top,* Christie's Images; *center,* Salisbury & S. Wilts. Museum; *bottom left,* In the collection of Richard Wright Antiques; photography by Anne Jackson.

page 276: *bottom left,* Provided by Richard Wright Antiques; photography by Anne Jackson; *bottom right,* In the collection of Richard Wright Antiques; photography by Anne Jackson.

page 277: *center right,* Jeffrey Dunn/ARS; *bottom left,* Christie's Images.

page 279: *bottom,* Provided by

Richard Wright Antiques; photography by Anne Jackson.

page 280: *top,* Provided by Richard Wright Antiques; photography by Anne Jackson; *bottom,* In the collection of Richard Wright Antiques; photography by Anne Jackson.

page 281: *top,* Provided by Caroline Edelman; photography by Caroline Edelman; *center,* Christie's Images; *bottom,* Christie's Images.

page 282: *bottom,* Jeffrey Dunn/ARS.

page 283: *bottom,* Courtesy of Skinner, Inc.

page 284: *top,* The Granger Collection; *bottom,* National Museum of American History, Smithsonian Institution.

page 285: *bottom,* Chris Ayers/ARS.

page 286: *top,* Teddy Bear Museum; *bottom,* Teddy Bear Museum.

page 287: *top,* Teddy Bear Museum; *bottom,* Teddy Bear Museum.

page 288: *top,* Christie's Images; *center,* Christie's Images; *bottom,* National Baseball Hall of Fame, Cooperstown, NY.

page 289: *bottom,* Jeffrey Dunn/ARS.

page 290: *bottom,* Archive Photos/Blank Archives.

page 291: *top,* Courtesy of Hake's Americana & Collectibles, York, PA ; *bottom,* Courtesy of Hake's Americana & Collectibles, York, PA.

page 292: *top,* Courtesy of Hake's Americana & Collectibles, York, PA; *bottom,* Photo of Elvis Presley memorabilia, one jumpsuit; obtained from the photography archive of Elvis Presley Enterprises, Inc. Used by permission, ©Elvis Presley Enterprises, Inc.

page 293: *top,* Corbis-Bettmann; *center,* Courtesy of Dunbar's Gallery; *bottom,* Christie's Images.

page 294: *top and bottom,* Jeffrey Dunn/ARS.

page 295: *top,* Courtesy of Skinner, Inc.; *center,* The Granger Collection; *bottom,* www.nostalgia.com.

page 296: *bottom,* Jeffrey Dunn/ARS.

page 297: *top,* Corbis-Bettmann; *bottom,* Corbis-Bettmann.

page 298: *top,* The Granger Collection; *center,* Corbis-Bettmann; *bottom,* The Granger Collection.

CHAPTER 10

page 301: *top left,* Christie's Images; *bottom right,* Coram Foundation, London/ The Bridgeman Art Library, London/NY.

page 302: *bottom left,* Dave Masucci/ARS.

page 303: *top left,* National History Museum, London/The Bridgeman Art Library, London/NY; *lower left,* The Granger Collection.

page 305: *top right,* Christie's Images; *center right,* Christie's Images; *bottom right,* Christie's Images.

page 308: *center left,* Corbis-Bettmann; *bottom left,* The Granger Collection.

page 309: *bottom right,* Chris Ayers/ARS.

page 310: *bottom left,* Dean Stevenson/ARS.

page 311: *top right,* The Granger Collection; *center right,* The Granger Collection; *bottom right,* Christie's Images.

page 314: *top left,* Christie's Images;

bottom left, The Granger Collection.

page 316: *center left,* Kean Collection/ Archive Photos.

page 317: *bottom right,* Dave Masucci/ARS.

page 318: *bottom left,* Jeffrey Dunn/ARS.

page 319: *bottom right,* Jeffrey Dunn/ARS.

page 320: *bottom left,* Swann Galleries, Inc.

INDEX

(Page numbers in *italics* refer to illustrations.)

A

Abrash, 238, *238, C-24*
Academic art, 141, 146
L'Accolade (Mène), 209
Acid-etched glass, *104,* 105–6
Acoma pottery, *98,* 99
Adam, Robert, 30, 32, *32,* 70
Adams, John Quincy, chair of, 16, *16*
Adam-style furniture, 2, *13,* 38, *39*
Adventures of Huckleberry Finn
     (Twain), 311, *311,* 314
Advertising:
     memorabilia, 292–94, *293, 294,*
        299, 300, *C-30*
     toy vehicles displaying, 275
Aesthetic Movement:
     ceramics, 96
     furniture, 5, 8, 16, *23*
     glass, 108
     mixed-metal wares, *51*
     silver, 66
"Aetatis" ("aet"), use of term, 132–33
Aetna Toy Animal Co., 286
Affleck, Thomas, 26
African-American dolls, 283
African-American quilts, 253, *253*
Agate, 147
Albert, Prince, 171
Album quilts, *247,* 249, *249,* 250,
     252, *253,* 254

Alcott, Louisa May, *C-32*
"Alfonzo" (teddy bear), *288*
Alice in Wonderland dolls, 279
Alice's Adventures in Wonderland
     (Carroll), 303–4, 312
Alice's Adventures Under Ground
     (Carroll), *303*
Almandine garnets (carbuncles), 158,
     174, *C-16*
Alphabet samplers, *255,* 256, *256,*
     260, *260, C-26*
Althof Bergmann, 273
Amber, 162–63, *C-16*
Amelung, John Frederick, 106, *106*
American ceramics:
     art potters and marks, 91
     porcelain, *80–82,* 81–83
     pottery, *88–94,* 89–93
American clocks, *182,* 185, *186, 188,*
     188–89, 190–91
American furniture, 1–2, *2, 3, 3, 6, 7,*
     9–11, 10, *14,* 16–17, *16–21,*
     21–22, 24, 25–31, *26–29,*
     40–42, *40–43, C-1*
     craftsmen, 26–27
     determining value of, 29–31
     distinguishing English furniture
        from, 32–33
     folk, 28–29, *29*
     further reading on, 43–44
     Philadelphia Centennial Exposition
        and, 6
     rural versions of, 25–28
     styles and periods of, 4–5

American glass, *100–103,* 101, 104,
     106, 106–7, *107*
     art glass, 105, *108,* 108–9, *109,*
        111, *111,* 112
American iron, 226–30, *226–30,*
     C-23
American pewter, *221, 222,* 222–23,
     224–25, *225,* 226, *226, C-23*
American silver, *45, 47–51, 53,*
     58–62, 59–68, *64–67,* 74, 75,
     75, 77, *77,* 78, *78, C-5–C-6*
     hallmarks on, 58–59, 74
     makers, 62, 65
     of seventeenth and eighteenth
        centuries, 59–64
     of nineteenth century, 64–67
     of twentieth century, 67–68
American War of Independence, 2, 57
American watches, 194, 196, 199
Amethysts, 157, *157, 160, 167,* 168,
     172, *C-15*
Amish quilts, 250–51, *251,* 252–53,
     254, *C-25*
Anchor escapements, *180,* 184
Andersen, Hans Christian, 315, *C-31*
Andirons:
     brass, 214–15, *215,* 216, 217,
        C-21, C-22
     iron, *226,* 227, 230
Aniline dyes, 242
Animalier bronzes, 206–7, *206–8,*
     209, 211
Animal-paw feet, 31
Animation cels, 292, 295–96, *C-30*

"Anno," use of term, 131
Annotations, in books, 304
Antimony, 222
"Antique," legal definition of term, 3
Apple butter copper kettle, 202
Appliquéd quilts, 247, 249, *249,* 250, *250, 252, C-25, C-26*
Aquamarines, 153, 160, *160, 164, C-16*
Armchairs, 3, *3, 11,* 16, *16, 23, 37*
Armoires, 36
Arrow Shirts, 293
Art. *See* Fine Art; Painting; Sculpture
Art Deco, 238
    bronzes, *205,* 208, 211
    furniture, 5
    glass, 110, 111
    jewelry, 148, 151, *153, 156,* 157, 173, 174–75, *C-17, C-18*
    mantel clock, *C-18*
    pocket watch, *198*
    silver, 67, *67, C-7*
    travel clock, 193, *193*
    wrought iron, 230
Art glass, 103, 105, *108,* 108–9, *109,* 111, *111,* 112
Artists:
    good and bad years of, 137–38
    reference sources on, 129
    see also Painting; Sculpture
Art Nouveau:
    bronze, *209*
    furniture, 5, 8, *35*
    glass, 110, 111, *C-11*
    jewelry, 165, 171, 173, 174, *C-17*
    pewter, 222, *C-23*
    pottery, 92
    silver, *49, 50,* 53, *C-6, C-7*
Art pottery, American, 90, 92
Arts and Crafts:
    American metalworkers, 219
    copper, 218–20, *219, 220*
    furniture, 5, 8
    jewelry, 165
    pottery, 90, 92
    Roycroft and, 27, *27,* 210, 218–20
    silver, 53, 66
Associated Artists, 108

Association copies, 304
Audubon, John James, 312
Auguste, Robert-Joseph and Henry, 71
Aurene, 107
Austrian furniture, 35, 36, *36*
Autograph albums:
    of Carnegie family, 319, *319*
    with "clipped" signatures, 316
Autographs, 312, *314,* 315, *316,* 317–20, *319, 320*
    on baseballs, *289,* 289–90, 300
    celebrity, 312
    facsimile or proxy, 304, 318-19, 321
    famous, 319–20
    of little value, 312
    presidential, 315, 318–19
    writing in script and, 319
    see also Signatures
Automata:
    clocks with, 178, 183, 192
    dolls, 276, *276*
Automotive advertising objects, 293
Automotive toys, 267, *267–69,* 275
Autopens, 319

B

Baby dolls, 280, 283
Baccarat, 110, *110,* 112
Backgammon, 271
Backplates, *12*
Bakelite, *C-16*
Baker, Arnold & Co., *214*
Balch, Polly, School, *259,* 260
Ball-and-claw feet, *13,* 42, *42*
Ball feet, *13*
Baltimore album quilts, 249, *249,* 250, 254
Banjo clocks, 190, 191
Banks, toy, 274
    cast-iron, *269,* 269–70, *270*
Barbedienne, F. K., 206, 207, 210
Barbies, Dirty, 283
Barbizon art, 136
Baroque:
    copper, 218
    furniture, 4, 6, 33, 38

Baroque pearls, 162
Barrett, Noel, 268, 270, 271, 299
Barrymore, Lionel, 135
Barye, Antoine-Louis, 206–7, *206–8,* 208, 210
Baseball memorabilia, *288–90,* 289–90, 299, *C-30*
Basket, soft-paste porcelain, *81*
Bateman family, 69, *69*
Batwings, *12*
Bauhaus, 5, 68
Baum, Charles, *C-15*
Bayer, Melchior, *72*
Bay Psalm Book, The, 311
Beads, 149
Beatles memorabilia, 291, 292, *292, C-30*
Beaux Arts furniture, 8
Bébé dolls, 278, *279*
Bedcovers (coverlets), *254,* 254–55, 261, 262
Bedroom suites, 9
Beds, *7,* 29, *C-3, C-4*
    headboard for, *35*
Beer steins, 99
Belknap, Zedekiah, 141, *141*
Belleek, American, *80, 81,* 82
Belle Époque (Edwardian):
    furniture, 8
    jewelry, 149, *153, 156,* 174
    silver, *C-5*
Bell toys, 267, 269
Belt buckles, advertising, 299, 300
Belter, John Henry, 27, 28, *28*
Benezit (Dictionnaire des Peintres, Sculpteurs, Desinateurs, et Graveurs), 129
Bennington pottery, 90–92, *94*
Bentalls Van, *C-27*
Benton, Thomas Hart, 139, *139,* 295
Berlin porcelain, 85, 87
Berlin work (sampler patterns), 259
Berninghaus, Oscar Edmund, *C-13*
Berryman, Clifford, *284*
Beryl, 156, 160
Bible, 312
    Gutenberg, 305, *305*
    toys associated with, 264, *264*

Biedermeier furniture, 5, 36, *36*

Bierstadt, Albert, *116*

Big Ben, 180

Bindings, 304, *308,* 309–10

Bing, 273, 285, *286,* 288, *C-28*

Bird groups, bronze, 211

Birds of America (Audubon), 312

Bisque, 82, 90

   dolls, *263,* 276, *277,* 279–80, 282, 283, 287

Black basalt, 89

Blanket, Navajo, *246*

Blanket chests, 29

Blocks, decorated with lithographed colored paper, 274

"Bloomed" jewelry, 169, 170, *170, 171*

Blown-molded glass, 101, 103, *103,* 113

Blue-and-white wares, *84,* 84–86, 99

Blue Fluted Lace pattern, 84

Blue Willow patterns, 84, *84*

Blunck, Andrea, 83

Boardman, Thomas D., *226*

Boardman and Co., *221*

Boats, toy, 268

Bogart, Humphrey, 295, 320

Bohemian glass, 103, 105, 113

Bombé chests, 34, 39

Bonalcosi, Pietro, 204

Bone china, 88, 95

Bonheur, Isidore, 207, 208

Bonheur, Rosa, 208

Bonnin and Morris, 81

Bookcases, 9, 37, 38

Book-club editions, 312, 313

Bookends, 231

Book plates, 304, *306*

Books, 301–2, *302,* 303–15, *C-31–C-32*

   bindings of, 304, *308,* 309–10

   categories of, 301–2

   children's, *303,* 303–4, 312, *314,* 315, 320

   condition of, 312–13

   covers and spines of, 307, *308*

   determining age of, 311–12

   determining value of, 312–15

   distinctions, or points, within editions of, 306, 307–8

   dust jackets of, 310–11, 313–14

   early drafts of literary works, 317

   first editions, 301, 302, *303,* 304, *305,* 305–8, *311,* 312, 313–14, 315

   further reading on, 320

   identifying edition of, 306–7

   illustrated, 304, 308–9, *308–10,* 315

   incunabula, 305, 312

   of little value, 312, 320

   potentially valuable, identification of, 307

   provenance of, 304

   publication date of, 307

   signed, 304, 307–8, 314–15

   tips from experts on, 304

Book worms, 313

Boos, Frank, 63, 74, 162

Bosch, Hieronymus, 134, *134*

Boston and Sandwich Glass Co., *100,* 107, *107*

Boston band pattern, 259

Boston Braves pennant, *288*

Boston State House, 218

Botanical illustratons, 309, *309*

Bottles, glass, *101,* 103, 106

Boucher, Francois, *118*

Boucheron, 173

Boudoir clocks, 194

Boulle, A. C., 35, 38, *C-4*

Boulsover, Thomas, 53, 224

Boulton, Matthew, 54

Bourgeault, Ron, 141

Bowls:

   glass, *100*

   mixed-metal, *51*

Boxes:

   gold-colored filigree, set with stones, 231

   original, of collectibles, 289

   original, of toys, 274

   slide-lid, *20*

   tin, 230

Bracelets, *150, 154,* 155, *155, 156,* 157, *164,* 165, *167,* 171, *171,* 174, *174,* 175

   see also Jewelry

Bracket clocks, 178, *187,* 187–88

   what to look for in, 190

Bracket feet, *13, C-1*

Braided rugs, 243, *243*

   Shaker, 244, *244*

Brass, 47, 54, 185, 201, 202, 211–17, *212, 214–16,* 221, *C-21–C-22*

   casting, 213, *213*

   determining age of, 216

   determining value of, 217

   furniture decorated with, 14, 38

   iron embellished with, 227–28, 230

Breakfast tables, *10, 33*

Breguet, A. L., 189

Brewster and Carver chairs, 1

Bridal quilts, 250

Brigden, Timothy, *224*

Bright-cutting, 52

Brilliant cut, *152,* 153, *153,* 168, 171

Briosco, Andrea, 204

Bristol Blue, *C-11*

Britain's Ltd., *269,* 274

Britannia metal, 54, 224

Bronco Buster, The (Remington), 203, *203*

Bronze(s), 47, 221, *C-21*

   animalier, 206–7, *206–8,* 209, 211

   casting, 204, *204*

   determining age of, 209

   determining value of, 209–11

   furniture decorated with, 16–17, 22

   gilt, *205,* 205–6, 211

   imitations of, 207–9, 210

   patina on, 203, 209, 210, 211

   reproduction, 209–10, 231

   signatures on, 208, 209

   tips from experts on, 210

   white metal copies of, 231

Brooches, *147-49,* 149, *153, 159, 161, 163, 168, 170,* 171, *172*

   see also Jewelry

Brooklyn Dodgers, 289

Brown, George W., & Co., *267,* 273

Brown, J. G., *140*

Brown, Robert, 63, *63*

"Brown wood," use of term, 19
Bru Jne et Cie, 278, *279*, 280, 283
Brush pot, Chinese porcelain, *80*
Bryan, William Jennings, 298
Buddy L, 268, *268*, 273, *275*
Buffalo Brewing Co., 294
Bugatti, Carlo, 35
Bugatti, Rembrandt, *207*, 208, *208*
Bun feet, *13*
Burlap, 243
Burn tests, 162, 241
Bus, toy, *275, C-27, C-28*

C

*Cabinet-maker's and Upholsterer's
    Guide, The* (Hepplewhite), 33
Cabinets, parlor or side, 9, *9*
Cabinet plates, *C-10*
Cabochon cut, 148, 154, *159*
Cabriole legs, *13*, 41, *41*
Calendar watches, 196, 198
Calligraphy, 146
Cameo compote, Silver Gallé, *48*
Cameo glass, 103, 113, *114*
Cameos, 148, *148, 163*, 168–69,
    168–71, 172, 175, *C-16*
    shell, 169, *170*, 175
Cameras, 300
Campaign collectibles, *297*, 297–300,
    298, C-30
    badges, 298, *298*
    buttons, *297*, 298, *298*, 299, 300
    hats, 298, 299–300
Canaletto, *118*
Candelabra:
    brass, *214*
    bronze, 206
    silver, 64, *77*
Candlesticks:
    brass, 212, 214, *214*, 216, *C-21*
    copper, 217, *217, 219*
    mantel clock with (girandole set),
        189
    pewter, *222*
    silver, 63–64, 74, *75*, 76
Canns or mugs, silver, 60, *60*, 61, *61*
Canvas, 117, 119–21

laying down, 120
    marks on, 121
    relining, 119–20
Cap guns and cannons, 274
Carat:
    of gold, 152, 164, 165
    of stones, 152
Carbuncles (almandine garnets), 158,
    174
Carder, Frederick, 107
Card (gaming) tables, 9, *9*, 22, *22*
Carette, 267, *267*, 273
Carlton house desks, 32
Carnegie autograph book, 319, *319*
Carnelian, *148, 168, C-16*
Carnival glass, 113
Carpets:
    use of term, 235
    see also Oriental rugs; Rugs
Carriage clocks, 177–78, 193–94,
    194
Carrie (King), 305
Carroll, Lewis, *303*, 303–4, 312
Cars, toy, 267, *267–69*, 275
Carter, Yough & Co., *200*
Cartier:
    clocks and watches, 193, 194, *198*
    jewelry, 149, 173, *C-17*
Cartledge, Charles, 82
Cartoon buttons, 299
Cartoons, animation cels from, 292,
    295–96, *C-30*
Caruso, Enrico, 300
Carving, on furniture, 17, *17–19*, 19,
    24, 39
Casablanca, 294, *295*
Casenelli, Victor, *C-14*
Cassatt, Mary, *116, C-14*
Castellani, 169, 173, *C-16*
Casters, on Shaker beds, 29
Casters, silver, 63
Casting:
    lost-wax, 204, *204*
    sand, 213, *213*
    silver, 51
Cast iron, 228–29, *229*, 231
    toys, 268–70, *269, 270*
Catalogue raisonné, 126

Caucasian rugs, 233–34, 235, 236,
    239, *239*, 242, *242*
Celebrity autographs, 312, 320
Centennial pieces, 6
Centerpieces:
    gilt-bronze, *205*
    silver, *75*
Center tables, 9
Ceramics, 79–99
    banks, 274
    determining age of, 94–96
    determining value of, 96–97, 99
    dolls. *See* China dolls
    folk, *89*, 93
    marks on, 79–80, 85, 91, 92,
        94–95
    see also Porcelain; Pottery
Chairs, *21, 35*, 36, *C-1, C-3*
    Adam, *39*
    American vs. English, 33
    armchairs, 3, *3, 11*, 16, *16*, 23, 37,
        C-3
    Chippendale, 3, *3*, 6, *12, 19, C-3*
    Classical, 24
    "fancy," 24
    Federal, *11*
    of John Quincy Adams, 16, *16*
    period vs. reproduction, 6
    Pilgrim-style, 1, *11, 12*
    with plain vs. carved knees, *18*
    Queen Anne, *1, 12, C-3*
    repairs to, 24
    Rococo Revival, 28
    sets of, 39
    Shaker, 29
    signs of wear and tear on, 8, 23
    tenons visible in, *14*, 16
    upholstered, 7
    Victorian, *43, 44*
    visual guide to styles in, *12–13*
    Windsor, *12*, 20, *20*, 25, *28*, 29
Chalice, silver, *77*
Chalk, colored, 117
Chambersticks, 214, *C-7*
    silver, 64
Champlevé, 170
Chaplin, Charlie, *293*, 295
Character dolls, *263, 276*, 287

Charcoal, 117

Charles X furniture, 36

"Charles" hose reel, *267*

Chase, Martha, 280

Chasing, 52

Checkers, 271, *271*

Chelsea Keramic, 91

Chemistry sets, 274

Cherokee Roses in a Glass (Heade), *115*

Cherry, 11

Chesterfield, Lord, 316

Chests of drawers, 23, 38, 39

  American vs. English, 33

  bombé, 34, 39

  French commodes, 34, *34,* 36

  Shaker, *29*

  underside of, *7*

  William and Mary, *39*

  see also Highboys

Chests-on-chests, 25, *C-1*

Cheyenne, The (Remington), 203

Chicago Land and Irrigation

  Exposition (1910), 99

Child dolls, 280

Children's books, *303,* 303–4, 313,

  314, 315, 320

Children's tableware, porcelain, *87*

China. *See* Ceramics; Porcelain; Pottery

China dolls, *263,* 276, *277,* 279–80,

  282, 283, *283,* 287

Chinese porcelain, *80,* 80–81, 82, 95

  blue-and-white, *84,* 84–86

  export wares, 83, *83,* 97

Chinese rugs, 238, *238*

Chinoiserie, 32

Chiparus, Demetre, 208

Chippendale, Thomas, 2, 28, 30, *30,*

  32

Chippendale furniture, 2, *2, 4, 13,* 24,

  42, *43, C-1–C-2*

  chairs, 3, *3, 6, 12, 19*

  tallcase clocks, 185

Chisholm, Nan, 120–21, 139

Christmas collectibles, 272, *272*

Christy, Howard Chandler, 309

Chryselephantine, 211

Chrysler, 293

Chrysoprase, 174

Church, Frederick Edwin, *C-13*

Churchill, Winston, 135, *135*

Circular saw marks, *7*

Circus sets, 272

Cire perdue (lost-wax casting), 204, *204*

  glass dolphin sculpture, *107*

Citrines, 159, *C-16*

Civil War diaries and letters, 315,

  316–17

Classical furniture, 2, 5, *10,* 11, 16,

  23, 24, 28, 36

Clemens, Samuel Langhorne. *See*

  Twain, Mark

Clocks, 177–94, *177–94, C-19–C-20*

  boudoir, 194

  bracket, shelf, and mantel, 178, 181,

    187–91, *187–90, C-19–C-20*

  carriage, 177–78, 193–94, *194*

  decorative cases of, 177–78, 181,

    185, 186, 189

  determining age of, 182–83

  determining value of, 183–84

  dial and hands of, 182, *182,* 184,

    185, 186

  further reading on, 200

  mass production of, 188–89

  with mechanized figures or scenes,

    178, 182, 183, *191,* 192

  movement of, *179,* 179–80, *180*

  novelty, *192,* 192–93

  painted faces on, 187

  regulator, 191, *191*

  repairs to, 183, 186

  repeating mechanisms in, 188, 193,

    194

  with reverse-painted panels, *188,*

    189, 190

  serial numbers on, 193–94

  signatures or labels on, 183–84,

    185, 189, 190, 194

  striking of, 180, 183, 187, 188,

    193, 194

  table, *172*

  tallcase (grandfather or longcase

    clocks), 177, *181, 182, 184–86,*

    185–87, *C-19*

  timeline for, 183

  travel, 193, *193*

wall, 178, *187,* 191, *191*

  winding, 180, 183

  see also Movements, clock

Clockwork toys, *266,* 267

Cloisonné enamels, 170, 174

Cloister and the Hearth, The (Reade),

  307

Closed settings, 153, 170, *170*

Cloth dolls, 277, *277, 280,* 280–81,

  296

Coalport, 88

Coates, Edmund C., *C-13*

"Coattail" political ephemera, 300

Cochiti pottery, 99

Coffeepots:

  pewter, 224, 225

  silver, *51, 54*

  tinned sheet metal, 228, *228, 229*

  tinware, 230

Coffee services, silver, *66, 77*

Cogswell, John, 26

Coins, silver standard for, 47

Cold-working, 203

Cole, Thomas, *127*

Colinet, Clare-Jeanne-Robert, 208

Collas, 210

Collected works by standard authors,

  320

Collectibles, 263–64, 288–300,

  C-27–C-30

  advertising memorabilia, 292–94,

    293, 294, 299, 300

  ephemera, *296–98,* 296–300

  further reading on, 300

  of little value, 300

  original boxes of, 289

  political campaigns and, *297,*

    297–300, *298*

  rock and roll memorabilia, 290–92,

    291, 292

  sports memorabilia, *288–90,*

    289–90, 299

  tips from experts on, 299

Colonial Revival furniture, 8

Colophons, 307

Color book illustrations, 309, 315

Columbus, Christopher, 311, *311*

Comb-back chairs, *12*

Coming Through the Rye (Remington), 203, *C-20*

Commodes, 34, *34,* 36, *C-4*

Communion service, pewter, *224*

Complin, George, *C-10*

Composition dolls, 283

Compotes:
    glass, *107*
    silver, *48, 52,* 78

Concert posters, *291,* 292

Coney, John, 62

Confectionery banks, 270

Connelly, Henry, *11*

Connoisseurship, 133–41

Consoles, 2, *32*

Constitution, USS, 218

Construction kits, 274

Construction techniques, *15,* 15–16, 24, 38

Continental furniture, 2, 9, *9,* 10, *13,* 16–17, 31, 32, 33–39, *34–37, C-4*
    craftsmen, 35
    determining age of, 37–39
    determining value of, 39
    styles and periods of, 4–5
    tips from experts on, 38

Continental glass, *110,* 110–11

Continental porcelain, 81, 82, 83, 84, 86–88

Continental silver, 47, 52, *52,* 53, *53,* 68, 70–73, *71, 72,* 74, *76, C-7*
    hallmarks on, *57,* 57–58, *72*
    makers, 71

Converse, Gordon S., 184

Cookbooks, 312

Cookware, copper, 217–18, *218,* 231

Cooper, James Fenimore, *308*

Coover, Chris, 315

Copper, 47, 201, 202, 203, 212, 217–20, *217–20,* 221, *C-22*
    Arts and Crafts movement and, 218–20, *219, 220*
    in mixed-metal wares, *50, 51,* 66
    silver plated, 53–54, 224
    weathervanes, 231, *231,* 232

Coral, 162–63, *163*

Cornelius, 214

Corundum, 154, 155, 174

Costumes, worn by R&R celebrities, 292, *292*

Cotton, burn test for, 241

Country furniture, 11

Courthouse Steps quilts, *248*

Court proceedings, records of, 303

Courvoisier Co., 295

Coverlets, *254,* 254–55, 261, *C-26*
    further reading on, 262

Cowbells, 231

Cox, Archibald, *222*

Cox, James, 299

Cradling, 121

Cranach, Lucas, I, *131*

Craquelure, 125, 139

Crayon, 118

Crazy quilts, *248*

Cream pitcher, silver, *45*

Creamware, 88

Creels, 290

Crocks, 92, 93

Cruet sets, silver, 63, *C-5*

Crystal, glass vs., 100–101

Cubic zirconia (CZ), 153–54

Cubism, 67, 138

Cuckoo clocks, *191,* 192

Culme, John, 46

Cup, covered, glass, *106*

Cup and cover, silver, *72*

Cup-and-trumpet legs, *13*

Cupboards, 29, 38

Cup plates, glass, 102

Cups, silver, 47, *47,* 73, 74

Curiosities of Glass Making, 101

Curran, Peter, 258

Curtis, Edward S., 310, *310*

Cushing, L. W., & Co., *231*

Cushing and White, 231

Cushion cut, 148, *152,* 168

Cut glass, *79, 100,* 104–5, 110, 112, 113

Cut-to-clear glass, *105, 113*

Cypriote glass, 111

D

Dali, Salvador, 137, *137*

Danish furniture, 36

Darley, Felix O. C., *308,* 309

Darrow, Charles, 271

Darwin, Charles, *303, C-32*

Dates:
    incorporated into rug designs, 245
    on paintings, 131–33

Daum, August and Antonin, 111, *C-11*

Davenport desks, *31,* 32

David, Jacques-Louis, *128*

Davis, John, 299

Davis, Martha Pease, *259*

Dawes, Nick, 81, 83, 86, 112

Day the Earth Stood Still, The, 295

Deal, 32

Dean, James, 295

Decanters, glass, *103–5*

Declaration of Independence, 320

Decorative Art, Fine Art vs., 116

Dedication copies, 314–15

Deeds, 303, 315

Degas, Edgar, *126*

DeHeem, Jan Davidsz, *C-13*

Deidrich, Hunt, 230

Deisroth, Barbara, 105, 217

De Kooning, Willem, 138, *138*

Delaunay, Nicolas, 71

Delftware, 90, 99

Demantoid garnets, *150,* 157, 158, *C-16*

Demi-parure, *160, C-16*

Demitasse set, silver, *67*

Demmen, Desire, *260*

Dennis, Thomas, *C-1*

Depression quilts, 251

Derr Family, *C-26*

Desk accessories, *221*

Deskey, Donald, 65

Desks, *31,* 32, 37, *C-1, C-2*

Despres, Jean, 173

Dessert service, porcelain, *87*

Devil jug, *89*

Diamonds, *147,* 148, *148, 150,* 150–54, *151, 153, 154, 156,* 157, *157, 161–63,* 167, *167,* 168, *170,* 171, *174,* 174–75, *C-16–C-18*
    carat of, 152
    clarity of, 151–52
    color of, 151
    simulants, 153–54

Diana (Saint-Gaudens), *206*
Diaries, Civil War, 315, 316–17
Dickens, Charles, 308
Dicky bear, 287
Dictionaries, 320
Dictionary of American Painters,
    Sculptors & Engravers (Fielding),
    129
Dictionnaire des Peintres, Sculpteurs,
    Desinateurs, et Graveurs
    (known as *Benezit*), 129
Dinglinger, Johann Melchior, 71
Dining room tables, 8, 31
Diorama, *265*
Dirigibles, toy, 268, *C-28*
Dirty Barbies, 283
Dishes:
    pewter, *226*
    see also Plates
Disks (records), 291, 300
Disneyana, 295–96
Dixon, James, 224
Dixon and Co., 54
DiZessel, *C-29*
Doat, Taxile, 92
Documents. *See* Manuscripts
Dolls, 263–64, *275–77,* 275–83,
    279–83, C-29
    character, *263, 276,* 287
    china, *263,* 276, *277,* 279–80, 282,
        283, *283,* 287
    cloth, 277, *277, 280,* 280–81, 296
    composition, 283
    condition of, 287, 288
    construction methods for heads of,
        279
    determining age of, 281–83
    determining value of, 283
    Disneyana, 296
    eighteenth-century, 276
    encyclopedia of, 287
    folk, 281, *281,* 283
    further reading on, 300
    great age not important for, 263
    makers, 278
    marks on, 278, 282, 287
    mechanical (automata), 276, *276*
    papier-mâché, 279, 283

peg (peg woodens), *275,* 277
physical characteristics of, 282–83
Raggedy Ann, 277, *277,* 281, *281*
repairs to, 287
tips from experts on, 287
wax, 276, 277
Dolphin feet, *13*
Dolphin sculpture, glass, *107, C-11*
Donald Duck collectibles, 296
Donatello, 204
Donne, John, 315
Double-weave coverlets, 254, *254*
Dovetail joints, *15,* 15–16, 24, 38
Dowels, 15, 38
Drawers, 23, 24, 38
    American vs. English, 33
    pulls for, *12, 13,* 14
    signs of wear and tear on, 8, *14*
Drawings, 116
"Drawing the line in Mississippi"
    (Berryman), 284, *284*
Dresden porcelain, 87–88
Dressing tables, 9, *14,* 17, *C-5*
Drop-leaf tables, *18*
Drops, *12, 13*
Druckman, Nancy, 120–21, 241,
    254, 257
Dumbwaiter, *37*
Dummer, Jeremiah, 62
Dumond, Frank Vincent, *C-12*
DuMouchelle, Lawrence, 211
Dunbar, Leila, 272, 289, 299
Dürer, Albrecht, *128,* 171
Durgin/Gorham, *67*
Dustcovers, 7
Dust jackets, 310–11, 313–14
Dutch decorative arts:
    furniture, 1, 9, *9,* 10, 31, 33, 35,
        38, 39
    silver, 58
    tallcase clocks, 186, *186, C-19*

E

Earrings and ear pendants, 149, *157,*
    159, 166, 167, 175
    see also Jewelry
"Earth Angel," 291

Eastlake, Charles, 30, *30*
Eastlake furniture, 8
Eaton, William Page, *21*
Eclectic furniture, 5
Edison, Thomas Alva, *C-32*
Edwardian. *See* Belle Époque
Egyptian Revival furniture, *44*
Egyptian-style watch fob, *200*
Eisenhower, Dwight, 248–49
Election tokens, 298
Electric trains, *267,* 268, 275
Electroplate, 54–55, 78
    gold jewelry, 166
    gilt bronze and, 205
Elephant motifs:
    in bronze, *207*
    in hooked rug, *243*
Elgin, 196, 197, 199
Elizabeth I, Queen, 310
Elkington Co., 54
Embossing, 51
Embroideries:
    mourning pictures, 257
    see also Samplers
Emerald cut, *152*
Emeralds, 150, *156,* 156–57, 160,
    171, 174, *C-16*
    simulants, 157
Empire furniture, 2, 5, 11, *18,* 33, 36,
    37, 38, *C-4*
Enameling, 52–53, *53*
    of glass, 103, 112, 113
    of jewelry, *170,* 171–72, *172,* 174
    of watch cases, 195, 198
Encyclopedias, 320
Endpapers, *306*
English brass, *214, 216,* 217
English ceramics:
    porcelain, 81, 82, *84,* 85, 88
    pottery, 88, 89, 90, 94, 95
English clocks, *181, 182,* 185, *187,*
    187–88, 189, 190, 191
English dolls, 277, 278
English furniture, 1, 2, 10, *14,* 16, 22,
    22, 30, *30, 31,* 31–33, *C-3*
    designers and craftsmen of, 30
    determining age of, 37–39
    determining value of, 39

distinguishing American furniture from, 32–33

further reading on, 43

styles and periods of, 4–5

tips from experts on, 38

English glass, 104, *104*, 112

English pewter, *221–23*, 222–23

English silver, *46, 54–56*, 60, 61, 63, *63*, 68–70, *68–70*, 73, *73*, *C-7*

hallmarks on, 55–57, *57*

makers, 69

English teddy bears, 284, 285—86

English watches, 194, 196

Engraved book illustrations, 308–9

Engraved glass, *79, 104*, 105, 106

Engraved silver, 52, 74, 76

Ephemera, *296–98*, 296–300

further reading on, 300

political, *297*, 297–300, *298*

EPNS (electroplated nickel silver), 45, 54–55

Erp, Dirk Van, 219, *219*, 220, *220*

Escapements, 180, *180*, 184

Escutcheons, *13*, 14

Etagères, 9, *9*

Etched glass. See Acid-etched glass

Etruscan-work, 169, 170, *C-16*

Ewer, silver, 68, *68*

Excelsior banks, 269

Ex-library copies, 313

Export porcelain, 83, *83, 84*, 84–86, 97

Exposition Internationale des Arts Décoratifs et Industriels Modernes (1925), 67

Eyeglasses, 300

F

Fabergé, 149, 170, *172*, 173, *C–18*

Fabric dating, 252

Faience, 90

Fairy Tales (Andersen), 315

Fallows, James, & Son, 273

Famille rose, 83, *C-8*

Famille verte, 83, *C-10*

Family record samplers, 256, *256*

"Fancy" chairs, 24

Farnell, J. K., 285–86

Fashion dolls, French, *277, 279*, 280, 282, *282*

Faulkner, William, 307, 311

Fausel, Alan, 120, 125

Favrile glass, 108, *C-11*

Feathers (inclusions), 155

"Fecit," use of term, 130

Federal-style furniture, 5, *7*, 11, *11*, 28, 40, *40*

tallcase clocks, 185

Feet (furniture), 38, 42, *42*

visual guide to styles in, *13*

Fenders, fireplace:

brass, 214, 215, 216, 217

iron, 230

Fesko, Colleene, 119, 133

Ffrench, James, 241

Field, Erastus Salisbury, 120

Fielding, Mantle, 129

Fiestaware, 99

Fine Art:

Decorative Art vs., 116

monetary hierarchy of media in, 117

see also Painting; Sculpture

Finlay, John and Hugh, *C-1*

Finish, on furniture, 20–21, 38

Finster, Howard, 142

Firebacks, cast-iron, 228–29, *229*

Fire marks, 228, *228*

Fireplace furnishings:

brass, 214–15, *215*, 216, 217

iron, *226*, 227, 228–29, *229*, 230

Fire pumper, toy, *274*, *C-27*

Firescreens, wrought-iron, 230

First editions, 301, 302, *303, 305*, 305–8, *311*, 312, 315, *C-32*

determining value of, 313–14

limited signed, 308

withdrawn, 304

Fisher, Alvan, *C-13*

Fisher, Jonathan, 142

Fishing collectibles, 290

Fishing Lady motif, 260

Fiske, J. W., Works, 229, 231

Fitzgerald, F. Scott, 302, *305*, 307, 311

Fitzhugh patterns, 83

Flagon, pewter, *221*, *C-23*

Flanigan, J. Michael, 32, 220

Flashed glass, 103, 113

Flasks:

glass, *103, 106*

pewter, *222*

pottery, *94*

Flatware, silver, 48, *53*, 55, 64, *64*, 74, 77, *C-6*

Flesh and the Devil, 295

Fletcher, Stephen, 20

Fletcher & Gardiner, 65

"Floating signature," 130

Flower book, 309, *309*

Flowerpot, pottery, *89*

Fluted legs, *13*

Folk art:

ceramics, *89*, 93

dolls, 281, *281*, 283

furniture, 28–29, *29*

jewelry, *175*, 175–76

metal, 230–32, *230–32*

painting, 120, 121, 135, 141–46, *143–45*

rugs, 241, 243–45, *243–45*

toys, 264, 265

Football cards, 290

Football games, 271

Forks, 48, 73

see also Flatware

45 rpm singles, 291

For Whom the Bell Tolls (Hemingway), 313-14

Fouquet, Georges, 173

Fowler banks, 269

Foxing, 122, 313

Frakturs, *145*, 146

Frames, 123–25, *124*

Franchi, Rudy, 296, 299

Frank, Jean-Michel, 35

Frankenstein, 294

Franklin, Benjamin, 228, 302

Free-blown glass, *79*, 101, *101*, 102, *102, 106*

French animalier bronzes, 206–7, *206–8*, 208, 209, 211

French decorative arts:

brass, *216*

clocks, 189, *189*, 191, 193, *193*

furniture, 2, 4–5, 10, *13,* 16–17,
    31, 32, 33–39, *34, 35, 37,* 37–39
gilt bronze, *205,* 205–6
glass, *110,* 110–11, 112
porcelain, 81, 83, 85, 86–87, 88
silver, 58, 70, 71, 72
French dolls, 276, *276, 277,* 278,
    279, 280, 282, *282, 283*
French jewelry, *170, 171*
"French plate," 213
"French polish," 38
French Provincial furniture, 36
French Revolution, 36, 70, 172
Froment-Meurice, François, 71
Frontispieces, *306*
Frost, Andrea Blunck, 74
Frosted glass, 103
"Fruit salad" (jewelry), *156,* 174, *C-17*
Fruit stand, silver, *65*
Fruitwood, 37
Furniture, 1–44, 116, *C-1–C-4*
    Adam, 2, *13,* 38, 39
    Aesthetic Movement, 5, 8, 16, *23*
    "antique," use of term, 3, 6
    antique or period, distinguishing
        used furniture from, 6–8
    Art Nouveau, 5, 8, *35*
    Arts and Crafts, 5, 8, 27, *27,* 220
    Baroque, 4, 6, 33, 38
    beds, *7,* 29
    bookcases, 9, 37, 38
    Chippendale, 2, *2, 3, 3,* 4, 6, *12,*
        13, 19, 24, 28, *30,* 32, 42, *43,*
        C-1, C-3
    Classical, 2, 5, *10,* 11, 16, *23,* 24,
        28, 36
    clocks as, 177–78, 181
    color of, 21–22
    condition of, 22–24
    construction techniques in, *15,*
        15–16, 24, 38
    decorative details in, 16–17,
        17–19, 19, 20, 24, 39
    determining age of, 3–8, 37–39
    determining value of, 17–25,
        29–31, 39
    Empire, 2, 5, 11, *18,* 33, 36, *37,* 38
    Federal, 5, *7,* 11, *11,* 28, 40, *40*

folk, 28–29, *29*
forms of, 9, 10
further reading on, 43–44
hardware on, 7, *7, 12–13,* 14–15,
    19, 20, 24, 25, 38
Hepplewhite, 2, *11, 12,* 16, 28, 30,
    30, 32–33
highboys, 1–2, *2,* 6, *6,* 9, *9,* 24,
    25, 41, *41,* C-1
inscriptions or labels on, 8, 39
Jacobean, 1, 4, 29–31
learning by comparing, 40–42
of little value, 44
Neoclassical, 4, 9, 32, 39
painting on, *20,* 21, *21,* 22, 24,
    25, 28
patina and finish of, 20–21, 38
"period," use of term, 3, 6
Pilgrim-style, 1, 4, *11–13,* 15
provenance of, 16, 18–19
quality of, 19–20
Queen Anne, *1,* 2, *2,* 4, 11, *12, 13,*
    38, 41, *41, C-3*
rarity of, 17–18
Regency, 5, *31,* 33
repairs to, 23, 24
reproduction, 6
revival styles in, 2, 5, 8, *28,* 32, 38,
    43, 44
Rococo, 4, 32, 33–34, *34,* 39, *C-4*
Shaker, 11, 29, *29,* 42, *42*
shrinkage on, 23, 38
size of, 24
styles and periods of, 4–5
tips from experts on, 24–25, 38
transitional pieces, 32
upholstered, 7, 23, 24, 33
"used," use of term, 3–6
Victorian, 5, 8, 9, 11, *12,* 16–17,
    24, *28,* 33, 38, 42, *42–44*
visual guide to styles, *12–13*
William and Mary, 1, 4, 10, *12,*
    13, 39, 41, *41*
wood in, 7, 10–11, 32, 36, 37, 38,
    39
see also American furniture; Chairs;
    Chests of drawers; Continental
    furniture; English furniture;

French furniture; Tables
Fusee movements, *179*

G

Gadrooning, 17, *17*
Gale, Benjamin, 6
Gallé, Emile, 35, 111, 112, *C-11*
Gambling collectibles, 290
Games, 271, *271*
Gaming (or card) tables, 9, *9,* 22, *22*
Ganado rugs, *245,* 246
Garbo, Greta, 295
Garden furnishings, iron, 228, 229,
    230
Gardens (inclusions), 156
Garner, John Nance, 299
Garnets, 148, *150,* 155, 157, 158,
    170, 174
Garrett, Wendell, 16, 202
Gasoline advertising objects, 293–94,
    C-30
Gateleg tables, 9
Gaugengigl, Ignaz M., 118, 119, *119*
Gaultier, François, 282
Gemstones. *See* Stones; *specific stones*
Gendje rug, *233*
Genealogies (samplers), 256, *256*
Genre painting, 119, *119,* 122, *122,*
    126, 130, *130, 132,* 140
*Gentleman and Cabinet-maker's
    Director, The* (Chippendale), 32
Geometric patterns, 234
    in quilts, *248,* 249, *251,* 252, *252,*
        253
    in rugs, *233, 234, 236,* 237, 239,
        239, 242, 243, *245,* 246
George II furniture, *37*
Georgian:
    cameos in, 168–69
    furniture, 4
German decorative arts:
    clocks, 190, 191, 192, *C-20*
    copper, 218, *218*
    furniture, 33, 36
    pewter, 222, *222*
    porcelain, 81, 82, 83, 84, 85, 86,
        87–88

silver, *52,* 58, 70–73, *72*

"German silver" (alloy), 54, 73

German toys, *264,* 265, 267, *267,* 268, 273

    dolls, *263, 275, 276,* 277, 278, 279, 280, *280,* 282, *C-29*

    teddy bears, 284–85

Gesso, 119

Gettysburg Address, 320, *C-32*

Gilding, 52

    on furniture, 17, 22, 39

    on glass, 103, 112, 113

Gillows, 30

Gilpin, Edmund, 196

Gilt bronze, *205,* 205–6, 211

Giorgione, *136*

Girandole set, *189*

Girl Skipping Rope banks, 270, C-28

Girl with Flowers, 143

Giuliano, 173

Glass, 1, 79–80, 99–114, 116, *C-11*

    acid-etched, *104,* 105–6

    American, *100–103,* 101, 104, 105, 106–7, *106–9*

    art, 103, 105, *108,* 108–9, *109,* 111, *111,* 112

    banks, 274

    blown-molded, 101, 103, *103,* 113

    colored, 103

    crystal vs., 100–101

    cut, *79, 100,* 104–5, 110, 112, 113

    cut-to-clear, *105, 113*

    definition of, 99–100

    determining age of, 111–12

    determining value of, 112–13

    engraved, *79, 104,* 105, 106

    European, *110,* 110–11

    free-blown, *79,* 101, *101,* 102, *102, 106*

    further reading on, 114

    gemstone simulants (paste), 153, 155, 156, 157, 170

    knobs, *14*

    in less than perfect condition, 112, 113

    manufacturing techniques for, 101–3, *102*

marks on, 79–80, 107, 112

ornamentation of, 103–6, 113

pressed, *100, 101,* 102–3, 104, 107, 110

repairs to, 104, 110

reverse-painted, 145

and silver compote, *48*

silver-mounted, 67, *67*

tips from experts on, 112

Glasses (drinking), *100, 103, 106, 111*

Glued joints, 15

Goblet, bronze, *209*

Goddard-Townsend School, 26, *26, 42, 42, C-2*

Gold, 47, *148,* 149, *150, 153, 156, 159–62,* 163, 164–65, *164–67,* 166, 167, 171, 174, *174,* 175, *C-16–C-18*

    carat of, 152, 164, 165

    frosted finish on, 169, 170, *170, 171*

    watch cases and watchbands, 198–99

    see also Gilding

Gold-filled jewelry, 149, 166, 175

Gold-plated silver, 52

Golf memorabilia, 290

Gone with the Wind, 294, 308

Goodyear, 293

Goofy collectibles, 296

Googly-eyed dolls, *280*

Gorham & Co., *49,* 55, 65, *65,* 67, *78, C-6, C-7*

Gothic furniture, 4

Gothic Revival furniture, 8, 32, 38

Gouache, 117

Governors, recent, letters of, 312

Goya, Francisco José de, 134

Graining, 21, *21*

Grande sonnerie, 193

Grandfather clocks. *See* Tallcase clocks

Grant, Ulysses S., 299, 304

Grapes of Wrath, The (Steinbeck), 295

Great Gatsby, The (Fitzgerald), 302, *305,* 311

Greeks, ancient:

    bronzes of, 203, 204

    silver of, 47

Greene, Charles and Henry, 27

Greiner, Ludwig, 278, 283, *C-29*

"Gretchen" doll, *263*

Griffen, Smith, and Hill, 90, *C-9*

Grisham, John, 302

Grove, George, *214*

Grueby Faience, 91, 92, *C-2*

Guilloche enamels, 170, *172*

Guitars, 292

Gutenberg, Johannes, 305, *305*

Gutenberg Bible, 305, *305*

Guzman, Kathleen, 299

Gwinnett, Button, 319–20

H

Hagen, Ernest, 10

Hairy-paw feet, *13, 19*

Half titles, *306, 308*

Hall, John, 269

Hall China, 99

Hallmarks, 55–59, 73

    American, 58–59, 74

    Continental, *57,* 57–58, 72

    English, 55–57, *57*

    on silver plate, 54, 55

    tip for deciphering, 58

Hammering silver, 50–51, 66, 73

Hancock, John, 319

Handbags, painted mesh, 175

Handel, George Frideric, *301*

Handel & Co., 109, *109*

Handles (hardware), *13*

Harding, Warren G., 319

Hardware, 7, *7,* 14–15, 19, 20, 24, 25, 38

    brass, 213

    iron, 227, 229, 230

    and normal wear and tear to furniture, *14, 23*

    visual guide to styles in, *12–13*

Harley-Davidson, 293, *293*

Harp legs, *31*

Harrison, Josiah, 230, *230*

Harrison, William Henry, *297,* 298, *298,* 319

Hartop, Christopher, 60, 73

Hawkes, Thomas, 107

Hay, John, 319
Hays, John, 3, 21, 24
Headboard, *35*
Heade, Martin Johnson, *115*
Hearst, William Randolph, 184
Hemingway, Ernest, 307, 311, 313–14
Henri, Robert, 133, *133*
Henry, Edward Lamson, *132*
Hepplewhite, George, 28, 30, 32–33
Hepplewhite furniture, 2, *11, 12,* 16, *30*
Herculaneum, 36
Herter, Gustave and Christian, 26–27, *C-2*
Heubach, Gebrüder, 278
Hicks, Edward, *144,* 145
Highboys, 1–2, *2,* 6, *6,* 9, *9,* 24, 25, 41, *41, C-1*
Hinges, 14
Hitchcock, General, *320*
Hobbs, Brockunier & Co., 102
Hobbyhorses (rocking horses), *265,* 265–66
Hoffmann, Josef, 35, *35, C-22*
Holbein, Hans, 171
"Holloware," use of term, 48, 222
Hollywood collectibles, *293,* 294–96, *295*
Homer, Winslow, *116*
Hooked rugs, 241, *243,* 243–45, *244, C-24*
Hooper, Henry N., 214
Hope, Thomas, 70
Hopi:
    dolls of, 281, *281*
    pottery of, 99
Horror film posters, 294, *295*
Horse-and-carriage weathervane, *230*
Horse-and-driver weathervane, *231*
Horse brasses, 213
Horse Guard (The Blues), *269*
Horses, carved, *265,* 265–66
Hose reel, toy, *267*
Hot-water bottle bears, 288
Houston, Samuel, 319
Howdy Doody collectibles, 299
Hubbard, Elbert, 220
Hubley, 273, *273*
Hummels, 99, 300

Humphrey, Maud, 293
Hunter-cased watches, 196, *197, C-20*
Hunting scenes, 134, *135*
Hurd, Jacob, 58, 60
Hurd, Nathaniel, 52

I

Ideal Novelty and Toy Co., 286, *286*
Illustrated books, 304, 308–9, *308–10,* 315
Imports, marked with country of origin, 14–15, 270
Impressionism, 128, 136
Inclusions, 151, 155, 156
Incunabula, 305, 312
Ingres, Jean-Auguste-Dominique, *146*
Inks, 318
Ink standishes, *221*
Inkwell, ceramic, *93*
Inlay, in furniture, 16, *17,* 20
Inscribed copies, 314
International Silver Co., *53,* 65
Irish decorative arts:
    furniture, 39
    glass, 101, 104, 110
Iron, 47, *214, C-23*
    cast, 228–29, *229,* 231, 268–70, *269, 270*
    determining age of, 229
    determining value of, 230
    rolled and tinned, 228, *228, 229*
    wrought, 14, 227–30
Ironstone, 90, *C-8*
Irving, Washington, 309
Islamic glass, 108
Italian decorative arts:
    furniture, 33, 35, 37, 38
    silver, 58
Ives, Blakeslee & Co., 273, 275
Ivory, 162, 172
    and bronze figures, 211
Ivory Soap, 293, *293*

J

Jackson, Andrew, 315
Jacobean furniture, 1, 4, 29–31

Jacobsen, Antonio, *C-15*
Jacquard coverlets, 254, *C-26*
Jade, 160–61, *C-17*
Jadeite, 160–61, *C-16*
Jamnitzer, Wenzel, 71
Japanese ceramics, 92, *96,* 99
Japanese toys, 274
"Japonesque" pieces, 66, *C-6*
Jars, pottery, *88,* 98, *98,* 99
Jarvie, Robert, 219, *219*
Jasper ware, 89
Jelly glasses, 113
Jensen, Georg, 71, 173
Jet, 162–63
Jewelry, 147–76, *C-16–C-18*
    appraisals of, 149
    Art Deco, 148, 151, *153,* 156, 157, 173, *174–75, C-17*
    Art Nouveau, 165, 171, 173, 174, *C-17*
    Belle Époque or Edwardian, 149, *153,* 156, 174, *C-17*
    "bloomed," 169, 170, *170, 171*
    bracelets, *150, 154,* 155, *155, 156,* 157, *164,* 165, *167,* 171, *171,* 174, *174,* 175
    brooches, *147–49,* 149, *153,* 159, *161, 163,* 168, *170,* 171, 172
    cameos, 148, *148, 163,* 168–69, *168–71,* 172, 175
    condition of, 149
    earrings and ear pendants, 149, *157, 159,* 166, 167, 175
    enameled, *170,* 171–72, *172,* 174
    further reading on, 176
    with little value, 175
    metals in, 163–66, 167
    mourning, 163, 172
    Native American, 165, *175,* 175–76, *176*
    necklaces, 149, *150, 153,* 155, *155,* 166, *166, 175, 176*
    organic materials in, 161–63, 168
    pendants, *156, 162, 170,* 171, *172*
    pins, 167, *172*
    precious stones (gemstones) in, 150–57, *C-16*

real vs. imitation, 149–50, 153–54, 162
Renaissance, 162, 170, 171
repairs to, 149, 157
Retro, *174,* 175, *C-18*
rings, *148, 151, 154,* 155, *155, 165,* 171, 172
selected makers and marks, 173
semiprecious stones in, 157–61, *C-16*
styles of, 148–49, 171–75
techniques in, 169–71
tips from experts on, 158
Victorian, 148, *148, 160,* 162, *163, 164,* 166, *166,* 167, *167,* 169, *169,* 171, *171, 172,* 172–74, *C-16*
watches as, 177, 195, 198, 199
see also Stones; *specific stones, organic materials, and metals*
Jewels:
pocket watches set with, 199
see also Stones; *specific stones*
Johnson, Isaac, *212*
Johnson, Joshua, 121
Joining, *15,* 15–16
Jonas, Joyce, 149, 158, 174
Jones, George, 90
Joplin, Janis, *291*
Josephine, Empress, 309, 316
Joyce, James, 308, *308*
Jugates, 299, 300
Jugendstil, 5
Jugs:
glass, *99, 100*
pottery, *89,* 93
Jumeau, *276,* 278, 280, 283, *283*

K

Kachina dolls, 281, *281*
Kalo, *50,* 65
Kämmer & Reinhardt, *263,* 276, 280, *280*
Kangaroo bracelet, 165
Karolik, Maxim, 144
Kas, 9, *9*
Kayserzinn, 222
Kazakh rugs, *236,* 237, 242, *242, C-24*

Kennedy, John F., 319
Keno, Leigh, 6, 22, 24–25
Keno, Leslie, 22, 24–25, 249, 250
Kent, Rockwell, 309
Kestner, Johannes Daniel, 278, 280, *C-29*
Kettles:
bronze, 203, *C-21*
copper, 202, 218, *218, C-22*
Kewpie dolls, 277, 278, *C-29*
Kid, The, 293, 295
Kiffer, Selby, 304, 307, 310
Kilim rugs, *236*
King, Stephen, 305
King Kong, 295
Kipling, Rudyard, 319
Kipp, Karl, 210, 219
Kirk, Samuel, & Son, 65, *C-5*
Kirman carpet, 240, *240*
Kitchen utensils, 201, 213
Klah, Hosteen, 246
Knickerbocker, 296
Knives, 48, 76
see also Flatware
Knobs, *13, 14*
Knox, Archibald, *77*
Kovshi, silver, 72, *72*
Kraus, Peter, 319
Kruse, Käthe, 280
Kuba rugs, 237, *238*
Kuharic, Gregory A., 218
Kurlikov, Orest, *76*

L

Lace, 261
Lackey, David, 96
Lacloche, *C-18*
Lacquer, 213
imitation, on furniture, 21–22
"Lacy glass," 102–3, *107*
Ladder-back chairs, *12,* 25
Lafayette, Marquis de, 206
Laguna pottery, *98,* 99
Lalique, René, 110–11, 112–13, *C-11*
as jeweler, 149, 173, *C-17, C-18*
Lambert, *276*
Lamerie, Paul de, 69

Lamps:
art glass, *108,* 108–9, *109,* 111, 112
copper, 220, *220*
Land grants, "Lincoln-signed," 318
Landscape paintings, *116,* 119, 126–27, *127, 129,* 137, 139, *139*
by folk artists, *143,* 144
watch faces set into, 192, *192*
Lane, Fitz Hugh, *C-14*
Lannuier, Charles-Honoré, 2, 26, *26*
Lanterns, 214
Lapel watch and pin, *199*
Lapis lazuli, 160
Larsen, Don, 289
Last of the Mohicans (Cooper), *308*
Lava carvings, 169
Laying down (a picture), 120
Lead, 202, 221
Leather-bound books, 310, 312, 320
Leaving Home (Henry), *132*
Leddel, Joseph, 52
Lee, Richard, *226*
Lee, Robert E., 315
Legs (furniture):
repairs to, 24
signs of normal wear and tear on, 8, 23
visual guide to styles in, *13*
Leleu, Jules, *205*
Lenox, 82
Letters, 302–3, 312, *314,* 315–17, *316, 317*
Lewis, Dianne, 171
Lewis, Mabel G., 92
Leyendecker, J. C., 293
Libbey, 107
Liberty & Co., *77,* 222, *222*
Liberty weathervane, *227*
Liddell, Alice, *303*
Lieberman, Gloria, 158
Life on the Mississippi (Twain), 311
Lighthouse-shaped coffeepots, 225
Lighting:
art glass lamps, *108,* 108–9, *109,* 111, 112
Arts and Crafts, 220
brass, 212, 214, *214,* 216
electric, 79

oil and gas, 214
  silver, 63–64, 74, *75, 76, 77*
  wrought-iron, 228, 229
Limited Edition Club, 308
Limited signed first editions, 308
Limners, 143–44
Limoges, 86–87, 88, 99
Lincoln, Abraham, 312, 318, 319
  Gettysburg Address drafts written
    by, 320, *C-32*
  letters written by, 315, 317, *317,
    320*
Lincoln, Mary Todd, 279
Lincoln Logs, 274
Lind, Jenny, 279
Linen canvas. *See* Canvas
Lion's-paw feet, *13*
Literary works:
  early drafts of, 317
  see also Books
Lithographed paper, toys decorated
    with, 266, 268, 271, 274, *274*
Lithography:
  color book illustrations and, 309
  stone, 295
Little Bull (Barye), *208*
Little Leather Library books, 320
Lladro ceramics, 300
Lockwood, Wilson, *C-14*
Log cabin quilts, *248, 249, 251,* 253
Longcase clocks. *See* Tallcase clocks
Lonhuda, 91
Lost-wax casting (*cire perdue*), 204,
    204
  glass dolphin sculpture, *107, C-11*
Louis XIV furniture, 4, 33, *C-4*
Louis XV furniture, 4, *C-4*
Louis XVI furniture, 4, *34,* 36
Louis XVIII furniture, 5
Louis Philippe furniture, 5
"Loupe-clean," use of term, 151
Lowboys. *See* Dressing tables
Luke, Timothy, 285
Lures, 290
Luri rugs, *234*
Luther, Louise, 108, 111, 112
Lutz, *C-27*

Maclean, Nicholas, 122
MacNeil, H. A., 211, *211*
"Made in" inscriptions or labels, 14–15
Madonna, 292
*Madonna and Child with the Infant
    Baptist* (Pontormo), *127*
Magic Skin baby dolls, 283
Magnussen, Erik, 67, *C-6*
Mah Jongg sets, 300
Mahogany, 10–11, 32, 36, 38
  panels, paintings on, 120
Maiolica, 90, *90*
Majolica, 89–90, *C-9*
Majorelle, Louis, 35, *35,* 111
Malmaison, 309, *309*
Mantel clocks, 178, 181, 187, 189,
    189, 190, C-19
  what to look for in, 190–91
Mantle, Mickey, 289
Manuscripts, 302–3, *303,* 313–20,
    C-31–C-32
  determining age of, 317–18
  letters, 302–3, 312, *314,* 315–17,
    316, 317, C-32
  of little value, 320
  musical score, *301, C-32*
  presidential, 315, 318–19, *C-32*
  ship's passports, 318
  tips from experts on, 315
  see also Autographs
Man with a Pink (Solari), *136*
Maps, on samplers, *255,* 256
Marble bases, for bronzes, 210–11
Marbles (toys), 300
Marie Antoinette, *275*
Mariner's Compass quilts, 253
Marinot, Maurice, 111
Märklin Co., 268, 273, 274, *274,
    C-27, C-28*
Marlborough legs, 13
Marquetry, 38, *C-18*
"Marriage," use of term, 20
Marseille, Armand, 278, *C-29*
Marshall family, 184
Martelé silver, 65, *C-7*
Martinez, Maria and Julian, *98,* 98–99

Marx, 273, *274, C-28*
Master's Hat (Wardle), *132*
Matisse, Henri, 308, *308*
Mazda Edison Lamps, 293
McCarron, David, 162
McCoy, 99
McGwire, Mark, 289
McKinley, William, 298
McKinley Tariff Act, 15, 270
McLaughlin, 271
Mechanical toys, *266,* 266–67, 296
  banks, *269,* 269–70, *270*
  bears, 285
  dolls (automata), *276, 276*
Medical kits, brass, 215
Medieval silver, 47, 52
Meeks, J. and J. W., *18*
Meissen, 81, 84, 85, 86, 87, 279, *C-8*
Meissonnier, Juste-Aurèle, 71
Memorabilia. *See* Collectibles
Mène, Pierre Jules, 207, 208, 209
Mennonite quilts, 251, *C-25*
Mercury, 205
Merry-go-round banks, 269
Messiah (Handel), *301*
Metals and metalwork, 201–32,
    C-21–C-23
  Arts and Crafts artisans, 219
  in Colonial America, 201–2,
    211–12, 222, 224–25, 231
  folk art, 230–32, *230–32*
  further reading on, 232
  hierarchy of, 47, 202
  imitation, 166
  in jewelry, 163–66, 167
  mixed-metal wares, *50, 51,* 66,
    66, 74
  tips from experts on, 210
  see also Brass; Bronze(s); Copper;
    Gold; Iron; Pewter; Platinum;
    Silver
Mettlach, 99
Mexican jewelry, 165
Michelangelo, 116, 204, 206
Michtom, Rose and Morris, 286
Mickey Mouse collectibles, 296
Micromosaics, *172*
Middle Ages, silver in, 47, 52

Mighty Mouse collectibles, 299
Mignot, Louis Rémy, *C-13*
Mihrab, 237, *237, C-24*
Military discharges, 312
Millegrain, 164
Miller Iron Co., 229
Mine-cut, *152,* 152–53, *153,* 168
Miniatures, die-cast, 274
Minton, 85, 88, 90, *C-9*
    Boyle, and, *C-8*
Mirror frame, American Belleek, *80*
Mirrors, 8, 24, 33
Mitchell, Margaret, 307–8
Mixed-metal wares, *50, 51,* 66, *66,* 74
Mobil, 294, 299, *C-30*
Modernism, 146
Modernist silver, 67–68
Mohrmann, John Henry, *C-15*
Moigniez, Jules, 207, *208*
Mondrian, Piet, 127, 138, *138*
Monet, Claude, 128, 136, *C-13*
Monkhouse, Thomas, *186*
Monopoly, 271
Monroe, Marilyn, 295, 320
Montanari, 278
Montre militaire, 197
Moore, Clement Clarke, *C-32*
Moorish-style furniture, *23*
Moose motif, in hooked rug, *244*
Morgan, J. P., 305
Morgan Lithography Co., 295
Morse, Nathaniel, 75
Mortimer Snerd's "hometown band,"
    274
Mortise-and-tenon construction, *14,*
    15, *15,* 16, 38
Moses, Grandma, 142
Moths, 234, 241, 288
Motorcycle advertising objects, 293, *293*
Mount Washington, 102, *102*
Mourning jewelry, 163, 172
Mourning pictures, 144–45
    samplers, 256–57, *257,* 259
Movable type, 305–6
Movements, clock, 178, *179,* 179–80,
    180, 181
    American vs. English, 185, 189
    detecting repairs to, 186

fusee, *179*
    spring-driven, 179–80, 186, 187–79
    value and, 183, 184, 186, 187
    weight-driven, 180, 184–87
    wooden, 185, 188
Movements, watch, 194, 195, *195,* 199
Movie memorabilia, *293,* 294–96, *295,*
    C-30
Movie stars, autographs of, 320
Mozart, Wolfgang Amadeus, *316, C-32*
Muffineer, silver, *70*
Mugs or canns, silver, 60, *60,* 61, *61*
Müller-Munk, Peter, 65, *C-7*
Multiples, 207
Mummy, The, 294
Murals, painted on canvas, 145
Myers, Myer, *59,* 62, *62, C-5*
Mystery clocks, *192,* 192–93

N

Nails, 14, 15, 16
Nampeyo, 99
Napoleon, 36, 196, 206, 316
Napoleon III furniture, 5
Nardin, Ulysse, *198*
Native Americans:
    book on, 310, *310*
    bronze kettles and, 203
    depicted in bronze, 211, *211*
    dolls made by, 281, *281,* 283
    jewelry made by, 165, *175,*
        175–76, *176*
    pottery made by, *98,* 98–99
    rugs made by, *245,* 245–46, *246,*
        C-24
Navajo:
    jewelry of, 175–76, *176*
    rugs of, *245,* 245–46, *246, C-24*
Necklaces, 149, *150, 153,* 155, *155,*
    166, *166, 175, 176*
    see also Jewelry
Neoclassical:
    clock, *189*
    furniture, 4, 9, 32, 39
    gilt-bronze centerpiece, *205*
    silver, 68–70, *C-7*
Neo-Egyptian furniture, 8

Neo-Grecian furniture, 8
Nephrite, 160, 161, *C-16*
Newcomb College, 91, *92,* 95, *95*
New England Glassworks, *79,* 102
New York Yankees, 289
Nichols, Maria Longworth, 91
Niello, 53
Nixon, Richard M., 299
Noah's Ark sets, 264, *264*
Nomadic rugs, 233–34, 236
North American Indian, The (Curtis),
    310, *310*
Novelty clocks, *192,* 192–93
Novelty watches, *178,* 195–96
Nymphenburg, 87

O

Oak, 10, 32, 39
Objets de vertu, 50
Odiot, Jean-Baptiste-Claude, 71, *C-7*
Ogee bracket feet, *13*
Ogee clocks, *188,* 189
Ohr, George, 91
Oil and gas advertising objects, 293–94
Oil paint, 116–18, 121, 122, 130, 139
    see also Painting
Old Church, The (Mondrian), *138*
Oldsmobile, 293
Onyx, 174
Opals, 159, *159, C-16*
Oriental rugs, 233–34, *233–40,* 235,
    236–43, *241, C-24*
    colors of, 242
    condition of, 241–42
    determining age of, 238–40
    determining value of, 240–43
    fineness of weave in, 240, 241
    fringes at ends of, 241
    further reading on, 262
    manufactured in village workshops,
        236, 236–37, *238*
    nomadic, 233–34, 236
    Persians, 233, 234, *234,* 235, 237,
        237, 240, *240*
    prayer rugs, *234,* 237, *237*
    silk, 236, 241
    tribal patterns in, 237

urban-made, 235, 237, *237*
Originality, in art, 127
Origin of Species, On the (Darwin), *303, C-32*
Ormolu:
  furniture mounted with, *34*
  gilt bronze, *205,* 205–6, 211
Otis, Bass, 309
Otsea, Mary Jo, 241, 242
Ott and Brewer, *81,* 82
Outsider Art, 142
Overlay glass, 103, *105,* 113, *113, 114*
Overshot coverlets, 254, *254*
Owl andirons, iron, *226*

P

Paderewski, Ignacy, 319
Pad feet, *13*
Painters, reference sources on, 129
Painting, 115–46, *C-12–C-15*
  artists' good and bad years and, 137–38
  authenticity of, 118, 126
  canvas and other supports for, 117, 119–22
  by celebrity painters, 135, *135*
  color in, 136
  condition of, 139–41
  connoisseurship and, 133–41
  dates on, 131–33
  determining age of, 116–25
  determining legitimacy of, 121, 125–33
  folk, 120, 121, 135, 141–46, *143-45*
  frames of, 123-25, *124*
  on furniture, *20,* 21, *21,* 22, 24, 25, 28, *C-1*
  further reading on, 146
  genre, 119, *119,* 122, *122,* 126, 130, *130, 132, 140*
  labels on, 121, 131
  landscape, *116,* 119, 126–27, *127, 129,* 137, 139, *139, 143,* 144
  laying down, 120
  monetary hierarchy of media in, 117
  originality in, 127
  plaques with "credits" of, 125

portraiture, 119, 126, *126, 131,* 132–33, *134,* 135, *136,* 141, *141–43,* 143–44
  prints vs., 120, 122
  religious, 126, 127, *127*
  relining, 119–20
  repairs to, 121, 139–41
  reproductions vs., 116, 125
  signatures and inscriptions on, *128,* 128–31, *129,* 132
  stamps on back of, 121
  still life, *115,* 134, 135
  stretchers of, 119, 120, 122–23
  subjects of, 126–27, 134–35
  technique in, 128, 136–37
  tips from experts on, 120–21
Painting clocks, 192, *192*
Pairpoint, 109, *109*
Palmer, Lillian, 219
Panda bears, stuffed, 287
Panels, paintings on, 117, 120, 121, 123
Paper, paintings on, 117, 120, 121–22
Paperback books, 320
Papermaking, 317–18
Paperweights, glass, 110, *110,* 112
Papier-mâché dolls, 279, 283
Parcheesi, 271
Parian, 82, 90, *C-9*
  dolls, 279
Paris Porcelain, 85, *C-8*
Parrish, Maxfield, 293, 309
Paste (glass gemstone simulants), 153, 155, 156, 157, 170
Pastel, *116,* 117, 121
Patent numbers, on toys, 270
Patina, on furniture, 20–21
Patriotic motifs:
  in quilts, *247,* 251, 253, *253*
  in samplers, 261
Patterson, Jerry E., 304, 309
Pavé, *159*
Peaceable Kingdom, The (Hicks), *144,* 145
Peachblow, 102, *102, C-11*
Peale, Charles Wilson, *C-15*
Peale family, 121
Pearls, 148, 149, 150, *159,* 161–62, *161–63, 170,* 171, 174, 175, *C-16*

Pearlware, *87,* 88
Pearlwork, 212
Peg dolls (peg woodens), *275,* 277
Pegs, 15, 37
Pen and ink, 117, 121
Pencil, 117, 118, 121
Pendants, *156, 162, 170,* 171, *172*
  see also Jewelry
Pendi Hatchlu, *234*
Pendule d'officier, 193
Pendulums, 184–85, 186, 187, 188
Penguins (R&R group), 291
Penn, William, 276
Pennyweight, 75
Pens, gold-colored, 300
Pen tray, copper with applied silver, *50*
Perfume sphere, silver-overlaid glass, *67*
Persian Qashqa'i bags, 235, *235*
Persian rugs, 233, 234, *234,* 235, 237, *237,* 240, *240*
Persistence of Memory (Dali), 137, *137*
Peter Pan in Kensington Gardens, 315
Petsy bears, 285
Pewter, 47, 201, *201,* 202, 217, 221–26, *221–26, C-23*
  determining age of, 224–25
  determining value of, 225
  marks on, 223, 224–25, 226
  painted, 225
  uses of, 222–23
Philadelphia Centennial Exposition (1876), 6, 66
Philippe, Patek, & Cie, *198*
Photography, 146
  book illustration and, 309, 310, *310*
Phyfe, Duncan, 2, 6, 10, *10, 12,* 26, *26,* 40, *40*
Pictorial quilts, 251–52
Pictorial rugs, 246
Pictorial samplers, 257, 258, *258–62*
Pieced quilts, 247, *247,* 248, *248*
Pieplate, pottery, *89*
Piercing, in silver, 52, *52, 56*
Pierotti, 278, *C-29*
Pier tables, 2, 9, *9*
Pie safes, 29
Piggy banks, *269,* 269–70, *270,* 274
Pig weathervane, *227*

Pilgrim-style furniture, 1, 4, *11–13*, 15
Pillbox, silver, *50*
Pinchbeck, 166
Pine, 7, 10
Pins, 167, *172*
    lapel watch, *199*
    see also Brooches; Jewelry
Pint measures, pewter, *223*
"Pinxit" ("P.," "Pinx.") or "Pictor,"
    use of terms, 131
Pipes, carved, 300
Piqué, 162
Pistol watch, *178*
Pitchers:
    ceramic, *82*
    glass, *113, 114*
    mixed-metal, *66*
    silver, *45*, 74
Planes, toy, 268
Plaques, painted porcelain, 83
Plaster figures, 99
Plates:
    collectors', 300
    maiolica, *90*
    pewter, 223, *223, 226*
Platinum, 47, *147, 148,* 149, *153,*
    156, 167, *174, 175*
    watchbands, 199
Plique-á-jour enamels, 170–71, 174, *C-17*
Plumbing, copper, 218
Plywood, 15
Pocket watches, *194,* 194–97, *195,*
    197–99, 198-99
    gold-filled, 175, 199
    heavy, 199
    see also Watches
Poe, Edgar Allan, 314
Poetry, 312
Poinçons d'Or, 171
Pointillism, *127,* 128
Points, 306, 307–8
Polishing:
    patination destroyed by, 210, 217
    silver, 76, 77
Political themes:
    banks with, 270
    campaign collectibles and, *297,*
        297–300, *298, C-30*

Pompeii, 36
Pontil marks, 101, 104
Pontormo, Jacopo da, *127*
Poole, Elisabeth, 239
Popes, 319
Poplar, 7, 10
Porcelain, 79–88, *80–87,* 90, 116, *C-8*
    American, *80–82,* 81–83
    blue-and-white wares, *84,* 84–86,
        99, *C-8*
    determining age of, 94–96
    determining value of, 96–97, 99
    Disneyana, 296
    dolls, *263,* 276, *277,* 279–80, 282,
        283, *283,* 287
    European, 81, 82, 83, 84, *84,* 85,
        86–88, *87,* 95
    export, 83, *83, 84,* 84–86, 97
    German mantel clocks, 190
    inspecting for damage, 96
    makers and marks, 85
    Parian ware, 82, 90, *C-9*
    pottery vs., 88
    soft-paste wares, 81, *81*
    timeline for, 86
    tips from experts on, 83
Porringers:
    pewter, *201,* 223, 224, *225*
    silver, 61–63, *C-5*
Portrait of an 83-Year-Old Woman
    (Rembrandt), *134*
Portrait of Sigmunt Kingsfelt (Cranach),
    131
Portraiture, 119, 126, *126, 131,* 132–33,
    134, 135, *136,* 141, *141, 142*
    by folk artists, *143,* 143–44
Portuguese furniture, 38
Postcards, 297
Posters, 316
    concert, *291, 292*
    movie, *293,* 294–95, *295, C-30*
Potter, Beatrix, 309, 314, *314*
Pottery, 79–80, *87–95,* 88–99, *97, 98,*
    C-9–C-10
    American, 88–94, *89–93*
    art, 90, 92
    determining age of, 94–96
    determining value of, 96–97, 99

figures, 94, *94,* 99, *C-9*
folk art, *89,* 93
marks on, 91, 92
Native American, *98,* 98–99
porcelain vs., 88
varieties of, 89–90
Pottier and Stymus, 27
Pratt, Matthew, *C-15*
Pratt, Wayne, 230
Prayer rugs, *234,* 237, *237*
Preiss, Ferdinand, 208
Presentation copies, 314
Presentation samplers, 257
Presentation silver, 49, *49, 70, C-5*
Presidents:
    autographs of, 315, 318–19
    glassware of, *103*
Presley, Elvis, 290–91, *292, 292*
Pressed glass, *100, 101,* 102–3, 104,
    107, 110
Primary woods, 10
Prints:
    paintings vs., 120, 122
    sepia-tone, painted over with oil
        paint, 145
Prior, William Matthew, 142
Prohibition memorabilia, 299
Provenance:
    of books, 304
    of furniture, 16, 18–19
Provincial furniture, *2,* 36, 38
Pueblo pottery, *98,* 98–99
Puiforcat, Jean, 71, *C-7*
Pulls (hardware), *12, 13,* 14
Pull toys, 267, 268, 269
Punch bowls, silver, 49, *49, 50*
Pyle, Howard, 309
Pyrope garnets, 158

Qashqa'i, Persian, 235, *235*
Quaker samplers, *259,* 260
Queen Anne:
    furniture, *1,* 2, *2,* 4, 11, *12, 13,* 38,
        41, *41, C-3*
    wooden dolls, 276, *C-29*
Queen's ware, 88, *C-10*

Quilts, 233, 234, *247–54,* 247–55, *C-25*
  album, *247,* 249, *249,* 250, 252, *253,* 254
  Amish, 250–51, *251,* 252–53, 254, *C-25*
  appliquéd, 247, *247,* 249, *249,* 250, *250, 252, C-25, C-26*
  crazy, *248*
  determining age of, 251–53
  determining value of, 253–54
  further reading on, 262
  materials in, 249
  patterns of, 249–51
  pictorial, 251–52
  pieced, 247, *247,* 248, *248*
  techniques and types of, 247–49
  tips from experts on, 254
  whitework, 250, *251*
  whole-cloth, 247, 248
Quinn, Anthony, 135

R

Rabbets, 39
Rabson, Susan, *260*
Race cars, toy, 275
Rackham, Arthur, 309, 315
Radio Flyer sleds, 300
Raggedy Ann dolls, 277, *277,* 281, *281*
Rago, David, 92
Rag paper, 317–18
Rag rugs, 243, *243,* 244
Railroad watches, 197
Rattlesnake, The (Remington), 203
Ravenscroft, George, 100–101
Raviro, Antoine-André, *C-20*
Razor's Edge, The, 295
Reade, Charles, 307
Reading copies, 301–2, 311
Récamier sofas, 9
Records, 291, 300
Redouté, 309, *309*
Redware, *88,* 89, 93, *C-10*
Reeding, 17, *17*
Regency, 70
  furniture, 5, *31,* 33, *C-3*
Regulator clocks, 191, *191*

Reitveld, Gerrit, 35
Religious motifs:
  mechanical banks with, 270
  memorabilia with, 300
  in paintings, 126, 127, *127*
Relining paintings, 119–20
Rembrandt, *126, 134*
Remington, Frederic, *140,* 141, 202–3, *203,* 210, 231, 309, *C-20*
Remmey family, *90*
Renaissance, 116
  bronzes, 204, 206
  copper, 218
  furniture, 4
  jewelry, 162, 170, 171
  pewter, 221
Renaissance Revival, 78
  furniture, 8, *43*
Renoir, Auguste, 136
Repeating mechanisms:
  in clocks, 188, 193, 194
  in watches, 195, *197*
Repoussé, 51, *51,* 52
Reproduction furniture, 6
Reproductions, paintings vs., 116, 125
Requiem (Mozart), *C-32*
Restoration:
  of furniture, 20–21
  of paintings, 139–41
Retro jewelry, *174,* 175
Revere, Paul, *52, 59,* 61, 62, *201,* 202, 218, 308–9
Revivale furniture, 5
Revival styles, in furniture, 2, 5, 8, *28,* 32, 38, *43,* 44
Ricci, 125
Richardson, Joseph, 62, *62*
Richardson, Nathaniel, *50*
Riley, John, *182*
Rings, *148, 151, 154,* 155, *155, 165,* 171, 172
  see also Jewelry
"Rite of Spring, The" (Stravinsky), *C-32*
Riviere & Sons, *C-32*
Robineau, Adelaide Alsop, 91, 92, *C-10*
Rock and roll memorabilia, 290–92, *291, 292, C-30*

Rockingham-glazed wares, 90, 92, *94, C-9*
Rocking horses, *265,* 265–66
Rockwell, Norman, 295, 309
Rococo furniture, 4, 32, 33–34, *34,* 39, *C-4*
Rococo Revival furniture, 8, *28*
Rodin, Auguste, 231
Rods and reels, 290
Roesen, Severin, *C-15*
Rohde, Gilbert, 65
Rolex, 197, 198
Rolled gold, 166
Rolling Stones, 292
Roly Poly, 272, *272*
Roman Bronze Works, 203, 210, 211
Romance film posters, 294, *295*
Romans, ancient:
  bronzes of, 203, 204
  glass of, *99,* 103, 108, 113
  jewelry of, 148, 149, 157
  silver of, 47, 48, 60
Rookwood, 91, 93
Roosevelt, Franklin D., 299, 319
Roosevelt, Theodore, *265,* 284, *284, 298,* 299
Rooster weathervane, *232*
Rose-cut, 152, *152, 153,* 168, 171
Rose medallion patterns, 83
Roseville, 92
Rosewood, 10, 38
Rossignol, 273
Rostand Manufacturing Co., *226*
Roux, Alexander, 27, *27*
Royal Copenhagen, 84, 279
Royal Crown Derby, 85, 88
Royal Doulton, 99
Roycroft, 27, *27,* 210, 218–20, *C-22*
Rubáiyat of Omar Khayyám, 310
Rubies, 150, 154–55, *154–56, 167,* 174, *174, C-16–C-18*
  simulants, 155
Rug fragments, 241
Rugs, 233–47, *C-24*
  American Indian, *245,* 245–46, *246*
  Chinese, 238, *238*
  collectible vs. decorative, 235–36
  flat-surface vs. pile, 235, *236*

folk, 241, 243-45, *243-45*
further reading on, 262
geometric patterns in, *233, 234, 236,* 237, 239, *239,* 242, 243, *245,* 246
machine-made, 234, 238, 240
repairs to, 241, 242
tips from experts on, 241
use of term, 235
see also Oriental rugs
Ruhlmann, Emile-Jacques, 35
Rundell, Bridge & Rundell, 69
Ruskin, John, 301–2
Russian furniture, 37, 38
Russian silver, 47, 52, 53, *53,* 72, *72, 76*
hallmarks on, 58
Rust, 211, 217
Ruth, Babe, *288*

S

Saber legs, *13, 23,* 24
"Sadware," use of term, 222
Saint-Gaudens, Augustus, 202–3, *206,* 208
St. Louis glass, *110*
Salt cellars, silver, *58,* 63
Salt-glazed wares, 89, 90, *90,* 91, 92, *93*
Samovars, 210, 231
silver, *76*
Samplers, 233, 234, 255–62, *255–62, C-26*
alphabet, *255,* 256, *256,* 260, *260*
American vs. English, 261
condition of, 261–62
determining age of, 258–59
determining value of, 260–61
family record, 256, *256*
further reading on, 262
materials in, 257–58
mourning pictures, 256–57, *257,* 259
pictorial, 257, 258, *258–62*
presentation, 257
tips from experts on, 257
types of, *256–57*

Sanchez, Gabriel, *311*
Sand casting, 213, *213*
Sandoz, Gerard, 173
Sandpainting rugs, 246, *246, C-24*
Sandwich glass, *100,* 107, *107, C-11*
knobs, *14*
Sangorski and Sutcliffe, 310, *C-31*
Santa Roly Dolly, 272, *272*
Santa sleigh, *273*
Sapphires, 150, 155–56, *156, 162,* 174, *C-16*
simulants, 151, 156
Sartori, Polly, 130
Satinwood, 38, *C-3*
Sauce boats, silver, *50, 62,* 63, *C-5*
Sautoir, *164*
Savery, William, 26
Saw marks, circular, *7*
Scandinavian decorative arts:
furniture, 36, 39
silver, 58
Schmertz Vergesen (Gaugengigl), 119, *119*
Schoenhut Co., 264, 265, *265,* 272, *272, C-28*
Science-fiction film posters, 294, *294*
Scientific instruments, brass, *212,* 215, *216*
Sconces, 214
gilt-bronze, *205*
tin, 231
Scooters, 274
Score, musical, *301, C-32*
Scottish grandfather clock, 184, *184*
Scrabble, 271
Screws, 7, 14, 15, 16
Sculpture, 116
bronzes, 201, 202–11, *203–7, 209, 211,* 217
white metal/spelter, 207–9
wrought-iron, 230
Secondary woods, 10, 23, 32, 39
Second Empire furniture, 5
Second impressions (printings), 306
Secretaire à abattant, 34
Secretary bookcases, 9
Self-help books, 312
Settee, *36*

Seurat, Georges, *127*
Seven Dwarf dolls, 296
78 rpm records, 291
Sèvres, 85, 86, 87, 97, 279, *C-4, C-8, C-9, C-10*
Sextants, 215
Seymour, John, 22, *22,* 26, *C-1*
Seymour, Thomas, 26
Sgraffito, *88, 89,* 93
Shade, W., *228*
Shag rugs, 244
Shaker:
braided rugs, 244, *244*
furniture, 11, 29, *29,* 42, *42*
Shakespeare, William, 304–5
Shayer, William, 130, *130*
Sheeler, Charles, 247
Sheffield plate, 53–54, *54,* 75, 77
Shelf clocks, 187, *188,* 188–89
what to look for in, 190
Shellac, 22, 38
Shell cameos, 169, *170,* 175
"She Loves You," 292
Shelving, 37
Sheraton, Thomas, 30, 33, *33*
Sheraton furniture, 2, *11, 12*
Sherman, William T., 319
Ships, toy, 274, *C-28*
Ship's passports, 318
Shiraz rugs, 237
Shirvan rugs, 239, *239*
Shop signs, 230–31
Shoulder-head dolls, 279
Shrinkage, on furniture, 23, 38
Sideboards, 40, *40,* 42, *42*
Sidechairs, *1, 19, 29*
see also Chairs
Signatures:
on brass, 216, 217
on bronzes, 208, 209
on clocks, 183–84, 185, 189, 190, 194
"floating," 130
on furniture, 8, 39
on paintings, *128,* 128–31, *129,* 130, *132*
see also Autographs
Signed books, 304, 307–8, 314–15

Signs:
 shop, 230–31
 tin, 293, *293*
Silk (inclusions), 155, 156
Silk rugs, 236, 241
Silver, 1, 45–78, 95–96, 116, *C-5–C-7*
 American, *45, 47–51, 53, 58–62,
  58–68, 64–67,* 74, 75, *75,* 77,
  77, 78, *78, C-5–C-6*
 bright-cutting, 52
 canns or mugs, 60, *60,* 61, *61*
 casting, 51
 centerpiece, *75*
 chalice, *77*
 chasing, 52
 coffeepot, *51, 54*
 coffee services, *66,* 77
 compotes, *48, 52,* 78
 Continental, 47, 52, *52,* 53, *53,*
  57, 57–58, 68, 70–73, *71, 72,*
  74, *76, C-7*
 cruet sets and casters, 63, *C-5*
 cup and cover, *72*
 cups, 47, *47,* 73, 74
 demitasse set, *67*
 design techniques for, 51–53
 determining age of, 73–74
 determining value of, 75–78
 embossing, 51
 enameling, 52–53, *53*
 English, *46, 54–56,* 55–57, *57,* 60,
  61, 63, *63,* 68–70, *68–70,* 73,
  73, C-7
 engraving, 52, 74, 76
 ewer, 68, *68*
 flatware, 48, *53,* 55, 64, *64,* 74, 77,
  C-6
 fruit stand, *65*
 further reading on, 78
 gilding, 52
 hallmarks on, 54, 55–59, 73
 hammering, 50–51, 66, 73
 holloware, 48
 jewelry, 149, 163, 165, 167, *167,*
  170, 171, *175,* 176, *176*
 kovshi, 72, *72*
 lighting, 63–64, 74, *75,* 76, *77*
 manufacturing techniques for,

   50–51
  in mixed-metal wares, *50, 51,* 66,
   66, 74
  muffineer, *70*
  piercing, 52, *52, 56*
  pill or stamp box, *50, C-6*
  pitchers, *45,* 74
  polishing, 76, 77
  porringers, 61–63, *C-5*
  presentation, 49, *49, 70, C-5*
  punch bowls, 49, *49, 59, C-5*
  recycling of, 45–46, 47–48, 70
  repairs or alterations to, 74, 76, 77
  salt cellars, *58,* 63
  samovar, *76*
  sauce boats, *50, 62,* 63, *C-5*
  slicer, *C-6*
  small collectibles, 50
  smell of, 158
  spinning, 51
  spoons, 46, *46, 47, 52, 53, 58,* 64,
   64, 73, *73,* 78
  sterling, silver plate vs., 74–75
  sugar basket, *55,* 73
  tankards, *55, 59,* 60, 63, *63,* 74
  tea accessories, 61, *61*
  tea caddy, *69*
  teapots, *45,* 73–74, *C-5*
  tea services, 64, 77
  tips from experts on, 74
  tobacco box, *48*
  trays, 75
  trophies, 49, *49,* 78
  tureens, 63, *70,* 77, *C-5*
  types of, 47–50
  weight of, 75–76
  wine coasters, *56*
Silver, Eric, 210
Silver-mounted glass, 67, *67*
Silver plate, 53–55, 213, 222
  antique (Sheffield plate), 53-54, *54,*
   75, 77
  on Britannia metal, 54, 224
  modern (electroplate), 54–55, 78
  sterling vs., 74–75
Silver standard, 47
Simon & Halbig, 277, 278, 280
Sinclair, 107

Sirolli, Larry, 38
Sleds, 300
Slide-lid box, *20*
Sloane, Jeanne, 49, 58, 68, 74
Smith, Al, 299
Snake jewelry, *159,* 171, 172
Snellenburg, Jonathan, 193, 196, 198
Snyders, Frans, *135*
Soar, Hank, 289
Socket-head dolls, 279
Sofas, 9, *C-2, C-4*
Sofa table, *31*
Soft-paste wares, 81, *81*
Solari, Antonio, *136*
Soldiers, toy, *269,* 274
Solon, M. L., *C-9*
Souvenirs. *See* Collectibles
Spade feet, *13*
Spanish-American War, 317
Spanish feet, *13*
Sparkle Plenty dolls, 283
Spatterware, 89
Speaking Dog banks, 270
Speeches, 315
Spelter/white metal, 207–9
Spinel, 153, 156
Spines, of books, 307, *308*
Spinning silver, 51
Spode, 85, *87,* 88
Spongeware, 89, *C-10*
Spoons, 48
  pewter, 223
  see also Flatware
Spoons, silver, 46, *46, 47,* 52, 64, *64,*
  73, *73,* 78
  coin, *58,* 78
  enameled, *53*
Sports memorabilia, *288–90,* 289–90,
  299, 300, *C-30*
Spring (Boucher), *123*
Squash-blossom necklaces, *175,* 176,
  176
Staffordshire figures, 94, *C-9*
Stamp box, silver, *50*
Staples, 15
Star (inclusions), 155
Star-pattern quilts, *247,* 251, *252,*
  253

Stebbins & Stebbins, *103*
Steiff bears, 284–85, *285, 287, 287,* 288, *288*
Steiner, 280
Stenciling, *21,* 22, *C-13*
Stereopticon cards, 300
Sterling standard marks, 56, *57*
Steuben Glass Works, 107, 112
Stevens, J. & E., Co., 269, *270, 273,* 274
Stickley, Gustav, 27, *27, C-2*
Stickpin, *172*
Stiegel, Henry William, 106, *106*
Still life painting, *115,* 134, 135, *C-13, C-15*
Stipple engraving, *104,* 105
Stone China, 90
Stone lithography, 295
Stones, 150–61, 168
    analyzing, 148
    books bound with, 310
    carat of, 152
    clarity of, 151–52
    color of, 151
    cut of, 148, *150, 152,* 152–53, 168
    inclusions in, 151, 155, 156
    precious (gemstones), 150–57, *C-16*
    semiprecious, 157–61, *C-16*
    settings for, 153, 170, 171–72
    synthetic or imitation, 151, 152–53, 155, 156, 157, 159
    see also Jewelry; *specific stones*
Stonewares, 89, *90, 93, C-10*
    salt-glazed, 89, 90, *90,* 91, 92, *93*
Storr, Paul, 69
Straight-molded legs, *13*
Stravinsky, Igor, *C-32*
Stretchers, 119, 120, 122–23
Strongboxes, iron, 227
Stuffed toys. *See* Teddy bears
Sugar basket, silver, *55*
Summer and winter coverlets, 254
"Sunday toys," 264, *264*
Sundials, brass, *212,* 215, *C-4*
Surmoulages, 210
Surrealism, *137*
Swedish furniture, 36

Swiss clocks and watches, 192, 195, 196, 198, *198*
Swivel-head dolls, 279
Syng, Phillip, Jr., 62

T

Tabernacle frame, *124*
Table clocks, *172*
Tablecloths, printed, 261
Table-cut, *151,* 152
Table mats, *245*
Tables, 29, *C-2, C-3*
    breakfast, *10, 33*
    center, 9
    console, 2, *32*
    determining age of, 8
    dining room, 8, 31
    dressing, 9, *14,* 17, *C-3*
    drop-leaf, *18*
    and forms characteristic of their era, 9
    gaming (card), 9, *9,* 22, *22*
    pier, 2, 9, *9*
    repairs to, 24
    sofa, *31*
    tilt-top, 25, 38, *43*
    tripod, 8, 15–16
    worktables, 9, 40, *40*
Tabriz rugs, 241, *C-24*
Taft, William Howard, 319
Tailor of Gloucester, The (Potter), *314*
Tale of Peter Rabbit, The (Potter), *314*
Tallcase clocks (grandfather or long-case clocks), 177, *181, 182, 184–86,* 185–87, *C-19*
    what to look for in, 186–87
Tamerlane (Poe), 314
Tammy, 257
Tankards:
    pewter, 223
    silver, *55, 59,* 60, 63, *63,* 74
Tank watches, 197, *198*
Tapered legs, square, *13*
Tapersticks, 214
Tapestries, 235
    French or Belgian machine-made, 261
Tchaikovsky, Pyotr Ilich, 319

Tea accessories, silver, 61, *61*
Tea caddy, silver, *69*
Tea kettle, copper, 218, *218*
Teapots:
    pewter, 223, 224
    porcelain, *81*
    silver, *45,* 73–74, *C-5*
Tea services, silver, 64, 77, *C-7*
Tea towels, printed Irish, 261
Technology books, 312
Teddy bears, 275, 284–88, *284–88*
    determining age of, 286–87
    determining value of, 288
    further reading on, 300
    tips from experts on, 287
Telescopes, brass, *216*
Tempera, 117
Templier, Raymond, 173
Tenniel, Sir John, 304
Tenons. *See* Mortise-and-tenon construction
Terry, Eli, *188,* 188–89
Texaco, 293
Textbooks, 320
Textiles, 233–62
    Arts and Crafts, 220
    coverlets, *254,* 254–55, 261, 262
    fragility of, 234
    further reading on, 262
    with little value, 261
    Navajo blanket, *246*
    printed, 261
    table mat, *245*
    see also Oriental rugs; Quilts; Rugs; Samplers
"That's All Right," 291
Theorems, 145
Thinker (Rodin), 231
3rd Hussars (The King's Own), *269*
Third Republic furniture, 5
Thomas, Seth, 189
Thomire, Pierre Philippe, *205,* 205–6, *C-8*
Tiffany, Louis Comfort, 92, 105, 107, *108,* 108–9, 111, *111,* 112, 173
Tiffany & Co.:
    bronze, *209, C-21*
    clocks, 190, 194

copper candlesticks, 217, *217*

furniture, *23, C-11*

jewelry, 154, *154,* 173, *C-18*

porcelain, 97

silver, *51,* 55, 65, *66, 75, 77, C-5–C-6*

Tiger Devouring an Antelope, A (Barye), *207*

Tilt-top tables, 25, 38, *43*

Timepieces:

  use of term, 180

  see also Clocks; Movements, clock; Watches

Time to Kill, A (Grisham), 302

Tin, 203, 221, 222, 230–31

  signs, 293, *293*

Tin-glazed ceramics, 90

Tinned iron, 228, *228,* 229

Tinplate toys, *266,* 266–68, *267,* 271, 274, *274,* 296, *C-27*

Tipped-in artwork, 304

Titanic, 310

  memorabilia from, 296, *296*

Title pages, 306, *306,* 307, *311*

Tobacco boxes:

  brass, *212, 216*

  silver, *48*

Todt Hill, Staten Island, New York, 143

Toe caps, 14

Tom Sawyer (Twain), *C-32*

Tompion, Thomas, *188*

Tondal's Vision (Bosch), *134*

Topalian, Mark A., 240

Topazes, 158, 159, *159,* 166, *166,* 168, 170, *C-16*

Tortoiseshell, 38, 162

Tourmalines, 155, 157

Toys, 263–75, *263–75, C-27–C-30*

  cast-iron, 268-70, *269, 270*

  condition of, 271

  determining age of, 270–71

  determining value of, 271–75

  further reading on, 300

  games, 271, *271*

  great age not important for, 263

  mechanical, *266,* 266–67, *269,* 269–70, *270,* 285, 296

  original boxes of, 274

  rarity of, 272–74

  repairs to, 272

  selected manufacturers of, 273

  teddy bears, 275, 284–88, *284–88,* 300

  tinplate, *266,* 266–68, *267,* 271, 274, *274,* 296, *C-27*

  wooden, *264, 265,* 265–66

  see also Dolls

Trains, toy, *267,* 267–68, 275, *C-28*

Tram car set, electric, *267*

Transfer printing, *84,* 96, 97

Transitional pieces, 32

Trapunto, 250, *251, C-25*

Travel clocks, 193, *193*

Traylor, Bill, 142

Trays, silver, 75

Tribal patterns, 237

Tricycles, 300

Trifid feet, *13*

Tripod tables, 8, 15–16

Trophies, silver, 49, *49, 78*

Troy ounce, 75

Truman campaign buttons, *297*

Tucker, 81, *82*

Tudric, 222

Tumblers, glass, *100, 106*

Tupperware, 300

Tureens, silver, 63, *70, 77*

Turkish Horse, The (Barye), 206

Turquoise, 158–59, *C-16*

Twain, Mark (Samuel Langhorne Clemens), 304, 311, *311,* 314, 319, *C-32*

  letter written by, *314*

Two Gray Hills rugs, *245,* 246

Tyler, John, *297*

Typewriters, 300

U

Ulysses (Joyce), 308, *308*

Unger Brothers, *66*

Union des Artistes Modernes, 173

Union Porcelain Works, 82, *82*

United States Pottery Co., 90

University City Porcelain Works, 92

Upholstery, 7, 23, 24, 33

Urban rugs, 235, 237, *237*

Urn-form chairbacks, *39*

Used furniture, 3–6

Utensils, kitchen, 201, 213

V

Van Briggle, Artus, 91, 97, *97, C-10*

Van Buren, Martin, 298

Van Cleef and Arpels, 173, *C-18*

Van der Weyden, Cornelius, 119, *119*

Van Gogh, Vincent, *C-12*

Vases:

  copper, *219*

  glass, *102, 104,* 105, 111, *111, C-11*

  pottery, *90,* 92, *92,* 95, *95,* 97, *97, C-8*

  silver, 76, *C-6*

Vegetal rugs, 246

Vehicular advertising objects, 293–94

Vehicular toys, 267–68, *267–69,* 269, 274, *274,* 275, *275*

Veneers, 7, 23, 38, 39

Venetian glass, *110,* 113, *C-11*

Verge escapements, *180,* 184

Vermeil, 52

Veronese, Paolo, *C-12*

Verrocchio, Andrea del, 171

Victoria, Queen, 163, 171, 172, 282

Victorian, 220

  ceramics, 87, 89–90

  furniture, 5, 8, 9, 11, *12,* 16–17, 24, *28,* 33, 38, 42, *42–44*

  hardware, 14

  hooked rugs, 245

  jewelry, 148, *148, 160,* 162, *163, 164,* 166, *166,* 167, *167,* 169, *169,* 171, *171, 172,* 172–74

  silver, *56,* 64

Vienna porcelain, 87–88

Vienna regulators, 191, *191*

Village workshop rugs, *236,* 236–37, *238*

Virgin and Saints (David), *128*

"Visit from St. Nicholas, A" (Moore), *C-32*

Voland, *281*

Volkmar, Charles, 91

W

Wagner, Honus, 290, *290*
Wahlgren, Francis, 302
Walker, Izannah, 280, *280*
Walker, William Aiken, 122, *122*
Wall clocks, 178, *187*, 191, *191*
Walnut, 11, 38
Walpole, Horace, 32
Waltham, 197, 199
Wardle, Arthur, *132*
Wardrobes, Dutch (kas), 9, *9*
Warming pans, brass, 215
Warner, A. F., *51*
War of Independence, 2, 57
Warrior and His Equerry (Giorgione),
   136
Washington, Booker T., *298*, 299
Washington, George, 318, 319, *C-32*
Washstand, *21*
Watches, 177, 178–79, 194–200,
   C-19–C-20
   determining value of, 183–84
   further reading on, 200
   ladies', 197, *198*, 199
   movements of, 194, 195, *195*, 199
   novelty, *178*, 195–96
   pocket, 194, *194–97*, *195*, *197–99*,
     198–99, *C-20*
   railroad, 197
   striking, 183, *194*, 195
   subsidiary paraphernalia for,
     199–200, *200*
   with two nested cases, 195
   what to look for in, 190, 198–200
   winding, 196, 198
   wristwatches, 197–98, *198*, 199
Watercolor, *116*, 117, 120, 121, 122,
   145
Waterford, 110, *C-11*
Watermarks, 318
Wax dolls, 276, 277
Weapons, 201
Weathervanes, *227*, 230, *230–32*,
   231–32, *C-22*, *C-23*
Weavings:
   coverlets, *254*, 254–55, 261, 262
   Navajo, *245*, 245–46, *246*

rag rugs, 243
   see also Oriental rugs
Webb, Thomas, and Sons, 113, *114*
Weber, Barry, 158, 165, 169
Weber, Karl, 65
Wedgwood, 85, 88, 89, 90, 99, 172,
   C-9
   Queen's ware, *C-10*
Wedgwood and Bentley, *168*
Wedgwood pattern (flatware), *53*
Weller, 91
Wellington, Arthur Wellesley, Duke
   of, 196
Wells, Clara, 65
Werkstatte, Wiener, 71
Weschler, John, 157, 166
West, Thomas, 58
"Whale's tails," *186*
Whatnots, 9, *9*
Whirligigs, *265*, 266
Whistler, James, 129, *129*
Whistler, Laurence, *104*
White Granite Ware, 90
White metal/spelter, 207–9
Whitework quilts, 250, *251*
Whiting and Company, 49, *C-5–C-6*
Whitney Museum, 247
Whole-cloth quilts, 247, 248
Wilde, Oscar, 66
Willard family, *185*, 188, 191
William and Mary:
   furniture, 1, 4, 10, *12*, *13*, *39*, 41,
     41
   clocks, *181*, *182*, *187*
Wills, 303, 315
Windsor chairs, *12*, 20, *20*, 25, *28*, 29
Windup toys. *See* Mechanical toys
Wine coasters, silver, *56*
Wineglasses, *79*, *103*, 105
Wine vessels, silver, 47
Winnie the Pooh, 285, 302
Wistar, Caspar, 106
Wistarburg Glassworks, *106*
Withdrawn first editions, 304
Witherell, Brian, 294
WMF Metal Company, 218
Woman (Blue Eyes) (de Kooning), *138*
"Woman's Rights" toy, *266*

Wonderful Wizard of Oz, The (Baum),
   C-31
Wood, Grant, 247
Wood and Perot, 229
Wood dolls, *275*, 276–77
Wood panels, paintings on, 117, 120,
   121, 123
Wood-pulp paper, 318
Woods, in furniture, 7, 10–11, 32, 36,
   37, 38, 39
Woodstock memorabilia, 291, *291*
Wood veneers, 7, 23, 38, 39
Woodworms, 37
Worcester, 85, 88, *C-8*, *C-10*
Worktables, 9, 40, *40*
World's fair memorabilia, 299
World War I, 197, 317
Wormholes, 37, 121
Wright, Charles, 68, *68*
Wright, Frank Lloyd, 27, *27*
Wright, Richard, 277, 282, 287
Wristwatches, 197–98, *198*, 199
Wrought iron, 14, 227–30
Wyeth, N. C., 309

X

X-ray banks, 269

Y

Yachting games, 271
Yarn-sewn rugs, 244
Yates, James, *223*
Yates & Birch, *223*
Yellow Submarine, 292
Yellowware, 89
Yomud, *C-24*

Z

Zavian, Berj, 155
Zeppelin, toy, 274
Zircons, 153, *C-16*
Zuccarelli, Francesco, 125
Zuni:
   jewelry of, 176, *176*
   pottery of, 99